How Mediation Works

Using conversation analysis to study the interaction between mediators and disputants, this study shows how mediation is used to resolve conflict in small claims and divorce mediation sessions. Angela Garcia explores the techniques mediators use to help disputants tell their stories, make and respond to complaints and accusations, and come up with ideas for resolving the dispute. By analyzing these techniques in their interactional context, she shows how they impact the experience and responses of disputants, and she demonstrates that mediator techniques can empower disputants, maximize disputant autonomy, and display a mediator's neutrality while, in some cases, the organization of talk in mediation may work against these goals. This book is the first to use conversation analysis to study how mediation works and how mediators can best help disputants.

ANGELA CORA GARCIA is Professor of Sociology at Bentley University. She conducts conversation-analytic research on mediation, emergency phone calls to the police, computer-mediated communication, air traffic communication, and political interviews and speeches. She is author of *An Introduction to Interaction: Understanding Talk in Formal and Informal Settings* (2013).

T0370767

Studies in Interactional Sociolinguistics

Founding Editor
John J. Gumperz (1922–2013)

Editors
Paul Drew, Rebecca Clift, Lorenza Mondada, Marja-Leena Sorjonen

How Mediation Works

Resolving Conflict Through Talk

Angela Cora Garcia

Bentley University, Massachusetts

CAMBRIDGE
UNIVERSITY PRESS

University Printing House, Cambridge CB2 8BS, United Kingdom

One Liberty Plaza, 20th Floor, New York, NY 10006, USA

477 Williamstown Road, Port Melbourne, VIC 3207, Australia

314-321, 3rd Floor, Plot 3, Splendor Forum, Jasola District Centre, New Delhi - 110025, India

103 Penang Road, #05-06/07, Visioncrest Commercial, Singapore 238467

Cambridge University Press is part of the University of Cambridge.

It furthers the University's mission by disseminating knowledge in the pursuit of
education, learning and research at the highest international levels of excellence.

www.cambridge.org
Information on this title: www.cambridge.org/9781009244985
DOI: 10.1017/9781139162548

© Angela Cora Garcia 2019

First published 2019
First paperback edition 2022

A catalogue record for this publication is available from the British Library

Library of Congress Cataloging in Publication data
Names: Garcia, Angela Cora, author.
Title: How mediation works : resolving conflict through talk / Angela Garcia.
Description: Cambridge, United Kingdom ; New York, NY : Cambridge University
   Press, 2019. | Series: Studies in interactional sociolinguistics | Includes
   bibliographical references and index.
Identifiers: LCCN 2019003349 (print) | LCCN 2019015694 (ebook) |
   ISBN 9781107024274 (Hardback) | ISBN 9781107024274 (hardback)
Subjects: LCSH: Mediation. | Conflict management.
Classification: LCC HM1126 (ebook) | LCC HM1126 .G36 2019 (print) |
   DDC 303.6/9–dc23
LC record available at https://lccn.loc.gov/2019003349

ISBN 978-1-107-02427-4 Hardback
ISBN 978-1-009-24498-5 Paperback

To the loving memory of my father, Angel Antonio Garcia, an immigrant to the United States of America. He was a kind and gentle man who devoted his life to his family and his work.

Contents

Acknowledgments

I would like to thank the mediators and mediation clients from the three mediation programs studied in this book. These mediation clients and mediators agreed to participate in this project and allowed me to videotape their mediation sessions. I would also like to thank the research assistants who did an outstanding job transcribing data when they were graduate students at the University of Cincinnati: Jennifer Baker Jacobs and Brent Shannon.

Some of the chapters in this book were based in part on previously published research articles. These articles analyzed only parts of the data sets, and in this book, the analysis has been expanded to include all of the data sets. Parts of the analysis in Chapters 2 and 3 are based on my 1991 paper in the *American Sociological Review* ("Dispute resolution without disputing: How the interactional organization of mediation hearings minimizes argument"). Part of the analysis in Chapter 5 is based on my 1995 paper in the *Journal of Sociology and Social Welfare* ("The problematics of representation in community mediation hearings: Implications for mediation practice"). Parts of the analysis in Chapters 6 and 7 were based on two papers in *Discourse & Society* (2000, "Negotiating negotiation: The collaborative production of resolution in small claims mediation hearings," and 1997, "Interactional constraints on proposal generation in mediation hearings: A preliminary investigation").

The people who taught me conversation analysis were wonderful teachers and inspired me to study and teach this topic: Janet Tallman at Hampshire College, Candace West at the University of California, Santa Cruz, and Don H. Zimmerman at the University of California, Santa Barbara. They set me on a path of researching and teaching conversation analysis that prepared me for the task of writing this book.

I would like to thank the National Science Foundation for a research grant that provided the funding for the collection of two of the data sets analyzed in this book (Law and Social Sciences program, grant SBR-9411224). I would like to thank Bentley University for a sabbatical during which much of the work for this book was done. My editor at Cambridge University Press, Paul Drew, has been so helpful with editing, suggestions, and advice as I put this book together; I can't thank him enough. His input has greatly improved this book. Thanks also to commissioning editor Helen Barton, to Holly Monteith for copyediting the manuscript, and to Alexandra Nickerson for creating the index.

1 Introduction

Approaches to Mediation

Minor disagreements and occasional conflicts between people are a common experience and a normal part of life. While such disagreements are typically handled or resolved informally by those involved, there are times when help must be obtained from others. In some cases, individuals utilize the legal system (for example, by filing a law suit or filing a case in small claims court). Other disputants may choose to utilize alternative dispute resolution approaches such as mediation or arbitration.

Mediation is an alternative to litigation which provides a nonadversarial approach to the resolution of conflicts and is used in a wide range of civil disputes.[1] The legal system and mediation both bring a third party into the dispute resolution process, have specific rules and procedures which must be followed, and give participants specific rights and obligations. However, institutionalized methods of conflict resolution such as these differ in several ways. First, disputants using mediation have the autonomy to negotiate their own agreements. While they have the help of the mediator in attempting to resolve their conflict, the mediator does not have the authority to make a decision for them.[2] When compared to adjudication, mediation empowers the disputant and provides them with a greater opportunity to express themselves and to represent their own interests (Charkoudian, Eisenberg, and Walter 2017; Ewert et al. 2010; Moore 1986). Second, mediation programs are designed to facilitate cooperation and compromise. Third, the help of the mediator and the design of the process work to lessen intensity of the conflict. When disputants choose traditional legal avenues such as lawsuits to resolve their conflicts, those modalities of dispute resolution may exacerbate the

---

[1] See Bishop et al. (2015); Borg (2000); Boulle, Colatrella, and Picchioni (2008); Conley and O'Barr (2005); Doneff and Ordover (2014); Ewert et al. (2010); Felstiner and Williams (1978); Folberg and Taylor (1984); Frenkel and Stark (2012); Moore (2014); Woolford and Ratner (2008). In the case of divorce mediation, McGowan (2018) argues that instead of offering mediation as an alternative to litigation, it should often be used in conjunction with litigation.

[2] See Boulle et al. (2008); Cobb and Rifkin (1991b); Doneff and Ordover (2014); Merry and Silbey (1986).

1

antagonism between the disputants.[3] Mediators believe that mediation can help disputants reach an understanding of each other's positions while reducing conflict between them and increasing the chances of reconciliation.[4]

Over the last two decades, mediation has become an increasingly prevalent method of conflict resolution (Gewurz 2001). Mediation is used in a wide range of conflicts, including divorce and family conflicts, small claims cases, and neighborhood, consumer, business, and workplace disputes. It has also been used to help resolve disputes in educational institutions and medical settings, and for victim–offender reconciliation and international conflicts.[5]

Mediation is used in many countries around the world including Canada, China, Denmark and other Scandinavian countries, Great Britain, Israel, Liberia and several other African countries, and the United States.[6] Mediation is likely to maintain its popularity, as it is more cost effective than many of the alternatives. In addition, disputants may learn skills for avoiding and resolving conflict by participating in mediation, and may be more likely to maintain relationships with the person with whom they were engaged in conflict if a mutually agreeable resolution is reached (Boulle et al. 2008).

In this chapter I first briefly describe mediation and its history. I then describe several types of mediation currently in use in the United States and other countries around the world. This is followed by a review of previous literature which investigates the effectiveness and fairness of mediation. I then describe the data sets to be analyzed in this book. The chapter concludes with brief chapter summaries.

Roots and Varieties of Mediation

Although only coming into common use by the general public since the 1960s and 1970s, mediation has a long history. It initially developed both in ancient China and Africa, and the idea has spread to many countries around the world.[7] In the United States, the first use of mediation was probably among Puritan

---

[3] See Cahn (1992); Carper and LaRocco (2016); Girdner (1985); Worley and Schwebel (1985).

[4] See Bottomley (1985); Boulle et al. (2008); Charkoudian et al. (2017); Dingwall (1986); Folberg (1983); and Roberts (1988) on the benefits of mediation for disputants. There are also benefits for the mediators (Malizia and Jameson 2018).

[5] See Alberts, Heisterkamp, and McPhee (2005); Bishop et al. (2015); Cohen (1995); Doneff and Ordover (2014); Edwards and Stokoe (2007); Irving and Benjamin (2002); Kressel (2007); Little (2007); McKenzie (2015); Pines, Gat and Tal (2002); Polkinghorn and McDermott (2006); Presser and Hamilton (2006); Saposnek (1983); Sellman (2008); Stokoe and Hepburn (2005); Stoner (2018); Szmania (2006); Szmania, Johnson, and Mulligan (2008); Trachte-Huber and Huber (2007); Wallensteen and Svensson (2014).

[6] See de Vera (2004); Liebmann (2000); Mikkelsen (2014); Pogatschnigg (2012); Savoury, Beals, and Parks (1995); Uwazie (2011); Zamir (2011).

[7] See Brown (1982); Folberg (1983); Gibbs (1963); Liebmann (2000).

settlers in the colonial period, while in the United Kingdom, mediation began to be used historically as early as in the 1600s (Roebuck 2017), for industrial and employment disputes in the 1960s, and for family conflicts in the 1970s (Liebmann 2000; Woolford and Ratner 2008). Mediation was used in industry as early as the late 1800s in the United States for labor issues and contract disputes (Kolb 1983). During the mid 1900s, an increase in the number of civil cases began burdening the legal system, resulting in a push to increase utilization of mediation as an alternative conflict resolution procedure (Folberg and Taylor 1984). Social and cultural changes during the 1960s and 1970s also made mediation an attractive alternative to adjudication (Folberg and Taylor 1984).

A burgeoning of organizations and services occurred during this period with the goal of providing mediation services to a wider range of people and types of civil disputes. For example, national organizations such as the American Arbitration Association, the Association of Family and Conciliation Courts, the Family Mediation Association, and the Federal Law Enforcement Assistance Administration began providing mediation and educating the public about mediation in the 1960s and 1970s.[8] Local and regional organizations also appeared, which provided mediator training and community and neighborhood mediation services, such as Community Boards in San Francisco and the Institute for Mediation and Conflict Resolution in New York City (Zondervan 2000). Mediation programs and philosophies have never been monolithic; each program had its own approach to mediation and used different techniques and procedures to conduct mediation sessions (Woolford and Ratner 2008).

There is a wide variety of approaches to mediation and perspectives on its purpose and goals (Goldberg, Brett, and Blohorn-Brenneur 2017; McEwen 2006). These include the shuttle diplomacy, conciliation, and panel approaches, as well as the deal-making and orchestration approaches to mediation. The Institute for Mediation and Conflict Resolution in New York City used the shuttle diplomacy approach.[9] Their mediations were run by a panel of mediators (Felstiner and Williams 1978). The mediation sessions they ran began with an opening phase in which mediators conducted introductions and described the mediation philosophy and process. The mediators then held a joint session during which the disputants communicated the problems that brought them to mediation. The panel of mediators then held a private conference among themselves to discuss the case, and then brought in each disputant

---

[8] See Brown (1982); Folberg and Taylor (1984); Frenkel and Stark (2012).
[9] See Boulle et al. (2008), Ewert et al. (2010), and Wahrhaftig (1983) for historical information; see Shun (2018) for a discussion of contemporary uses of similar approaches.

in turn for private conferences with the mediators. The disputing parties were only brought back into a joint session when the panel believed a possible resolution had been identified (Felstiner and Williams 1978; see also Woolford and Ratner 2008).

While the shuttle diplomacy approach consists almost entirely of individual caucuses, other mediation programs conduct mediation in a joint session, using individual caucuses only when necessary. For example, the Community Board in San Francisco practiced what they call the "conciliation" model of mediation (Wahrhaftig 1983). The Community Board mediation program strived to not just resolve specific conflicts but to teach disputants how to resolve conflicts themselves. The joint session model of mediation was considered more beneficial than the shuttle diplomacy model for achieving this goal.

Most mediation programs encouraged or required disputants to represent themselves (Greenwald 1978), but there were some which required disputants to be represented by attorneys. For example, in mediation sessions run by the Philadelphia County Court of Common Pleas, panels of three attorneys served as the arbitrators and the disputants were represented by attorneys (Cerino and Rainone 1984). Some contemporary mediation programs also use attorneys as mediators, representatives of the disputants, or both (see, for example, Abramson 2005; Frenkel and Stark 2012; Mantle 2017).

There are also variations in mediation procedures which depend on the nature of the dispute being mediated. Consumer disputes may be resolved effectively in a relatively short mediation session of an hour or two in length (Cerino and Rainone 1984), while more complex disputes such as divorce and child custody mediations may require a series of sessions in order to reach agreement (Thoennes and Pearson 1985). While divorcing spouses typically have attorneys representing them, the attorneys usually play a behind the scenes role rather than attending the mediation sessions (Bahr 1981). This is one reason why mediation is a less expensive method of divorcing.

Differences in mediator style result in different degrees and types of intervention in the dispute resolution process. The "orchestrating" style of mediation was found in the context of state and federal labor mediation (Kolb 1981). The orchestrating mediator works as a facilitator or go-between, working to represent the positions of one side of the dispute to the other side. Kolb found that the "deal-making" style of mediation involved more intervention. This type of mediator engaged actively in the process, at times arguing with disputants, taking positions on issues or proposals for resolution, and working to achieve a fair outcome.

Today, a variety of new programs, organizations, and approaches to mediation have emerged. While the most common approach is facilitative mediation, the narrative and transformative approaches to mediation also have adherents and advocates and will be discussed here as well.

Facilitative Mediation

Facilitative mediators try to help disputants resolve their conflict while working to maintain disputant autonomy. While they may at times provide advice and information, they try to stay neutral and let disputants reach their own agreement.[10] They work to facilitate the mediation process and the interaction that occurs within the session. The stages of facilitative mediation typically include "opening the session, setting ground rules, gathering information, defining issues, exploring options, generating movement by forceful persuasion, and achieving agreement" (Bush 2013: 434).

The mediator role is stronger in facilitative mediation than in transformative mediation (see below). Woolford and Ratner (2008) note that facilitative mediators take active steps to encourage cooperative communication between the disputants rather than arguing. They note that mediator techniques such as summarizing disputants' positions or reformulating their statements may be effective. The mediation sessions that are analyzed in this book follow a facilitative approach to mediation.

A videotaped role play of a workplace mediation provides an example of a facilitative mediation (Merchant Dispute Resolution Center 2006). The two co-mediators in this session use a facilitative approach to resolving a dispute between a supervisor and one of the midlevel managers who works under him. The mediators begin with ground rules and a description of the mediation process. They ask the disputants not to interrupt each other, and to take notes instead. They ask them to avoid name-calling. The mediators state that they will work to be unbiased. Each party begins with a brief opening statement (they start with the complainant) in which they describe their issues. When one disputant interrupts the other, a mediator sanctions them for interrupting, and reminds them to take notes if there is anything they want to respond to later. They then begin the information-gathering phase. The mediators ask the disputants to describe the situation they are in and how it has affected them. The mediator uses paraphrases to reframe disputants' complaints in a more constructive direction. At one point a disputant speaks directly to the opposing disputant to make an accusation. The opposing disputant immediately denies the accusation. This initiates a short argumentative exchange. The mediator intervenes, but uses questions to redirect the conversation rather than sanctioning them for arguing or interrupting. The mediators help the disputants articulate their problems and the underlying interests each disputant has. They write the problem statements on an easel and ask the disputants to brainstorm ideas for resolution. They specify that the ideas can be anything they can think of,

---

[10] See Bishop et al. (2015); Boulle et al. (2008); Ewert et al. (2010); Frenkel and Stark (2012); Seaman (2016); Xu (2018).

and that they will not be held to anything they may suggest. After they have generated a list, the mediator asks them to see if any would work. The disputants select the solutions they prefer, and the mediators help the disputants write up the agreement. During the agreement-writing phase the ideas for resolution are clarified and elaborated as necessary.

Narrative Mediation

Narrative mediation is an approach based on the premise that listening to and understanding the stories disputants tell provides the key to resolving the conflict and improving the relationship between them.[11] The role of the mediator is to assist the disputants in telling their stories and understanding the nature of the problems they face. The belief is that this experience will help them create a more positive relationship with each other (Winslade and Monk 2008). Ewert et al. (2010) describe the narrative approach as follows:

LeBaron's view is that every person's self-image, belief system, and sense of meaning are based on the stories that have surrounded him or her since birth. These formative stories are endlessly diverse and equally valid. The narrative mediator deals with a conflict situation by trying to discover the formative stories belonging to each disputant. Having done that, the mediator helps each party break down their stories into their main elements and then reconstruct these elements into a larger narrative that integrates their own and the other party's interests. The mediator's main activity, in this scenario, is to gain the parties' trust and build rapport between them, so they can understand one another's stories. Through this process, parties are freed from the trap of their own socialization stories. (Ewert et al. 2010: 62)

The result of the narrative mediation process should be for the mediator to help participants construct a new story which is more positive and beneficial for both sides of the dispute (Bishop et al. 2015). This narrative model is more likely to be useful for disputes involving participants with ongoing relationships (such as divorce and family mediation), rather than problems between those with temporary or short term relationships (such as those typically resolved in small claims court mediations).

Transformative Mediation

The main goal of transformative mediation is to accomplish social change by empowering disputants through a process which enables them to learn how to resolve their own disputes (Bishop et al. 2015; Seaman 2016; Woolford and Ratner 2008). The transformative mediator works to

---

[11] See Boulle et al. (2008); LeBaron (2002); Seaman (2016); Winslade and Monk (2008).

help the parties recognize their interests and to help them develop their skills in communication and problem solving. Thus empowered, they can make appropriate decisions for themselves. This approach emphasizes mediation's educational function, and how mediation can transform individuals, groups, and society as a whole. (Ewert et al. 2010: 61)

In transformative mediation "the mediator's work focuses not on guiding the parties toward a solution to specific problems, but on supporting them in a constructive interaction about their situation and disagreements without focusing on problem solving per se" (Bush 2013: 431).[12] Transformative mediators are something like interactional coaches, as they work to help participants shift toward more positive interactional styles (Bush 2013). Bush (2013) writes that in transformative mediation, instead of controlling the process through facilitating disputants' progress through the stages of mediation, the mediator supports their communication by reflective listening (without rewording or reformulating their statements). Transformative mediators believe that they should be providing summaries of issues and arguments, and "highlighting decision points – but letting the parties decide" (Bush 2013: 444). In addition, transformative mediators are trained not to suppress arguing or interrupting between the disputing parties (Bush 2013).

There are several ways in which the transformative mediation session differs from the facilitative sessions described above (and from the data analyzed in this book). A videotaped example of a transformative mediation session provides an example of transformative mediation (Institute for the Study of Conflict Resolution 2011). Instead of describing the mediation procedure and setting ground rules in her opening, the transformative mediator tells the disputants, who are parents, that they will have a conversation to help them get a better understanding of their situation and their issues, and to give them the opportunity to listen to each other. The mediator's role is to support them and help them have the best conversation they can. The disputants are allowed to speak directly to each other. The mediator does not interrupt them, even if the discussion gets a little heated, but does take advantage of pauses or breaks in the discussion to summarize each disputant's position and perspective.

The summary work this transformative mediator does is different from that typically done by facilitative mediators in that she will more often reflect back the person's statements using the exact words and phrases that they used. She is much less likely to paraphrase or reframe their perspectives, and instead acts as a "mirror," holding each parent up to themselves so that they can clearly see their own position as well as the other parent's position. The mediator avoids making suggestions or sharing her own ideas for resolution. She uses caucuses

---

[12] See also Bush and Folger (2004); Bush and Pope (2002).

during the session in which she speaks to each parent privately. The mediator also highlights emotions when they are displayed and labels them for the disputants (Institute for the Study of Conflict Resolution 2011).

The mediation sessions studied in this book fit squarely in the facilitative mediation model as opposed to a transformational or narrative model (Hanley 2010). There is individual variation between mediators in their approach to the session, and in the degree to which disputants are allowed to deviate from the official structure of the mediation session. For example, as the analysis in this book will show, divorce mediation tends to provide disputants greater interactional autonomy and self-direction within the sessions than does small claims mediation.

Previous Research on Mediation

While mediation is marketed as empowering disputants to resolve their disputes in a nonadversarial setting, there are several factors which may impede the ability of mediators to achieve this goal. For example, the extent of mediator control over the production of ideas for resolution of the dispute as well as the challenge of potential power imbalances or differing levels of interactional competence between disputants, are potentially problematic for the fairness and utility of mediation as a conflict resolution procedure.[13] Such findings about the sources of mediation's strengths and weaknesses are important for mediation practitioners and for researchers evaluating the effectiveness of mediation.

Of the many types of disputes that can be resolved via mediation, the two most well known are divorce mediation and small claims mediation. The analysis in this book will cover both of these types of mediation and will explore the similarities and differences between them. Small claims mediation sessions tend to be comparatively brief, and typically require only one mediation session. They often involve disputants who will not necessarily have contact with each other after the conflict is resolved (e.g., a shopkeeper and a customer). With divorce mediation, on the other hand, the participants know each other well and the issues typically take several sessions to resolve. If the couple has children, the issues should be resolved such that the parents can remain on speaking terms after the divorce. These differences in the nature of the disputes and the relationships between the parties are reflected in and reflexively shape the interactions that occur in the two settings.

---

[13] See Cobb and Rifkin (1991a); Garcia (1995; 2010); Greatbatch and Dingwall (1989); Mayer (2004).

While advocates of mediation are very enthusiastic about its benefits, some argue that the strengths of mediation are also to some extent its weaknesses.[14] For example, although mediation attempts to protect the autonomy of disputants, less powerful disputants may be more disadvantaged in mediation than in other legal processes. The informality of the process of mediation may enable more forceful or otherwise powerful disputants to have an advantage (Bottomley 1985; Wing 2009). Some also question the possibility or desirability of true mediator impartiality.[15]

Mediation programs see fairness and neutrality of the mediator and the autonomy of the disputant as core values of the process.[16] These goals may be achieved through a variety of different methods and within a range of different styles and modes of mediation. While mediation programs differ in the degree of active intervention of the mediator in the interaction, there is consensus that mediators should not pressure disputants or treat them differently; these actions can lead to perceptions of bias on the part of the disputants. In all types of mediation:

[Mediators should] remain – and *appear* to remain – impartial and balanced with respect to competing positions, and disinterested and nondirective with respect to the content of any agreement. Mediators may influence the *process* – for example, seeing to it that both parties have equal opportunities to tell their stories, that both parties understand the perspective of the other, that both parties treat one another with civility, or that neither party is coerced into agreement – but mediators should not leave their mark on the *content* of the resolution … According to the official ideal of neutrality, [mediators] must resist the impulse to agree or disagree with one or the other party, to refute or support positions, to challenge and contradict, or to bolster and confirm. (Jacobs 2002: 1406)

Mediators are trained to avoid taking sides in the dispute, but there are several ways that bias could be conveyed unconsciously.[17] For example, unequal attention could be unintentionally displayed through talk, tone of voice, or body language (Shailor 1994). Because mediation is less formal and more flexible than court proceedings, inequality of treatment of the disputants can occur more readily.

---

[14] For example, see Bottomley (1985); Cobb and Rifkin (1991a); Garcia (1995); Merry (1989).

[15] For example, see Bishop et al. (2015); Kishore (2006); Mayer et al. (2012); Mulcahy (2001).

[16] See American Arbitration Association et al. (2005); see also Alberts et al. (2005); Boulle et al. (2008); Burton (1986); Center for Dispute Settlement (1988); Doneff and Ordover (2014); Donohue (2006); Douglas (2012); Frenkel and Stark (2012); Folberg and Taylor (1984); Jacobs (2002); Kressel (2000); Maggiolo (1985); Menkel-Meadow et al. (2011); Poitras and Raines (2013); Shailor (1994); Zetzel and Wixted (1984); Zumeta (2006).

[17] See Garcia et al. (2002); Jacobs (2002); Poitras (2013); Poitras and Raines (2013); Roberts (2008); Shailor (1994).

In spite of these potential challenges, research shows that mediation is perceived as fair and unbiased by the majority of participants. For example, Polkinghorn and McDermott (2006) found very high rates of agreement with statements that the mediator was neutral and the mediation procedures were fair. Wissler (2002) found similar results, with strong majorities believing that the process was fair and that mediators were neutral and impartial. However, studies show that at least some participants report dissatisfaction with the fairness of the process or neutrality of the mediator.[18]

In sum, a significant number of disputants in mediation perceive at least some degree of unfairness and mediator bias during the process. In addition, some of these studies may tend to overestimate the rates of satisfaction, for example by combining the "somewhat satisfied" and "very satisfied" categories (e.g., Bingham et al. 2009). This approach may obscure some of the disputant experiences that were problematic – something about the fairness of the mediation process led the client to check the "somewhat satisfied" box instead of the "very satisfied" box; it is not clear that these two experiences are equivalent. Although the dissatisfied clients are clearly in the minority, they are a significant portion of mediation clients. A disputant who perceives bias or unfairness might not choose mediation in the future or may not recommend it to others. In this instance, the mediator's goals of providing a fair and unbiased process have not been met.

Research on how disputant react when they experience bias during a mediation session reveals that these perceptions are rarely shared with the mediator, and rarely revealed during the mediation session.[19] On the rare occasions on which a disputant revealed perceptions of bias during a mediation session, it resulted in the termination of the mediation (Garcia, Vise, and Whitaker 2002; Jacobs 2002). These two studies used a conversation-analytic approach to directly examine the interaction in the session. This approach enables researchers to study mediation techniques directly and to examine how disputants respond to actions they perceive as unfair or biased. Most research on bias and unfairness in mediation uses survey or interview methods and therefore does not examine the interaction itself or the specific mediator actions that may have led to these perceptions.[20]

---

[18] See Bahr (1981); Benjamin and Irving (1995); Brett et al. (1996); Chandler (1990); Depner, Cannata, and Ricci (1994); Gaughan (1982); Gaybrick and Bryner (1981); Herrman et al. (2006); Irving and Benjamin (1992); Kelly (1989); Kelly and Duryee (1992); Meierding (1993); Neves (2009); Pearson and Thoennes (1985); Saposnek et al. (1984); Waldron et al. (1984).

[19] For example, see Charkoudian and Wayne (2010); Polkinghorn and McDermott (2006); Wall and Dewhurst (1991); Wissler (1995; 1999; 2002; 2004; 2006).

[20] For example, see Alberts et al. (2005); Brett et al. (1996); Donohue, Drake, and Roberto (1994); Herrman et al. (2006); Wissler (2002; 2006).

Interviewing mediators can provide useful information about the process of mediation (e.g., Granzner-Stuhr and Pogatschnigg 2012). However, survey or questionnaire-based research does not provide access to the actions of participants during the interaction in the mediation session (Dingwall 1986). While Kolb's (1981) study of mediator style involved both interviews and direct observation of what mediators did in the hearing, Gerhart and Drotning's (1980) study surveyed disputants after the completion of the mediation session. Their responses were therefore based on their impressions and memories of mediator style during the session rather than on direct observations of mediator's actions.

Surveys rely on participants' recollections of what happened; these post hoc reports are unlikely to provide the details needed to understand the interaction during the session.[21] Some studies combined post hoc surveys with direct observation of mediation sessions, but in these cases general categories of behavior (such as mediator's use of topic changes or paraphrasing disputant's utterances) tend to be coded rather than analyzing the use of these actions in context.[22]

In sum, much of the previous research on mediation has been based on research approaches which do not adequately investigate the interactional process of the session. An understanding of the mediation process on an interactional level must be obtained before comparative, simulation, or evaluative studies can be most fruitful. We need to discover how mediation works (or does not work, as the case may be).

Interactional Approaches to the Study of Mediation

There is increasing awareness that the interactional process of mediation helps facilitate the creation of agreement in mediation sessions. For example, there are differences in how mediators ask questions, use active listening techniques, or participate in brainstorming or "problem solving" in search of a solution (Bush 2013). There is also interaction research that explores disputants' actions during mediation sessions (e.g., Stokoe 2003). Previous research on mediation as an interactional event has suggested several potential sources of bias and nonneutrality in mediation including (1) the priority given the first speaker's story (Cobb and Rifkin 1991a); (2) the control mediators have over whether to discuss client's concerns (Greatbatch and Dingwall 1989); (3) the techniques mediators use to restate or reframe a client's position (Garcia

---

[21] For example, see Alberts et al. (2005); Polkinghorn and McDermott (2006); Shapiro and Brett (1993); Stimec and Poitras (2009).

[22] See Alberts et al. (2005); Charkoudian and Wayne (2010); Gale et al. (2002); Green et al. (2007); Greenwald and Krieger (2006); Herrman et al. (2006); Wall and Dewhurst (1991).

1995); and (4) the inequalities in speaking turns and mediator responses to client's turns (Garcia et al. 2002; Jacobs 2002).

Heisterkamp (2006b) identified several techniques for maintaining and displaying mediator neutrality. He found that mediators may explicitly identify themselves as a neutral mediator, paraphrase a disputant's remarks to display an unbiased understanding, and use perspective-display sequences (Maynard 1992) to get disputants' perspectives on the table. In addition, mediators can use footing shifts (Goffman 1981) to convey neutrality in the session (Heisterkamp 2006a; 2006b; Jacobs 2002).

A discourse analytic investigation of the effectiveness of community-based mediation was undertaken in a series of papers published by Sara Cobb and Janet Rifkin in the 1990s. Cobb and Rifkin (1991a) found that the way mediation sessions were organized and facilitated prevented the goal of mediator neutrality from being achieved. The disputant who got the first opportunity to tell their story has a privileged position in terms of setting the agenda and framing the meaning of events and actions described. The mediators they studied reinforced the influence of the first story by focusing on that disputant's issues and positions as they facilitated the session. This failure to elicit and facilitate the second disputant's story on an equal basis with the first made it hard for the second disputant to challenge the moral framework established by the first disputant. The mediators were therefore unable to construct a truly neutral mediation process (Cobb and Rifkin 1991a; see also Zamir 2011 for an analysis of similar problems in an environmental mediation). For these and other reasons, the assumption that mediators can achieve neutrality is problematic (Cobb and Rifkin 1991a; Mayer 2004).

Cobb and Rifkin (1991b) elaborate their critique of the neutrality of mediation through a study based on open-ended interviews of mediators and analysis of videotaped mediation sessions. They argue that the way neutrality in mediation is typically defined leads to practical problems in creating a truly neutral mediator role. For example, mediators they interviewed might describe how they maintained neutrality by siding with a weaker party in a dispute. They work to make the process fair by balancing power between the parties. Cobb and Rifkin (1991b) analyze the concept of neutrality in mediation as "impartiality" or "equidistance." They note that impartiality is typically conceived in terms of the mediator's perspective rather than in terms of their actions. They conclude that the mediator therefore actually has a lot of power in the mediation session and may inadvertently play a role in determining the outcome of the process instead of merely facilitating the process.

Cobb's (1993) article on empowerment in mediation uses interview data to construct a critique of the application of disputant empowerment in community and family mediation. The mediators she interviewed described empowerment of disputants as accomplished by their efforts to fairly facilitate the process while being impartial and working to balance power between the disputants. Cobb (1993) critiques the balancing power approach because it imposes the will of the mediator on disputants. The problem with controlling the process of mediation is that the mediator often inadvertently ends up controlling the content of the dispute. Finally, mediators' goal of maintaining neutrality may be perceived as directly contradictory to the goal of balancing power. In addition, individual differences in interactional skill affect disputants' ability to effectively convey and support their position and their version of events in a coherent narrative.[23] For example, Garcia (2010) showed how a disputant's skill in constructing her opening story affected the opportunities for the opposing disputant to present his case and rebut the first disputant's arguments.

In their role as facilitators of the session, mediators may control the topics that are addressed and the order in which they are discussed. Greatbatch and Dingwall's (1989) study of British divorce mediation found that mediators can shape the outcome of mediation through the control of topic shifts, what they refer to as "selective facilitation." While maintaining a display of neutrality by not taking positions during the session, the mediator can thus still have influence over the discussion of the issues or the creation of proposed solutions. In a subsequent study, they also found that divorce mediators' attempts to facilitate the session by asking questions or focusing the topic of talk may be resisted by disputants (Greatbatch and Dingwall 1994).

Other research has investigated how the interactional organization of mediation differed from the interactional organization of ordinary conversation. Mediation facilitated the creation of agreement between disputants while minimizing the occurrence of arguing between them by limiting direct address between the disputants (Garcia 1991). On the other hand, divorce mediators may allow the divorcing spouses to talk directly to each other rather than directing their remarks to the mediators (Greatbatch and Dingwall 1997). In addition, divorce mediators at times allowed extended arguing exchanges between the spouses when these exchanges did not become problematic. The spouses were sometimes able to wind down these argumentative exchanges themselves without the overt assistance of the mediator.

The divorce mediation sessions Greatbatch and Dingwall (1997) studied differ from the small claims data Garcia (1991) studied in several ways. In particular, in their data the ground rules of the mediation process did not restrict the disputants' right to speak (Greatbatch and Dingwall 1997), whereas in Garcia's data set disputants were instructed to avoid interrupting each other and to speak to the mediator rather than to each other. Greatbatch and Dingwall

---

[23] See Cobb (1993); Cobb and Rifkin (1991a); Poitras and Raines (2013).

(1997) showed that mediators helped disputants disengage from arguing by intervening to reframe or refocus the talk, interventions that served to restore mediator-addressed utterances. Disputants accomplished self-exit from argumentative exchanges by such techniques as refraining from speaking in response to an argumentative utterance, responding to what the disputant said but in a remark addressed to the mediators, saying something that indicated a refusal to engage in disputing, or providing an explanation instead of an argumentative response.

These previous studies reveal that in order to fully understand mediation and how it works, a direct examination of the interactional process within the session is necessary. These types of studies can also address the issues of equity, neutrality, and autonomy raised by critics. These findings suggest that the institutional role and authority of mediators in the session do not ensure that they are in control of every aspect of the session – what ends up happening in the session is also impacted by the disputants' willingness to cooperate with or resist the mediators' attempts to facilitate the ongoing process of the session.

This book will extend and expand on these prior research studies which work to understand mediation as an interactional process. I will show how the work being done by mediators to facilitate the creation of agreement between disputing parties is done through an interactional organization that supports the goals and constraints of mediation. I will explore how mediators do the work of facilitating the session, and how disputants both cooperate with and resist the efforts of the mediators. In addition, I explore how the mediators' actions as they facilitate the session work to increase or impede the goals of disputant autonomy and mediator neutrality in the dispute resolution process. I will use conversation analysis, an approach to the qualitative analysis of interactional data that developed out of ethnomethodology, to investigate how participants interact in mediation sessions. The interactional organization of mediation creates opportunities for dispute resolution at the same time as it provides for problematic actions, such as mediator bias, the exercise of power over disputants, and resistance of disputants to mediator attempts to facilitate the session fairly.

Theoretical Perspective and Analytical Approach

This book takes an ethnomethodological approach to the study of the process of mediation. Ethnomethodology investigates how people accomplish social action and social organization, and works to discover and understand the procedures and techniques people use to do this (Garfinkel 1967; Heritage 1984a; Silverman 1993; von Lehm 2014). The main concern of ethnomethodological research is to discover how people create and orient to the social organization or social setting in which they are participating (Heritage 1987: 231).

Conversation analysis is an ethnomethodological approach to the study of interaction which involves the qualitative analysis of talk in a variety of contexts.[24] Foundational research on how ordinary conversation is conducted, such as how turn taking is done (Sacks, Schegloff, and Jefferson 1974), how troubles in talk are repaired (Jefferson 1974), and how preference organization works (Schegloff, Jefferson, and Sacks 1977), have formed the basis of understanding participants' actions in many different types of interactions and institutional settings (e.g., Arminen 2005; Boden and Zimmerman 1991; Drew and Heritage 1992).

Conversation analysts study what participants do in interaction, and interpret systematic patterns in what they do as evidence of the rules and procedures participants follow to accomplish conversational interaction. The sequential context of utterances as they are produced in the interaction, the interactional context (type of institutional or informal context, nature of the participants, and reason for the interaction), and the physical and temporal contexts are all potentially relevant to the participants (Goodwin and Duranti 1992). Analysts, therefore, must analyze talk in its naturally occurring setting.[25]

Instead of interview data, participant observation, or coding schemes, conversation analysts rely on tape-recorded interactions. Detailed transcripts of recorded interactions are necessary because the subject of conversation analysis is not accessible by casual contact with the data and because interaction is accomplished and coordinated through precise placement of actions (Jefferson 1979; Schegloff 1979; West and Zimmerman 1982). The transcription system used was developed by Gail Jefferson (see, e.g., Atkinson and Heritage 1984; Jefferson 1984a; 2004a). These transcripts are not only verbatim records of the words participants use, they are attempts to reproduce as precisely as possible how participants say what they say. The transcripts include symbols indicating such characteristics of the talk as timing of utterances, presence of pauses, and the use of shifts in volume, drawing out of syllables, and other techniques to indicate stress or emphasis. Nonlinguistic utterances (such as sighs, laughs, and exclamations) are also transcribed. The transcription symbols used in this book are described in the appendix.

The conversation-analytic method has been applied to the study of how work is done through talk. Work in a wide range of institutional settings, such as medical, legal, media, and emergency service settings, has been investigated using this approach.[26] Conversation-analytic studies of talk in institutional

---

[24] See Arminen (2005); Heritage (1984a); Heritage and Clayman (2010); Sacks (1992); Sacks et al. (1974); Schegloff (2007); Sidnell (2010); ten Have (2007).

[25] See Heritage (1987); Heritage and Atkinson (1984); West and Zimmerman (1982).

[26] For example, see Atkinson and Drew (1979); Clayman and Heritage (2002); Heritage and Maynard (2006); Hutchby (2006); Maynard (1984); Peräkylä (1995); Whalen and Zimmerman (1998); Zimmerman (1984).

settings explore how the institutional context, roles, procedures, expectations, and constraints affect and are manifested through the actions of participants on a turn by turn level.[27] The intersection between institutional roles and the activities that occur in that setting can also be investigated with this method.[28]

In this book I analyze how participants do "mediation work" – discussing issues under dispute and working to create an agreement both parties can accept. In the context of this study of mediation, I am not interested in whether the participants reach a decision, but in how they reach that decision. By using the conversation-analytic method, we not only discover how work is done through talk in a particular institutional setting, but also discover its strengths and weaknesses. In the remainder of this chapter I will first describe the research settings for the three data sets analyzed in this book, and then summarize the chapters of the book.

The Research Settings

The data for this study come from three sources: (1) eleven mediation hearings videotaped from a county-run consumer complaints program on the West Coast, (2) eighteen mediation sessions from five multisession divorce and family mediation cases videotaped in the Midwest, and (3) fifteen small claims mediation hearings videotaped in the Midwest.[29] In this section of the chapter I will describe the three mediation programs studied and the procedures I used to collect the data in each setting.

Mediation programs vary in many ways, such as the number and role of the mediators, the organization of the session, the amount and type of direct contact between the disputants, and the presence or absence of lawyers.[30] Thus no claim is made for the representativeness of the mediation programs studied in this book (or for any other mediation program) to be regarded as "typical" mediation programs. However, this is not to imply that the mediation programs studied here are deviant or atypical. All three of these programs follow the guidelines of the American Arbitration Association, and thus share characteristics with many other mediation programs.

---

[27] For example, see Boden and Zimmerman (1991); Drew and Heritage (1992); Fairhurst (2007); Maynard (2003); Psathas (1995); Rouncefield and Tolmie (2011).
[28] See Boden and Zimmerman (1991); Button (1992); Halkowski (1990); Heritage (1984a); Heritage and Greatbatch (1991); Schegloff (1992).
[29] The two Midwest data sets were collected with support from my 1994 grant from the "Law and Social Sciences" program at the National Science Foundation (grant SBR-9411224).
[30] See Bahr (1981); Bishop et al. (2015); Cerino and Rainone (1984); Doneff and Ordover (2014); Felstiner and Williams (1978); Greenwald (1978); Thoennes and Pearson (1985); Wahrhaftig (1983).

The West Coast Data

The West Coast data were collected from a mediation program run by the Consumer Affairs office of a county in a western US state. When small claims court cases were deemed appropriate for mediation, they were referred to this mediation program. The program handled a wide range of cases, including consumer complaints, landlord–tenant disputes, and a variety of interpersonal issues such as family or neighborhood conflicts.

During the time these data were collected in 1987, this program had been operating for about nine years. Mediation was a voluntary process in this program, so both disputants must agree to participate. Because of this, there was not a high rate of participation in the mediation program. Only one or two mediations were held each month. However, compliance with the agreements made in mediation hearings was reported to be high (based on the low number of complaints about compliance after the hearings occurred). If noncompliance occurred, the disputants could take their mediated agreement to Superior Court to have it enforced.

I videotaped all nine hearings (plus two follow-up sessions) held during a six month period in 1987, a total of about twenty hours of videotape. The mediation sessions in this collection ranged from forty minutes to three hours in length, with a typical session running about an hour. A total of twenty-seven people participated in the sessions (some disputants brought colleagues, family members, or friends as co-disputants or for support).

The hearings in the sessions I recorded included three consumer complaints cases. One of these cases involved a carpet company (the "Patched Carpet" mediation), one involved an auto repair shop (the "Vehicle Repair" mediation), and one involved a company that made custom dresses (the "Custom-Made Dress" mediation session). Two of the hearings involved disputes between neighbors. The "Neighbors" mediation hearing involved two neighbors disputing about noise and harassment complaints, and the "Property Line" mediation involved two neighbors disputing about the use of land between their houses. There were three mediation hearings involving family members. In the "Two Brothers" mediation hearing two brothers disagreed about whether to sell the house they had inherited from their mother, in the "Blended Family" mediation a father and his ex-wife's new husband disputed about child care and transportation arrangements for three children, and in the "Joint Custody" hearing the father and his ex-wife disputed about child care and visitation arrangements. Finally, there was one landlord–tenant mediation hearing. In the "Childcare Center" mediation a landlord and his tenant were in disagreement over rents due and other financial issues resulting from a failed partnership in a childcare business.

The mediators in this program are volunteers from the community who receive five days of training from the director of the program. The hearings are almost always facilitated by two mediators working as a team. In this data set one session (the "Joint Custody" session) was led by a single mediator. The director made an effort to match the areas of professional expertize with the nature of the dispute. For example, the "Property Line" dispute was handled by two mediators with experience in real estate and construction.

The disputants in this mediation program are allowed to bring a lawyer with them (none of the disputants in these data did so), but lawyers are not allowed to speak during the hearing. The disputants are expected to represent themselves. The disputant filing the complaint is referred to as the "complainant," and the opposing disputant is referred to as the "respondent." Either side may bring witnesses or written statements to support their case.

These hearings have five stages: opening, storytelling, discussion, resolution generation, and closing. In the opening stage of the hearing, the mediators conduct introductions of all participants, describe the process of mediation, and have the complainant produce a brief statement of the complaint. During the storytelling phase the mediators ask first the complainant, and then the respondent to tell their version of what happened. These stories can be quite extensive and may last from ten to thirty or more minutes. A question-and-answer period typically follows each disputant's story, and private caucuses with individual disputants may also be used. If the disputants reach agreement on a solution to the issues under dispute, the mediators write up the agreement, which the disputants then sign.

The goal of the mediation process is to help the participants resolve the dispute by reaching a mutually agreeable settlement. If the disputants are unable to resolve the dispute through mediation, the mediators become arbitrators and decide for them.[31] Their decision is binding on both parties. The advantages of this mediation/arbitration program over litigation include privacy (mediation records are not public, while the records of small claims court cases are) and cost-effectiveness (the service is free and lawyers are not necessary). Another advantage is that both complainant and respondent get to speak for themselves and state their cases, something they might get little opportunity to do in court.

Data Collection. Permission for the study was obtained from the director of the mediation program, and before each hearing began I explained the study to the participants, and both the disputants and the mediators signed

---

[31] Arbitration is an alternative dispute resolution procedure in which the arbitrator has the power to make decisions on the disputants' behalf if they are unable to create an agreement on their own (American Arbitration Association 2016; Notz and Starke 1978). Arbitration is sometimes used independently (Greenspan, Brooks, and Walton 2018) but may also be used as a second step if mediation does not result in an agreement (see Barsky 2013; Bishop et al. 2015; Doneff and Ordover 2014; Maggiolo 1985).

consent forms. Participants agreed to have their mediation sessions videotaped, with the understanding that they could ask to have taping stopped at any time. Informal interviews were conducted with some of the mediators and with the director of the program, in order to obtain background information on the program and the perspective of mediators on their approach to mediation.

Recording Equipment. It should be noted that in 1987 the equipment used for video-recording was not only much more cumbersome but also more difficult to use than the types of recording devices in use today. I used a single color video camera to cover the table at which the participants were seated, and a cassette tape recorder as a backup in case the video camera failed at any point (fortunately this did not occur). Since I had only one camera, I had to use a handle to shift the direction of the camera as different people spoke; at times I focused it broadly on the group as a whole, and at times I turned the camera to focus in on the current speaker. Because of this, it was not always possible to study the nonverbal behavior of nonspeaking participants.

The equipment used to record the hearings required me to be in the room during the hearings in order to run the equipment. I made every effort to behave unobtrusively while recording the mediation hearings (Webb et al. 1981), including facing away from the table and watching the hearing on a monitor instead of staring at participants directly. I wore headphones to check the volume levels of the recording. The control lever for moving the camera enabled me to shift the camera's view while watching the hearing on a small monitor instead of turning my head to face the participants. In short, I did my best to convey that I was "unavailable for interaction."[32]

Thus, even though I was in the room during the mediation hearing and attending to every thing that happened, these measures appear to have been successful in being as unobtrusive as possible. Several disputants told me, during breaks from their mediation hearing, that they had forgotten that they were being videotaped.

Midwest Small Claims Mediation Data

Fifteen small claims mediation hearings were video recorded at a mediation program in a Midwest city in 1994. The Midwest small claims mediation program was funded by the county and city, and had a paid director, paid mediators, and several paid staff members. Once a person calls or walks in and registers a complaint with the receptionist, the opposing party is contacted

---

[32] See Goffman (1963); Maynard (1984); Schegloff (1968).

and a hearing scheduled. Cases were also referred to the mediation program directly from the small claims court.

In this program mediation was used as an alternative to small claims court. If the disputants did not reach a resolution in mediation, they were taken back to small claims court and their case was heard by a judge that day. The mediation sessions were facilitated by a paid mediator. If more than one person was involved in the case, two or more people could participate on each side of the dispute. Disputants were not allowed to bring persons not directly involved in the issue into the session. These mediation sessions lasted from twenty minutes to an hour and a half, with about forty-five minutes being a typical length.

I learned about this mediation program from the friend of a colleague who worked as a mediator for this program. The director of the program was initially concerned with how the study might affect the confidentiality of the mediation hearings. After I gave her copies of my research proposal and consent forms, the director consulted with other members of her staff. She then suggested several changes in procedures and revisions to the permissions forms. We were able to come to an agreement about these confidentiality issues and human subjects protection procedures, and the study was approved.

In the Midwest small claims program, the decision as to which specific hearings to videotape were made by practical rather than theoretical concerns. I had two graduate student research assistants working with me who were funded by the National Science Foundation grant. Given our teaching and class schedules, there were only a couple of mornings a week we were available for taping. Another constraint was the preferences of the mediators. There were five or six mediators handling small claims cases at this time, and all agreed to participate in the study. However, after one of the mediators had the experience of being videotaped, she said it distracted her from her work, and asked not to be videotaped in the future. Therefore on days when that mediator was on duty, we did not collect data. There were also three or four occasions on which one of the disputants declined to participate in the study. So we were not able to record all of the hearings during the time we were collecting data.

The Setting. Not all of the hearing rooms were large enough to set up the video equipment sufficiently far back from the table in order to cover all participants. Because of this we selected one of the larger rooms to set up the video equipment. When disputants arrived for their hearing, they were first shown into a smaller room by the mediator, and left with me or one of the research assistants. We quickly described the research project and gave them copies of the permissions forms. If they were interested in participating in the project, they read and signed the forms. If not, we thanked them for their time and immediately left the room so the mediator could begin their hearing.

The mediator would step out into the hall during this process so that disputants would not feel under pressure to agree to participate.

We made a backup audio copy of the hearing at the same time we video recorded it. The research assistant (or, in some cases myself), sat in the room to supervise the video camera and make sure it was still operating, and to turn over the audio cassette tape when necessary. The research assistants were instructed to remain silent and direct their attention to the equipment or their notes so that the mediation participants would be less likely to be self-conscious.

The Organization of the Hearings. The mediators had a set routine for beginning each hearing. First, the participants were asked to sign a form saying that they understood that their small claims case had been referred to mediation, and that they were not obligated to resolve it there. After performing introductions, the mediator then briefly described the purpose of mediation and how the hearing would be organized. Unlike the West Coast mediation hearings described above, the mediators in the Midwest mediation program were not arbitrators. If the mediation was unsuccessful, the disputants would return to small claims court.

The mediator emphasizes that the mediation hearing is confidential, and sets ground rules for the hearing (such as asking the disputants not to interrupt and to direct their remarks to the mediator rather than each other). The mediator then typically asks the person who filed the suit (or, the person who filed the first suit, since in some cases there was a countersuit), to make an opening statement in which they explain what the problem is and tell their story of the events.

During the remainder of the hearing, the mediator typically asks questions of the first disputant, and then lets the opposing disputant tell their story. A more general question-and-answer period follows. At some point the mediator initiates the transition to the problem-solving stage of the hearing, in which she or he attempts to elicit suggestions for resolution from the disputants, or to produce such suggestions himself or herself. Mediators use caucuses when there appears to be a stalemate, when they have something they want to say to only one party, or when the discussion is unproductive or argumentative (Goldberg et al. 2017).

Midwest Divorce and Family Mediation Data

The Midwest divorce mediation program was run by the "Arnold Institute," a nonprofit organization which provides a wide range of services to families and children. Most of their cases involved divorcing parents with children, although services were also provided to nonmarried couples. The divorce mediations were led by teams of family practice mediators who had both mediation and family counseling training. The co-mediator was typically a trained family counselor who was working to achieve their certification as a family practice mediator. This certification process involved a combination of classroom training and service as a co-mediator with a trained mediator. Each session lasted from one to one and a half hours, and each couple typically participated in between three and five mediation sessions.

Access to the Setting. Because of the confidential nature of divorce mediation hearings, access to this setting was challenging, and took a number of back and forth discussions over procedures and consent forms in order to accomplish. Privacy and voluntariness were both of great concern to the Arnold Institute. The agreement to collect data included the restrictions that the videotapes would not be made available to mediation clients, and would not be shown in undergraduate classes or in conference presentations in the region. The Arnold Institute requested and was given copies of the videotapes for mediator training purposes.

Data Collection Procedure. Mediation clients at the Arnold Institute were sent a letter informing them that a study was in progress and that they might be asked to participate when they arrived for their session. When participants arrived for their first session, I met them in the waiting room area, briefly explained the study to them, gave them copies of the permissions forms, and asked if they would be willing to participate. Three couples declined to participate. If both spouses agreed, they read and signed the permissions forms and were introduced to their mediators who took them upstairs to a room where the recording equipment was already set up.

Equipment and Recording. The video camera was set up in the room so it could get all four participants on camera at the same time. We arranged the chairs (which were placed around a low table) so that the disputants' faces would appear directly on the tape, and the mediators would be recorded in profile. With one camera it was not possible to get direct shots of all participants' faces. In addition, a small portable tape recorder was used, with a microphone on the small table, to get a backup copy of the audiotape. This tape recorder and microphone were of high quality, and produced a better sound quality than that achieved by the video camera (although the SVHS video camera was also of high quality and produced a very good audio record). Because of this, we used the "backup" audio tapes as our main source for making the transcripts. Initially, we had decided that myself or a research assistant would have to be in the room during the hearing to do the videotaping. However, the modern (for that time) video camera was so reliable that we soon became convinced that this step was not necessary. We then began a practice of having the research assistant set up the equipment and turn it on, then leave the room shortly after the hearing had begun, when they were sure everything was working properly. This procedure did cost us one session, however. There was one session where the video camera failed because the research assistant had not set up the equipment properly, so we had to rely on the audio backup.

Data Preparation. A number of different research assistants helped with the transcription of the data from the Midwest mediation programs. I checked each transcript and made changes as necessary. The pauses were timed by means of a stop watch, providing accuracy within about two to three tenths of a second. Pseudonyms were used for all names and addresses of individuals and organizations.

Recent Examples of Mediation

In addition to the three data sets analyzed in this book, I directly observed or viewed the video tapes of an additional ten mediation sessions which occurred within the last ten years. The purpose of these observations was to evaluate the extent to which the approach to mediation used currently is similar to that used during the 1980s and 1990s.

I observed five divorce mediation sessions facilitated by a professional mediator in 2012. This experience enabled me to evaluate the extent to which divorce mediation today is similar to that used in the last two decades. This professional mediator worked alone rather than with a co-mediator. In addition, this mediator was more directive in terms of topics to be discussed than were the mediators in the Midwest and West Coast data sets.

I also watched five publicly available DVDs of mediation sessions in order to get a sense of how similar current mediation practice is to the mediation sessions analyzed in this book.[33] Some of these were recordings of actual mediation sessions, and the others were role plays or reproductions of mediations with actors playing the roles of the disputants with a genuine mediator. These mediation sessions were not analyzed for this book for several reasons. First, because they were produced and made publicly available for educational purposes, we can assume that they were selected because they are "exemplary" examples of mediation rather than typical mediations. Second, because they come from four different sources and from mediation programs with a variety

---

[33] See Fighting Fair (2006; 2010); Merchant Dispute Resolution Center (2006); Program on Negotiation (2009–2010).

of approaches they do not constitute a coherent collection of data. Third, because at least three of the recorded sessions were role plays, the interaction is not necessarily the same as it would have been if they were recordings of actual sessions. However, they are useful as a comparison to show the extent to which the mediation sessions studied in this book are similar to mediation sessions as currently conducted by a wide range of mediation programs. Since these five sessions were all recorded within the past several years, they provide current examples to compare with the data sets analyzed in this book (which were collected during the late 1980s and mid 1990s). They provide assurance that the basic interactional structure of mediation has not shifted significantly since the data analyzed in this book were recorded. These publicly available mediations include two workplace mediations, two family mediations, and a landlord–tenant mediation.

Training and Experience as a Volunteer Mediator

I completed three different mediation training programs in the 1990s, and served several times as a volunteer mediator for a nonprofit organization and for a university. These experiences helped me better understand the job of mediator, and gave me an appreciation of the challenge of responding to issues as they arise during the mediation session. I have also participated in one mediation session as a disputant. This experience gave me an appreciation of the challenges of participating in a mediation session and working to make compromises.

Chapter Summaries

In this book I explore the interactional organization of mediation sessions from a conversation-analytic perspective. I will analyze the three data sets described above, expand and extend previous research, and investigate unexplored aspects of mediation such as mediator teamwork and how divorce mediation differs from small claims mediation.

Some of the chapters in this book were based in part on previously published research articles. Each of these previous articles analyzed only parts of the data set, and in this book the analysis has been expanded to include all of the data sets. Parts of the analysis in Chapters 2 and 3 are based on my 1991 paper in the *American Sociological Review* ("Dispute resolution without disputing: How the interactional organization of mediation hearings minimizes argument"). Parts of the analysis in Chapter 5 are based on my 1995 paper in the *Journal of Sociology and Social Welfare* ("The problematics of representation in community mediation hearings: Implications for mediation practice"). And finally, parts of the analysis in Chapters 6 and 7 were based respectively on two papers in *Discourse and Society* (2000, "Negotiating negotiation: The collaborative production of resolution in small claims mediation hearings" and 1997, "Interactional constraints on proposal generation in mediation hearings: A preliminary investigation").

In Chapter 2 I analyze the interactional organization of mediation sessions and describe their turn-taking system and participation framework. The turn-taking system of ordinary conversation is a basic structure which is varied to produce other types of interactions, often through prespecification of some or all of the turn-taking parameters (Sacks et al. 1974). I analyze how participants display an orientation to the speech exchange system of mediation, and how mediators work to maintain this interactional organization in the face of disputant departures from it. The chapter concludes with a comparison of the interactional organization of the small claims and divorce mediation cases. In the divorce mediation sessions a hybrid format, combining aspects of the mediation format with a more conversational turn-taking procedure and participation framework, also occurs.

One of the goals of mediation is de-emphasizing the adversarial nature of the situation and encouraging cooperation and compromise. In an earlier study of the West Coast data I showed how participants accomplish these goals of dispute resolution while minimizing arguing and working to avoid the escalation of arguments (Garcia 1991). Chapter 3 analyzes how argumentative talk in mediation is minimized in all three data sets. The chapter begins with an analysis of how arguing occurs in ordinary conversation, to show how the speech exchange of mediation creates an interactional environment which minimizes the production of arguments. Because the interactional organization of mediation differs from that of ordinary conversation in key ways, disputing techniques routinely used in arguments can not typically be used. This interactional organization facilitates the discussion of issues and the negotiation of agreements without unproductive arguing or escalating into conflict. Arguments in mediation are avoided or minimized by how accusations and denials are placed and constructed and by a speech exchange system which provides for the delay of responses to accusations. I also analyze the brief exchanges of argumentative talk that occur in these data and show how disputants and mediators work to manage and exit from them.

The techniques mediators use to solicit and facilitate the production of disputants' opening statements or stories describing the dispute are investigated in Chapter 4. Different methods of determining which disputant goes first and of soliciting disputants' stories are used in the small claims and divorce mediation programs studied. Once such stories have been solicited, mediators facilitate their production with a range of techniques and interventions. In addition, I show how the solicitation of the second disputant's story differs from the solicitation of the first disputant's story.

This chapter also examines the interactional techniques disputants use in their opening stories to present a strong case and to counter opposing disputants' claims. While some of the resources available to disputants to construct persuasive stories (such as the presentation of various types of evidence and claims of fairness, reasonableness, and trustworthiness) can be used by both disputants, the teller of the first story has certain advantages in that they can more readily use preemptive moves. The first disputant can both describe the conflict and report events that led up to the dispute, and also preemptively respond to projected defenses or counteraccusations that might be eventually made by the second disputant. However, the analysis of these data shows that there are also some advantages to being the second disputant, such as the opportunity to selectively respond to only those complaints or accusations that can be responded to advantageously.

A major mediator technique in facilitative mediation is to repeat, paraphrase, or summarize disputant's statements, positions, or stories. Mediators use a range of techniques to respond to and convey disputant's positions. How these differing formulations and practices affect the process of negotiation, disputant autonomy, and mediator neutrality in both small claims and divorce mediation sessions are addressed in Chapter 5. These reformulations can show the disputant that they have been heard correctly, articulate the disputant's position in a way that the opposing disputant can hear and understand, and reframe or repackage positions in order to give disputants new ways of thinking about issues.

However, while functional for mediation in several ways, these types of mediator interventions may conflict with mediation values. One of the main advantages of mediation over other forms of conflict resolution is that disputants get to tell their own story instead of having a lawyer speak for them or a judge control the process. When mediators represent disputants, they may interfere with the autonomy mediation has promised. In this chapter I show how mediators also engage substantially in the disputants' communicative processes as they tell their stories, respond to the positions of the opposing disputant, and discuss possible resolutions of the dispute.

Chapters 6 and 7 investigate how the interactional organization of mediation both facilitates and constrains how disputants and mediators participate in the proposal-generation process. Chapter 6 begins with an analysis of how mediators solicit the disputant's ideas for resolution of the dispute. I show how the mediator's choices for how to construct proposal solicits impact the parameters of the disputant's responses. General solicits leave the type of proposal open. Specific solicits work to elicit new ideas not yet suggested, related to a specific issue or topic, or which change or elaborate an existing proposal (Garcia 2000).

Although disputants can resist mediator solicits by avoiding or delaying production of proposals, a mediator may pursue proposal production by reissuing or revising the proposal solicit. This pursuit may make it difficult for disputants to avoid producing a proposal. The fact that there is flexibility in how and when proposals are produced raises questions about the degree of mediator control and disputant autonomy in this important aspect of the dispute resolution process. For example, disputants may differ in their skill in resisting mediator solicits or in finding or creating good places for their proposals.

While in facilitative mediation the mediator is supposed to facilitate disputants' discussion of substantive issues rather than engaging in the substantive issues themselves, in these data mediators often participate in the production of ideas for resolution of the dispute. In Chapter 7 I show how mediators' production of suggestions for resolution can be problematic. Mediators must work to display their orientation to the norms of mediator neutrality and disputant autonomy as they formulate these suggestions. Mediators use a variety of techniques to present their proposals as suggestions rather than proscriptions (e.g., by using mitigation techniques or formulating the suggestion as an informational question rather than as a proposal). Disputants, on the other hand, are free to make proposals. They typically formulate them as "offers" or "position reports" by directly or indirectly conveying their support for the idea (Garcia 1997). This chapter includes a comparison of how proposals are produced in divorce and small claims mediation sessions. The proposals produced in the divorce and family mediation sessions were more likely to be collectively oriented and to be produced in quasi-conversational or hybrid exchanges involving both disputants.

The use of a team of co-mediators is a common practice in mediation, and more than half of the sessions in these data were facilitated by teams of two co-mediators. In Chapter 8 I investigate how co-mediators effectively coordinate their actions with each other while facilitating the mediation session. I first examine how failures of mediator teamwork can occur. I found three types of misalignment between co-mediators in these data: activity misalignment, substantive misalignment, and interactional misalignment. Most of the co-mediation work in these data was successful, with co-mediators displaying a shared orientation to the mediation process and modeling cooperative behavior for the disputants. These displays of mediator alignment are accomplished through the use of silence, explicit negotiation, expressions of agreement, paraphrasing, sentence completions, and-prefaces, and complementary actions.

Chapter 9 summarizes the work of this book and discusses the implications of these findings for how research on mediation should be done. The strengths and weaknesses of mediation as a conflict resolution procedure are revealed by this type of analysis of how it works. The detailed in-depth understanding of the interactional process provided by conversation analysis enables us to understand the similarities and differences between small claims and divorce mediation sessions. Mediation's reliance on the procedures of conversational interaction creates opportunities for conflict resolution, as well as for the exercise of power, bias, competition, and resistance. The use of the conversation-analytic approach therefore reveals not just how mediation works and how it achieves its official goals, but what its weaknesses are and how contingencies can be exploited by participants for strategic purposes. I conclude with a consideration of the implications of these findings for future research on mediation, as well as for mediation clients and practitioners.

2   The Interactional Organization of Mediation

The mediators in these data play major roles in shaping the interaction that occurs in the sessions. This chapter therefore begins with a discussion of how mediators open the session and explain the ground rules of the mediation process and expectations for disputant behavior. In a previous study of the West Coast small claims mediation program, I found that disputants were instructed to address their remarks to the mediators, to avoid interrupting each other, and to wait until solicited to speak by a mediator (Garcia 1991). This interactional organization was functional for the process of conflict resolution because it enabled participants to constructively discuss problems while minimizing the occurrence and escalation of arguing. This chapter extends that previous research by incorporating the analysis of all three data sets. I will show how mediators display their orientation to the speech exchange system of mediation through their facilitation of the session and management of departures from the turn-taking system.

This chapter also investigates some key variations in interactional organization between the different mediation programs studied, in particular between the small claims and divorce mediation programs. The divorce mediation sessions, especially in later sessions of these multisession cases, at times have a more conversational structure than is typical in the small claims mediation sessions. I describe and contrast this "hybrid" style with the typical mediation format and show how it incorporates elements of both conversational and mediation speech exchange systems.

Mediation Session Openings

The mediator's approach to opening the session and explaining the process of mediation to the disputants has an impact on the interactional organization of the session and its subsequent effectiveness in solving problems and creating agreement. The specific instructions mediators give to disputants in the opening portion of the hearing vary from program to program and from mediator to mediator.[1] How the mediators opened the sessions and explained the mediation procedures differed in the small claims and divorce mediation programs in these data. In the small claims programs, the mediators facilitate introductions, have disputants sign the agreement to mediate, briefly describe the process of mediation, and then solicit the first disputant's story or statement of the problem.

The process of opening the session is more extensive in the divorce mediation cases. Divorce cases take several mediation sessions to complete, because there are more issues to resolve and since children are involved, the issues may be more complex. There are also more documents to sign in the opening portion of the session. Mediation divorce cases may therefore require longer descriptions of the mediation procedures than do the small claims sessions. I will first describe the opening stage of a small claims mediation, and then contrast this with the opening of a divorce mediation case.

Small Claims Mediation Session Openings

The introductory stage of the small claims mediation sessions in these data is fairly consistent from one mediation to another. This consistency reflects the philosophy of the mediation programs and the effectiveness of the training programs the mediators have completed. In this section I will use one mediator's introduction to the session to illustrate how openings were handled in these small claims mediation sessions.

The mediator began the session by conducting introductions and asking the disputants what they would like to be called during the hearing (not shown). She then explained the agreement to mediate form. After the disputants signed that document, the mediator began describing the mediation process (Excerpt 2.1):

Excerpt 2.1 Washer Dryer Midwest Small Claims Mediation, p. 2

```
60  Med:  Thuh purpose of mediation is tuh bring together people >who
61        have uh dispute?< (0.3) .h Give them an opportunity tuh sit
62        down? (0.5) .h talk about it? (0.5) listen >tuh thee other< parties?
63        (0.4) .h And see if they can voluntarily resolve it through an
64        agreement. (0.8) .h As I said over in thuh courthouse, if you don't get
65        it worked out here? (0.4) .h you will go back? (0.4) .h and proceed
66        tuh trial, (0.3) this morning.
```

[1] See Boulle et al. (2008); Doneff and Ordover (2014); Ewert et al. (2010); Frenkel and Stark (2012); Madonik (2001); McCorkle and Reese (2015); Picard (2016); Tracy and Spradlin (1994).

The mediator's explanation of the mediation process includes a discussion of the voluntary nature of mediation (lines 63–64). If the disputants do not reach agreement they will return to small claims court where their case will be heard by the judge (lines 64–66). This reassures the disputants that they will not be forced to come to an agreement in mediation.

The mediator's explanation of the nonadversarial nature of mediation (lines 67–78) is illustrated in Excerpt 2.2.

Excerpt 2.2 Washer Dryer Midwest Small Claims Mediation, p. 2

67 Med: (0.6) .h THERE ARE some advantages in resolving uh dispute
68   through mediation, (0.4) .h as opposed tuh submitting uh case tuh
69   trial! (0.6) .h If it goes tuh trial? (0.9) °one of° one party wins, one
70   party lo:ses! (0.3) °That's° that's thuh nature (0.4) .h of thee
71   adversarial system. (0.6) .h Half thuh people who walk into uh
72   courtroom? are going to lose their cases! (0.5) .h And NOBODY'S
73   sure which side that's gonna be. (0.6) .h In mediation, what we're
74   going tuh do is see if there's some possible middle ground, (0.6) .h
75   that you all can find so that everyone can walk away (0.4) .h
76   rea:sonably satisfied with thee outcome. (0.4) .h But not uh winner
77   loser kind of °concept, >So this is uh little different way of<° (0.4)
78   approaching uh problem.

The mediator emphasizes the benefits of a nonadversarial approach to conflict resolution, explaining that a middle ground can be reached instead of having one side win and the other side lose (lines 69–70 and 76–78). The goal of finding a middle ground is apparent in most of the mediation sessions in these data. While compromise is an appropriate value for a mediation program, there are some cases in which one side's position is genuinely superior to the other's. Under those circumstances, or where at least one party believes that those are the circumstances, it may not be feasible or desirable to reach a compromise.

Excerpt 2.3 shows the mediator explaining the benefits of the autonomy disputants have in mediation:

Excerpt 2.3 Washer Dryer Midwest Small Claims Mediation, p. 2

79 Med: (0.6) .hh ANOTHER ADvantage <is that> (0.6) .h IF IT
80   goes tuh trial? thuh referee? (1.0) >who acts in th' capacity of uh
81   judge,< (0.5) .h will control thee outcome. (0.4) and thuh ter:ms
82   (0.5) of thee outcome. (0.7) .h Here? you all are in control °of that.°
83   (0.8) .h This will be resolved thuh way you want it resolved? (0.5)
84   .h not thuh way uh third party wants it tuh be worked °out.°

The disputants have the power to reach an agreement or to decide not to reach an agreement. The mediation process also has the advantage of being confidential (Excerpt 2.4). This aspect of mediation is of particular interest to business owners, who often do not want a public display of customers' dissatisfaction with their services:

Excerpt 2.4 Washer Dryer Midwest Small Claims Mediation, p. 2

```
85  Med:  (1.0) tch .h SO >there are< there are some °distinct advantages (0.4)
86         in in uh resolution through thuh hearing.° (1.2) .h What you say in
87         here is confidential. (0.5) .h If you go back tuh trial, I don't go back
88         and talk thuh referee? (0.4) .h So: you can be as upfront in here as
89         possible.
```

In Excerpt 2.5 the mediator explains the mediation process (lines 90–94) and the role of the mediator (lines 94–98). The mediator is there to facilitate the process, not to make a decision for the disputants. This excerpt also shows how mediation differs from trials (lines 99–102):

Excerpt 2.5 Washer Dryer Small Claims Mediation, p. 2

```
90  Med:  (0.6) .h WHAT WE'LL do? I'll ask each of you (0.6) .h tuh talk
91         about (0.6) YOUR perspective on thuh on thuh °situation?° (0.5) .h
92         °What brought you tuh court today?° (0.4) .h u:m (0.7) When we've
93         explored that? (0.5) I will then ask each of you (0.3) to suggest ways
94         it could be worked out! (0.7) .h As uh mediator! (0.6) I don't impose
95         an agreement on anyone? (0.5) .h I don't even make suggestions?
96         (0.6) uh as to uh possible outcome? (0.4) .h unless: you either ASK
97         my assistance? or you're close to: (0.5) .h uh resolution and maybe
98         some of my (0.4) input would be helpful to you! (0.4) .h u:m
99         But it isn't uh mini trial. (0.4) I don't act as uh (0.4) referee?
100        or uh judge? or an attorney °here?° (0.7) .h So: (0.9) HOPEfully
101        you'll be able to: (0.5) to find uh way to get this resolved so that you
102        can all (0.8) .h °y'know, be° (0.6) be satisfied with thee outcome.
```

The mediator explains that the primary difference between mediation and small claims court is that the mediator has no authority to make a decision.

Mediators in these small claims mediations differ in their approach to the ground rules for behavior during the session. Some mediators articulate an explicit prohibition against interruptions, while others wait to see how the interaction unfolds. They may then ask disputants not to interrupt each other. In Excerpt 2.6 the mediator explains her "ground rules" for the process (lines 103–107).

Excerpt 2.6 Washer Dryer Midwest Small Claims Mediation, p. 2

```
103 Med:  (0.4) .hh TO INSU:RE that thuh hearing? (0.9) proceeds in uh civil?
104        a:nd we hope uh productive way, (0.3) .h I do ask participants to
105        agree to uh couple uh ground rules. (0.4) .h particularly at thuh
106        beginning? (0.7) That you speak tuh me? (0.4) not each other? (0.4)
107        .h and not interrupt when somebody else is °talking.° (0.5) .h Tish,
108        are those agreeable?
109        (0.5)
```

110 Tish: You bet!
111   (0.4)
112 Med: Thank you. [John? Thanks!   ] (0.7) Anna? (0.5) Thank you
113 John: [°Yeah.° °°Mm hm!°°]
114 Med: (0.4) .h LET'S GET STARTED THEN! (0.4) um (0.8) .h TISH?
115   would you like tuh begin? I HAVEN'T LOOKED in thuh jacket
116   so I don't know what thuh problem is? (0.5) Can you talk about it
117   °uh little bit?°

The mediator asks the disputants to direct their remarks to her rather than to each other, and to avoid interruptions (lines 106–107). After this description, the mediator solicits the disputants' agreement to participate in the mediation session as outlined (lines 107–108, 112). After the disputants agree to the ground rules, the mediator begins the session by soliciting the complainant's story (lines 114–117).

In sum, the small claims mediators communicate that they are acting as facilitators of the session. Disputants are almost always instructed to direct their remarks to the mediator instead of to each other, and to not interrupt each other. The small claims mediation session is thus largely a series of alternating two-party exchanges between the mediator and each disputant individually, with the mediator acting as liaison between the opposing disputants.

Divorce Mediation Session Openings

There are several ways in which the opening stage of divorce mediation sessions differs from the small claims cases discussed above. First, the divorce mediation sessions are led by teams of two co-mediators instead of a single mediator. Second, divorce mediation involves multiple sessions, which also impacts how the process unfolds. Third, since the disputing parties in these divorce mediation cases all have children, they will have continuing interaction with each other after their divorces have been finalized. The mediation process must therefore enable the participants to maintain productive communication with each other after the divorce.

Excerpt 2.7 illustrates how the divorce mediators typically handled the opening stage of the first session. Mediator A is the lead mediator and plays a major role in the opening stage of the session. She begins the session while handing out literature and documents to the participants (lines 12–17). The "Arnold" Institute referred to in line 12 is the nonprofit organization which runs the mediation program.

Excerpt 2.7 Jon and Liz Midwest Divorce Mediation, Session 1, p. 1

12 MA: This is uh PACKet of information about?, (1.2) A:rnold?, (0.4) and
13   has one of our newsletters and .h (0.5) there's ALso in there?, (0.4)
14   an agreement tuh mediate! (1.3) And I'll be h (1.2) walking

15   through that! with you?, (0.8) and asking you again tuh (0.1) si:gn.
16   (1.0) uhm (1.4) this agreement! tuh mediate, (0.4) So, if you
17   HAVE questions as I'm going alo:ng?, (1.1) just bring 'em up.

While in the small claims sessions mediators typically instructed disputants to direct their remarks to the mediator instead of to each other and to refrain from interrupting, some of the divorce mediators specifically invited the spouses to participate actively in the session and to ask questions when necessary. In Excerpt 2.7, Mediator A explicitly gives the spouses permission to interrupt to ask questions (lines 16–17). She then begins to explain the mediation process (Excerpt 2.8):

Excerpt 2.8 Jon and Liz Midwest Divorce Mediation, Session 1, p. 2

30 MA: All right we:ll?, .hh (0.5) Harrison County only refers people that
31   they (0.2) think (0.5) have (0.5) hope of (1.0) settling things on
32   your o:wn, (0.5) without having .hh (0.3) your law:yers settle it or
33   (0.7) thuh court (0.4) make uh recommendation. (0.4) [So   ]
34 ?:   [°Mm]hmm°
35   (1.0)
36 MA: Hopefully we will be able tuh talk things ou:t and you'll be
37   able tuh reach agreements: and (0.8) keep yourselves outta thuh
38   court. (0.7) 'cause thuh court can be more stressful than this:! So.
39   (0.7) tch (0.5) I ha' (0.2) I hope! that you'll be able tuh make some
40   progress here. (1.1) ahm (1.2) Mediation is meant tuh be uh
41   cooperative process. (1.3) .h which mea:ns tha:t thhh uhm we
42   hope that you'll both feel that you can say >whatever you need tuh
43   say< in he:re?, (0.3) and?, feel that you're hea:rd?, (0.4) both by
44   each other and by us:.

Mediator A emphasizes the difference between having their divorce settled by the court and negotiating an agreement themselves. She first addresses how this autonomy benefits them (lines 30–40). She then explains that mediation is a "cooperative process" and notes that the spouses will be able to speak as needed (lines 40–44).

Mediator A goes on to explain how the mediators will manage the process (Excerpt 2.9, lines 45–50):

Excerpt 2.9 Jon and Liz Midwest Divorce Mediation, Session 1, p. 2

45 MA: (1.0) .hh uhm (0.7) tch (0.9) What we try tuh do is ma:nage thuh
46   pro:cess. Which means, we try tuh help thuh two of you!
47   communicate (1.2) and uh maybe reflect back tuh you what we've
48   hea:rd?, (0.6) and uhm (1.0) possibly offer you suggestions? (0.8)
49   if that's helpful? (0.3) or tell you (1.0) u:h what we know about:
50   parenting arrangements and that kinda thing:, with thi- thee ages of
51   your children, (0.4) and I don't (0.4) know at this time what they
52   are .h (0.8) uhm (1.4) tch (0.5) But we will not be making

53   decisions for you. (0.6) no:r do we make any recommendation to
54   thuh court. (1.0) tch .h In fact thee only thing we tell thuh court is:
55   that you ca:me he:re, (0.8) .h and that there was fu:ll agreement,
56   (0.7) pa:rtial agreement, or no agreement. (0.6) And it's uh simple
57   check off. (0.9) So we don't give thuh court any information about
58   you. .h (0.4) And we don't have any information about you from
59   thuh court. (0.7) except your names and addresses. (1.0) tch So
60   (0.8) uhm (0.5) w- (0.5) we're supposed tuh try tuh remain
61   neu:tral?, (0.8) uhm (0.5) When you hire uh lawyer, your lawyer is
62   your personal advocate. (1.2) We have to try tuh m' (1.0) remain
63   as neutral as me- as we ca:n and help both of you (0.4) to (1.1)
64   look at your situation and try tuh make (good) decisions.

As in the small claims cases, the mediator explains the main aspects of mediation. She notes that the mediators will not make decisions for the spouses, and will not share any information with the court (lines 52–59). Mediator A's description of the divorce mediation process differs from some of the small claims mediations in that she states that the mediators will try to remain neutral (lines 59–64). The neutrality issue was not always explicitly addressed in the introductory stages of the small claims sessions. Another difference is that Mediator A raises the possibility that the mediators will offer suggestions or helpful information (lines 45–50); in many facilitative mediation programs mediators are not supposed to offer substantive suggestions.

After this general introduction to mediation, Mediator A then discusses each item on the agreement to mediate (not shown). This document covers issues such as whether the couple's children will participate in the mediation process, what role their lawyers will play, how financial issues will be mediated, what happens if they reach an impasse, and what fees will be charged. Mediator A then has both spouses sign the agreement to mediate.

Once the documents are signed, Mediator A first acknowledges receipt of the signed documents ("thank you."; Excerpt 2.10, line 194), and then transitions from the introductory to the substantive stage of the session by asking the spouses to describe their daughter: "tch So what can you tell us about Bethany?" (line 194).

Excerpt 2.10 Jon and Liz Midwest Divorce Mediation, Session 1, p. 5

194 MA: Okay!, thank you. (1.1) tch So what can you tell us about Bethany?
195   (1.7)
196   What's she like.
197   (3.8)
198   Who wants tuh start.=
199 Liz: =uh=heh=huh!
200   (0.9)
201   .h °Oh God [[this is awful°?)]
202 Jon: [Very caring   ] 'n very giving?,

Note that Mediator A does not start by soliciting a story from one disputant or asking one disputant what the problems are, as would typically happen in a small claims mediation session. Instead, she begins the session by treating the spouses as a unit rather than as opposing disputants. When neither spouse replies (line 195), Mediator A revises and reissues the question (line 196). When neither replies to this second question (line 197), she asks them "Who wants tuh start.=" (line 198). By beginning the substantive portion of the session with a question about the couple's daughter, their child is made the focus of the divorce mediation process rather than any problems or differences of opinion between the spouses (although of course these will be addressed in the mediation).

Summary

In their opening remarks the mediators display their expectations for how the disputing parties will conduct themselves during the session. While both divorce and small claims mediation sessions differ markedly from ordinary conversation, they also differ in some ways from each other. There is at least a claim of increased flexibility and freedom to volunteer to speak in the divorce mediation sessions compared to the small claims sessions. While disputants in small claims mediation sessions are typically instructed not to interrupt each other, and to direct their remarks to the mediators, divorce mediators may specifically invite both spouses to ask questions at will. Once the session has been opened and the participants have signed the agreement to mediate, a mediator will begin the substantive stage of the session. In the small claims sessions, this typically means that the complainant's story or opening state- ment will be solicited. In the divorce mediation cases, the substantive stage of the session typically begins with a discussion of joint concerns. In the next two sections of this chapter, I first analyze the typical interactional organization of talk in mediation sessions. This section focuses on an investigation of the turn-taking system and participation framework of mediation. The final section of this chapter addresses how the interaction in divorce mediation differs from that in small claims mediation.

The Turn-Taking System of Mediation

In ordinary conversation, exchange of speakership and opportunities for others to take turns occur frequently, and length of turn, type of turn, and topic of talk are free to vary (Sacks et al. 1974). Participants construct their turns such that their possible end points ("transition relevance places") are projectable by recipients, who can by this means determine when turn transition is relevant (Sacks et al. 1974). At this point, a current speaker may select a next speaker.

If he or she does not, a next speaker may select himself or herself, and if that does not happen, a current speaker may continue and select himself or herself for another turn (Sacks et al. 1974).

The interactional organization of talk in mediation sessions differs from ordinary conversation. The order of speakership in mediation is preset for several types of actions during the session. Mediators typically speak first, using their role as facilitators to open the mediation session (as described above). Disputants typically wait until selected by a mediator to speak. When solicited by a mediator to make an opening statement or to tell their story, the disputant may continue speaking until the story is done or the mediator initiates another action (such as asking a question). A disputant who has the floor to tell their story may use the 'current speaker selects self' option (Sacks et al. 1974) to resume talk after mediator questions during their story.

Disputants in both of the small claims programs and the divorce mediation program studied here typically displayed an orientation to the speech exchange system of mediation by remaining silent during opposing disputants' utterances, unless solicited by a mediator. For example, in Excerpts 2.11 and 2.12 the divorcing parents' participation is invited through mediator solicits. In Excerpt 2.11, Mediator A first solicits Darryl's perspective on how his daughter Melody is doing (lines 1219 and 1221):

Excerpt 2.11 Belinda and Darryl Midwest Divorce Mediation, Session 1, p. 56

```
1219  MA:  What do you hear Dad? (0.3) How [duh-  ] what are you hearing
1220  Dar:                                 [Hunh?]
1221  MA:  from Melody?
1222       (1.3)
1223  Dar: I don't hear much at all from her on that kind uh thing she hasn't
1224       really talked to me about it. She- talks to her mother I suppose.
1225       (0.3)
1226  MA:  Mm hm=
1227  Dar:           =But to me she seems, .hh (0.2) you know other than just
1228       normally shy: she seems uh perfectly well adjusted
1229       (0.3)
1230  MA:  M[m hm]
1231  Dar:  [lit   ]tle girl.
1232       (0.2)
1233  MA:  Mm hm
1234       (0.7)
1235  Dar: And uh (0.2) does well in schoo:l and? (0.8) y'know?, plays piano
1236       and (0.6) plays with her friends and (0.8) just perfectly normal!
1237       (0.2)
1238  MA:  Mm hm
1239       (0.4)
1240  Dar: Kind of uh (0.2) just
1241       (2.3)
```

Darryl's remarks are addressed to the mediator rather than to his wife Belinda. During Darryl's response, Belinda remains silent. Mediator A produces continuers (lines 1226, 1230, 1233, and 1238), thus actively constructing his role as the addressed recipient of Darryl's turn.[2] Next, Mediator A solicits Belinda's perspective on her daughter (Excerpt 2.12, line 1242).

Excerpt 2.12 Belinda and Darryl Midwest Divorce Mediation, Session 1, p. 56

```
1242  MA:   And Mom? (Tell me about) Melody?,
1243        (0.9)
1244  Bel:  tch I've uh much different [vi::ew] of [thuh situation]
1245  MA:                             [Ye:ah]    [Okay      ]
1246        (0.1)
1247  MA:   'kay wh[at  ]
1248  Bel:         [Uh:] .hh (0.7) it's true, she's uh very shy child. uh very
1249        conscientious: u:hm (0.4) tch bu:t! (0.2) uh worrier. uh worry wart.
1250        u:h About uh year! ago, it just (0.3) well I guess it was mo:re than uh
1251        year ago, because- .h (0.5) about uh year ago I moved, (0.5) into
1252        our de:n.
1253        (0.3)
1254  MA:   Mm hm=
1255  Bel:             =Just moved out. .hh Okay, so- Melody had problems
1256        before! that: u:hm (1.1) what- in- what- thuh pediatrician eventually
1257        uh diagnosed as anxiety! disorder. .hh She unh she could not sleep!
1258        She would wake me u:p, in thuh middle of thuh night, ringing her ha-
1259        ah-ah-nds, .hh >O:h I can't sleep I can't sleep< ((in falsetto)) And
1260        then d- see:ing things in her roo::m?, .hh a:nd that just- (0.2) panic
1261        panic disorder.
```

Belinda prefaces her response by announcing that her perspective differs from her husband's (line 1244). She then goes on to paint a much more severe picture of Melody's psychological problems than was conveyed by her husband (lines 1248–1252, 1255–1261). Belinda addresses her remarks to the mediators, and Darryl remains silent during her response, even though it differs markedly from his perspective. Mediator A again participates by using continuers (line 1254) and other brief interjections (lines 1245 and 1247), thus positioning himself as the addressed recipient of Belinda's turn.

In short, even though the spouses have strong differences of opinion relative to their daughter, each waits to talk until solicited by a mediator and follows the turn-taking system of mediation rather than interrupting or arguing with each other. When disputants wait for a mediator solicit before responding to an

---

[2] Continuers or "minimal responses" can display attention and active listenership to a speaker's utterance. See Fitzgerald and Leudar (2010); Goodwin (1986); Heritage and Clayman (2010); Jefferson (1984c); Schegloff (1982).

opposing disputant's complaints or accusations, the possibility of arguing is minimized because arguing requires adjacently placed oppositional utterances.

Disputants in the small claims mediation programs typically do not speak during an opposing disputant's story. For example, in Excerpt 2.13, John does not speak during Kris's story until selected to speak by the mediator. Once he has answered the mediator's question, he returns to silence, and the complainant's story resumes.

Excerpt 2.13 Electric Bill Midwest Small Claims Mediation, p. 10

```
246 Kris:   um (0.5) Okay in? (0.4) in JuLY? (0.3) because John had been
247         staying thERE, and paying? (0.5) thuh bills, and taking >care of
248         everything. .hh< (0.4) thuh landlord Tommy? (0.4) had told Kurt?
249         (0.5) that he would let John have thee apartment.
250         (0.5)
251 Med:   Okay,=
252 Kris:        =So: (0.6) Kurt was okay with that. He moved in with me.
253         (0.6) .h a:nd so: (0.5) John to- I: presented John with thi:s? which I
254         have uh copy of, John had thee original, (0.4) of thuh final bill?
255         (0.7) >And 'uh gas and< electric.
256         (0.5)
257 Med:   Which was: twenty six [dollars? (            )]
258 Kris:                        [Uh=hunh- no: hundred] and twenty two,
259         sixty nine.=
260 Med:             =paid- (0.2) have you seen that? (0.3) John?
261         (0.8)
262 John:  >Oh yes.<
263         (0.4)
264 Med:   Okay?
265         (0.4)
266 Kris:  I HANDED him thee original. (0.5) .h u:m (0.3) he told me?, (0.3)
267         he was going tuh take care of it?, (0.4) he also told thuh landlord
268         he was gonna take care of it,
```

The respondent (John) remains silent during Kris's turn, and does not speak until solicited to do so by the mediator (line 260). Note that the mediator's utterance in line 260 interrupts Kris's opening statement-in-progress, thus displaying that rights to speak are based on institutional role. A mediator may interrupt a disputant's ongoing turn or story, but a disputant is expected to wait until invited to speak.

When one disputant has the floor to tell their story, the opposing disputant is expected to wait until that story is complete and their response is solicited by the mediator. However, the mediators may intervene in a disputant's ongoing story to ask questions, refocus the topic, or perform other actions. After a mediator intervention, the interrupted disputant typically uses the current speaker selects self turn-taking option (Sacks et al. 1974) to resume telling

their story. Excerpt 2.14 shows the mediator asking questions during Sue's
opening statement. After answering each question, Sue resumes telling her
story-in-progress.

Excerpt 2.14 Dog with Fleas Midwest Small Claims Mediation, p. 10

```
197  Sue:   And yet thuh dog was not picked up by (1.0) Anybody, (0.3) you
198          know (0.3), in this family, wife or husband. It was (0.3) another
199          woman, I don't know who it was. (0.7) uhm (1.2) There's uh
200          timespan of (0.8) when she >picked it< up, (0.7) to whenever they
201          received the dog, (0.3) that anything could of happened. They
202          indicated that=
203  Med:               =How do you know there's uh timespan?
204          (0.8)
205  Sue:   Well, I mean (0.7) they weren't home yet and they had somebody
206          else pick up thuh dog. It was uh week lapse, between thuh ti:me .hh
207          that they took thuh dog to thuh vet and thuh time that it left my
208          kennel. (0.6) For flea treatment. It was two weeks between thuh time
209          it left my kennel to thuh time that they had flea killers come. (0.8)
210          Okay, (0.3) thuh dog walked down thuh sidewalk (0.6) from my
211          kennel (0.4) to their vehicle. Whoever picked it up. .hh uhm. (1.2)
212          They indicate that thuh dog doesn't go outside much and they're
213          saying that, there's no other way >you know< that it could get fleas,
214          but thuh dog walked down my sidewalk when it left, (0.5) even if it
215          sits on their deck at home, (1.0) it can get fleas. (0.5) And yet when
216          she called me, (0.5) it was at least four or five days [after thuh fact ]
217  Med:                                                          [When you say]
218          she- who do you mean?
219          (0.2)
220  Sue:   His wife.
221          (0.2)
222  Med:   °Yeah°=
223  Sue:           =In other words, (0.7) THE ONLY dealing that I had with
224          this gentleman was at thuh very end. At thuh beginning of
225          September, when he came to see me. All thee other problems were
226          with his wife. Not only on thuh telephone, (0.7) but threatening
227          letters, and visits to thuh kennel ...
```

The mediator freely selects himself to speak to ask questions during Sue's
story (lines 203 and 217–218). In both cases, Sue first answers the mediator's
question and then selects herself to speak to resume telling her story-in-
progress.

Participants can also display an orientation to the turn-taking system of
mediation by explicitly invoking it. For example, in Excerpt 2.15, Stan gives
up his right not to be interrupted by his ex-wife Karen (lines 496–501), thus
displaying his orientation to the expectation that the opposing disputant is not
supposed to interrupt a disputant's story.

Excerpt 2.15 Joint Custody West Coast Family Mediation, p. 21

```
495  Stan:  Actually:?, u::hm, (0.4) I'm gonna- (0.2) give you uh little
496         bit °of (0.4) kind of uh BA:ckgrou:nd?, you know and allow
497         KA:ren tuh interject, because I beLIE:VE!, (0.4) .hh
498         this is a:ll, (0.2) true and FAIR, (0.2) there's: really (0.2) .hh
499         nothing SLA:NTED this is- (uh-) (in) factual so:: (0.2) yuh- you
500         (0.2) think that (0.2) s:omething is (0.1) amiss here, (0.2) u:h,
501         I'm allo:wing her tuh ( . ) .h interject!, (0.2) (What
502         [was ne   ]:xt). .hh Okay, Karen and I as of Octo:ber, have
503  Med:   [(°Okay )]
```

Explicit displays of orientation to the speech exchange system of mediation such as this are unusual in these data. Typically, disputants remain silent during the opposing disputant's statement not because they have nothing to say, but because they are following the instructions of the mediators to remain silent during the opposing disputant's turns. This restraint based on institutional role is a key way that mediation differs from ordinary conversation.

Participants' orientation to the turn-taking system of mediation is also displayed by the use of requests for permission to speak. While Schegloff (1980) noted that requests for permission to speak are often preliminaries to projected actions rather than literal requests for permission, in some interactional contexts they work as devices to get the floor.[3]

Disputants in mediation sessions direct requests for permission to speak to the mediator rather than to the opposing disputant, and routinely wait until a positive response has been received before beginning their interjection. For example, Excerpt 2.16 shows Bob using a request for permission to speak during his brother Herbert's story about their sister's distress during a car ride with Bob.

**Excerpt 2.16 Two Brothers West Coast Small Claims Mediation, p. 14
(Garcia 1991: 823)**

```
303  Herb:  She was: very very upset about that! and (0.1) .h (0.4) made it
304         perfectly clear that she didn't want (0.1) anything °that had° to do
305         with Bob! (0.3) °after tha:t?°=
306  Bob:                           =COULD I- (0.1) could I a:sk a question
307         °at this point?° ((Bob moves gaze to the mediators))
308         (0.1)
309  MB:    °Sure!°
310         (0.2)
311  Bob:   Was: (0.3) wa:s: (0.2) he:r: (0.9) u::h inte:nt, in °you know?, uh°
312         (0.3) Did it SOU:ND to you: that she was TE:LLing you:?, . . .
```

---

[3] For example, in televised news interviews, requests for permission to speak are sometimes used by interviewees who begin an utterance before they have been given the floor by the interviewer. See Clayman and Maynard (1990); Greatbatch (1988); Heritage and Greatbatch (1991).

Instead of responding directly to Herbert, which could have resulted in an adjacently placed denial of Herbert's accusation that Bob's driving had upset their sister, Bob asks the mediators for permission to ask a question (lines 306–307). He shifts his gaze to the mediators during this utterance. After Mediator B gives permission (line 309), Bob asks Herbert a question (lines 311–312). Bob thereby displays an orientation to the speech exchange system of mediation by not selecting himself to speak when the opposing disputant has the floor. He did not directly address the opposing disputant (his brother Herbert) to produce his rebuttal until given permission to do so by the mediators.

Mediators do not always grant disputant's requests for permission to speak. In Excerpt 2.17, Bud's request for permission to speak to get the floor to make a rebuttal during Sue's first story is denied:

Excerpt 2.17 Dog with Fleas Midwest Small Claims Mediation, p. 12

```
252  Sue:  All thuh dogs have their own inside stall and outside run. (0.5) Okay-
253        it's concrete- they're not (0.3) on thuh ground. (0.8) Okay (0.4) so
254        they have access to thee inside and thee outside. (0.8) We're air
255        conditioned, we're, (1.3) you know, °heated depending on thuh time
256        of thuh year.° (0.4) Now like I say, I'd personally, did thuh dog on
257        thuh day it left, because they came back early, (0.8) there was some
258        problem with thuh date. (0.3) uhm We weren't expecting them till uh
259        week later, and they called up and said they were home. (0.5) I made
260        uh special effort that day to- to get that dog done and out, even
261        though we weren't expecting it to leave.
262        (1.0)
263  Bud:  May we brief- uh rebut uh now or (°maybe should we wait°)
264        (0.1)
265  Med:  Wa- What I'd like to do sir is to give Sue here an opportunity to
266        speak and then I will °come back to you.° (0.8) uhm This is not uh
267        trial, I'm not here to make uh judgment.
```

Bud produced a request for permission to speak in line 263. The mediator denied Bud's request and asked him to wait (lines 265–267). The mediator's denial of this request displays his orientation to the speech exchange system of mediation, in which disputants have differential rights to speak depending on whether they have the floor to produce their story or opening statement. The use of requests for permission to speak illustrates how the mediator's role as facilitator of the session enables them to place limits on the autonomy of disputants. The mediator's right to facilitate the session gives them discretion over which complaints or accusations may be responded to immediately and which must wait to be addressed.

Mediator sanctions are another way that participants display their orientation to the speech exchange system of mediation. Previous research has shown that mediators may sanction disputants for self-selecting to produce an oppositional response to the opposing disputant's turn (Stokoe 2003), for persisting to talk on unproductive topics (Greatbatch and Dingwall 1994), and for arguing (Garcia 1991). Excerpt 2.18 illustrates how a mediator can display an orientation to the turn-taking system by sanctioning disputants. When Gesa addresses a question to the opposing disputant Val (lines 468–469 and 471–472), the mediator intervenes and explains that directly addressing the opposing disputant is not allowed (lines 470, 473, 475, 477–478; see also lines 481–482 and 485).

Excerpt 2.18 Sewer Fumes Midwest Small Claims Mediation, p. 22

```
468  Gesa        =.HH I- I like tuh ask first, (0.4) you occupied thee: (0.4)
469              apartment for fou:r yea:rs and I want=
470  Med:                                    =.HH [NOW]
471  Gesa:                                        [I    ] wondered (0.4)
472              [how ] lo:ng [ago it  ] was.
473  Med:        [Okay]       [you go.]
474              (0.3)
475  Med:        This is not uh cross exa[mination you-  ]
476  Gesa:                               [.h I mea- I 'em] I'm=
477  Med:                                               =YOU CAN'T ASK
478              QUE:S[TIONS: of him.          ]
479  Gesa:            [>Oh I-< I can't (say uh)] no:thin'.
480              (0.1)
481  Med:        .hh No! pa:rt of what you agree:d to: .hh was u:h- that you would
482              speak tuh me no:t to each other.
483              (0.3)
484  Gesa:       >Okay. So. O[kay<]
485  Med:                    [This ] isn't uh mini tri:al.=
486  Jake:                                  =°°>Uhkay.<< °°
487              (0.4)
488  Gesa:       .h! Okay hh!
```

The mediator's interventions in Excerpt 2.18 serve to remind the disputants of the ground rules of the session.

In a small claims mediation session about an unpaid electric bill, the mediator sanctions Kris for speaking during her ex-roommate John's story without being first selected to speak (Excerpt 2.19). Kris's interjection in line 345 is an adjacently placed oppositional utterance which was formulated directly, and hence is an arguing move.

Excerpt 2.19 Electric Bill Midwest Small Claims Mediation, p. 13

```
333  John:  I was payin' thuh gas and electric?, (0.3) °th'° phone, a:nd thuh
334         rent. (0.5) .h Kurt was: (0.6) gettin:g uh HUNdred and fifteen
335         dollars (0.5) approximately, monthly, (0.3) for general assistance.
336         (0.7) .h eh He was TOLD by his: (0.4) doctors, that he was
337         allowed to work at any time!, (0.6) prior! to- (0.8) July. (0.5) °prior
338         tuh June. an'-° (0.5) a:nd he- (0.4) cared not to go out and get uh
```

```
339          job? (0.4) and (0.4) help me in any sort of thuh way.=
340 Med:                                          =Were you
341          working at that time?
342          (0.4)
343 John:    Yes I was.
344          (0.4)
345 Kris:    That (0.2) that's an incorrect statement.=
346 Med:                                          =Um (0.4) °well that° (0.4)
347          °uh- uh- ih-° (0.3) k Kurt waited real- (0.3) I mean John
348          [waited real] patiently while you talked?
349 Kris:    [Uhkay.    ]
350          (0.5)
351 Med:     .h Um d'you want uh piece uh paper? °duh° (0.3) take [note ]s.
352 Kris:                                                          [Yeah.]
353          (0.3)
354 Kris:    Please.
```

This excerpt shows that it is acceptable for a mediator to intervene in a disputant's story. For example, the mediator asked John a question in lines 340–341, which he answered in line 343. However, when the opposing disputant (Kris) selects herself to produce an utterance challenging John's statement (line 345), the mediator latches a response to that utterance and asks Kris to wait (lines 346–348). He then asks her if she wants paper so she can take notes (line 351).

In sum, disputants' departures from the turn-taking system of mediation may lead to mediator sanctions. These sanctions enable mediators to maintain control over when disputants participate and respond to each other. Participants in the mediation sessions in these data typically interact within the turn-taking system of mediation rather than a conversational speech exchange system.

The Participation Framework of Mediation

The participation framework refers to how participants construct their utterances to address specific recipients or subsets of recipients (Goffman 1981). For example, a speaker can direct their remarks to an addressed recipient, with others present being "bystanders" or "nonaddressed recipients" of the utterance. The utterance itself could be "authored" by the speaker, or "animated" on behalf of another. Speakers can shift their relationship to the utterance they are producing by means of footing shifts. For example, in television news interviews, the interviewer may identify confrontational information as being authored by another by attributing the statement to a third party.[4]

---

[4] See Clayman (1988; 1992); Clayman and Heritage (2002); Goffman (1981); Goodwin (1987).

The participation framework in mediation hearings differs in several ways from other institutional settings and from ordinary conversation. While mediators can address any participant in the session, disputants typically address their utterances to the mediators rather than to each other. The mediator is the primary recipient of the utterance, and the opposing disputant is treated as an overhearing audience or unaddressed recipient.

Disputants in mediation typically construct their utterances to address the mediator by referring to the opposing disputant in the third person. Nonverbal behaviors such as gazing at the mediators instead of the opposing disputant can also convey who is the addressee. In Excerpt 2.20 the respondent Rich directs his remarks to the mediator and treats the complainant as an unaddressed recipient of his utterances.

Excerpt 2.20 Vacation Pay Midwest Small Claims Mediation, p. 10

```
210  Med:  Anything like that.° °Okay.° .h I'm not here to do thuh referee's job.
211        .hh U:hm (0.7) what's goin' on.
212        (0.9)
213  Rich: .hhh well, HHH! what happened is: h (0.4) u:h, (2.2) Miss Sa:nders
214        is: (0.3) is absolutely right, sir, with (0.5) thuh vaCAtion?, (1.1) tch
215        u:h (1.1) after >one year vaca-< after one >year of wo:rk,<
216        >they are tuh< gettuh week's paid vacation. then- ih- during thuh
217        second year.
218        (0.6)
219  Med:  unh hunh
220        (0.1)
221  Rich: uhm (0.7) .h on her (1.3) third year anniversary, of (1.0) August
222        sixth nineteen ninety four?, (0.9) tch she did have- t- two: years of
223        vacation coming up, (0.3) between August six' nineteen ninety fou:r,
224        and August six' nineteen ninety five!, (0.3) she had- two weeks: of
225        (0.1) paid vacation. (0.1) .h sometime, (0.2) during that time period.
```

The excerpt begins with Mediator A soliciting Rich's opening statement (lines 210–211). In Rich's response, he addresses Mediator A in the first person ("sir" in line 214) and refers to the opposing disputant in the third person. Rich refers to her by her name ("Miss Sanders" in line 213) and by pronouns ("her" in line 221, and "she" in lines 222 and 224). Ms. Sanders is also included in the plural pronoun "they" (line 216), where Rich is referring to Ms. Sanders and the other employees in the same job category.

When conducting one-on-one exchanges with individual disputants, mediators also typically refer to the opposing disputant in the third person. For example, in Excerpt 2.21 the mediator asks Bill a question on behalf of his former tenant Jessica (lines 628–629). The mediator speaks on Jessica's behalf because the participation framework of mediation does not provide for Jessica to address Bill directly.

Excerpt 2.21 Broken Lease Midwest Small Claims Mediation, p. 29

```
623  Med:  Would you accept anything LESS than th' twelve hundred and
624        three dollars you're asking for?
625        (1.1)
626  Bill: °I don't believe so.°
627        (2.9)
628  Med:  U:M (0.4) Jessica! (0.4) wanted (0.3) to know where you got
629        thuh figure uh nine hundred and fifty dollars °from.°
630        (1.0)
631  Bill: U::h just hh three months rent? (0.6) h is nine hundred and (0.3)
632   ᐟ    six days rent fifty?
```

Note that Bill's response (lines 631–632) is directed to the mediator, not to Jessica. In the participation framework of small claims mediation, issues under contention are typically discussed via a mediated interaction rather than directly between the principals in the dispute.

In sum, while interaction in mediation is closer to a conversational speech exchange system than other types of legal proceedings, such as trials or hearings, its turn-taking system and participation framework differ from these types of interaction. Mediators facilitate the sessions such that for much of the time disputants direct their remarks to the mediators. Disputants typically wait until selected by a mediator to speak rather than speaking directly to each other. Disputants have extended periods during the session in which they can tell their stories in turn, explain their positions, and answer questions. By these actions, participants create and maintain a unique speech exchange system which facilitates the work of conflict resolution. However, some disputant intrusions can occur without derailing the mediation process. In the next section I discuss how mediators respond to disputants' intrusions into an opposing disputant's turn space.

Nonproblematic Disputant Intrusions

While disputants typically displayed an orientation to the speech exchange system of mediation by waiting until solicited to speak or by requesting permission to speak, there were occasions on which self-selection during an opposing disputant's turn to talk did occur. Problematic intrusions (typically arguing moves), will be discussed in Chapter 3. In the current chapter I analyze those intrusions which were not treated as problematic or as violations of the speech exchange system. In these data five types of nonproblematic disputant intrusions were found: error repairs, sentence completions, brief oppositional utterances, informational questions, and the provision of relevant information.

Error Repair. In some instances error repair (Jefferson 1974) of an opposing disputant's utterance was allowed to stand without sanction or intervention by a mediator. For example, in Excerpt 2.22 a disputant interjects during an opposing disputant's turn without being selected to speak. This interjection accomplishes repair of the opposing disputant's utterance:

Excerpt 2.22 Vehicle Repair West Coast Small Claims Mediation, p. 49

```
1110  Dan:  I've met mechanics tellin' me that uh water pump hou:sing,
1111        (0.1) on thuh {Car Brand Name} (0.5) NE::ver (0.2)
1112        cr[ack.  ]
1113  MA:      [°(Um ]hmh) (0.5) °Um [hmh.]
1114  Dan:                          [((sni]ff))
1115        (0.5)
1116  MB:   h (0.2) D'you agree that? Tim?
1117        (0.5)
1118  Tim:  WA:ter pumps have uh- °eh- are probuh'ly one uh thuh
1119        CO::Mmon, (.) replacements:=
1120  Dan:                            =>No no no,< thuh pump, not
1121        th[uh hou:se] system.
1122  Tim:    [(       )]
1123        (0.3)
1124  Tim:  tch=.hh (.) Thee:: thuh HOU:sing itself I'm gonna say, is::
1125        something that is not very usual. (.) >I will agree with that.<
1126        I'm only been dealing with them for about ni::ne years: now in
1127        {Car Brand Name} products.< (0.2) .hh u::hm.
1128        (0.2)
1129  MB:   Do you agree with Da:n, that it rarely occurs:?
1130        (.)
1131  Tim:  It's it rarely occurs it is not at all common[place.]
```

Tim, an employee of the auto repair shop, states that water pump repairs are common (lines 1118–1119). The opposing disputant Dan interrupts Tim to correct an error (lines 1120–1121). The mediators do not sanction this self-selected utterance, and Tim goes on to agree with Dan on this issue (lines 1124–1127). Dan's interruption is clearly constructed as an error repair rather than an oppositional utterance, and Tim's response treats it as a repair rather than an arguing move.

Sentence Completion. Although rare in these data, sentences completions were also treated as nonproblematic intrusions into an opposing disputant's floor space (Excerpt 2.23):

Excerpt 2.23 Camera Repair Midwest Small Claims Mediation, p. 15

```
316  Pete:  I called her and I said (1.8) and it was you and I talked that time (0.3)
317         I'm sure (0.6) u:h (1.0) and I told you I would le:t you: (0.4) have
318         thuh whole thing for seventy five dollars. (0.6) And: her answer was:
319         (0.7) that uh I'll call you back. (1.0) And then she didn't (0.5) call me
320         back 'cause she said (0.3) it's not
321         (1.0)
```

```
322  Cindy:  Acceptable.
323          (0.8)
324  Pete:   Acceptable. (0.4) Yeah.
325          (3.4)
326  Med:    No:w (0.6) who gave permission tuh go ahead and fix thuh camera?
327          (1.2)
328  Pete:   We had to (0.3) repair (0.5) anything it's broken we had to repair it so
329          we can give 'em uh estimate. (0.3) Now if they don't [want it done ]
```

Pete's pause in line 321 was clearly hearable as a within-turn pause, thus suggesting an error avoidance move (Jefferson 1974). Cindy, the opposing disputant, selects herself to speak without requesting permission and provides a candidate completion of Pete's utterance ("Acceptable."; line 322). Pete accepts Cindy's suggestion by repeating it and confirming it ("Acceptable. (0.4) Yeah."; line 324). The mediator does not sanction Cindy's brief intrusion. By placing it so that it did not interrupt the prior speaker, Cindy's sentence completion can be heard as a helpful interjection rather than as oppositional or argumentative. Also note that by using completion intonation in line 322, Cindy indicates that her brief utterance is complete, and she is not using this interjection as a way to wrest the floor away from Pete.

Brief Oppositional Utterances. As will be shown in Chapter 3, oppositional utterances produced by opposing disputants can lead to direct disagreements which may escalate to arguing. Arguing is typically treated as problematic by mediators and is usually avoided or repaired (Cobb 1994; Garcia 1991). However, occasional oppositional utterances may be allowed to stand unsanctioned by mediators if they are brief and placed so as not to interfere with the flow of the interaction. In Excerpt 2.24, Kelly interjects to disagree with her husband Mike's claim that she has driven with their children in the car after drinking alcohol:

Excerpt 2.24 Mike and Kelly Midwest Divorce Mediation, Session 1, p. 65

```
1471  MB:    What else would you want.
1472         (2.0)
1473  Mike:  I I- couldn't ask! (0.6) y'kno[w for anything °more.°]
1474  MA:                                  [If she's drinking and ] driving?
1475         (0.6)
1476  MB:    That's different.
1477         (0.1)
1478  MA:    That's [different.]
1479  Mike:         [Yes it is ] different.
1480         (0.3)
1481  MA:    A[nd esPECIALLY      ] if you can show that she's doing it
1482  Mike:  [Very much °different.°]
1483  MA:    with thuh children.
```

```
1484          (0.3)
1485 Mike:    Yes:=
1486 Kelly:   =°Never.°=
1487 Mike:              =[>Very much<] different.=
1488 MA:                              =Then you- (0.3) then
1489          you've got uh big [(problem). ]
```

Kelly's brief interjection in line 1486 is a direct disagreement with the position Mike has taken. Her oppositional utterance is spoken very quietly and is pronounced with completion intonation. While its placement immediately after Mike's "Yes:" (line 1485) and its directness clearly mark Kelly's disagreement as an oppositional move, she produces it in a way which displays that she is not attempting to wrest the floor from Mike.

Information-Seeking Questions. Brief utterances formulated as information-seeking questions are another type of disputant intrusion into an opposing disputant's turn space that may go unsanctioned by mediators. Excerpt 2.25 occurs at the point in the hearing when the respondent Rob is engaged in making his opening statement. The complainant Bryan interjects with a brief question in line 234:

Excerpt 2.25 Roommates Midwest Small Claims Mediation, p. 10

```
226 Rob:   tch NOW, (0.5) thuh- (0.4) lease that is (1.5) u:h, (0.8) being
227        disputed right now was signed before this DATE.
228        (0.6)
229 Med:   Uh huh?
230        (1.9)
231 Rob:   Whi:ch (0.5) since both leases were executed, (1.1) this should
232        terminate both of 'em.
233        (2.2)
234 Bry:   You feel?
235        (0.7)
236 Rob:   I feel.
237        (0.7)
238 Med:   Uh huh? .h (0.4) A::nd uh (1.8) when was: (0.5) thuh second lease
239        signed?
240        (0.9)
241 Rob:   Thuh SECond lease was signed on (0.7) I believe it's June?
242        twelfth?
```

Rob briefly answers Bryan's question in line 236, but there is no further direct talk between them. This direct exchange between the disputants is not sanctioned by the mediator.

The mediator then provides a minimal response (line 238 "Uh huh?"), thus positioning himself as a recipient of Rob's turn. The mediator then uses an and-preface (Heritage and Sorjonen 1994) to return to the previous action-in-progress, Rob's opening statement. He does this by asking Rob a question about the lease (lines 238–239).

As with some other types of brief intrusions, the mediator let this intrusion pass, perhaps because it was a brief question. However, it differs from some other intrusions in that although the question was ostensibly information-seeking, and could easily be heard that way by the mediator, it could also be heard as an implied criticism of Rob's position.

Provision of Relevant Information. Disputants who self-selected to speak during a disputant's turn were typically not sanctioned by mediators if their utterance produced immediately relevant information. For example, after Darryl complains about medical expenses for their three children (Excerpt 2.26, lines 1156, 1158, 1160–1161), his wife Belinda interjects that "Eighty percent's covered.=" by insurance (line 1163).

Excerpt 2.26 Belinda and Darryl Midwest Divorce Mediation, Session 1, p. 53

```
1156  Dar:  [Be      ]cause when I see thuh kind of money that's: spent on it,
1157  MA:   [°Mm hm°]
1158  Dar:  it[s just]
1159  MA:    [Is it ] covered by (ex  )=
1160  Dar                            =Some of it is? and some of it isn't
1161        (y'know        then) °I guess we probably throw: in°
1162        (0.3)
1163  Bel:  Eighty percent's covered.=
1164  Dar:                        =thrown thousands 'n thousands uh
1165        dollars into thu:h (0.4) quote, ca:re of Ma:rcu:s [over    ] thuh
1166  MA:                                                     [Mm hm]
1167  Dar:  years and and .hh I hadn't seen: (1.0) any results tuh (that would)
1168        justify, (0.4) you know?, (0.7) that kind of expenditure
```

While Belinda's interjection can be heard simply as the timely provision of relevant information, it is also a subtle rebuttal of Darryl's contention that the health care for their children is very expensive. By means of this brief interjection, Belinda was able to insert her perspective into the discussion without derailing Mediator A's exchange with Darryl, and without attracting a mediator sanction. The placement and formulation of her utterance, along with its brevity and completion intonation, minimize its disruptiveness to Darryl's ongoing turn.

In sum, disputant interjections when an opposing disputant has the floor may be allowed without mediator sanction if they are brief, relevant, and appropriately placed. If oppositional, they should not be openly oppositional, or likely to incite escalation of the disagreement into arguing. As mentioned in the introduction to this chapter, the speech exchange system of the divorce and family mediation sessions may differ from the format of the small claims mediation sessions. It is to these variations in interactional organization that we now turn.

The Interactional Organization of Divorce Mediation Sessions

While both the small claims and divorce mediation sessions in these data are examples of the facilitative approach to mediation, there are differences between the two types of mediation which impact their interactional organization in several ways. In this section of the chapter I discuss two of these main differences, first, the use of a "hybrid" format which combines elements of the speech exchange systems of mediation and ordinary conversation, and second, the interactional impact of designing divorce mediation cases to be completed over a series of sessions rather than in one session.

The Hybrid Mediation Format

Previous research on a range of institutional contexts has shown that in order to better achieve the tasks of the interaction, participants may shift from an institutional to a conversational turn-taking system or may combine elements of both. For example, a study of interaction between air traffic control and airplane crews shows that they switched from a highly structured form of talk for routine exchanges, to a more conversational, hybrid form of interaction during emergencies (Garcia 2016). Another study found that the interactional organization of HIV counseling sessions consist largely of a "quasi-conversational" speech exchange system, using questions and answers which are common patterns of turn exchange in ordinary conversation to best transmit and discuss sensitive personal information (Peräkylä and Silverman 1991).

In this chapter I use the term "hybrid" speech exchange system to refer to those parts of mediation sessions in which participants depart from mediation format and interact in something closer to a conversational speech exchange system. This includes segments of talk in which disputants address each other directly. As Greatbatch and Dingwall (1997) found in their study of British divorce mediation, the Midwest divorce and family mediation sessions studied here have segments of talk in which the interactional organization is closer to a conversational speech exchange system than to the typical mediation format. In these segments of the sessions, disputant self-selection and direct address may occur unproblematically. Some mediators in the divorce cases explicitly gave permission for the spouses to ask questions rather than waiting for the mediators to select them to speak. However, even though disputants may be at times addressing each other directly, the presence and actions of the mediators make the structure of the interaction different from an ordinary conversational exchange. In this section of the chapter I describe the use of this hybrid format in the divorce mediation sessions.

In Excerpts 2.27 and 2.28 the divorcing spouses shift between the mediation format described in the initial sections of this chapter and a more conversational speech exchange system. Rather than addressing all turns to the mediators, in Excerpt 2.27 six turns are directly exchanged between the spouses (lines 1139–1151).

Excerpt 2.27 Dave and Kim Midwest Divorce Mediation, Session 1, p. 52

```
1135  MB:     °°Good.°° (2.0) HOW 'BOUT with his graduation coming up?
1136           (1.7) ub- <Are there um> (0.7) tch (0.7) °y'know decisions you
1137           need tuh make about° (0.5) °I dunno.< school ri:ng? or >is 'at
1138           I guess 'at was last year when he was uh jun[ior. um° .h]
1139  Kim:                                               [°I think we] did? we
1140           did uh° ring already? (0.5) You did pictures already?
1141           (0.4)
1142  Dave:   No! I haven't ordered 'em yet?
1143           (0.6)
1144  Kim:    °You haven't?°
1145           (0.2)
1146  Dave:   °No!°
1147           (1.2)
1148  Kim:    °He said he picked 'em out!°
1149           (1.0)
1150  Dave:   Well! We talked about it uh little bit. °But I haven't° °°ordered
1151           it.°°
```

In lines 1139–1140 Kim addresses a question about their son's graduation photographs directly to her husband Dave. Dave responds in line 1142, and Kim asks two follow-up questions, both of which are answered by Dave (see lines 1144–1151). There are several aspects of this segment which are conversational in nature, especially when compared to the interactions in the small claims mediation cases which follow mediation format more consistently. The spouses select themselves and each other to speak, and they speak directly to each other several times. This occurred without escalation into arguing, and without mediator intervention.

However, the interaction in this excerpt differs from a conversational speech exchange system in several ways. First, Mediator B is still engaged in the interaction and works to facilitate the discussion, for example by introducing the topic of talk (see her lines 1135–1138). Note that it took some work for the mediator to get this new topic off the ground. There is a two-second pause in line 1135 during which neither spouse volunteered to speak. When Mediator B completed her question in line 1135, neither spouse responded (note the 1.7 second pause in line 1136). The mediator then hesitated and repaired her turn to produce a more specific question (lines 1136–1137). This question was also unsuccessful in eliciting a response. Mediator B then extended the question (lines 1137–1138). At this point Kim produced a response (beginning in line 1139).

As the exchange continues (Excerpt 2.28), the interactional organization shifts from direct address between the spouses back to a more typical mediation format. Mediator B again actively engages in the exchange:

Excerpt 2.28 David and Kim Midwest Divorce Mediation, Session 1, p. 52

```
1152              (1.3)
1153   Kim:    tch=.h I'm planning uh graduation party for him back home in
1154              Sleighdale.
1155              (0.8)
1156   MB:     °°Mmkay?°°
1157              (0.3)
1158   Kim:    °Um° (0.2) °In June?°
1159              (0.6)
1160   MB:     °°Mm hm.°°
1161              (1.2)
1162   Kim:    'Cause we don't have any relatives °here.°
1163              (0.4)
1164   MB:     °Okay.° (1.1) .h So is 'ZAT somethin' that you kind uh
1165              coordinate? (0.5) Not not that Dave would attend? but- it's-
1166              just so (0.5) .h he doesn't have something (0.7) else planned for
1167              that particular day? [°or do you (        )°]
1168   Kim:                            [tch um I don't know] if he's mentioned it to
1169              you or not.
1170              (0.6)
1171   Dave:   tch .h °Yeah uh he he mentioned to me and 'at's° (0.3) °that's
1172              fine.° (0.8) °Great.°
1173              (2.7)
1174   MB:     °°Okay.°° (3.5) .h What about (0.3) um (1.1) tch (0.5) °school
1175              conferences. How's that?° (1.0) °D' you know about?
```

After a 1.3 second pause (line 1152), Kim shifts the topic to her son's graduation party (lines 1153–1154). This announcement is relevant to the overall topic Mediator B had introduced – their son's impending graduation from high school. Kim's topic shift is formulated as an announcement rather than as a question, and does not elicit a response from Dave. Instead, Mediator B provides a slightly delayed minimal response (line 1156), thereby performing an active listenership role. Mediator B's continuer solicits Kim to continue speaking.

Mediator B provides minimal responses or continuers (Fishman 1978; Schegloff 1982) on several occasions, thereby constructing her involvement as a recipient of disputants' utterances (e.g., see also line 1160). These actions display Mediator B's work in facilitating the interaction between the spouses and keeping the discussion focused on the work of the session. Her institutional role in the process differs from that of the disputants, and this role is reflected in her actions in this portion of the session (Halkowski 1990). At this point in the excerpt, the disputants are no longer speaking directly to each other. Mediator B and Kim are now engaged in a dyadic exchange, with Kim directing the topic and the mediator supporting her production of that topic (lines 1153–1162).

After that exchange, the mediator returns to a more active role. Mediator B makes an unsolicited suggestion about how Dave and Kim could handle their son's graduation party to avoid scheduling conflicts between them (lines 1164–1167). Instead of responding to the mediator, Kim immediately addresses a question directly to Dave (lines 1168–1169). She accomplishes this change of addressee by using the pronoun "he" to refer to their son, and using "you" to refer to her husband Dave. After receiving his response, both spouses remain silent (2.7 second pause in line 1173). The mediator allows sufficient time for either spouse to choose to develop this topic further. When no further responses are forthcoming, the mediator shifts the topic to the children's school conferences (lines 1174–1175).

In sum, there are several aspects of Excerpts 2.27 and 2.28 which are consistent with the speech exchange system of ordinary conversation. At times the disputants address each other directly, select themselves or each other to speak, introduce subtopics or refocus topics, and engage in question-and-answer exchanges with each other. These actions occur without sanction by a mediator. However, there are also a number of ways in which the excerpts reflect the speech exchange system of mediation. A mediator chose the initial topic, asked questions and made suggestions, engaged in direct exchanges with individual disputants, and provided minimal responses or continuers to display active listenership.

Through these minimal responses Mediator B can also retrospectively reconstruct a disputant's turn as directed to themselves as well as to the opposing disputant. Thus, although there are a number of times in the divorce mediation sessions in which there are extended sequences of direct address between disputants, this does not mean that the speech exchange system of mediation has been abandoned. Mediators are always present, are at least an overhearing audience, and are also recipients of disputants' utterances. They can intervene in the exchange as necessary to redirect or focus talk.

In sum, the hybrid mediation format consisted of segments of talk in which disputants addressed each other directly without sanction from mediators, using current speaker selects next and next speaker selects self turn-taking options to get the floor to speak rather than routinely waiting for mediator solicits. Mediators intervened or worked to restore mediation format when necessary. These hybrid segments occurred more often in the divorce mediations than in the small claims mediation sessions. For some disputants in the divorce mediation sessions a hybrid interactional format could be used for cooperative, even collaborative, efforts at communicating and problem solving.

The Interactional Impact of Multiple Sessions

Another way in which the divorce and family mediation sessions differ from
most of the small claims mediation sessions in the data is that the divorce
mediation cases involve multiple sessions. In the Midwest divorce mediation
program, each couple participates in between three to five or more mediation
sessions rather than in a single session. When a mediation is conducted over
multiple sessions, the level of conflict and interactional style can change
throughout the process because of developing comfort with mediation, trust
in the ability of the mediators, and progress being made on issues under dispute. In addition, some progress in resolution of issues may be made between
sessions without the help of the mediators. There are several ways in which
having multiple sessions may change the nature of what occurs during the
mediation session.

Excerpts 2.29 and 2.30 illustrate a transition in how the spouses respond to
mediator questions in Session 1 and Session 4, respectively. During the first
session there are several instances of conflict and arguing between the spouses.
During Session 4 there is much less conflict and there are also several instances
in which the spouses act as a team and collaborate. Excerpt 2.29 shows one of
the instances of conflict between Mike and Kelly which emerged during the
first session:

Excerpt 2.29 Mike and Kelly Midwest Divorce Mediation, Session 1, p. 27

```
587 Mike:  Envir- their environment? (0.6) y'know the:y? adapt tuh that. .h
588        (0.6) and if (0.6) you have taught them that those things are wrong,
589        that those things are wrong >that those sings are wrong!< .h (0.3)
590        an' 'en you introduce those things as .h (0.5) >well it was wrong
591        then °but it's not wrong°< °°now!°° (0.7) I mean THAT'S uh
592        struggle that they have! .h (0.4) what- (0.7) it [is  ] uh struggle!
593 Kelly:                                                  [No.]
594 Mike:  [°(for them).° ]
595 Kelly: [I'm not sayin'] that it's not wrong tuh them! I'm not tellin' them
596        that it's not wrong! (1.1) °And° they're sayin' jus' like they're sayin'
597        thuh same with th' cigarettes! we're tellin' 'em! (0.5) .h that's
598        wrong! don't s:moke cigarettes! (0.5) don't drink! .h (0.4)
599        whatever! .h (0.4) we've always taught 'em that! they've been
600        around it before? other people?
601        (0.6)
602 Mike:  They'd not been around thuh alcohol? (0.6) that I know of? that I
603        never took 'em? .h (0.8) My children never saw an open container
604        of alcohol, in their life! that I ever knew!
605        (0.7)
606 Kelly: >That's not true!<
607        (0.3)
```

```
608  Mike:  That I [ever knew! ]
609  Kelly:        [You would-] >you would leave 'em< with your brother at
610         uh (0.3) at- at thee um (1.1) u:h (1.6) crystal lake! (1.0) You told
611         me! (0.6) you told me! .h (0.5) you left Randy and Robert there!
612         (0.9)
613  Mike:  They spent thuh day with my fishin' stuff but that [°there-°]
614  Kelly:                                                     [And he] had
615         it-! they told me! (0.4) he had it!
616         (1.3)
617  MA:    >'S okay well is 'ere uh< uh prohibition in your church?
618         (0.5)
619  Mike:  Yes 'ere [is. ]
620  MA:             [say]ing that alcohol is evil? or
621         (0.2)
622  Mike:  °Yes it is.°
623         (0.2)
624  MA:    Okay.=
```

While Mike is engaged in producing an extended turn explicating why he thinks his wife Kelly's drinking hurts their children, Kelly selects herself to speak to disagree with his position. In line 593 she produces a direct, unmitigated disagreement ("No."). She goes on to explain how Mike is misunderstanding or misrepresenting her position (lines 595–600). This unsolicited intervention initiates a sequence of arguing between the two participants, continuing with Mike's rebuttal in lines 602–604, and Kelly's challenge of it in line 606. The arguing continues through line 615. After a pause (line 616), Mediator A asks an informational question which works to restore mediation format by having the disputants address her directly instead of speaking to each other.

Excerpt 2.30 is from the fourth session of Mike and Kelly's divorce mediation. At this point in the process the disputants have already reached agreement on many of the major issues under dispute. In addition, they have met with each other between mediation sessions to discuss and come to agreement on some of the details of their parenting plan. In this excerpt they are reporting these agreements to the mediators, who then write them on the easel they use to take notes during the sessions. In this excerpt, when a mediator asks a question, both participants often answer. As the excerpt begins, Mike is raising the issue of how they have decided to handle their children's college expenses (lines 981, 983, and 985).

Excerpt 2.30 Mike and Kelly Midwest Divorce Mediation, Session 4, p. 46

```
981  Mike:  °And now. modification. domination)? co[llege ] education
982  MB:                                           [What?]
983  Mike:  expens:e?
```

```
984              (0.4)
985   Mike:   Is gonna be uh split?
986              (2.4)
987   MB:     How 'bout deciding where thuh kids go tuh °college.°
988              (0.1)
989   Mike:   That'll be up t[uh them.]
990   Kelly:                  [Tha'll be] up tuh them?
991              (0.4)
992   MB:     Okay.
993              (0.7)
994   Mike:   I[f they pick uh really          ] expensive one then they'll
995   Kelly:   [°We're gonna let them decide.°]
996   Mike:   be: (0.3) it'll be like °henh!° .h!
997              (0.7)
998   Kelly:  Yo[u better get uh scholar]ship.=
999   Mike:      [Better get uh jo:b!     ]     =[Okay? you g ]otta be
1000  MB:                                        =[Mm hm yeah!]
1001  Mike:   re[al sm ]art? (0.3) play good ball? .h=
1002  MA:       [Right.]
1003  Kelly:                                  =eh henh
1004          [>henh henh henh<]
1005  Mike:   [hh! .h              ]
1006             (1.0)
1007  Kelly:  tch Right.
1008             (0.5)
1009  MA:     .h (0.6) So yo- (0.5) [>so what are you] saying about thee<
1010  Mike:                         [And that's       ]
1011  MA:     expenses then?
1012             (0.4)
1013  Mike:   We're splitting those.
1014             (0.4)
1015  Kelly:  °For college yes.°
```

Both spouses respond to Mediator B's question in line 987 about where the children will go to college, and to Mediator A's question in lines 1009 and 1011. In both instances Mike and Kelly's responses display their agreement on these issues. There is also evidence of supportive use of format tying. Incorporating partial repeats into oppositional utterances is referred to as "format tying" (Goodwin 2006; see also Coulter 1990). For example, in line 989 Mike answers Mediator B's question about where their children will go to college, and Kelly overlaps his turn at a point at which she can project its completion; her utterance repeats his almost exactly (line 990). Kelly also produces a supportive sentence completion of one of Mike's utterances. His utterance-in-progress from lines 994 and 996 is incomplete, he pauses and laughs, then pauses again. Kelly produces a sentence completion in line 998 "Yo[u better get uh scholar]ship.=", which although different from what Mike ends up saying in line 999, displays that she shares Mike's perspective on what their children should expect in terms of financial support from them for college. The couple is displaying a united front on this issue for the mediators.

Another way the spouses display cooperation with each other is through humor. For example, when Mike comments that their children will have to get scholarships by being real smart or playing good ball (lines 999, 1001), Kelly responds with laughter (lines 1003–1004). In line 1005 Mike joins in with laughter implicative particles.[5] Kelly then explicitly expresses agreement with his sentiment (line 1007). This type of cooperation is very different from much of the interaction between the spouses in the earlier sessions of the mediation which was at times quite confrontational.

In sum, the multiple session approach to divorce mediation can enable the spouses in a divorce mediation case to make progress on issues outside the session, thus changing the nature of the interaction in the session. Disputants can then report progress and agreements to the mediators rather than having the mediators lead a discussion of areas on which they disagree. Of course, it is also possible that interactions between sessions could make things worse and increase conflict, but this was not the pattern typically observed in these data.

This analysis of the interaction in the divorce mediation sessions shows both some commonalities with the small claims mediation sessions, and some key differences. The hybrid format allows the participants to utilize the conversational speech exchange system when useful, and the multiple sessions enable the participants to make progress between sessions and to display improved communication between each other as the mediation process proceeds.

Discussion and Conclusions

Compared to other types of legal proceedings such as trials, hearings, and tribunals,[6] the interactional organization of mediation sessions is closer to a conversational speech exchange system in that disputants have extended periods during which they can tell their stories, ask questions, and explain their positions. Nevertheless, the turn-taking system and participation framework of mediation differ from that of conversational interaction in several ways. This chapter has shown that in both the divorce and small claims mediation sessions, participants consistently follow the patterns of turn exchange and participation framework outlined in Garcia (1991) for much of the session. For small claims cases, and for much of the divorce mediation

---

[5] See Glenn (2003; 2010); Jefferson (1979); Potter and Hepburn (2010) on laughter invitations and laughter particles.

[6] For example, see Atkinson and Drew (1979); Burns (2000); Lynch and Bogen (1996); Matoesian (2005); Pomerantz (1987).

sessions, disputants typically direct their remarks to the mediator and wait until solicited by a mediator to speak. Disputants display their orientation to the speech exchange system of mediation by using requests for permission to speak, and by refraining from intrusions into an opposing disputant's story or turn, unless the intrusion is brief, relevant, and done in such a way as to avoid escalation of conflict.

The divorce mediation sessions differed from the small claims mediation sessions in that the mediators conveyed that they were more open to disputant questions during the session and did not generally ask the disputants to address the mediators rather than each other (although this was nevertheless the format of the interaction for much of the divorce mediation sessions). In divorce mediation, and at later points in some of the small claims cases, there are segments of talk which have a hybrid format, with some aspects of the speech exchange system of mediation combined with aspects of conversational interaction. While there are times during some divorce mediation sessions when disputants speak directly to each other, the mediators were present as addressed or unaddressed recipients of these utterances and frequently intervened in these hybrid exchanges with such actions as questions, topic redirects, or minimal responses.

3   Minimizing and Managing Argumentative
     Talk in Mediation

The interactional organization of mediation minimizes arguing by separating accusations and denials, and providing for selective responses to accusations and the mitigation of accusations and denials. Argumentative exchanges that occurred were brief (typically no more than two to three exchanges of pairs of oppositional utterances), and were often sanctioned by mediators when they occurred (Garcia 1991). While Greatbatch and Dingwall (1997) found that in British divorce mediation sessions mediators allowed disputants to speak directly to each other for extended exchanges, even when arguing occurred, they also found evidence of mediators sanctioning disputants for arguing (Greatbatch and Dingwall 1994).[1] These findings suggest that mediators make judgment calls as to when arguing between disputants should be allowed.

In the current chapter I extend the analysis of argumentative talk in mediation to the entire data set and investigate how the interactional organization of mediation minimizes arguing. In addition, I will show how mediators and disputants in these data manage and exit from arguments when they occur. Since those who end up participating in mediation have been unable to resolve their conflict through direct communication, the chapter begins with an analysis of how arguing occurs in ordinary conversation. This type of interactional organization will then be contrasted with how arguing is done in mediation. I will show how the speech exchange of mediation creates an interactional environment which minimizes the production of arguments, by (1) providing for the delay of responses to accusations and (2) facilitating the formulation of mitigated and indirect accusations and denials. The techniques used to mitigate the production of accusations in these data included third person attributions of blame, elision, and displacement of the agent, as well as various techniques for downgrading the accusation. In the last two sections of this chapter I analyze how disputants and mediators work to manage and curtail brief exchanges of argumentative talk that occasionally occur in these data.

---

[1] See also Jenks, Firth, and Trinder (2012); Smithson et al. (2015); Vasilyeva (2010).

Disputing in Ordinary Conversation

Previous research on arguing in ordinary conversation shows that it involves adjacent, directly addressed exchanges of oppositional turns.[2] Similar patterns of arguing occur in some institutional settings (see Hutchby's 1996a, 1996b analysis of arguments on radio talk shows). Arguing often involves repetition of parts of the previous speaker's utterance (Goodwin and Goodwin 1987). Incorporating partial repeats into oppositional utterances is referred to as "format tying" (Goodwin 2006; see also Coulter 1990). Escalation of volume, acceleration, and denying or negating the previous speaker's utterance are common in arguments (Brenneis and Lein 1977). Research on children's arguments showed that arguments often involve aggravated rather than mitigated disagreements (Goodwin 1983; Maynard 1985a; 1985b).

Once begun, it may be difficult to disengage from an argument because accusations or complaints make return accusations, counterassertions, or denials relevant (Coulter 1990; Dersley and Wootton 2001). Since the speech exchange system of ordinary conversation does not restrict who can speak to whom (Sacks et al. 1974), participants engaged in arguments typically use argumentative techniques like repetition, escalation, and format tying in utterances addressed to each other. This may lead to escalation because the opposing disputant is selected as next speaker or can select himself or herself as next speaker to produce an oppositional response in an adjacent next turn.

In ordinary conversation, one way arguments can be avoided is through formulating or placing disagreements with a prior speaker to demonstrate its dispreferred status (Pomerantz 1975; 1984). However, Pomerantz (1984) noted that for some utterance types there is a preference for disagreement. For example, she found that disagreements with self-deprecations were preferred, presumably because support for one's co-interactant could be better demonstrated by such disagreement. Similarly, accepting a compliment puts the recipient in the awkward position of praising himself or herself (Pomerantz 1978a). Recipients may manage this situation by producing compliment acceptances in a dispreferred format, for example by downgrading the compliment or deflecting the compliment with a shift of referent. Accusations and denials are another category of action which operates contrary to the preference for agreement. If a dispreferred structure were used for a denial, its delay or absence might be interpreted as an admission of guilt.[3]

Dersley and Wootton (2000) argue that since agreement sometimes occurs during arguments, it is inaccurate to describe arguments as having a preference

---

[2] See Dersley and Wootton (2000; 2001); Theobald (2013); Williams (2005).
[3] See Atkinson and Drew (1979); Heritage (1984a); Kotthoff (1993); Pomerantz (1984); Schegloff (2007).

for disagreement. However, if a denial is produced without mitigating techniques such as accounts or explanations that might lead to resolution of the difference of position between them or lessen their face-threatening impact, the state of disagreement may escalate. By denying an accusation, a direct disagreement with the prior speaker is created. This action may lead to the initial accuser reissuing the accusation, potentially provoking a continuation of the exchange of oppositional utterances.

A disagreement that is delayed or displaced is a mitigated disagreement (Pomerantz 1975; 1984), and therefore works against the escalation of conflict. However, when participants in ordinary conversation are engaged in arguments, denials are preferred second pair parts for accusations, and therefore typically are produced quickly and without accounts or other mitigating techniques (see also Kotthoff 1993).

Excerpt 3.1 illustrates how the speech exchange system of ordinary conversation facilitates the escalation of arguments. During a mediation session between Stan and his ex-wife's husband Nick, Nick played a tape recording of an argument that occurred in Nick and Karen's house. During this argument, Karen and her ex-husband Stan argued about a child support check on which Nick had written an insulting comment.

Excerpt 3.1 Blended Family West Coast Mediation, p. 24 (Garcia 1991: 820)

```
538  Stan:   I want to talk to you ( )=
539  Karen:                  =I DI:DN'T: (0.3) HAVE
540          ANYTHING,=
541  Stan:                   =YOU HAD (RIGHT) TO DO WITH IT!
542  Stan:   [(YOU ARE ALWAYS)]
543  Karen:  [YOU KNOW THAT IS] BULL I DIDN'T
544  Stan:   [YOU ALLOWED IT   ]
545  Karen:  [(      see it       )]=I DIDN'T EVEN DO THAT CRAP I
546          DIDN'T SEE THAT.
```

Stan's first turn in this excerpt is produced at a conversational volume, neither noticeably loud or noticeably quiet (line 538). Karen escalates the volume in her oppositional response (lines 539–540), and Stan's response to Karen matches the increased volume of her utterance (line 541). Both participants speak loudly until lines 545–546, at which point Karen escalates the volume of her speech to an even higher level.

Also note that in lines 539–540 Karen produces direct and unmitigated denials of responsibility: "=I DI:DN'T: (0.3) HAVE ANYTHING,=". Stan counters this claim in line 541 with an oppositional utterance: "=YOU HAD (RIGHT) TO DO WITH=IT! ..." Karen's response overlaps this utterance and denies Stan's accusation: "[YOU KNOW THAT IS] BULL I DIDN'T ..." It is the turn-taking system of ordinary conversation which enables participants to place such oppositional responses contiguously. In Excerpt 3.1 accusations are responded to quickly and without delay; in the context of an argument denials are the preferred response to accusations.

In sum, the interactional environment of an argument within the speech exchange system of ordinary conversation enables the use of disputing techniques to initiate, maintain, or escalate the disagreement. However, as was shown in Chapter 2, the interactional organization of mediation differs from that of ordinary conversation. The interactional organization of mediation works against the use of the disputing techniques that occur in arguments in ordinary conversation. In the next sections of this chapter I will show how the speech exchange system of mediation facilitates dispute resolution while enabling participants to minimize the occurrence or escalation of arguments.

Minimizing and Managing Arguing in Mediation

While arguing does occasionally occur in mediation sessions, in order to engage in arguing participants must depart from the turn-taking system of mediation and rely on the flexibility of the turn-taking system of ordinary conversation. Several aspects of the interactional organization of mediation enable participants to produce accusations and denials while avoiding arguments. First, accusations and denials are not adjacency pairs in mediation. Accusations therefore do not engender oppositional responses as next actions because denials are not immediately relevant. Second, the institutionalized delay of denials provides for selective responses to accusations, potentially reducing the number of issues requiring resolution. Third, disputants typically address both accusations and denials in utterances directed to mediators instead of to the opposing disputant. The opposing disputant is therefore not the addressed recipient of the oppositional utterance. These characteristics of mediation are part of an interactional context in which accusations and complaints tend to be mitigated rather than produced in an aggravated form which may lead to an argumentative exchange. Therefore, the occurrence of adjacent and directly addressed oppositional utterances that constitute arguing are minimized in mediation.

The Separation of Accusations and Denials

As shown in Chapter 2, the interactional organization of mediation minimizes adjacent exchanges between disputants. Arguing techniques which depend on adjacency can therefore not be used in this context. In the speech exchange system of small claims mediation, the respondent typically waits to speak until the complainant's story is complete and his or her response has been solicited by the mediator. This interactional organization prevents disputants responding adjacently to any accusations that might be produced without departing

from the turn-taking system of mediation. In addition, mediators may ask
disputants questions during and after their story, thus further delaying the
opposing disputant's response to any accusations or complaints that have been
made. Responses to accusations are therefore not the relevant next action after
an accusation in the context of mediation, and may in fact be significantly
delayed. For example, in Excerpt 3.2 Nick produces some challenging accusations and complaints about his stepchildren's biological father, Stan (lines
701–702, 704, 708–709).

Excerpt 3.2 Blended Family West Coast Mediation, p. 30

```
690  MB:    °(Okay) (5.0) Is thee i:ssue just as thee issue that you don'- duh
691         thah- (0.5) you have these- these ki::ds: and that you can't get
692         along?, or is it thee issue that thuh money's not the:re? >is it it:<
693         (0.5)
694  Nick:  tch U:::HM (2.5) I think theh i:ssue is: (3.3) U:::HM (2.1) I-
695         I mus' SA:Y that- O::Ften (0.7) U:::H (2.1) we are able tuh get
696         alo::ng we are a:ble to: (0.4) at least, comple:te thuh business at
697         ha:nd:, whi[ch=is    ]:
698  ?:               [Um hmh]
699         (.)
700  MB:    °Um hmh=
701  Nick:          =Bu:t (0.4) thuh pro:blem seems tuh be these incidents
702         that crop up (0.5) once in uh whi::le, [wher    ]e (0.4) HE IS (.)
703  Stan:                                         [((sniff))]
704  Nick:  verbal- (.) verbally:: and perhaps physically abusive!
705         (.2)
706  MB:    Um hmh.
707         (0.2)
708  Nick:  A::nd du::h (0.5) you kno:w?, it's s'no:t ONly with ME::, you can
709         s:ee how he talks with his ex [wi:    ]fe!,
710  Stan:                                [((sniff))]
```

Nick accused Stan of being physically and verbally abusive. Note that
Stan's response to Nick's accusations and complaints does not occur adjacently to those utterances. Instead, he waits until a mediator solicits his
response (Excerpt 3.3, line 720).

Excerpt 3.3 Blended Family West Coast Mediation, p. 30

```
711         (.)
712  MB:    °Um hmh=
713  Mark:          =AND THAT has HAppened in front uh thuh kids, (0.6)
714         uh NUMber of ti:mes a::nd, I- you know I- (0.8) I- just think it's
715         really SA:d for them.
716         (.)
717  MB:    °Um hmh, (.) °Um hmh!=
718  Stan:                        =((blows nose))
```

```
719          (0.2)
720   MB:   °tch (0.3) °Duh you wanna respond?°
721          (0.4)
722   Stan:  YEA:H, I sure wou:ld, I have uh whole bunch uh things tuh
723          talk about. (0.3) u:::hm, (0.2) Thee issue ('s ha::nds) (0.5) i::s:
724          (0.5) I: (0.2) have uh- uh very strong paternal dri:ve. (0.7) A::nd
725          (0.2) NI::CK, (0.4) °(h) has conTI:Nually- (0.7) for FI:ve yea:rs
726          (0.1) interferred, (.) with thuh raising of my children.
```

When Stan does produce his response to Mark's accusation, he directs his response to the mediators rather than to Nick, referring to Nick in the third person (lines 722–726).

Denials of accusations are at times substantially delayed in mediation. For example, Excerpt 3.4 shows a complainant (Bud) producing a number of accusations about the respondent Sue, the owner of a dog kennel, in his opening statement. Sue's denials of these accusations and complaints do not occur until later in the hearing.

Excerpt 3.4 Dog with Fleas Midwest Small Claims Mediation, p. 4

```
67   Bud:  I brought thuh suit for (1.9) very extreme expenses and (1.1)
68          problems related to (1.7) uh dog, our puppy that was placed in her
69          care (0.6) when we went on vacation this past summer.
70          (0.4)
71   Med:  Mmhm
72          (0.3)
73   Bud:  It came back (0.7) very infested with fleas, in which (0.5) I believe
74          (0.2) was not something to expect from uh good kennel. (1.2) Went
75          to uh lot of expense. (0.4) I have documents (0.6) that (0.6) spending
76          uh lot of money on. (0.9) And uh lot of time. (1.3) And I believe that
77          we should be reimbursed for that because of their (0.2) poor
78          housekeeping and their (0.3) and their (0.6) unsanitary (1.3) efforts
79          of taking care of uh (0.4) of uh young dog.
80          (1.3)
81   Med:  How long was th- (0.2) thuh dog in thuh kennel
```

There are several complaints against Sue in this opening statement. For example, Bud complains about "very extreme expenses" (line 67), that his dog was infested with fleas (line 73), and that the kennel was unsanitary (line 78). Sue does not reply to these accusations until later on in the hearing (Excerpt 3.5). At this point in the mediation hearing the mediator has solicited Sue's opening statement and it is her turn to tell her story:

Excerpt 3.5 Dog with Fleas Midwest Small Claims Mediation, p. 10

```
193   Sue:  °It wasn't just one other time.° (0.9) This time that he's indicating
194          thuh dog went home after uh ten day stay, thuh dog was groomed,
195          and flea bathed thuh day that it went home. (0.4) I know, when it
```

196   walked out my door, (0.3) that it was not infested with fleas. (1.0)
197   And yet thuh dog was not picked up [by   ] (1.0) Anybody, (0.3) you
198 Med: [nnfff]
199 Sue: know (0.3) in this family, wife or husband. It was (0.3) another
200   woman, I don't know who it was. (0.7) uhm (1.2) There's uh
201   timespan of (0.8) when she picked it up, (0.7) to whenever they
202   received thuh dog, (0.3) that anything could of happened. They
203   indicated that=

Sue has finally responded to Bud's accusations, explaining why the dog could not have gotten fleas while at her kennel, and why he most likely got fleas somewhere else. Her response is an explanation of why she was not responsible for the problems with the dog rather than a direct denial or an oppositional turn in an argument.

In sum, because denials in mediation are delayed, and not produced as second pair parts to accusations, they are not positioned as disagreements with an immediately prior utterance. One potential source of dispute escalation is therefore removed from these mediation sessions. Any denial of an accusation or response to a complaint will occur later on in the session, and usually in response to a mediator solicit rather than as a direct denial of an accusation. Accusations and denials in mediation are therefore much less likely to provoke escalation into argument than when produced in the context of an ordinary conversation.

Selective Responses to Accusations

In ordinary conversation, failure to respond to an accusation would imply guilt, because denials are the preferred responses to accusations in this context. However, in mediation sessions the lack of an immediate response to an accusation does not imply guilt, because the speech exchange system of mediation is designed to avoid exchanges in which disputants reply directly to each other. The requirement that the respondent wait to address accusations and complaints thus facilitates the resolution of conflict by allowing the option of selectively responding to accusations. A disputant may choose to respond only to the more important accusations, or may ignore accusations that are problematic for his or her position. For example, in the small claims mediation between two neighbors disputing about noise and harassment complaints, Ms. Kemper had accused Nancy of verbally assaulting her and of damaging the lawn. Several of Ms. Kemper's accusations were never responded to by Nancy.

If an opposing disputant fails to respond to an accusation, the one who made the accusation may pursue a response by reissuing the accusation. Excerpts 3.6 and 3.7 show a complainant (Dan) making an initial accusation to which the respondents do not reply. Dan reissues the accusation later in the hearing in a second attempt to get a response. In his opening statement, Dan had accused the mechanic at the repair shop of accidentally breaking his vehicle's water pump housing. The opposing disputants do not respond (Excerpt 3.6):

**Excerpt 3.6 Vehicle Repair West Coast Small Claims Mediation, p. 14
           (Garcia 1991: 830)**

298	Dan:	And THEN 'EE said- (0.1) u:h (0.1) he called me up about uh
299		DA:Y after- it was (three 'clock) s'pose tuh pick it up. (0.4) He
300		said you gottah <u>leak</u> in your water pump (0.8) housing now. (1.2)
301		I said well, I didn't <u>have</u> uh leak when I brought it <u>in</u> here. (0.6)
302		<u>So</u>, I din' kno:w!, (0.1) what- what thuh- (0.1) th' <u>pro</u>:blem was
303		<u>here</u>. (1.1) u::h (0.6) And it TURNED OU:T that it <u>NEE</u>:ded aye:
304		aye- thuh- WAter- (0.3) thuh <u>water</u> pump housing was cracked.
305		(0.6) Now <u>I</u> don't know whether that was: (0.3) was <u>cracked</u> (0.2)
306		whether- when thuh me<u>CH</u>Anic was <u>work</u>ing on it?, .h <u>or</u> it was
307		cracked before I brought it in, but it wasn't <u>leaking</u> when I
308		brought °it in.° (0.1) D'at I kno:w. (0.4) I <u>woulduh</u> seen
309		puddles in my driveway.

At a later point in the mediation hearing, Dan raises the issue of the broken water pump housing a second time:

**Excerpt 3.7 Vehicle Repair West Coast Small Claims Mediation, p. 48
           (Garcia 1991: 830)**

1075	Dan:	We're A:lso for<u>get</u>ting thuh WAter pump was not leaking when
1076		I brought it <u>in</u> there! (0.5) <u>Some</u>body could uh WHACKed it
1077		with uh HAMmer for all <u>I</u>: know!

In the mediation sessions in the three data sets, disputants typically did not attempt to reissue accusations that had been ignored by the opposing disputant. In mediation sessions in which a number of accusations and complaints are made, this selective reissuing of accusations may result in a reduction of the number of issues that need to be addressed. When responses to accusations are delayed rather than avoided, opportunities for arguing are minimized because there may be fewer issues over which to engage in disagreement.

The Formulation of Accusations and Denials

Mediators emphasize the nonadversarial nature of mediation during the opening stage of the hearing, and disputants often display an orientation to this norm by mitigating accusations and complaints. In these data disputants use third person attributions of blame, elision or displacement of the agent, and other mitigation techniques to downgrade accusations.

Third Person Attributions of Blame. Since disputants' utterances in mediation are addressed to the mediators rather than the opposing disputant, third person attributions of blame are routine in these data. Addressing an accusation or complaint directly to the opposing disputant, while addressing them with the pronoun "you" or with their name can only be done by violating the speech exchange system of mediation.[4] For example, in Excerpt 3.4, Bud uses third person attributions of blame when describing his complaints against Sue, the owner of the kennel where his dog was boarded.

Bud addresses his utterance to the mediators and refers to the respondent Sue with the pronouns "her" (line 68) and "their" (lines 77 and 78). He avoids directly accusing the opposing disputant. The Mediator provides a minimal response in line 71, thus demonstrating that he interprets Bud's utterance as addressed to him rather than to Sue. By her silence at this juncture, Sue displays her understanding that Bud's utterance was not addressed to her.

As Pomerantz (1978b) has shown, third person formulations of attributions of blame may be less threatening to face. With the third person attributions of blame that are used in mediation, the substance of the dispute and accusations and denials can be discussed without creating an argumentative exchange as might emerge in an ordinary conversation.

Elision of Agent. Accusations in mediation sessions are often constructed with the agent elided. This is most often done by using the passive voice. At times, an utterance in the active voice is produced but the agent of the action (person being accused) is implied but not stated. Pomerantz (1978b) found similar patterns of interaction in ordinary conversation, in order to enable participants to mitigate the impact of accusations and complaints. Note that in both interactional contexts, the elision of the agent can be done because the co-interactants understand who is the referent of the accusation. For example, in Excerpt 3.8 Dan produces a complaint and explains what the problem was while implying the respondent's role in the problem rather than directly stating their identity.

Excerpt 3.8 West Coast Data, "Vehicle Repair" Small Claims Mediation, p. 3, (Garcia 1991: 831)

```
47 Dan:  U:::H (0.3) .h LODDAH thee U::h (0.5) thuh la- thuh LAbor that
48       was u::hm (0.2) .hh conducted on thuh motor home was: was not
49       done in uh- in uh profe:shional (1.6) °in uh° (0.8) wa:y!, (0.2)
50       >°I mean° basic'ly.< (0.3) °it wasn't, tuh° comple:ted,
51       professionally ih wasn't- .hh it is MY uh- in MY: estimation
52       ih wasn't completed at all!
```

---

[4] In ordinary conversation, attributions of blame are typically produced separately from the description of the problem (Pomerantz 1978b).

In Excerpt 3.8, Dan uses the passive voice when summarizing his complaint against the repair shop, who did the faulty repairs on his vehicle, a mobile home. Dan elides the agent instead of formulating these complaints in the active voice (e.g., "The repair shop did not complete the work."). By not referring explicitly to the blamed party in the complaint itself, the complaint is mitigated, and a defense or denial from the blamed party is not immediately relevant.

Displacement of Agent. Instead of eliding the agent, a disputant can formulate their accusation such that the identification of the opposing disputant is separated from the accusation itself. This displacement can be accomplished through how the utterance is constructed, or through delay or hesitation. For example, in Excerpt 3.9 Vince constructs his opening statement in a way which separates his identification of Mary Lou (who sold him the house) from his description of the problems with the house that he is complaining about.

Excerpt 3.9 Real Estate Midwest Small Claims Mediation, p. 3

```
49  Med:   .h °kay-° UM (1.8) VINCE?, >why don't you get us< started?, (0.3)
50         ho:w?, are you and Mary Lou acquainted with each other, °and° what
51         happe:ned?
52         (0.9)
53  Vinc:  We purchased uh hous:e (0.8) <from Martha Lou>,
54         (1.1)
55  Med:   °Um kay°
56         (0.7)
57  Vinc:  u::h (0.7) When we took OCcupancy. (0.6) of thuh house. (0.7) .h it
58         wa:s (0.4) full. (0.5) of (0.7) old clothes, (0.8) canned items, broken
59         furniture .h (0.4) >trash just of-< (0.7) all kinds. We had to: (0.6) .h
60         it took me! five HOURS, in which just tuh clean up thuh house so
61         we could prepare t' paint it? (0.8) .h take all this stuff down tuh thuh
62         (0.7) garage. (0.7) Now I had no problem with 'at?, (0.5) but
63         the:n?, (0.5) we had t- pa:y?, (0.5) to have everything hauled off (1.0)
64         all thuh garbage >taken away and it was< actually °uh° truckload and
65         uh ha:lf. .h (0.3) We've only asked Mary Lou t' pay for thuh one
66         truck load that was all her items.
```

In response to the mediator's question (lines 50–51), the complainant Vince first explains Mary Lou's role in the dispute (line 53). After a pause (line 54) and a mediator continuer (line 55), Vince continues his opening statement by beginning to outline the problems with the house that are part of his complaints against Mary Lou (lines 57–65). In this part of his story he does not refer to Mary Lou directly with a name or pronoun. He instead makes the house the subject of his sentences and describes its condition and what he found there. He does not refer to Mary Lou directly again until he has completed the complaint portion of this utterance and added a statement in which he explains his actions (why he is asking Mary Lou to pay for part of the hauling fee; lines 65–66). By separating the identification of the agent (Mary Lou) from the wrongdoing he is describing (leaving the house in poor condition), he mitigates the complaint against her while still communicating the facts required to justify his position (that she should pay for half of the hauling fees).

Mitigating Accusations. Accusations can also be mitigated by various techniques to downgrade their severity. In Excerpt 3.10 Dan's initial formulation of his complaint employs several techniques to downgrade his accusation.

Excerpt 3.10 Vehicle Repair West Coast Small Claims Mediation, p. 4
(Garcia 1991: 832)

```
60  MA:   °Okay.° (0.2) Improper mechanic[cal   ] work:?
61  Dan:                            [Yeah-]
62        (0.1)
63  Dan:   Ye:ah im::proper u::h (3.2) tch work completed by thuh
64         mechanic I would imagine, PArt of it was done, (0.2) u::h
65         (0.4) okay, (1.2) but there were- (0.2) two or three things that
66         were (0.2) thah weren't (0.1) completed (0.1) properly.
```

Dan first specifies the person who performed the improper work ("thuh mechanic"; lines 63–64). He then immediately qualifies this with an uncertainty marker (Heath 1992): "I would imagine," (line 64). After the uncertainty marker Dan goes on to further downgrade his complaint. He acknowledges that some of the work was done correctly ("PArt of it was done, (0.2) u::h (0.4) okay,"; lines 64–65). Dan's continuation of his turn reinforces his complaint, but also mitigates it by minimizing the severity of the problem: "two or three things that were (0.2) that weren't (0.1) completed (0.1) properly." (lines 65–66). This formulation is a hedged or understated form of "were completed improperly" (Huebler 1983).

Summary

Disputing techniques in ordinary conversation depend on a locally managed turn-taking system (Sacks et al. 1974) and participation framework that allow participants to directly address each other in adjacent utterances. In ordinary conversation, denials can be placed immediately after accusations and formulated with explicit attributions of blame; this placement provides the interactional context for escalation into argument. On the other hand, the interactional organization of mediation works to minimize the use of disputing techniques. In this chapter I showed that in mediation sessions, denials are not positioned immediately after accusations. By placing oppositional utterances apart from the utterance they are responding to, opportunities for escalation into arguing are minimized. In addition, the delay of responses to accusations can lead to some of the accusations never receiving responses. This can reduce the number of complaints and accusations being dealt with in the mediation session, which in some cases can be helpful for the facilitation of dispute resolution. Finally, since accusations are typically produced in utterances addressed to the mediators rather than to the opposing disputant, third person references to blamed parties are used which mitigate the accusation. Finally, the cooperative and nonadversarial normative order of mediation encourages disputants to formulate their accusations less strongly than possible. This mitigation work provides a further deterrent to escalation into a dispute.

Taken together, these aspects of the interactional organization of mediation minimize the occurrence of arguing in the context of mediation. Mediation is therefore often able to resolve conflicts between disputing parties who were not able to resolve their dispute informally. I now turn to those occasions on which disputants in mediation address each other directly. I will first examine those instances of direct address which do not escalate into arguing, and then analyze how mediators manage arguing when it occurs.

Disputant Direct Address and the Emergence of Arguing

While the speech exchange system of mediation enables indirect communication between disputants with mediators serving as liaisons between them, direct exchanges between opposing disputants do occasionally occur. As shown in Chapter 2, certain types of brief interjections by an opposing disputant may occur without mediator challenge. Longer nonargumentative exchanges or even direct disagreements between disputants may occur without mediator intervention if they are brief, constructive, and relevant. Direct exchanges between disputants tend to occur in the later portions of the mediation session, after both disputants have produced their opening statements. These direct exchanges are more common in the divorce mediation sessions than in the small claims mediation sessions, consistent with Greatbatch and Dingwall's (1997) findings. In this section I analyze direct exchanges between disputants, starting with argumentative exchanges from which disputants self-exit, and then discussing those in which mediators assist disputants in exiting from arguments.

Disputant Self-Exit from Brief Argumentative Exchanges

As described in Chapter 2, disputants in the small claims mediation sessions are not supposed to speak during an opposing disputant's story unless solicited by a mediator. However, in Excerpt 3.11 the participants engage in two exchanges of turns in which they self-select to speak in order to disagree with each other. The discussion does not escalate into arguing and the disputants end the direct exchange without assistance from the mediators. Greatbatch and Dingwall (1997) refer to this process as disputant "self-exit."

Excerpt 3.11 Two Brothers West Coast Mediation, p. 40

```
903  Herb:  tch .hhh And uPO:N coming ho:me, hhhh hu:hh (0.2) we found our
904         bro:ther, (0.5) cooking, (0.2) food out of our (0.6) out of OUR
905         u:h, refrigerator, and burning, our firewood, .hh and I'd like tuh
906         sa:y that my sister does have fu:ll right of, (0.2) any, (0.2)
907         appli:ance in thuh house!, and she's well awa:re of how tuh work
908         thuh heater. (0.1) but says that she doesn't like tuh use it
909         sometimes, (.) she has her electric blanket in her roo:m and she's:
910         very con°tent °with it.°
911         (0.1)
912  Bob:   Thuh FI:REwood we split. (0.5) Agreed? (0.4) We- we split
913         tha:t fifty fifty when you say our firewood, I hope you mean
914         your fi:rewood and my firewood, okay?
915         (0.4)
916  Herb:  No, I consider it my si:ster's firewood, 'cause she's thuh one that
917         really paid °for it.°
918         (0.2)
919  Bob:   We:ll!, (0.2) (I've been-) (.) I've (.) brought thuh house from
920         fifty fi:ve degree:s, (0.4) to seventy two degree:s, and she was
921         sitting in front uh thuh fire place, so- (0.1) was- (0.1) .h
922         duh you? (0.2) .h whah was my behavior, do you think got- (.)
923         u:hm, out of ha:nd?
924         (0.8)
925  Herb:  Yes I believe so!
```

As the excerpt begins, Herbert is complaining that Bob entered his house uninvited, ate food from his refrigerator, and burned his firewood (lines 903–910). Bob then selects himself to speak during a pause within his brother's story, thus departing from one of the conventions of the speech exchange system of mediation. Bob's utterance in lines 912–914 is directed at Herbert, and challenges a statement of fact in his story. Note that in this utterance Bob does not deny using the firewood, but rather claims that he owns half of it. Bob's interjection at this point is therefore a partial denial of the accusation that Herbert is making. While Bob's question in lines 912–914 has a preference for agreement (Sacks 1987a), his brother Herbert produces a "no" response (lines 916–917). Bob then continues the disagreement between them by prefacing his reply with a disagreement-implicative "We:ll!," (line 919; Hutchby 1996a; 1996b; Pomerantz 1984). However, instead of further challenging Herbert about the ownership of the firewood, Bob explains that he used the fire wood for the benefit of their sister, who lives with Herbert. Bob's question is constructed with a preference for disagreement (lines 919–923).

Herbert again produces a dispreferred response ("Yes I believe so!"; line 925), thus denying that what Bob did was right.

However, although Bob and Herbert have directly exchanged two pairs of turns in which they at least partially disagree with each other, their disagreement does not escalate into an argument. As the exchange continues, Bob ends the sequence by telling Herbert to continue his story ("Go on!"; line 927).

Excerpt 3.12 Two Brothers West Coast Mediation, p. 40

```
926           (0.5)
927  Bob:   Go on!
928           (0.4)
929  Herb:  U::hm (0.4) UPON entering thuh house, and (.) like seeing what
930           had been go:ing on, (0.3) we u:h (0.4) we got uh RENtal
931           refrigerato:r (0.2) and he decided h that thuh door didn't close just
932           right, so he propped it up under thuh front, (0.4) .h so thuh door
933           would close. u:hm .hh hh We'd seen uh few things that- (0.3) you
934           kno::w w' were juss: (0.2) weren't ready tuh see: (.) you know, we
935           saw that twenty minutes::: I had twenty minutes tuh prepare for
936           thuh mee::ting, and here's my bro:ther, .hh (.) with thuh (0.2) front
937           DOo:r wide open uh (0.4) thuh fire blazing and, and (0.2) our food
938           cooking on thuh °sto:ve! (0.3) tch And my sister, was then agai:n
939           uh little bit upset, (.) I won't say she cry:ing, or- (0.2) really upset
940           over thuh situation, just that BO:b, had come to thuh DOO:R,
```

Bob's self-exit from the disagreement is accomplished without conceding that Herbert's perspective is correct. Herbert then continues his story, which is addressed to the mediators rather than to his brother. Note, for example, that Herbert refers to Bob in the third person – "he" in line 931, "my bro:ther" in line 936, and "BO:b" in line 940). Mediation format has therefore been restored, without the active assistance of the mediators.

Mediator-Assisted Exit

While the disputants in Excerpts 3.11 and 3.12 above accomplish self-exit from a direct disagreement, mediators sometimes intervene in direct exchanges between disputants. Excerpts 3.13 and 3.14 show an extended sequence of direct address between opposing disputants which initially does not escalate into argument. The disputants exchange a total of nine pairs of turns directly with each other before a mediator intervenes, after the exchange has started to escalate.

This mediation involved the owner of a vehicle and the repair shop which had failed to repair it correctly. One of the issues under contention was the repair shop's work on the vehicle's air conditioning system. During the discussion of this issue, Dan accused the repair shop of having an unqualified

technician work on his vehicle. As Excerpt 3.13 begins, Respondent A defends
the shop's work by explaining the qualifications of the technician who worked
on the vehicle (lines 895–902).

Excerpt 3.13 Vehicle Repair West Coast Small Claims Mediation, p. 39

895 RA: He::'s (0.5) he's got certificates that are probably an inch thick from
896   s: {Car Brand} schoo::ls, that he's attended. .hh He's ASE
897   approved, he's u:h (0.2) tch u::h I guess smo:g licensed!, (0.3)
898   u::h (0.3) you kno:w, which u:::h (0.2) you know I mean uh (0.2) ee:-
899   e:ven though he's uh young fella, probably be (uh'out) twenty- (0.3)
900   f:our years old?, (0.2) .hh u:::h (0.5) u::h (0.7) I wouldn' I would
901   question your: your: deduction, and your theories about his
902   h[is (qualifications.)]
903 Dan: [Was he   ] certified tuh work on air conditioning?
904   (0.9)
905 RA: u::h I would assu:m:e, I've- I've ye:ah! (0.2) ye:ah, I
906   would assume he was. (0.2) Sure. (0.2) Well, sure. Most- (.) most
907   technicians are. (.) I mean it's not (.) that (.) complicated uh
908   system. .hh as I said before. (0.2) you know, you can over loo:k:
909   aye, or- or mi:ss aye u:h (0.2) and for aye detector aye piece of
910   electronic equipment doesn't pick up uh leak:?, (.) that might be
911   there, or it's so: minu::te!, that it doesn't pick it up.
912   (0.3)
913 Dan: Well basically I wanted tuh find out what was wro:ng with it.
914   (0.4) And I didn't get any- (0.3) any °answers.
915   (.)
916 RA: Well! you- it takes: (.) first of all, we cha:rge u::h .h uh labor charge
917   to insta:ll thee equipment tuh testing: thee thee pressure gauges:, and
918   we charge for thuh freon to insta:ll in thuh unit,=
919 Dan: =That's fine.
920   (0.1)
921 RA: A:nd, which you hah- and we have to get thee en: system is empty: .h
922   you HAve tuh recharge thuh sy:stem and put duh fluid back i:n, tuh
923   try tuh find a:ye, a:ye le::ak:! (0.2) .h u:::h- (0.4) Once thuh system
924   is fully CHA:rged, then you test for thuh leak! yuh- If there i:s no
925   leak!, or our detector doesn't pick up uh leak! .hh we can't just shot
926   gu:n thuh jo::b!, I mean you can't go through and replace e:very
927   seal!, .hh and replace e:very compo:nent, that can leak! within an
928   air conditioning unit. .hh I mean thuh co:st for something like that
929   would be- it- would be astrono:mical!
930   (0.6)
931 Dan: >Okay so what duh-< (0.2) >what duh you< 'vi:se people tuh do:

In line 903 Dan interrupts Respondent A's explanation to challenge the
technician's qualifications to work on air conditioning systems. Respondent
A's response is somewhat equivocal – he begins with delay (line 904), hesitation markers, and qualifiers (lines 905–906; see Clayman 1993; 2001 on

evasive answers). He does not definitively answer the question as to whether this particular technician was certified to work on air conditioning systems. Instead he explains why someone might fail to find a leak (lines 908–911). Dan's response to this utterance is disagreement implicative ("Well . . ."; line 913). He goes on to complain that the problem with the air conditioning system was not diagnosed (lines 913–914).

Respondent A's response to this utterance is also rejection-implicative ("Well! . . ."; line 916). However, although the two disputants are disagreeing with each other, directly addressing each other, and making and responding to complaints, they are not arguing, and their interaction is not escalating in intensity. By formulating their disagreements as dispreferred responses (Pomerantz 1984), they avoid shifting to an argumentative frame. They do not use interruptions, increased volume, name-calling, or format tying (Goodwin 1984) to escalate the disagreement. In fact, when Respondent A completes the first point in his defense (that they charge for the Freon and the work of detecting the leak – lines 916–918), Dan self-selects to express agreement ("That's fine."; line 919). After a brief pause, Respondent A signals the continuation of his turn in line 921 by using an "and-preface" (Heritage and Sorjonen 1994). He follows this with an explanation of the procedure for finding leaks in air conditioning systems, as well as the alternatives when no leaks are found (lines 921–929). This explanation works to justify the shop's lack of action in the face of the "no leak" finding on Dan's vehicle.

Their discussion is relevant to the topic at hand and produces information which can help the participants understand each other's positions. This exchange is therefore productive for the mediation process and does not require mediator intervention. By refraining from actively intervening in this discussion, the mediators display that they are not mechanically enforcing rules, but are instead using the rules as tools when needed. However, even when they remain silent, their presence and the potential for mediator intervention distinguishes the entire exchange from a conversational speech exchange system (per Chapter 2).

The discussion continues in this vein, with Dan questioning or challenging Respondent A's answers, and Respondent A providing answers, explanations, or evidence to counter those questions or complaints (not shown). Excerpt 3.14 picks up the discussion of this topic a few minutes later, when the discussion begins escalating to an argument.

Excerpt 3.14 Vehicle Repair West Coast Small Claims Mediation, p. 42

```
965  RA:   Of- (.) u::h, four hundred °dollars! (0.4) I mean you could
966        a:lMO::ST buy another air condi:°(tion)ing unit for that kind uh
967        money. (0.3) I m' it's that
968        (0.1)
```

```
969  Dan:  Well [THAT's] what I KINDA wanted tuh KNO:W, but
970  RA:        [(        )]
971  Dan:  tu:h air conditioner didn't work?, (.) Do I needed uh whole
972        ne:w one or what did I need!
973        D[at's what I wanted tuh find out.]
974  RA:    [Well! it's RA::re, that you     ] need uh
975        (.)
976  MA:  [Maybe you have] tuh (.) fill it (.) three TI:mes, tuh find out.
977  ?:     [°(              )]
978        (.)
979  RA:  Buh [we h]a:ve tuh FI:nd it,
980  MA:      [(So) ]
981        (.)
982  MA:  °(Ye[ah])
983  RA:       [A: ]n' a:n' a:n' wuh- you kno:w?, (0.6) We're SOrry we
984        missed it!, I mean, it's no fun for u::s! (0.2) (    I mean)=
985  Dan:                                              =Well ih
986        WA:SN' any fun ME: or thuh whole-
987        (.)
988  RA:  Well sure!=
989  Dan:          =(Thuh thing/family) [(              )]
990  RA:                                [And I:: understa]:n' that.
991        (0.4)
992  Dan:  Well I'm juss' GLA:::D I picked it up 'stead uh my WI:f::e.
993        (0.8)
994  MA:  This is uh big headache in thuh restaurant business with °(respect to
995        it for uh while) and thuh lea:ks that drove us cra:zy were in thuh
996        radiator!, (0.5) This is thuh (like) ra:diator in your ca::r and A:ny
997        one=[uh th    ]ose! (0.4) can
998  ?:      [(        )]
999  MA:  LEA:k (0.5) an- (0.2) FI:NDing it was uh son of uh gun
```

Mediator A finally intervenes in the discussion (line 976). Mediator A's intervention is not a sanction; it is an elaboration or reinforcement of the point Respondent A has been making about why the leak detection process is not always successful, and why other alternatives (e.g., replacing the entire air conditioning system) are not feasible or desirable. The next several turns exchanged between the disputants are somewhat escalated in terms of disputing intensity. Their utterances are almost all latched or overlapped, indicating an increase in pace (lines 983–990). In addition, Dan makes additional complaints. For example, he reiterates a previous concern about what could have happened if his wife had picked up the vehicle rather than himself (line 992). Since there was also a problem with how the brakes on the vehicle were repaired, he was worried that an accident could have occurred.

The mediator's next intervention refocuses the topic back to the issue of leaks. He addresses it indirectly by telling a story about an experience he had with leaking radiators when he was running a restaurant. He indirectly argues that it can be hard to find leaks (lines 994–999). By beginning his turn with "This is uh big headache in thuh restaurant business with °(respect to it for ...";" (lines 994–995), Mediator A presents his utterance so that "this" performs a dual function. First, it appears to indexically connect his utterance to Dan's prior turn in line 992. However, his turn also refers further back in the exchange and refocuses disputants' attention to the issue of detecting leaks rather than just the complaints Dan has articulated in these recent turns. Mediator A thus performs a subtle topic redirect while at the same time providing additional evidence in support of Respondent A's position. He implies that the shop's failure to find the leak in the air conditioning was not necessarily a sign of incompetence or of an incorrectly performed job. Mediator A's intervention in lines 994–999 also serves to restore mediation format, in which mediators facilitate the session and disputants speak when selected to do so by mediators.

In sum, the examples above have shown how at least some disputants can directly discuss the issues under dispute without escalating into arguing. While they disagree with each other and contest each other's positions at times, the talk can remain civil and responsive throughout. On other occasions, when disputants engage in direct address of the opposing disputant, arguing may emerge. In the next section I analyze the range of resources available to mediators to intervene in emerging arguments between disputants.

Mediator Responses to Emerging Arguments

While extended arguing sequences are rare in these data, there are some arguing sequences which extend for more than two or three exchanges of pairs of turns. I will examine how mediators may intervene in these argumentative exchanges to prevent escalation or to redirect disputants to more productive talk.

As shown in Chapter 2, mediators can respond directly to emerging arguments with sanctions. In this section I will show how argumentative exchanges can also be broken up by interjecting responses between disputants' argumentative utterances. By interrupting or talking over argumentative exchanges, mediators can refocus attention onto other issues while officially ignoring the argument. Mediation format can also be restored by asking questions to redirect talk and restore mediator address. Mediators may also rephrase or repeat a disputant's previously expressed position in order to help the arguing disputants hear what each other is saying. In addition, mediators can use continuers or minimal responses to insert themselves into the interaction as an active listener. The examples in this section will illustrate these and other mediator techniques for responding to emerging arguments.

Minimal Responses and Topic Shifts

Mediators can manage emerging arguments and display their recipiency of disputant's utterances through the use of minimal responses or continuers. This technique can work to transform the argument from a dyadic argumentative exchange between two disputants to a mediated exchange, thus separating disputants' oppositional utterances which otherwise would be adjacent. For example, in Excerpts 3.15 and 3.16 a mediator intervenes in an emerging argument between a divorcing couple. As Excerpt 3.15 begins, Belinda is discussing therapists she and her husband could engage.

Excerpt 3.15 Darryl and Belinda Midwest Divorce Mediation, Session 2, p. 14

```
277  Bel:  A:ND UH, (0.4) y'know I I hh °do see somebody and ha:ve for
278         two years and um (1.2) tch (1.0) not that I'm opposed (0.5) to to
279         seeing somebody >again° I wasn't< very impressed with her.
280         °And um I I did get uh name of of uh ma:n .hh that works, for
281         them. which I told Darryl about who I heard is very good with u:m
282         chemical dependency. (0.5) °u:m .hh kinds of things° which, that's
283         what (0.5) °alcoholism is that's thuh kind of home he grew up in°
284         (0.7) °um°
285         (0.8)
286  Dar:  That's just not tru-h-e! Bel-h-inda!
287         (0.3)
288  Bel:  What!
289         (0.1)
290  Dar:  You you can sa-h-y that bu-h-t it's simply not true!=
291  Bel:                                          =What!
292         (1.1) What. What isn't true.
293         (0.4)
294  Dar:  That I grew up in uh home with alcoholism as uh problem! It's just
295         not true.
296         (0.3)
297  Bel:  I believe it was.
298         (0.4)
299  Dar:  Well you weren't there. .hh My father became had uh drinking
300         problem as he got older and thuh family was gone y'know=
301  MA:                                                          =Ye:ah
302         (0.4)
303  Dar:  And but- when we were children he wasn't (0.8) wasn't an
304         alcoholic. He [worked] every day, went to work regular,
305  MA:                 [Ye:ah. ]
```

The mediators remain silent for several exchanges of pairs of argumentative turns (lines 286–300). As Darryl's turn in line 299 begins, he turns his gaze toward Mediator A and directs his utterance to him. In line 301 Mediator A latches a minimal response to the end of Darryl's turn ("=Ye:ah").

When "yeah" is used as a listener response it often presages a transition to speakership (Jefferson 1978). When Darryl continues his explanation after this interjection (lines 303–304), the mediator produces a second minimal response – this time in overlap with Darryl's turn (line 305). Mediator A's use of active listening techniques here successfully supplants Belinda's participation in the exchange. However, as Excerpt 3.16 shows, the argument resumes at the next possibly complete turn constructional unit. The disputants continue the argumentative discussion for several more turns (lines 306–321).

Excerpt 3.16 Darryl and Belinda Midwest Divorce Mediation, Session 2, p. 14

```
306  Dar:  [never missed work?]
307  Bel:  [He went he went tuh] work every day [I know-  ]
308  Dar:                               [He never-] he never came
309        home drunk?
310        (0.2)
311  Bel:  I don't think that's [((thuh thee issue)]
312  Dar:                       [He was thuh kind] uh guy that would come
313        home and, worked- (0.4) ten hours uh day six days uh week
314        and when he got home after ten hours uh work .h he'd drink uh
315        quart or two uh beer!
316        (0.3)
317  Bel:  I've ta[lked I've ha:d uh lot of talks with your mother Darryl]
318  Dar:         [A:nd what you (   ) you can (0.3) people          ] can
319        call that alcoholism but I didn't think [it was      ]
320  Bel:                                    [Your moth]er t- has told me,
321        many times when he [did not, come home at a:ll!   ]
322  MA:                      [Well these thuh kind of things] that you can:
323        relate to (0.5) whomever you select .hh uh uh I'd like to just u:m
324        (1.2) ask you: (0.7) about thee: (0.4) thuh- (0.7) it's thee uh (0.5)
325        it's thuh city personnel (0.6) I mean uh
326        (0.9)
327  MB:   E. [A. P.    ]
328  MA:      [Employee] Assistance [(he'll have)]=
329  MB:                            [Yeah-    ]=
330  Bel:                                    =°Uh huh.°=
331  Dar:                                           =Yeah.
332        (0.4)
333  MA:   An- a:nd and d'you have uh CHoice in that plan as tuh who you
334        see or?=
335  Dar:        =I dunno! (0.8) w-h-e should ask 'em (man) it's just uh,
336        somethin' 'at's some kind of uh=
337  MA:                              =Yeah.=
338  Dar:                                   =program that that they's
339        thuh city set up I guess (so) .hh=
340  MA:                              =Mm hm.
```

Mediator A interrupts Belinda's turn-in-progress (lines 322–325). His utterance is produced in overlap with Belinda's prior turn, thus effectively ending the argumentative sequence. Mediator A begins his turn with a disagreement-implicative "Well" (Pomerantz 1984). He conveys that the issues they are discussing are not relevant for mediation, and then shifts the topic to the issue of getting a therapist for the family from Darryl's employee assistance plan (lines 323–328). Mediator A thus effectively ends the argument about whether Darryl's father was an alcoholic by making a topic closure move followed by a transition to a related topic. After this intervention, the disputants abandon their argument and their direct address of each other. Mediation format has been successfully restored by mediator intervention.

Strategic Interruptions, Questions, and Sanctions

Mediators in these data can assist disputants in exiting from argumentative exchanges by using strategic interruptions, questions, and sanctions. A strategic interruption is an interruptively placed utterance which works to supplant another speaker's production of an utterance which is problematic in some way. In previous research I found that strategic interruptions were used by mediators to preempt a disputant's rejection of a proposal (Garcia 1989). In the data analyzed in this book they are also used to interrupt argumentative exchanges. Excerpts 3.17 and 3.18 illustrate how a mediator can use a strategic interruption in the context of an argumentative exchange to redirect the discussion to a related topic and restore disputant address of the mediators. In Excerpt 3.17 Mike accuses his wife Kelly of driving after drinking alcohol (lines 1337–1338):

Excerpt 3.17 Mike and Kelly Midwest Divorce Mediation, Session 3, p. 62

```
1337  Mike:   But. y'know- have y' ever (0.4) °y'know° (0.7) °drinkin'?° (0.8)
1338          while you were drivin'!
1339          (0.4)
1340  Kelly:  °Nope.°
1341          (0.8)
1342  Mike:   Never?
1343          (0.3)
1344  Kelly:  °Never.°
1345          (0.3)
1346  Mike:   °Michael Bolton concert!°
1347          (0.5)
1348  Kelly:  °Nope?°
1349          (0.4)
1350  Mike:   °No?°
1351          (0.5)
1352  Kelly:  °No-°
```

```
1353          (1.4)
1354   Mike:  °°(mm)°° °<And I know that->°
1355          (0.9)
1356   Kelly: And that's uh [hearsay      ] again!
1357   Mike:              [°those thing°]
1358          (0.3)
1359   Mike:  °if- if- it's hearsay when [your best      ]
1360   Kelly:                            [(And you GOT-)]
1361   Mike:  friend? (0.3) tel[ls me]
1362   Kelly:                  [No  s]he was NOT my best friend OBviously!
1363          (0.5)
1364   Mike:  Obviously? (mph! ye[s she is)        ]
1365   MA:                       [IF YOU FOUND] OUT THAT RANDY was
1366          (0.2) um .h tch (0.6) drinking with his friends would you blame
1367          that on Kelly?
```

After Kelly denies Mike's accusation (line 1340), he reissues it several times in different ways (lines 1342, 1346, 1350). Kelly resists Mike's attempts to pursue this accusation by repeated denials. The mediators stay silent during this exchange, but when the talk starts escalating to a heated argument (lines 1354–1364), Mediator A intervenes. She interrupts the argument-in-progress to ask a hypothetical question about the couple's eldest son Randy (lines 1365–1367). Mediator A's question is clearly directed at Mike, and selects him as next speaker (she refers to Kelly in the third person). Note Mediator A's use of loudness in her interruption; Mike drops out and lets her have the floor.[5] Excerpt 3.18 shows the mediators again intervening in a disputant's arguing move:

Excerpt 3.18 Mike and Kelly Midwest Divorce Mediation, Session 3, p. 62

```
1368          (0.6)
1369   Kelly: °Definitely.° (0.7) °He would.°
1370          [>I know he would.< ] I KNOW [he would.   ]
1371   MA:    [Okay let him answer.]
1372   MB:                                 [Let him! let] him! °answer.°
1373          (1.1)
1374   MB:    Especially if she didn't know about. °Would you blame it on
1375          Kelly?°
1376          (0.3)
1377   Mike:  I don' know that it- was is Kelly's fault. (0.3) If he was getting it
1378          from her hou:se? .h (0.4) and it was uh- an accessibility? (0.4)
1379          part of it.
```

[5] See Schegloff (2000); West and Zimmerman (1977; 1982); Zimmerman and West (1975).

Even though Mediator A's question (Excerpt 3.17 above, lines 1365–1367) was addressed to Mike, Kelly responded to it argumentatively (lines 1369–1370). The mediators then both sanction Kelly for speaking out of turn (lines 1371 and 1372). Mediator B then reissues the question (lines 1374–1375), and Mike answers it (lines 1377–1379). Note that in Mike's answer he follows mediation format and directs his answer to the mediators, referring to Kelly in the third person. The arguing sequence between Mike and Kelly has thus been interrupted by the mediators and replaced with talk consistent with mediation format.

Deflection from Arguing by Focusing on Facts

Another mediator technique for managing argumentative sequences is to redirect the disputants by refocusing attention to the facts under dispute. For example, in Excerpt 3.19 the mediators intervene in an ongoing argument by repeatedly working to refocus the disputants on information that was shared earlier in the session. In this part of the mediation session, the divorcing couple is trying to decide how to divide their household goods and furniture. Mediator A then intervenes in the discussion (lines 1654–1655):

Excerpt 3.19 Mike and Kelly Midwest Divorce Mediation, Session 2, p. 75

```
1647  Kelly:  But see there's not an everything! I >don' know where you're<
1648          [gettin'] everything! There's [not that much!]
1649  Mike:   [Well ]                     [but there's- re ]frigerators and 'uh
1650          stove, there's thee other [livin' room  ] set? .h=
1651  Kelly:                            [Thuh sto:ve?]     =Well
1652  Kelly:  [we won't get in [to where thuh stove] came from.]
1653  Mike:   [there's bedroom [sets? there's      ]
1654  MA:                     [And I also      ] heard her  ] say °she's
1655          willing tuh let you have thuh stove.°
1656          (0.7)
1657  Mike:   I don't- uh- I- I've already got
1658          (0.2)
1659  MB:     You [have thuh ] stove.=
1660  Mike:      [thuh stove.]
1661  Kelly:                        =Thank y' se[e? t]hat's what he's
1662  Mike:                                    [I do-]
1663  Kelly:  doin'!=
1664  Mike:       =Wel[l now no! not at a]ll! I'm just saying=
1665  MB:           [And then also    ]
1666  Kelly:                                       =mmhh!=
1667  MB:                                               =I've
1668          also heard her sa:y? °that- she's willing tuh let you have towels!
1669          (1.3) y'[know]
1670  MA:           [And ] tools.
```

```
1671          (0.2)
1672  MB:     And tools.
1673          (0.6)
1674  Mike:   And then she keeps half thuh towels an- (0.4) 's things like that and
1675          half thuh tools.
1676          (0.3)
1677  MB:     Are you keep[ing it?]
1678  Kelly:             [Well I] don't want any °tools.° (0.3) period. (0.2)
1679          No! (0.6) >I [don' need any uh those.<  ]
1680  MB:                 [>You don't even wanna<  ] screwdriver or something?
1681          (0.6)
1682  Kelly:  h!=
1683  MA:     =Hamm[er?]
1684  Kelly:       [If ] I needed one screwdriver or uh hammer I? I'm
1685          sure I can borrow 't from my neighbor.=
1686  MA:                                   =°Okay.°
1687          (0.1)
1688  MB:     °O[kay.°]
```

Mediator A's intervention in lines 1654 and 1655 is not a sanction or activity redirect, it is a reminder directed to Mike that Kelly has already offered to let him have the stove. She thus refocuses attention on the facts rather than on the argumentative exchange in progress. At the same time, she uses the strategic interruption strategy analyzed above to interrupt the argument-in-progress. As the discussion continues, Mediator B reminds Mike that Kelly has offered to let him have towels (lines 1165, 1667, and 1668). Mediator A extends that utterance by reminding Mike that Kelly has also offered to let him have household tools (line 1670). In short, most of the mediators' interventions in this argumentative sequence work to redirect the discussion by providing facts that are relevant to the issues under dispute. Their contributions, by their placement, at least temporarily break into the argumentative exchange between the disputants. They eventually succeed in redirecting the disputants from their argument and restoring mediation format.

The disputants then speak to the mediators rather than to each other (lines 1674–1688). Note that in line 1674 Mike begins directing his remarks to the mediators and referring to Kelly in the third person rather than addressing her directly. Kelly's subsequent utterances are also directed to the mediators. An argument has been terminated, not by mediator sanctions, but by timely mediator intervention in the substance of the dispute.

Stepwise Departures from Mediation Format to Arguing

While mediators have the freedom to self-select to speak at any point in the session, they do at times refrain from intervening in what look like arguing exchanges between disputants. However, when the structure of these arguing exchanges are closely examined, there are typically reasons for withholding mediator intervention. For example, on some occasions there is a stepwise departure from the turn-taking system of mediation to a quasi-conversational hybrid structure. In these cases, even though one disputant may be producing adjacent oppositional utterances directed to the opposing disputant, the other disputant may be maintaining mediation format and addressing the mediator. The interaction thus does not have the structure of arguing.

Excerpts 3.20–3.22 illustrate how the departure from mediation format to arguing can occur through a stepwise departure from the turn-taking system and participation framework of mediation. In this small claims mediation, two former roommates are in disagreement over who should pay an electric bill. Excerpt 3.20 begins toward the end of the mediation session. As the excerpt begins, the participants are following the conventions of the speech exchange system of mediation, but they progressively depart from this organization.[6] For example, in the initial portions of Excerpt 3.20, John argues directly with Kris, while Kris continues referring to John in the third person and directing her utterances to the mediator. This exchange is therefore conducted in a hybrid format (described in Chapter 2). It has elements of both mediation format and the speech exchange system of ordinary conversation.

Excerpt 3.20 Electric Bill Midwest Small Claims Mediation, p. 50

```
1285  Med:   Okay. What are you- what-? (0.6) what about this. He says he
1286         can't °af°ford it.
1287         (0.9)
1288  Kris:  HE MIGHT NOT BE ABLE TO NOW! but when I got this bi:ll?,
1289         (0.4) which (0.3) was thuh final notice?, (0.5) it says right here,
1290         thuh FInal bill prepared on June six(th)? (0.3) .h He was not
1291         making child support payments. (0.7) and whatEver other
1292         payments he was making then. He was not making those then. He
1293         could have paid it when he said he would. (2.1) And I know since
1294         then?, he's bought furniture?
1295         (0.6)
1296  John:  [Nah I haven't.]
1297  Kris:  [He's bou      ]ght?, (0.5) °uh- uh pff u:hh°
1298         (0.3)
1299  John:  I:?, my- MY APARTMENT IS COMPLETELY empty?
1300         (1.1)
1301  John:  I[t's   ] completely empty. My mother
1302  Kris:  [Well,]
```

<hr>

[6] This pattern is similar to what has been found in television news interviews, in which participants can progressively depart from the speech exchange system of interviews (Clayman and Heritage 2002; Clayman and Whalen 1988/89).

```
1303  John:  [bought me uh kitchen t      ]able? (0.4) I was given uh couch,
1304  Kris:  [from what I':ve been to:ld?,]
1305  John:  (0.3) .h and I have uh green tee: vee:.
```

Excerpt 3.20 begins with the mediator using a question to redirect the
disputants' attention to substantive issues regarding the electric bill (lines
1285–1286). The mediator paraphrases John's previous statements (not
shown) that he can not afford to pay the bill. Kris responds by rejecting this
argument (lines 1288–1293). Note that up to this point, John follows mediation
format and remains silent during Kris's utterance, even though she accuses him
of being able to pay the bill.

After a 2.1 second pause in line 1293, Kris makes the claim that John has
spent money on furniture (lines 1293–1294), thus arguing that he has discre-
tionary funds he could have used to pay the electric bill. In line 1296 John
produces a direct denial of Kris's accusation. John thus violates mediation
format by selecting himself to speak when not solicited by a mediator and by
producing an oppositional utterance (a denial of an accusation). This denial
occurs at the same time Kris continues her ongoing turn, and is overlapped by
it. After Kris hesitates (end of line 1297), John speaks again and elaborates his
denial (line 1299), supporting his position that he has not spent money on
furniture (lines 1299, 1301, 1303, and 1305). Kris overlaps John's turn with a
rejection-implicative "Well," (line 1302), and then continues with the beginning of a rebuttal in line 1304.

As the exchange continues, Kris completes her rebuttal (Excerpt 3.21, line
1307). This rebuttal was directed to the mediator and is interrupted by John as
he responds to her challenge (lines 1308–1310).

Excerpt 3.21 Electric Bill Midwest Small Claims Mediation, p. 50

```
1306         (1.2)
1307  Kris:  Well (0.2) what I was told [was: that he has      ]
1308  John:                             [Well you can come up] and look at it
1309         yourself, and s:ee!, (0.6) for what you was told is °it's°
1310         far[ther than from (facts uh reality.)]
1311  Kris:     [tch I mean it- it went as     f]ar as: (0.4) thuh FAct that he:
1312         (0.3) thought that we still had keys tuh thuh place, (0.4) .h and
1313         asked thuh landlord tuh change thuh locks because,
1314         (0.4)
1315  John:  Wouldn't you have?
1316         (1.1)
1317  Kris:  No!
1318         (0.4)
1319  John:  No. [(    )]
1320  Kris:      [I would]'ve tru:sted you!,
1321         (0.4)
1322  John:  °Oka-h-y.
```

Note that in Kris's line 1307 she preserves some elements of mediation format. For example, she refers to John in the third person, thus formulating her utterance as directed to the mediator, even though she is responding to the substance of John's previous turn. On the other hand, John's response to her incipient rejection of his denial has departed completely from mediation format and addresses the opposing disputant directly in an oppositional utterance. He is constructing an argument within the speech exchange system of ordinary conversation. John begins his turn with "Well" (line 1308), and departs from mediation format by addressing Kris directly with the pronoun "you" (line 1308) instead of indirectly with a third person pronoun. He also uses argumentative format tying (Goodwin and Goodwin 1987).

Some mediators in these data reacted much more quickly to cut off emerging arguments, while others waited longer, as long as the discussion was relevant to the topic at hand and productive for the disputants. In these excerpts the mediator waits and lets Kris and John discuss these issues directly. One reason for the silence of this mediator may be that it takes the participation of two disputants for a potential argument to escalate. Up to this point, Kris's contributions retain much of the mediation format which prevents escalation into arguing. For example, in lines 1311–1313, as Kris responds to John's challenging rebuttal, she maintains mediation format by addressing the mediator rather than the opposing disputant. Note that Kris again refers to John as "he" in line 1311.

John produces another argumentative move in line 1315. His question challenges Kris's criticism of him for changing the locks on the apartment (lines 1311–1313). Note that John's line 1315 is addressed directly to Kris, referring to her as "you," and it is placed in a pause within her turn rather than at a transition relevance place. Kris denies this accusation in line 1317, with a very direct and unmitigated "No!". However, note that there is a 1.1 second pause prior to her denial, so it is at least somewhat delayed. Also, she does not continue speaking after producing her denial, so she does not add further material to the argument. John's response in line 1319 is unfortunately partially inaudible, but also begins with "No." This formulation suggests that he is continuing his oppositional approach. Kris's "[I would]'ve tru:sted you!," (line 1320) is both a criticism and an attempt to take the moral high ground by claiming that she would have been a more trusting friend than he was. At this point, both disputants are actively engaged in arguing with each other.

Excerpt 3.22 shows the mediator responding to this shift by intervening. After a pause (line 1323), the mediator begins an intervention (line 1324), but is interrupted by Kris who produces another argumentative move directed at John.

Excerpt 3.22 Electric Bill Midwest Small Claims Mediation, p. 50

```
1323        (1.0)
1324 Med:   Alright [can]
1325 Kris:         [I   ] didn't change thuh lock on my house! and you have
1326        thuh key tuh my house?,
1327        (0.5)
1328 John:  °(Well?)
1329        (0.5)
1330 Med:   Um (0.4) You know it's: ten o'clock, and we've been at this for
1331        about forty five minutes. Again I have (thuh) question. (0.5) .h Is
1332        there uh way that you could co:me to: .h (0.3) uh middle ground
1333        here? or do you nee:d uh judge tuh make uh decision
1334        [about [hearing who's ri]ght or wrong? ]
```

Kris is now using "you" to address John directly, a further departure from the speech exchange system of mediation (lines 1325–1326). After this escalated interruption and John's disagreement-implicative turn beginning (line 1328), the mediator again intervenes. She asks the disputants whether they feel they can resolve their dispute in mediation or whether they need to go back to small claims court (lines 1330–1334). The mediator thus attempts to move the disputants to the resolution phase of the hearing. This move also serves to break into the argument-in-progress by inserting the mediator's utterance within the ongoing argument. These excerpts have shown how disputants in mediation sessions can progressively depart from the speech exchange system of mediation by independently violating the conventions regarding disputant direct address and waiting to be solicited by a mediator to produce a response.

In sum, the mediators in these excerpts made judgment calls as to whether or when to actively intervene in direct argumentative exchanges between disputants. Mediators have the option of sanctioning disputants for arguing, but may choose to avoid sanctioning in favor of a less intrusive type of intervention or to withhold intervention as long as the argument is constructive and does not escalate. Mediator interventions can range from watchful silence, asking questions, redirecting topics, or using strategic interruptions to forestall further argumentative talk. They can use continuers or minimal responses to transform argumentative utterances from direct address of an opposing disputant to address of a mediator (by displaying their role as recipient of the utterance). They also at times use a strategy of repeating relevant facts from earlier in the session to help guide disputants to end their disagreements over these issues. All of these methods of intervention were at times effective in restoring nonargumentative mediation format.

Discussion and Conclusions

This chapter has shown that the interactional organization of mediation differs from ordinary conversation in ways that minimize arguing and provide for the management of arguments when they do occur. Disputants contribute to this outcome by how they position and formulate complaints, accusations, and denials in the course of the mediation session. Disputants can depart from the speech exchange system of mediation during the session and engage in direct exchanges with the opposing disputant. At times disputants are able to engage in such direct exchanges without arguing, while in other situations arguing does emerge. When arguments occur, both mediators and disputants have a variety of techniques at their disposal to avoid or end the arguing and move disputants back to the speech exchange system of mediation. While arguing in a mediation session is not necessarily helpful for the dispute resolution process, direct discussion about areas on which disputants disagree may at times be helpful. Mediators allow arguing only when it does not escalate into overt conflict and when it is productive and relevant. Mediators have a variety of techniques for managing and ending arguments, and for discouraging their escalation.

4 Disputants' Opening Statements and Persuasive Arguments in Mediation

After completing the introductory stage of the session, mediators typically ask each disputant in turn to make an opening statement or tell their "story" (Boulle et al. 2008; Frenkel and Stark 2012). The first storyteller in the mediation hearing works to present his or her own position favorably, while showing how the opposing disputant was wrong (Cobb and Rifkin 1991a; see also Stokoe and Hepburn 2005).

Most mediators strive to be aware of the potential for differences between disputants in power or competence. Individual characteristics of the participants such as gender, education, or social status may have an impact on their ability to engage successfully in a mediation session (Landau 1995; Neumann 1992). Even though mediators are trained to try to assist the less advantaged disputant in a process called "empowerment,"[1] in the context of a mediation session it is often difficult to identify power differences between disputants.[2] Effective mediators must attend to the power of the interactional context and the interactional techniques disputants use to influence both the opposing disputant and the mediator.

This chapter begins with an analysis of the techniques mediators use to solicit and facilitate disputants' opening statements. I will show that different methods of soliciting disputants' stories or descriptions of the problem are used in the three mediation programs studied. In addition, I will show how the solicitation of respondent's stories differ from complainant's stories. I then turn to the techniques disputants use to construct strong arguments in their opening statements and to support their claims with evidence. I investigate how the interactional organization of mediation presents different opportunities and constraints for first and second disputants.

---

[1] See, e.g., Barsky (1996); Gewurz (2001); Regehr (1994); Tjosvold and van de Vliert (1994).
[2] See Beck and Frost (2007); Beck and Sales (2001); Morrill and Facciola (1992); Singer (1992); Wing (2009).

Soliciting the First Disputant's Opening Statement

There are a variety of ways mediators can open the substantive portion of the session.[3] The three mediation programs studied here each have different protocols for deciding which disputant will be the first to produce an opening statement or story. In this section I discuss how this work is done in the small claims and divorce mediation data sets.

Soliciting Disputants' Opening Statements in Small Claims Mediation

In the West Coast and Midwest small claims mediation programs, the story of the disputant who had filed the case was typically solicited first. In the West Coast mediation program, after the introductory stage of the session, the complainant was asked for a brief description of the claim or problem to be mediated, as well as a brief statement of the resolution requested. Since most of the cases in this consumer affairs mediation program were small claims cases, the resolution requested was often a monetary amount. This process was very brief in some hearings, while in others considerable discussion was required to narrow down the problems under dispute to a brief statement. After the documents were signed, the lead mediator solicited the complainant's opening statement. In the Midwest small claims mediation program, the mediators went straight from the introductory stage of the session to solicitation of the complainant's opening statement, without the intermediary step of first soliciting a statement of the claim.

There was some variation in how mediators solicited the first storyteller in these small claims mediations. Excerpt 4.1 shows the mediator explaining that the complainant will go first, followed by the respondent's story. When this approach is used, both participants know what to expect and understand why one party has been selected to speak first.

Excerpt 4.1 Vehicle Repair West Coast Small Claims Mediation, p. 1

```
33  MA:  As FAr as thuh general GROUnd ru:les are concerned .h thuh
34       CLAIMant- (0.2) will tell (0.2) his story!, (0.2) without
35       interruption. (0.4) °'kay? and then thee °(uh-) respondent will tell
36       their story!, (0.2) without interruption.
```

Some mediators solicit the complainant's story first, but do not explain why they are selecting that disputant to go first (Excerpt 4.2):

---

[3] See Bishop et al. (2015); Doneff and Ordover (2014). See Frenkel and Stark (2012) for examples of simulated mediation openings in mediation session facilitated by attorneys.

Excerpt 4.2 Borrowed Camera Midwest Small Claims Mediation, p. 3

```
38  Med:  'Mkay .hh Marissa? Why don't you start us off, how are you
39        acquainted with Jolene and what's [been goin'] on?
40  Mar:                                    [u:h Well,  ]
41        (0.4)
42  Mar:  I know Jolene because I work with Jolene at Parker's Rest'rant.
43        (0.4)
44  Med:  Oka:y?
45        (0.4)
46  Mar:  'Kay, u:h (0.6) we been friends for (1.1) I guess two years? maybe?=
```

The mediator selects the first disputant by saying "Marissa? Why don't you start us off," (line 38). This formulation makes it sound as if the choice of first storyteller is somewhat random, rather than conveying that it is the complainant who goes first. This approach may leave the mediator open to perceptions of bias (Garcia et al. 2002).

Some mediators asked the disputants to choose who should go first. Excerpt 4.3 shows the mediator soliciting the first story by asking the participants who would like to begin (line 52).

Excerpt 4.3 Camera Repair Midwest Small Claims Mediation, p. 3

```
49  Med:    U:h (0.5) You need thuh matter tuh be reso:lved and that's what court
50          is for. (0.5) uhm (1.8) .hh Also I ask that when whe- one person's
51          speaking thuh rest of you all remain quiet (0.4) You're a:ll gonna be
52          given ample opportunity tuh speak. (1.1) Who would like tuh begin?
53          (1.5)
54  Cindy:  It doesn't matter.
55          (1.9)
56  Med:    You wanna [start ma'am?]
57  Cindy:            [Okay.      ]
```

When neither party accepts the invitation to go first, the mediator reissues his solicit (line 56) by addressing Cindy directly. Cindy accepts the invitation (line 57).

In sum, there are three options for soliciting opening statements in these small claims mediation programs. First, the mediator may solicit the complainant first, and explicitly communicate the reasons for this to the disputants. Second, the mediator may solicit the complainant first, but not explicitly communicate this to the disputants. Third, the mediator may ask the disputants to volunteer to go first. These choices about how to solicit the first opening statement may be consequential for participants' perceptions of the fairness of the process. If a disputant does not know why the other disputant is being solicited first, they may feel they are being slighted.

Soliciting Disputants' Opening Statements in Divorce Mediation

Mediator solicits of disputant's first stories in the divorce mediation sessions differ from those in small claims mediations in several ways. First, in the Midwest divorce mediation program the mediators did not distinguish between complainants and respondents. Instead of treating the spouses as on opposing sides in a dispute, the norm was to begin the session by treating the divorcing couple as a unit. One way this was done was by directing a question to both spouses. For example, in the first session of Mike and Kelly's divorce mediation, the mediator opened the substantive portion of the session with a question directed to both spouses (Excerpt 4.4, lines 133–135). When neither spouse responds (note the 4.3 second silence in line 136), Mediator A reissues her solicit by asking for a volunteer to go first (line 137).

Excerpt 4.4 Mike and Kelly Midwest Divorce Mediation, Session 1, p. 7

```
133  MA:    >Well would you like< to each tell us: (0.9) what it is that brought
134          you tuh mediation? and (0.9) what your goals might be for? (0.5)
135          >entering intuh this< process?
136          (4.3) ((Mike turns head to look at Kelly, then Kelly turns to look at Mike,
              then both turn gaze to Mediator A and smile.))
137  MA:    °Who would like tuh go first.°
138          (1.1) ((Mike shrugs and smiles at Mediator A))
139  Mike:  .hh Honestly u::h (2.3) I guess: (0.7) through thuh court. (0.8)
140          °was: uh°
141          (0.9)
142  MA:    Thuh [court      ] twisted your arm uh little bit.
143  Mike:       [(bowmp-)]
144          (0.1)
145  Mike:  Well? I don't think so not really. u:m (0.7) We'd talked before.
146          (1.1) And I think °for thuh° majority of thuh (0.9) properties (0.9)
147          that type uh thing? .h (1.0) °u:m° (0.7) °we can come to:° (1.6) .h
148          °°um°° (0.7) an adequate mutual agreement on °things.° (0.7)
149          °A:nd° .h (1.3) it hh! was probably gonna be less expensive on
150          both of us: h °to:: do this° <than to:: go with: through> with thee
151          attorneys:? and things like that? .h (1.2) A::n' h hopefully? u:m
152          (1.3) uh lot less time consuming. (0.7) °°u:m°° °As far as things
153          go? that° (0.1) °we can agree on things?° (0.8) .h and I think
154          °for thuh most part uh° (1.1) eh (0.8) we'll find ouhht! ((laughs))
155          But uh .h (0.5) °I think that we'll agree on° .h (0.6) thuh majority
156          of- (0.6) °everything.°
```

There are several ways this divorce mediation session opening is less adversarial than the typical small claims mediation. First, Mediator A's opening question specifically asks for both spouse's perspective on why they are in mediation. Second, in the silence after Mediator A's question (in line 136) the spouses defer to each other in terms of who wants to go first. During this silence, Mike turns his head to look at Kelly, then Kelly turns her head to look at Mike. Both then turn their gaze to Mediator A and smile. After Mediator A's second invitation in line 137, Mike shrugs and smiles at Mediator A, and then goes first (line 139). Third, when Mike does take the floor to answer the question, he uses a plural pronoun ("we" in lines 145, 147, 153–155) and a collective formulation ("both of us" in line 150) to refer to himself and his wife. While expressing uncertainty as to the extent to which they will agree (line 154), Mike makes a qualified assertion that "°I think that we'll agree on° .h (0.6) thuh majority of- (0.6) °everything.°" (lines 155–156). The actions of both the mediator and Mike in this excerpt display a collective orientation to the spouses rather than treating them as adversaries.

In the one exception to this approach, a mediator selected one spouse to speak first rather than producing a collective solicit. Excerpt 4.5 shows Mediator A beginning the substantive portion of the session by conveying that he was randomly selecting Darryl (Excerpt 4.5, lines 217–218). By saying "well no magic in this" (line 217), Mediator A conveys that the selection of Darryl to speak first was not deliberate:

Excerpt 4.5 Belinda and Darryl Midwest Divorce Mediation, Session 1, p. 15

```
217  MA:  tch Let's just kind of hhh well no magic in this let's start with you
218       Darryl. What? (0.1) What kind uh things would y:ou like tuh have
219       accomplished (0.4) in mediation what would you hope to come out
220       of it. °to come out uh this.°
221       (2.0)
222  Dar:  I don't really have any (0.3) hopes tuh come out [hnh=hnh=hnh=hh]
223  Bel:                                                  [Um hm         ]
224  Dar:  Who knows what would happen I'm
225       (0.2)
226  MA:  Mm hm
227       (0.2)
228  Dar:  here by request.
```

By soliciting the perspective of one spouse first, Mediator A elicits an individual response rather than trying to elicit the perspective of both spouses (as in Excerpt 4.4). Darryl conveys that he is "here by request" (line 228), leaving it open as to whether he's in mediation as a response to a court referral (as is the couple in Excerpt 4.4) or whether his spouse has requested his participation.

Summary

In all three mediation programs studied in this book, a mediator begins the substantive portion of the session with a question directed to one or both disputants. In the small claims mediation programs the mediation sessions are almost always opened by a solicit of the complainant's opening statement. Occasionally, the mediator asks the disputants to decide who will go first. In the Midwest divorce mediation cases, very different techniques are used to open the mediation sessions. While in one case the mediator started by randomly selecting one spouse to go first, in the other cases the mediators began by asking a question of both disputants. These questions were about topics of common interest, such as the couple's children or their goals for the mediation process.

One of the implications of these differences in mediators' solicitation of disputants' opening statements is that the small claims sessions typically begin with a starker separation between the two disputants. Their relationship as opposing disputants (complainant and respondent) is emphasized and reinforced by how the statements are solicited. On the other hand, the mediators in the divorce mediation sessions typically begin with a collective approach which engages both parties. The fact that the spouses are in disagreement on at least some issues surrounding the divorce is therefore de-emphasized initially. Instead, an issue on which they have common ground (such as their children) is addressed first. In general, the small claims mediations therefore start out with an adversarial approach while the divorce mediations start out with a more collective approach to the relationship between the opposing disputants.

Facilitating Disputants' Opening Statements

The extent of mediator intervention in a disputant's opening statement is related to how that statement was constructed and presented. Two opening statements will be compared to illustrate the range of variation in mediation intervention. The first opening statement, in which the complainant read a statement she had prepared in advance, did not elicit any mediator interventions, while the second example elicited considerable mediator intervention.

Opening Statements with Minimal Mediator Intervention

Only a couple of disputants in these data brought a written opening statement with them, and in only one mediation was the disputant allowed to read her entire statement out loud. The mediators in this case remained silent until the disputant had finished reading her statement. When given the floor to tell her opening story, Mrs. Centerville begins with an apology for getting the respondent's name wrong (Excerpt 4.6, lines 134–137). She then begins reading her prepared statement (starting in line 137) which explains what happened and summarizes her complaint.

Excerpt 4.6 Patched Carpet West Coast Small Claims Mediation, p. 6

131 MA: O::kay!, I think we're ready tuh go: u:hhhhh (0.3) Mrs.
132   Centerville if you want to.
133   (0.2)
134 Cent: Okay may I first say that- (0.2) at no ti:me have I been
135   informed that it was Mister PORter not Mister PORterville so you
136   will forgive me for referring to Mister PORter in this: (0.2) u::h
137   that I have °written. (0.2) .hh We made uh contract of sa::le.
138   (1.5) with Mister Po:rter of Atop Carpets on March twenty first
139   nineteen eighty six to purchase carpet for our ho:me located forty
140   two fifty three: (0.2) Acorn Street. for uh space forty five in
141   Sanna Christo California. .hh This carpet was laid at thee above
142   address on April thuh fourth, nineteen eighty six and was paid for
143   by uh check, .h of deposit for one thousand on March twenty first
144   nineteen eighty six and by Vi:sa, .h for thee reMAInder: of one
145   thousand six hundred and fifty three dollars and twenty one cents
146   foll:owing thee installation of carpet on four four, eighty six. .h

The statement is clear and well written, and covers all the major points needed to understand the situation that led to the dispute. The mediators do not interrupt, ask questions, or provide minimal responses during her statement. The first part of Mrs. Centerville's statement (lines 137–146) gives the basic facts of the carpet installation. Excerpt 4.7 shows the continuation of her statement where Mrs. Centerville begins to describe how the problem with the carpet emerged and was handled.

Excerpt 4.7 Patched Carpet West Coast Small Claims Mediation, p. 6

147 Cent: LATE April, I noticed uh little part in thuh carpeting, and thuh
148   walking area, between thuh dining room and thuh family room
149   seemed to have raised uh uh- have uh raised area. .h And early
150   May while vacuuming, we realized that uh portion of this carpet
151   was loose, and coming apart. .h We called Atop Carpets an-
152   inqui:red for thee owner. (0.2) Mister son- Jim PO:Rter.
153   bu-huh-uh was to:ld, he was not available hh he left uh phone
154   number, we left uh phone number for him to return our call. .h
              ((50 lines omitted))
205   .h Receiving no phone call from him, I was very upset, and
206   contacted thuh Better Business Bureau (on) Sanna Christo:. (0.3)
207   They contacted Mister Porter and I received thuh following
208   reply from them. (0.4) STATing he wou-h-h-ld no-h-h-t: (0.2)
209   replace thuh carpeting. (0.3) (that) thuh FA:ctory would not
210   replace thuh car°peting. (0.2) In November I wrote uh- (.)
211   letter to thuh District Attorney consumer affairs, .h as thuh Be-h-
212   tter Bi-h-zness office, advi-h-sed me tuh do so-h-h, (0.1) or take
213   it to an attorney. (0.2) This why this complaint has been filed.
214   (0.4) I feel Mister Porter should stand behi:nd thuh carpet and

215   installation that he se:lls, I do not feel uh person should spend
216   two thousand six hundred and thirty one dollars, .h and have carpet
217   which is vi:sibly patched as our carpeting i:s.

In this written statement Mrs. Centerville produces a chronological narrative of events which documents the problems that occurred, how she and her husband learned about the problems (while vacuuming), how they tried to get help from the carpet company (through repeated phone calls), and how the efforts the company made to remedy the problem were inadequate. Mediator intervention was not necessary during this statement because it was well-ordered, relevant, informative, and concise.

After Mrs. Centerville finished reading the statement, there was an eight second pause (Excerpt 4.8, line 218). Mediator A then thanked Mrs. Centerville and complimented her on her statement's completeness (line 219). The mediators then asked several questions about the carpeting (starting in line 221).

Excerpt 4.8 Patched Carpet West Coast Small Claims Mediation, p. 6

218   (8.0)
219 MA: Thank you, that seems uh very complete run down!
220   (0.4)
221 MB: (One) question (uh) (.) is this uh high (loss/loft)?, carpet, or ih- e-
222   h- h-ye s' uh li'l hard tuh tell [(   )]
223 Cent: [Uh hunh] it is uh sculptured,
224   (.)
225 MB: (hunh)=
226 Cent: =but not rea:lly high (lof').

This excerpt shows that when a disputant's opening statement is well designed, little or no mediator intervention is required during its production. A well designed opening statement includes a clear description of the problem. Most statements construct a chronological account of events and identify the major participants in the dispute. The only case in which there was no mediator intervention in a disputant's opening statement in these data was that described above in which the complainant read a prepared statement. All of the other opening statements required at least some mediator intervention to facilitate their production.

Opening Statements with Mediator Facilitation

Most disputants' opening statements required at least some mediator intervention to get necessary information on the table in an effective way. The amount of help mediators provided to facilitate the production of a disputant's opening statement was closely tied to how the disputant told their story. For example,

Excerpts 4.9 and 4.10 show how a mediator worked to assist a complainant in the production of her opening statement. Excerpt 4.9 begins with the mediator soliciting Tish's opening statement (lines 95–98). Tish identifies herself and the respondents (Anna and John) in terms of their categorical identities as landlord and tenants (line 100). She then begins telling the story of the installation of the plumbing for the washing machine which led to her filing the small claims case against her tenants. The mediator facilitates Tish's telling of this story with several types of interventions, including questions, continuation prompts, and minimal responses or continuers.[4]

Excerpt 4.9 Washer Dryer Midwest Small Claims Mediation, p. 5

```
95   Med:  (0.4) .h LET'S GET STARTED THEN! (0.4) um (0.8) .h TISH?
96          would you like tuh begin? I HAVEN'T LOOKED in thuh jacket
97          >so I don't know what thuh problem is? (0.5) Can you talk about it
98          °uh little bit?°
99          (0.7)
100  Tish: tch HHHHH! I AM! (0.8) Anna and John's landlord? (0.5) when 'ey
101         came to me to rent an apartment in Springfield? (1.0) they LIKED
102         thee apartment? (0.5) .h however, it did not have uh washer dryer
103         hook up! (0.7) .h They: (0.8) wanted tuh move i:n? but they not
104         move in unless there was uh washer dryer hook up! (0.5)
105         [.h        ] So in thuh course o:f thuh conversation, (1.1) .h I:
106  Med:  [°°'kay.°°]
107  Tish: agreed tuh have it in within thuh first couple weeks after they
108         moved in!
109         (0.6)
110  Med:  °Okay.°
111         (0.1)
112  Tish: We agreed to: (0.7) u:h my partner? (0.6) who's out? in thuh waiting
113         room, (0.5) .h u:h he agreed to thee installation?
114         (0.6)
115  Med:  °Mm hm?°
116         (0.1)
117  Tish: tch And that (0.7) .h we: (0.7) u:h (0.3) Jay Bee Properties, myself
118         and my partner? (0.5) .h would split? (0.4) thee installation bill
119         with thuh new tenants, John and Anna Grant!
```

The mediator produced minimal responses or continuers at several points where Tish's turn-in-progress was possibly complete. In lines 106 and 110 she used "okay" as a listener response. The use of "okay" may serve as a continuer, but can also indicate a move to closure or an indication that one is ready to move on to another topic (Barske 2009; Beach 1993). Because of its placement

---

[4] See Fitzgerald and Leudar (2010); Goodwin (1986); Heritage and Clayman (2010); Jefferson (1984c); and Schegloff (1982) on continuers and minimal responses.

and intonation, the mediator seems to be using it as a continuer in lines 106 and 110. In line 113, Tish uses questioning intonation to solicit a response, and the mediator responds with the continuer "°Mm hm?°" in line 115. These minimal responses/continuers serve to encourage the complainant to continue with her story, while displaying the mediator's status as the addressed recipient of these utterances.

As the exchange continues, the mediator asks four questions to clarify her understanding of what happened and to help Tish establish a time line of events (Excerpt 4.10, lines 121–122, 125, 129, 133–134, and 138).[5]

Excerpt 4.10 Washer Dryer Midwest Small Claims Mediation, p. 5

```
120        (0.6)
121  Med:  °Okay.° WAS 'AT WRITTEN intuh thuh lease?
122        a[greement? or]
123  Tish: [No it was     ] not!
124        (0.1)
125  Med:  >That was apart< from thuh
126        (0.3)
127  Tish: Yes!
128        (0.3)
129  Med:  °lease agreement.° .h when [uh-    ]
130  Tish:                            [ANNA] was not there! (0.5) John and
131        I shook on 'ee agreement.
132        (0.6)
133  Med:  °Okay.° (0.2) .h WHEN (0.4) just tuh give me some time line! (0.7)
134        when approximately did this occur.
135        (0.9)
136  Tish: tch u::h I'd say that was around June uh last year.
137        (0.6)
138  Med:  Ninety four?
139        (0.4)
140  Tish: Yes!
141        (0.5)
142  Med:  °Mm ka:y.° (1.8) A:nd s:ubsequently the:n
143        (1.5)
144  Tish: tch u::h (0.7) .h Thuh tenants moved in? (0.6) .h u:h Robby
145        went ahead, and (0.4) huh CHUM! did thuh hook up, (0.5) .h
146        It took hi:m (1.0) three or four days? 'as it considerable amount of
147        time? (0.4) .h (0.6) tch John was there part uh thuh time, (0.3)
148        during that. (0.4) .h uh He hooked up, (0.5) he had put in
149        two hundred and twenty?
```

---

[5] Polanyi (1985) noted that stories are constructed to convey an understanding of the order in which things occurred.

Some of the mediator's questions were attempts to get additional information about things Tish has reported. For example, the mediator asked whether the agreement between Tish and her tenants was "WRITTEN intuh thuh lease? a[greement?" (lines 121–122). After that issue is clarified, the mediator asks for information about the dates various events occurred, which helps construct a shared understanding of the chronology of the events (lines 133–134). In line 142 the mediator produces a continuation prompt ("A:nd s: ubsequently the:n") which gives the floor back to the complainant to continue telling her story after the series of mediator questions. Tish responds by continuing her story (lines 144–149).

Summary

The first disputant's opening statement is almost always a narrative constructed on the spot, rather than a prepared document. Typical mediator responses to these statements include questions, topic redirects, continuers or minimal responses, and continuation prompts. While mediators typically intervene in the opening statement as it is being produced, the nature and extent of a mediator's facilitation work is related to how the disputant constructs his or her opening statement. In short, there is a relationship between the type and amount of work done by the mediator and the way in which the disputant presents their statement. The best approach to mediator facilitation of disputant's stories will therefore depend on how well the mediator's approach matches with the disputant's style, format, and skill in producing their opening statement.

Disputants differ greatly in their skill in constructing opening statements and creating convincing arguments to support their claims. One way in which mediators can help to balance power between disputants is by using the types of interventions shown above. Through these interventions the mediator helps the disputants who need help to produce a complete and coherent story and to clarify their position. The work of facilitating the production of disputant's opening statements is thereby one of the ways in which mediators can empower disputants. The disputants also have resources at their disposal to produce strong and persuasive opening statements. It is to an investigation of these techniques that I now turn.

Constructing Strong Opening Statements

Disputants in mediation sessions use a variety of techniques to maximize the effectiveness of their opening statements. They can construct chronological accounts or narratives, present evidence to support their claims, and use formulations which enable them to claim the moral high ground or impugn the standing of the opposing disputant (Garcia 2010). Disputants in these data use several types of evidence in their opening statements to support complaints and accusations they are making against the respondents and to make it more difficult for the respondents to defend themselves in their subsequent statements. Photographs, physical objects, and documents were frequently presented as evidence to support claims made in the disputant's statement. Disputants also used the quoted or reported speech of others and told stories describing how facts were ascertained to support claims they were making in their opening statements.

Stories or Narratives

The primary method of constructing opening statements was through stories or narratives that describe events. These stories, by conveying a coherent sequence of events, demonstrate how the disputants reached their conclusions and are themselves a form of evidence in support of the disputant's position. For example, in Excerpt 4.11 the complainant Dan accuses the auto repair shop of accidentally breaking his vehicle's water pump housing. He does this by telling a story which shows how he knows the water pump housing was not broken prior to his visit to the repair shop.

**Excerpt 4.11 Vehicle Repair West Coast Small Claims Mediation, p. 14
          (Garcia 1991: 830)**

```
319  Dan:  U:::HM (0.9) And THEN 'EE said- (.) u:h (.) he called me up
320        about uh DA:Y after- it was (about three 'clock) s'pose tuh pick it
321        up. (0.4) He said you gottah leak in your water pump (0.8)
322        housing now. (1.2) I said well, I didn't have uh leak when
323        I brought it in here. (0.6) So, I didn't kno:w!, what- what-
324        thuh- (.) th' pro:blem was 'ere. (1.1) u::h (0.6) And it TURNED
325        OU:T that it NEE:ded aye: aye- thuh- WAter- (0.3) thuh water
326        pump housing was cracked. (0.6) Now I don't know whether that
327        was: (0.3) was cracked (0.2) whether- when thuh meCHAnic was
328        workin' on it?, .h or it was cracked before I brought it in, but
329        it wasn' leaking when I brought °it in.° (0.1) D'at I kno:w.
330        (0.4) I woulduh seen puddles in my driveway.
```

Dan reports that he did not see puddles of water in his driveway prior to bringing the vehicle in for repair (line 330). This observation supports his contention that the water pump housing was not broken when he brought the vehicle to the dealership. The absence of puddles is not something he could have photographed and brought to the mediation session, because he did not know the water pump housing was broken until after taking the vehicle to the repair shop. He relies on his memory of the appearance of the driveway and the absence of water under the car. Puddles on his driveway would have been an anomalous event that he would have noticed. It is the narrative of this sequence of events which constitutes the evidence in support of his position.

Quotes and Reported Speech

The use of reported speech can be an effective technique to provide evidence because quotes give the impression of a more precise recounting of what was said than is achieved by summarizing or describing what was said.[6] Reported speech can either be direct, in which the speaker animates another's words in the form of a quote, or indirect, in which the speaker paraphrases another's words (Holt 1996; 2000). Disputants in these data often used quotes or reported speech in their opening statements in order to provide evidence to support their claims. A wide range of people were quoted in these data, including witnesses, family members, experts, or at times, even the opposing disputant. Quoting an expert can be stronger than a simple denial because it brings in a voice other than the two disputants engaged in a disagreement. In "he said/she said" types of arguments (Goodwin 1980) participants can become stuck in arguing back and forth. In Excerpt 4.12 Vince uses reported speech to buttress his claims about Mary Lou's promise to vacate the house he purchased from her:

Excerpt 4.12 Real Estate Midwest Small Claims Mediation, p. 40

```
869  Vince:  [.hh ] As for thuh date she said she was gonna get out?, we were
870          to:ld, in our clo:sing. (1.1) .h th' following people were present!
871          (0.6) my WIFE? mySELF! my real estate agent! .h thuh
872          closing attorney from thuh bank! Mary Lou's real estate agent!
873          and her friend? she has sitting in thuh lobby!
874          (0.5)
875  Med:    °Mm [hm?°]
876  Vin:         [.h   ] Mary LOU:! >even before< thuh closing bega:n!
877          proceeded tuh tell me, (0.5) .h we take OCcupancy on thuh
878          nineteenth? We've already hired uh moving company? t' co:me!
879          (0.4) on thuh nineteenth! and get everything out! (0.7) .h THAT is
880          and SHE SAID yo:u may take OCcupancy!
881          (0.1)
882  Med:    Mm hm?
883          (0.1)
884  Vin:    on thuh nineteenth! (0.5) [.h an'] MA'AM? (0.3) I have about five
885  Mary:                            [No.  ]
886  Vin:    people! who will all tell you thee exact same sto:ry, (0.4)
887          be[cause they] were in that room!
```

---

[6] See Holt (1996; 2000); Stokoe and Edwards (2007); and Wooffitt (1992).

Vince makes a footing shift in line 877 and animates Mary Lou's words (Goffman 1981). He also specifies who was in the room to witness this statement (lines 870–873). Vince reports that Mary Lou did not vacate the house on time, and describes the conversation in which she had promised to be out of the house by a particular date. He reports what Mary Lou said (lines 877–880), part of which is presented as a direct quote ("We've already hired uh moving company? . . .": lines 878–879). This use of reported speech may preempt a possible defense from Mary Lou when she gets the floor to respond, because it will be harder for her to claim that she did not say those words.

Moral Claims

Disputants in mediation sessions have been shown to denigrate opposing disputants by blaming them for various types of inappropriate actions and attitudes (e.g., Borg 2000; Merry 1990; Smithson et al. 2017). Disputants in mediation sessions can also strengthen their statements by showing the extent to which they have been reasonable, accommodating, fair, or morally blameless in their interactions with the opposing disputant. For example, Excerpt 4.13 shows the complainant Dan Barclay working to present himself as a good person. He begins by referring to a phone call from Tim (Respondent B) who is an employee of the auto repair shop.

Excerpt 4.13 Vehicle Repair West Coast Small Claims Mediation, p. 13

```
295  Dan:  And I I was getting phone calls from Tim. (0.2) You know,
296        saying that this needed be this that- th- they- took thuh brakes
297        apart, (.) a:nd duh (0.4) we'll start w'uh brakes, .hhh they took
298        (did) thuh wheels apart and (.) started checkin' everything out
299        they said thuh calipers were froze up becaus:e probably. (.) not uh
300        lottah u:se and I- I I wen' along you know, I'm fair.
301        (0.1) I wen' along with that. .hh That's FI:ne, but it turned out
302        tuh be: that- one uh th'dru:ms was ba:d.
```

Dan states that he went along with the repair shop's unexpected discovery that his brakes needed repairing because "I'm fair." (line 300). Dan continues with "I wen' along with that. .hh That's FI:ne," (line 301). He thus presents himself as not only fair but also as accommodating and reasonable. However, the continuation of his turn "but it turned out . . ." (lines 301–302) shows that his trust was broken when another unexpected problem with the vehicle emerged – the brake "drum."

In Excerpt 4.14 from the same mediation hearing, Respondent A uses a chronological narrative to respond to Dan's story and to present a counter-complaint. Respondent A, an employee of the auto repair shop, had previously complained that Dan (Mr. Barclay) had stopped payment on his check for the repairs (not shown). Here Respondent A makes moral claims to present the repair shop as trustworthy.

Excerpt 4.14 Vehicle Repair West Coast Small Claims Mediation, p. 27

```
609  RA:  .h A::nd du::h (0.7) then all of uh sudden, u::::h there was
610        thuh conversation about thuh fact that- (0.3) we::ll, (0.2) I'm
611        not gonna pay for any of your labor!, (0.2) I'm gonna pay you for
612        thuh parts. (0.2) .h And that obviously was not tu:h (0.2) .h
613        satisfactory, as far as I was concerned. (0.2) e::h We entered in
614        to: this agreement with Mister u:h Barclay .hh u::::h (0.4) u:h in
615        good faith!, (0.3) he signed thuh repair order. (0.4) We have
616        updates on thee repair orders, and everything was done uh- uh as it
617        should be! (0.4) u::hm (0.4) Then all of uh sudden he's- uh
618        somebody's gonna deci:de, (0.2) u::h (.) again: (.) u:h what is
619        gonna be PAid, and how it's gonna be paid, and .h and I guess
620        that's well, why we're here! (0.5) u::hm.
621        (0.2)
622  MB:  >Duh you have thuh bi:ll with you?<
```

In support of his position that Dan should pay the bill, Respondent A claims the high moral ground. He points out that the repair shop made a "good faith" agreement with Dan (lines 613–615). He also notes that "We have updates on thee repair orders" (lines 615–616) and "everything was done uh- uh as it should be!" (lines 616–617), thus displaying that the repair shop followed the appropriate procedures for getting customer approval to make repairs.

Another type of moral claim that can be made is that of fairness. Excerpt 4.15 shows Stan arguing that visitation time with his children should be shared equally with his ex-wife; he invokes a concept of fairness that is based on both spouses getting the same amount of time.

Excerpt 4.15 Joint Custody West Coast Family Mediation, p. 44
(Garcia 1996: 205)

```
1059  Stan:  =Okay? (0.1) Tit is for TAT here. .h u::hm, .hh (0.2) I
1060         do not agree with, (0.5) three DA:ys:?, (0.5) uh week. (0.4)
1061         Thursday FRIDAY SA:Turday? (0.8) By my uh- (0.2)
1062         calcula:tions, Thursday tuh Friday is twenty four hou::rs,
1063         Friday tuh Saturday is: (0.2) is forty eight. (0.3)
1064         I've had them FIFty hours in uh week. (0.5) There'r uh
1065         hundred and sixty eight hou:rs in uh week. Twenty four times
1066         seven. .hh That's less than thi:rty!, percent uh thuh ti:me!, (0.2)
1067         .hh and I, (0.2) you know?, I mean, (0.2) we- (.3)
1068         thuh bo:ttom line here is what constitutes rea:sonable. (0.4) .h As
1069         outlined in this petition, .hh (0.1) and I belie::ve, (0.4) for me
1070         tuh see my twins, (0.6) le:ss than thirty percent: (0.4) of thuh
```

1071   ti:me?, (0.4) is is uh VE:ry reasonable, (0.6) I'm I'm not
1072   A:Skin' for (.3) .h you know SAturday a:nd Sunday I'm
1073   asking 'em for .h (0.1) like- thee A:Fternoon on SA:turday, an'-
1074   an'- Thursday and Friday evenings and tha:t's i:t:.

Stan makes an argument based on a model of fairness that is tied to equality of treatment (Garcia 1996; Gilligan 1982). He argues that since he and his wife have joint custody, his request for "le:ss than thirty percent:" of the twins' time "is uh VE:ry reasonable," (see lines 1059–1974). He thus argues that he is being both fair and reasonable.

In sum, there are a variety of types of evidence disputants can use to support their claims and interpretation of events, including photographs, documents, objects, quotes and reported speech, narratives, and moral claims to justify or support positions they have taken. The way the complainant's statement is constructed is consequential for the options the second disputant has in responding to it.

Preemptive Moves

The complainant in a mediation session has an opportunity to constrain the second disputant's options for presenting a strong case, because he or she is the first to tell his or her story (Cobb and Rifkin 1991a). Interactionally competent disputants can construct their opening statement to not only describe the problem and the sequence of events that occurred, but to preemptively address defenses or counteraccusations that might be made by the opposing disputant (Garcia 2010). There are a range of interactional techniques that can be used strategically to limit the opposing disputant's defensive options.

A complainant can thus preempt or frame the respondent's options when they eventually get the floor to tell their story.[7] The use of preemptive moves can make the respondent's struggle to defend himself or herself and to reclaim the high moral ground more challenging. For example, a complainant may present evidence to defend himself or herself against an accusation the respondent might make, before it has been produced. The respondent can still make that accusation when he or she gets the floor, but this point will be made in an interactional context in which it has already been rebutted.

---

[7] Preemption may also occur in in ordinary conversation. For example, Schegloff (2005) found that participants often apologize for "complainables" before a complaint has been expressed; their utterance projects the complaint to come. See Gill, Pomerantz, and Denvir (2010) and Stivers and Heritage (2001) for analyzes of preemptive moves in doctor–patient interactions and Atkinson and Drew (1979) on prospective accusations in legal settings.

A number of complainants in these data use preemptive moves to manage projected accusations, counteraccusations, or defenses that respondents might produce when it is their turn to tell their story. Excerpt 4.16 shows a complainant (Ms. Kemper) constructing a complaint against the respondent (Ms. Nancy Randalls) to convey evidence that Nancy was responsible for vandalizing her car. She presents a photo of her car as evidence that the car was soiled with paint and garbage (Excerpt 4.16):

Excerpt 4.16 Neighbors West Coast Small Claims Mediation, p. 21

```
483  Kemp:  They had given her pai:nt:!, (0.3) uh month previous. (0.8) (then)
484         (0.2) and she di:d (0.2) corroborate at thuh time that it was: thuh
485         kind of paint:, (0.2) that thee apartment uses.
486         (0.8)
487  MB:    Thuh manager did?
488         (0.2)
489  Kemp:  Ye::s[:    ]
490  MB:         [(Th]ank you).
491         (0.3)
492  Kemp:  tch (0.2) She later retracts that statement at thuh request of Miss
493         (Randalls). (0.2) u::hm. (0.5) So she will change thuh statement
494         on thuh (cop report).
```

Ms. Kemper reports that the manager of their apartment complex had given Nancy paint on a previous occasion (lines 483–485), implying that this was the same paint that was used to vandalize her car. This statement about the paint works to document her claim that Nancy was responsible for the vandalism. After making this statement, Ms. Kemper then reports that the apartment manager retracted her statement at Nancy's (Ms. Randalls) request (lines 492–494). Note that reporting this retraction weakens Ms. Kemper's claim that it was Nancy who vandalized her car. However, preemptively responding to a potential defense that Nancy may eventually make may ultimately strengthen her position. By saying "at thuh time" (line 484) Ms. Kemper tries to support her perspective by showing that the manager's original statement was made shortly after the vandalism occurred. She thus implies that the manager's later retraction of her statement was due to Nancy's influence.

Similarly, in Excerpt 4.17 the complainant (Mrs. Centerville) presents several types of evidence in her opening statement to preempt possible defenses that the respondent (Mr. Jim Porterville) might produce when it is his turn to speak.

Excerpt 4.17 Patched Carpet West Coast Small Claims Mediation, p. 7

```
166  Cent:  So thee installer proceeds to remove (.) aye square, about twenty,
167         by twenty, and glued it into thee existing carpet. (0.2) telling u:s,
168         I don't believe it will sho:w once you walk on it uh while. (0.3)
169         .h Needless to say, we were not happy, paying two thousand six
```

```
170          hundred and fifty three dollars for carpeting, .h and having: aye
171          PA:tch: (0.3) done, in thuh walking area. (0.3) Now this was taken
172          from (0.2) standing above °(ih) looking do:wn .h by just uh
173          regular camera.
```

Mrs. Centerville shows a photograph of the patched carpet to the mediators as evidence to support her claims (Excerpt 4.17, lines 171–173). Mrs. Centerville also presents evidence by reporting the actions and words of relevant parties (lines 166–171). The reported actions and speech show that the patch was put in by Mr. Porterville's employees. Taken together, these actions make it more difficult for Mr. Porterville to claim that his firm was not responsible for the problem she is complaining about or that the problem does not exist.

Preemption of an opposing disputant's defense against complaints and accusations can also be done through the presentation of physical or documentary evidence. In Excerpt 4.18, the complainant Marissa is trying to get the respondent Jolene to repay a personal loan and to return a borrowed camera. During her opening statement, Marissa describes an occasion on which she and a friend went to Jolene's house and knocked on her door, but Jolene did not respond – even though music was audible from inside her apartment. In addition to telling this story during her opening statement, Marissa brought a notarized affidavit from this friend. The friend's report is therefore part of the evidence she presents to show that Jolene tried to avoid paying back the loan and returning the camera (Excerpt 4.18).

Excerpt 4.18 Camera Loan Midwest Small Claims Mediation, p. 13

```
270 Mar:  So my friend, after she sees that, (0.5) .hh runs back up tuh her
271        apartment, (0.7) knocks on her door again! (1.0) All of uh sudden!
272        (0.6) thuh music, (0.5) that was previously on!, (0.6) wasn't playin'
273        no more.
274        (0.4)
275 Med:  Okay so it [sounds like] you (0.2) you think that d'u:h [she was]
276 Mar:              [A:n' she-  ]                              [she was]
277        avoidin' [me! I mean     ] I can expect something from uh child
278 Med:           [°avoiding you.°]
279 Mar:  that's (0.4) ten years old! Not from some mature woman.
280        (0.5)
281 Med:  What=
282 Mar:       =And [and I do have uh notari           ]zed
283 Med:            [What is it that you have in your hand?]
284        (0.4)
285 Mar:  statement. (0.4) tuh that fact.
286        (0.2)
287 Med:  This is from your friend?
288        (0.3)
289 Mar:  Yes:.
```

In this excerpt Marissa effectively used a document to support her story and to attempt to preempt Jolene's possible future denials.

In sum, disputants can construct their opening statements such that possible denials, rebuttals, or counteraccusations that could be made by the opposing disputant are answered in advance or preempted. Disputants in these data often made preemptive moves, working to project potential accusations or claims that could be made by the opposing party, and preemptively presenting evidence to controvert them prior to their production. The use of these preemptive moves is possible because of the interactional organization of mediation, since the opposing disputant is expected to wait until the complainant's story is complete and his or her response has been solicited by the mediator. If mediation sessions were conducted in a more conversational format, the second disputant would be able to respond to problematic claims more expeditiously and effectively.

The use of these techniques can create a challenging environment for the opposing disputant's response. As Cobb and Rifkin (1991a) argue, the position of the second disputant in a mediation session is not the same as that of the first disputant. In the next two sections I explore the solicitation of the second disputant's opening statement, and the advantages and disadvantages of being the second disputant in the mediation session.

Soliciting the Second Disputant's Opening Statement

The mediators must work to close the complainant's opening statement before transitioning to the respondent's story. As advised in mediation textbooks,[8] the mediators in these small claims mediations typically summarized or paraphrased the complainant's story and then asked questions to clarify any remaining issues. Mediators also often let complainants add to their statements before soliciting the respondent's opening statement.

Excerpts 4.19 and 4.20 illustrate how mediators respond to and work to close down a complainant's story prior to soliciting the respondent's story. As Excerpt 4.19 begins, the mediator responds to Bud's story with a series of questions:

Excerpt 4.19 Dog with Fleas Midwest Small Claims Mediation, p. 8

152 Med: [I misunderstood] that's what you meant that th- (0.2) the total two
153   trips was two hundred and twenty dollars.
154   (0.5)
155 Bud: Correct.
156   (1.6)

---

[8] For example, see Boulle et al. (2008) and Frenkel and Stark (2012).

157 Med: Is thuh dog cured?
158   (0.9)
159 Bud: No (0.4) but- (0.3) almost, but not quite.
160   (0.5)
161 Med: Besides fleas, is there anything else wrong with thuh dog?
162   (0.2)
163 Bud: No
164   (1.1)
165 Med: °Mm hmm° (2.0) How old is thuh dog?
166   (3.3)
167 Bud: About uh, (0.5) fifteen months. (1.0) sixteen months, maybe
168   (younger).
169   (0.5)
170 Med: °Okay°
171   (3.0)
172 Bud: He was uh (0.9) uh (0.4) just about (0.6) uh little under uh year (0.7)
173   when he was there.

The mediator asks Bud several questions to clarify information provided in his opening statement (lines 157, 161, and 165). As the exchange continues, the mediator initiates the transition to the respondent's opening story (Excerpt 4.20). First, he thanks Bud for his opening story (line 175). This "thank you" serves a dual purpose – both thanking Bud and marking the end of his story. The mediator then announces that he will summarize Bud's story (lines 175–176) and "give Sue here an opportunity to speak." (lines 176–177).

Excerpt 4.20 Dog with Fleas Midwest Small Claims Mediation, p. 8

174   (3.2)
175 Med: Ahmm hmm ((coughs)) (4.6) Thank you Bud. (0.3) What I want to
176   do is just briefly summarize what you've told me. (0.2) And give Sue
177   here an opportunity to speak. (0.7) You're telling me that (0.2) uhm
178   (0.3) over thuh summer, (0.5) °I don't° for about ten to fourteen days
179   you left your- your dog over with uh (0.9) Sue's kennel. (0.6) A:nd
180   when you got thuh dog back, (0.2) thuh dog had fleas. (0.7) A:nd
181   what you're suing here today for is (0.8) nnhh ((sniffs)) (0.9) thee
182   expense that, arose because of that. (0.4) What you had to do to thuh
183   house, (0.3) and pet bills (0.3) and inconvenience to those costs. (0.4)
184   uhm (1.4) >You're telling me thuh dog was about< fifteen months
185   old.
186   (1.0)
187 Med: Thank you Bud. (0.9) >Sue what's going on?
188   (1.1)
189 Sue: Okay (0.4) [uhm] (2.2) It was exactly ten days . . .

The mediator briefly summarizes Bud's opening statement in lines 177–185. Bud does not intervene during this summary, although there are clear transition relevance places in lines 179, 180, 182, and 183 where Bud could have intervened. Bud also does not respond during the one second pause after this summary (line 186). The fact that Bud does not question or repair the mediator's summary indicates its adequacy. The mediator thanks Bud a second time and then solicits Sue's response (line 187).

Not all mediator attempts to close down a complainant's stories and open the way for soliciting the respondent's opening statement are immediately successful. Complainants may resist attempts to close down their stories, in which case mediators may make several attempts to accomplish this transition. In Excerpts 4.21 and 4.22, Marissa repeatedly resists the mediator's attempts to close down her opening statement.

Excerpt 4.21 Camera Loan Midwest Small Claims Mediation, p. 17

```
365  Mar:  That was fo:r (1.8) basically for not havin' (0.8) thuh money
366        returned tuh me and my property y'know?, .h [bu:t      ]
367  Med:                                          [Thuh has]sles?
368        (0.3)
369  Mar:  Yeah! Thuh hassles did every thi:ng, and comin' all down her:e, .hh
370        u:m (0.6) s: (0.5) Takin' ((Marissa bangs table)) it intuh court?
371        >Thuh money that I've had uh s-< (0.2) y'know spend out?, y'know.
372        (0.4)
373  Med:  Mm hm:? (0.7) °Mm hm?° .hh Oka:y! .hh What I'd like tuh do now
374        is to give Jolene uh chance tuh >talk. unless< y'have something else
375        y'wanna add.
376        (0.5)
377  Mar:  Um (0.3) ALso: um (0.5) if I may, (0.7) here. (1.0)°
378        ch-ch-ch-choo:-choo:.hh° (0.3) °hm!° ((hums)) (1.3) I did send
379        Jolene aye statement, (1.2) in thuh mail. I (do) have thee original?,
380        (1.1) copy?, it says after several attempts tuh get my hundred and
381        fifty dollars cash and my camera?, . . .
```

In Excerpt 4.21 the mediator moves to close Marissa's story so she can solicit the respondent (Jolene's) opening statement (lines 373–374). However, the mediator provides one more opportunity for Marissa to add something before making this transition. She latches a qualifier to her utterance ("unless< y'have something else y'wanna add."; lines 374–375). Marissa accepts this invitation to continue by presenting further evidence to support her claims (lines 377–381).

A few minutes later, the mediator makes a second attempt to close down Marissa's story and solicit Jolene's opening statement (Excerpt 4.22, lines 448 and 453–455).

Excerpt 4.22 Camera Loan Midwest Small Claims Mediation, p. 21

```
444  Mar:  Y'know I figured? (0.6) I was gonna be nice enough? (0.3) I'd help
445        her out! (0.9) y'know? I had (0.4) thuh money unfortunately
446        at ha:nd, to (1.0) be nice enough tuh loan it to her.
```

447   (0.3)
448 Med: .h But why don't-=
449 Mar: =And (0.6) and I mean (0.6) .hh I could say well- I
450   lent her uh thou:sand dollars!, (0.3) but I didn't. All I loaned 'er was
451   uh hundred and fifty? And 'at was it!
452   (0.8)
453 Med: .hh Why don't we give Jolene uh chance tuh respond tuh
454   some uh thuh things that you've said. .hh And also tell us what's
455   happened as she sees it. (1.4) °'kay?°
456   (0.5)
457 Jol: (°chum!°) Well first of a:ll?, u:m (0.9) Marissa and I used tuh be
458   friends?, but (0.2) I: (0.4) was living with someone:? and I have five
459   kids? (0.6) .hh a:nd I had three jobs?, .hh So- there WAS not much
460   time for Marissa! (0.4) She was like uh telephone friend. (0.4) And I
461   was Marissa's friend because (0.6) Marissa had- (0.4) no friends.
462   (0.6) .hh I mean tuh sit at ho:me?, and never have thuh phone ring?
463   (0.5) .hh and I'm thuh kind of person that will be uh friend to anyone.

The mediator displays an orientation to Marissa's apparent reluctance to end her story in lines 448 and 453–455. The mediator's use of the pronoun "we" creates an alignment with Marissa.[9] While perhaps helpful to Marissa in this context, the use of this pronoun may also exclude the respondent Jolene from the alignment.[10] The mediator then formulates her move to transition to Jolene's opening statement as a suggestion rather than a directive ("Why don't we . . ."; line 453). By formulating this transition attempt as a question, the mediator explicitly provides for a response from Marissa. The mediator's use of a tag question "°'kay?°" (Sidnell 2010) in line 455 solicits Marissa's approval of the move to transition to Jolene's turn to talk. Marissa displays her agreement with this transition by remaining silent (line 456). After a brief pause Jolene begins her opening statement (line 457).

In sum, before a mediator can solicit the respondent's opening statement, work must be done to close down the complainant's statement and close down any question-and-answer sequence that occurred after that statement. Especially if emotions are running high, it may be difficult for a disputant to cease describing and elaborating the problem as they see it (Poitras and Raines 2013; see also Gulbrandsen, Haavind, and Tjersland 2018; Lieberman 2016). Difficulty in closing down the first disputant's story and moving disputants to the opposing disputant's story is therefore common. Part of the mediator's work in

---

[9] In Muntigl's (2013) study of psychotherapy counselling sessions with couples, he found that there was a relationship between a therapist aligning with one of the clients and resistance on the part of the other client.

[10] See Garcia et al. (2002) for an analysis of a bias accusation against the mediator which emerged in this hearing.

facilitating the session is managing these transitions between disputants' stories. Once a disputant's story has been solicited, the mediator also has a role to play in facilitating its production.

The Interactional Consequences of Going Second

As discussed in Chapter 2, in mediation sessions the respondent typically waits until the complainant's story is complete and a mediator has solicited their opening statement before responding to it. This interactional organization is functional for mediation because it minimizes the possibilities for arguments. The disputant's denial of an accusation or rebuttal of an argument will not occur immediately, thus preventing the adjacent exchange of oppositional utterances which can escalate into argument.

While previous research by Cobb and Rifkin (1991a) convincingly argued that the first disputant in a mediation session has certain advantages over the second, there are also advantages to going second.[11] For example, Hutchby (1996a) analyzed arguments in radio talk shows and found that while the first position arguer must both state a position and justify it, the second-position arguer is not under the same constraints to present arguments or evidence in support of his or her position. Their response is thus less vulnerable to attack or challenge by the first position arguer, because they have not revealed as much that could be challenged.

Similarly, the order of the opening statements in mediation sessions is potentially consequential because the second disputants' story is often a response to accusations made by the complainant (Cobb and Rifkin 1991a). The second disputant can construct their response to the first story in order to challenge its claims and moral framework; their success in doing so may be related to their interactional competence (Garcia 2010). Mediators may need to work to empower the second disputant in challenging the first disputant's story. If this goal is not achieved, Cobb and Rifkin (1991a) argue that mediation is not truly a neutral process, due to the advantage the first disputant's story produces.

Being the second disputant to tell their opening story can also provide advantages in mediation. While first disputants to tell their story are free to formulate their story as they wish, they also have the responsibility of producing a coherent account of what happened. The second disputant, on the other hand, does not have to repeat or revisit the details of the chronological account. Instead, he or she can frame his or her opening statement as a response to selected elements of the complainant's statement (per Cobb and Rifkin 1991a).

---

[11] See Arminen (2005); Hutchby (1996a; 1996b); Sacks (1992).

The respondent can choose which of the complainant's points to address and in what order to address them. They can also construct their story more efficiently by relying on what has already been said to provide a context for their remarks, indexically framing their statement in relation to the first disputant's statement.

For example, in Excerpt 4.23 Respondent A could have retold the history of the complaint from his point of view, but instead he chooses to use his opening statement to respond to key elements in Dan's story.

Excerpt 4.23 Vehicle Repair West Coast Small Claims Mediation, p. 21

```
471 RA:  I u:h (0.3) first of all, I'm thuh service manager, (.) at thuh
472       dealership, a:nd du:h (0.1) I didn't have that much ss S:UH contact
473       with Da:n, at thuh ti:me, (.) a::nd, nor his wi:fe. (0.4) u:::h eh TIM
474       LO:rd: is our- (.) service advi:ser and he handled thee (.) thuh
475       JO::B from, (0.2) from thee outset. tch=.hh U:::h (0.8) 'd'ere's uh-
476       couple things I: would like to comment on. (0.2) u:::h .hh (0.8)
477       Whe::n (0.7) DAN was ca:lled, and was told that thee water pump
478       housing:, (0.2) was lea:king, (0.2) °and du:h there I guess:° (0.5)
479       profusely, or: o:r, whate:ver, U::h .hh u::h, when he came dow:n
480       and he picked up thuh car:, right before thuh coach, (0.4) °uh
481       before it was adequately road tested. (0.5) .hh A:::h (0.7) I'm sure
482       that had HAD we had completed thuh JO:::B, (0.4) and had (.)
483       road tested thuh coach, (0.2) and had go:ne ba:ck an'- an' double
484       checked things uh I'm sure we would have caught things such as
485       thuh brake line that was leaking! (0.5) .h You know, there was uh
486       big lottuh if's, and what if, an' an' an' what HAVE you!, (.) u:h
487       (0.2) Brake systems are equipped tuh, as s:you may know, with uh,
488       double reservoirs: s: systems. And thuh reason for that is that if it
489       looses thuh fluid in one system it has uh BACKup system. (0.3) .h
490       u:::h (.) Of course we don'- we don' li:ke to rely: on thuh back up
491       system, .hh=
```

Respondent A, the senior employee of the auto repair shop, first provides institutional identifications for himself and Tim (Respondent B), a mechanic at the shop (lines 471–475). He then uses a preface to set up his audience for more than one point (lines 475–476; "'d'ere's uh- couple things I: would like to comment on.").[12] The first item on his list is the issue of the water pump housing, which is one of the main items under dispute ("Whe::n (0.7) DAN was ca:lled, and was told that thee water pump housing:, (0.2) was lea:king,"; lines 477–478). Respondent A refers to several facts that were in Dan's story, including the repair shop's phone call to Dan and the fact that the water pump housing was leaking. His story is indexical (Garfinkel 1967), because it relies on Dan's previously told story in order to make sense.

---

[12] See Goodwin (1984) and Jefferson (1990).

Respondent A then produces several rebuttals to complaints Dan made in his initial statement. First, he argues that the problems with the vehicle were Dan's fault because he picked it up before it had been road tested. Specifically, he argues that the shop would have caught the problem with the brake line (lines 479–485). Second, he argues that Dan's complaints against the dealership were based largely on hypotheticals – what might have happened rather than what did happen (lines 485–486). Third, he argues that even if the shop had missed the problem with the brake line, there likely would not have been a failure of the brakes, because braking systems have built in redundancy (lines 487–491). In short, rather than using his opening statement to retell the history of the relationship between Dan and the repair shop from his perspective, or to revisit the history of the repairs that were done, Respondent A uses his opening statement to efficiently produce three major defenses to Dan's accusations or complaints.

Another approach used by some respondents is to use their opening statement to identify and correct errors in the first disputant's story. Excerpt 4.24 shows the respondent Sue responding to Bud's opening statement, rather than creating her own account of the events.

Excerpt 4.24 Dog with Fleas Midwest Small Claims Mediation, p. 9

```
181  Med:  >Sue what's going on?<
182         (1.1)
183  Sue:  Okay (0.4) [uhm] (2.2) It was exactly ten days=
184  Med:              [nnff] ((sniff))              =MHM HMM
185         ((cough))
186         (0.5)
187  Sue:  that thuh dog was at my place. (0.8) He indicated that thuh dog had
188         been there once before. (0.9) The dog boarded with me three other
189         times before that and was groomed (1.1) five (0.2) °times by me
190         before that.° (0.9) °Okay.°
191         (0.2)
192  Med:  Hmm mhm
193         (0.3)
194  Sue:  °It wasn't just one other time.° (0.9) This time that he's indicating
195         thuh dog went home after uh ten day stay, thuh dog was groomed,
196         and flea bathed thuh day that it went home. (0.4) I know, when it
197         walked out my door, (0.3) that it was not infested with fleas. (1.0)
198         And yet thuh dog was not picked up [by   ] (1.0) Anybody, (0.3)
199  Med:                                    [nnfff]
200  Sue:  you know (0.3), in this family, wife or husband. It was (0.3) another
201         woman, I don't know who it was. (0.7) uhm (1.2) There's uh
202         timespan of (0.8) when she picked it up, (0.7) to whenever they
203         received thuh dog, (0.3) that anything could of happened.
```

The mediator solicits the respondent's opening statement in line 181, using an open-ended solicit ("<Sue what's going on?>") which leaves Sue free to formulate her opening statement as she wishes. Sue begins her statement by correcting errors in Bud's statement, and responding to some of the accusations Bud made. First, she contradicts Bud's claims about how often and how long the dog boarded at her kennel (lines 183, 187–189). Second, she contradicts Bud's claims about how often the dog was groomed at her kennel (189–190). She then argues that the dog had been at her kennel more often than Bud had claimed (line 194). However, the significance of these corrections is not in the number of times the dog was boarded or groomed, since those facts are probably irrelevant as to whether the dog got fleas at the kennel on the particular occasion in question. Rather, Sue's challenges serve to raise doubt about the accuracy of Bud's opening statement, thus making an implicit challenge to the reliability of his claims.

Sue then goes on to explicitly deny Bud's accusation that the dog got fleas at her kennel (lines 196–197). She provides evidence to support her denial (lines 198–203). Sue argues that since Bud's employee picked up the dog rather than himself or his wife, this employee could have taken the dog somewhere where he could have been exposed to fleas.

Some disputants used their second story position to selectively respond to accusations. In Excerpt 4.25 Kelly takes advantage of her position as second storyteller to focus on only one of the many issues and problems her husband Mike addressed in his opening statement. Previously, Mike had spoken extensively about many of his concerns and raised a number of contentious issues, including his belief that Kelly abuses alcohol. As the excerpt begins, Mediator A invites Kelly to respond to Mike's "concerns" (lines 546–547).

Excerpt 4.25 Mike and Kelly Midwest Divorce Mediation, Session 1, p. 25

```
546  MA:     Okay. .h D' y' wanna speak to any uh thuh concerns that Mike
547          brought up? °Kelly?°
548          (0.8)
549  Kelly:  U:m? (0.7) chu=hum! .HH chu=HUM! (0.8) tch (0.3) Thee only
550          thing? (0.8) he says? (0.7) um (1.7) yeah they've been brought up
551          like that? (0.7) But (1.9) it's not (0.6) like (1.5) I dunno 'f he-
552          he's thinkin' that it's like we (1.0) have uh PARTY every night?
553          or what! .h (0.6) That's not true. (0.6) But if I wanna have uh
554          beer or so in my house! (0.6) I oughta be allowed to, it's not
555          against thuh law? .h (0.5) It's not (0.7) it's not? (1.9) it's not
556          somethin' that, I mean I'm not drinkin' uh (0.6) in- (0.5) to- (0.6)
557          tuh drink and, get drunk!
558          (0.7)
559  MA:     °°Right.°°
560          (0.4)
561  Kelly:  Y'know. So .h (0.6) That's not
562          (0.8)
```

```
563  MA:     's not criminal activity.=
564  Kelly:                    =That's [right!]
565  Mike:                            [No! ] ab[solute]ly not.
566  MA:                                       [Right.]
```

Kelly's opening statement rebuts Mike's complaints about her consumption of alcohol and his repeated accusations that she has been abusing alcohol. She makes three points in her defense. First, that her alcohol consumption is only occasional (lines 551–553), second, that alcohol consumption is not against the law (lines 553–555), and third, that she is not drinking to drunkenness (lines 555–557). Her opening statement thus relies on Mike's opening statement and uses it as a foundation to directly and clearly deny his accusations. Note that she does not have to retell the story of all of the problems they have experienced in their marriage, nor does she choose to respond to every complaint or accusation Mike has made during his extensive opening statement. Instead, she focuses on what she considers the most important issue.

Some disputants may construct a second story which builds on the first disputant's story, but design it in such a way that the implications of the story are different. For example, in Excerpt 4.26 the respondent (Mr. Jim Porterville) produces a very brief statement in response to the complainant's (Mrs. Centerville) opening statement. While not presenting any evidence to challenge Mrs. Centerville's complaints or accusations, he puts a different "spin" on her story.

Excerpt 4.26 Patched Carpet West Coast Small Claims Mediation, p. 11

```
252  MA:   How 'bout it, Jim?
253        (0.6)
254  Jim:  We:ll, (0.9) she has had uh very hard six months. (.) (Buh) first of
255        a:ll, (0.2) .hh=(chuh!) I'd like to apologize for bein' °late. (1.2)
256        °(Y'know) °ih's just one uh those thi:ngs. .hh u:::h (1.5) I think
257        it should be fairly obvious: from her, LEtter (0.8) .h °or from >her
258        statement< that tu:h (0.5) .h there has been (0.2) lots of action (0.2)
259        >on thee uh (.) carpet.< (0.6) u:::h (0.4) We had (0.2)
260        representatives ou:t, (1.2) we've- been back numerous times:,
261        >you know, to try and u:hm (0.3) .h satisfy thuh customer.< °'t's
262        prima:rily what it i::s: (0.2) u::hm (4.5) it is SAid in (thuh word
263        of Mike Manna donoh), (0.4) uh We have tried u::h (0.5)
264        there's only so many things >you can do do (uh/it) (0.1) u::h after
265        you keep going ba::ck, and >I- it- (duh) it's like uh< uh ba:d
266        piece uh steak, instead of getting better it- it thuh more you
267        me:ss with i-heh-t! thuh worse it ge-h-ts. (.) That type uh
268        situation. (.) .h u::hm (3.0) tch (5.0) I don' really feel like
269        there's u::h much that can be (0.4) or (.) in fact should be done.
270        (0.3) °u::h But I'm I'm sittin' here. h
```

While admitting that there is a problem with the carpet, Mr. Porterville does not admit that there is anything that he should do about it (lines 263–269). His opening statement spins Mrs. Centerville's chronological account of her encounters with his carpet company as evidence that his company has done a lot to try to solve the problem ("h there has been (0.2) lots of action (0.2) >on thee uh (.) carpet.< ..."; lines 258–259). By saying that he has had representatives out to her house numerous times (lines 259–260), Mr. Porterville implies that his company has been very responsive to Mrs. Centerville's concerns. However, recall that in Mrs. Centerville's opening statement (Excerpt 4.7), her description of each contact with Mr. Porterville's company was designed to show that the firm was unresponsive (hence many attempts to contact them were required). She detailed the repeated efforts she made to get them to respond to her complaints. In addition, note that Mr. Porterville does not respond to every claim that Mrs. Centerville made. For example, Mr. Porterville does not respond to Mrs. Centerville's claim that he has failed to return her phone calls (Excerpt 4.7).

Jim Porterville also makes moral claims in his opening statement. He works to present himself as a responsible business owner, and characterizes his firm's actions as efforts to try to satisfy the customer (lines 259–261). He then argues that doing more work on the carpet would make it worse rather than better (lines 262–267). He closes his opening statement with an upshot: "I don' really feel like there's u::h much that can be (0.4) or (.) in fact should be done. (0.3) °u::h but I'm I'm sittin' here. h"; lines 268–270). By saying he's "sitting here," Mr. Porterville conveys that he is open to other positions and willing to listen.

In sum, there are both advantages and disadvantages to being the respondent in a mediation session. The second disputant can selectively respond to accusations and complaints, and can organize his or her opening statement to respond to accusations in the most powerful way possible. In addition, the second disputant can use the same techniques that first disputants use to construct persuasive arguments and provide evidence in support of them. Even when mediator solicits of second disputants' opening statements provide a great deal of latitude for how the respondent constructs their opening statement, respondents often begin their statements with a rebuttal of specific accusations or complaints. The choice to narrow the focus of their opening statements therefore seems to be a strategic choice on the part of second disputants rather than an inherent problem with the organization of mediation sessions. In addition, not having to spend time laying out all of the details of a case could be seen as an advantage of going second. The ground work has already been laid by the complainant's opening statement, so the second disputant can use that statement as a resource to build upon indexically.

Discussion and Conclusions

In sum, there are several ways mediators can solicit and facilitate disputant's opening statements, and disputants can work to create strong opening statements. Mediators solicit opening statements from each disputant in turn in small claims mediations. The mediators in these data varied in the degree of transparency they displayed in terms of how they selected which disputant should speak first. The divorce mediators typically opened the mediation session by soliciting collective responses to questions or topics of concern to both spouses, thus creating a less adversarial context for the discussion that follows than occurred in the small claims mediation session.

The degree of mediator intervention in disputants' opening statements varied depending on how well they were constructed. Well-constructed opening statements clearly conveyed the nature of the problem that led to the dispute, the chronology of events, and the roles of the participants. Mediators worked to help facilitate the production of opening statements largely by asking questions during and after the production of the statement, and by using minimal responses and continuers to display recipiency and comprehension and to encourage continuance.

While constructing a narrative which conveyed a coherent description of the chain of events leading to the conflict, disputants used various types of evidence, ranging from physical objects or photographs to direct or indirect quotes of the opposing disputant or other witnesses to events. Disputants often used these types of evidence to preemptively defend against accusations that the opposing disputant might make when they eventually got the floor. The first disputant to tell their story thus has many advantages in terms of being able to frame the opposing disputant's statement.

However, it is also clear from these data that disputants in the second storytelling position are not necessarily disadvantaged by their position in the mediation session. In fact, there are some ways in which being in the second storyteller position is an advantage. The respondent has a wide range of resources for taking advantage of being second to create strong responses to complainants' stories. First, the respondent does not have to use their opening statement to retell the narrative that has been constructed by the first storyteller. Instead, they can selectively respond to those aspects of it which are most useful to them in conveying their side of the case. This approach can enable them to make a strong defense against any accusations or complaints that were made. They can also selectively respond to accusations, focusing on those they feel are most important or that they can most effectively deny. Some respondents used their opening statement to correct errors in the complainant's statement, thus challenging their credibility. Finally, they could tacitly accept the facts of the complainant's story, but put a different interpretation or spin on it, thus creating a more favorable impression for their side of the dispute.

These findings have practical implications for disputants in mediation sessions by revealing which methods of constructing their opening statements may advance their interests in the dispute. The choices available to mediators are more complex, because they are working to adhere closely to the goals and constraints of their role in facilitative mediation. However, it bears considering whether relying on facilitation results in a fair outcome for the session if the disputants are unequally skilled in the interactional techniques described in this chapter. The question then becomes what can facilitative mediators do to balance the power between disputants. Noticing and working to address power imbalances between disputants related to social statuses or individual characteristics is typically part of mediator training.[13] Mayer (2004) notes that participant's power in mediation is not unidimensional; rather it is due to such factors as the individual's role in the institution or social role, the nature of the situation the interaction is occurring within, and each individual's characteristics and strengths and weaknesses. The results of this chapter suggest that mediators should also consider how to balance power due to interactional competence and position in the mediation session (first or second storyteller). Mediators must also be alert to the challenge of attempting to balance power without challenging their display of neutrality.[14]

Mediators should be trained to notice the techniques and issues discussed in this chapter so that they can decide how to respond to them as they are occurring. Mediators should attend to the interactional techniques that are used by disputants to construct their statements and to present evidence, in order to maintain balance between the two disputants, especially if the interactional skill of one disputant is significantly greater than the other, and to prevent the use of such techniques from distracting attention from the facts and events involved in the dispute. Mediators should also be alert to the use of preemptive techniques and intervene as needed to keep disputants focused on their version of events rather than anticipating the opposing disputant's potential actions.

Mediators in small claims mediation sessions would do well to make sure disputants understand why one disputant is going first, or consider routinely allowing the disputants to choose who goes first. In order to defuse the power of the first storyteller to set the agenda of the session and decide how to define the problem, the mediator could have both disputants produce brief summaries of the problem before each disputant's full opening statement is solicited. This would enable both disputants to have some impact on the direction and agenda

---

[13] For example, see Landau (1995); Neumann (1992); Roberts (2008); Ver Steegh (2008).
[14] For example, see Garcia (1995); Garcia et al. (2002); Kolb and Kressel (1994); Rifkin, Millen, and Cobb (1991).

of the session before the complainant's opening statement begins. Another approach might be to have both disputants work together to construct the chronology of events before either has the chance to make their opening statement (see Winslade and Monk (2008) for additional suggestions). It might be beneficial for small claims mediators to use techniques similar to those used by the divorce mediators in terms of opening the session by addressing a question of common interest to both disputants; this may reduce the distance between the two sides and create a less adversarial atmosphere for the discussion to follow.

In sum, this chapter has demonstrated the challenges for mediators as they solicit and facilitate disputants' opening statements in mediation sessions. Some disputants may be reluctant to end their opening statements, requiring significant effort to get them to close down their stories. More reticent disputants may need mediator questions or clarification requests to help them construct and produce them effectively. There are also disputants who may be proficient in the use of interactional techniques for effective presentation of evidence and for constructing arguments in persuasive ways; they may need little help or intervention during their opening statements. Mediators should tailor their interventions to suit differences in disputants' interactional skills and be prepared to work to support weaker participants.

5   Mediator Representation of Disputants' Positions

One of mediation's main advantages over other forms of conflict resolution is the autonomy it provides disputants. Disputants in mediation have the opportunity to tell their own story instead of having a lawyer speak for them, and are helped to create their own agreement instead of having a judge or arbitrator decide for them. While mediators work hard to protect disputants' autonomy and maintain neutrality relative to the dispute, they also have the responsibility for facilitating the session (Burns 2007). Several previous studies have identified potential problems with mediators' facilitation of the process of mediation which may interfere substantially with disputants' autonomy. For example, by controlling topic shifts during the session, a mediator can influence the discussion of problems and proposals while officially remaining neutral.

Through such "selective facilitation," divorce mediators may move the disputants toward one potential approach and away from the concerns of the other disputant (Greatbatch and Dingwall 1989).

When disputants have the floor to make an opening statement and tell their story about what happened, they are representing themselves. However, as seen in Chapter 4, even these opening statements are generally facilitated by the mediators. Throughout the session, as mediators facilitate the discussion of issues and suggestions for resolving the dispute, a disputant's self-representation differs from self-representation in ordinary conversation. In the speech exchange system of mediation, disputants typically wait until selected to speak by the mediator instead of selecting themselves as next speaker. In addition, their utterances are typically addressed to the mediators rather than to each other. This interactional organization has an impact on the placement and formulation of disputants' self-representations. It also provides opportunities for varying degrees of mediator intervention in their representations.

There is much variability in the amount of control mediators and mediation programs exert over the dispute resolution process (Kolb 1981; 1983). In transformative mediation approaches, mediators are instructed to limit themselves to using almost identical words and phrases to reflect the disputants' views and statements.[1] However, in facilitative mediation programs such as those analyzed in this book, mediators rarely reflect back exactly what was said, instead using paraphrases or summaries which reproduce the substance of a disputant's story or position.[2] Mediators may also make statements consistent with a disputant's expressed position, but which go beyond merely rephrasing what was actually said. This is referred to as "reframing" the disputant's position (Boulle et al. 2008; Gilman 2017; Gray 2006; Livingood 2016). Reframing is regarded as a more intrusive mediator technique than paraphrasing or summarizing:

> Reframing involves restating comments (1) to give them a more positive tone; (2) to eliminate blame and accusation, (3) to reflect underlying interests, fears, concerns, needs, values, or goals, and (4) to reveal common ground between the parties. (Ewert et al. 2010: 81)

Mediators' summaries of disputant positions are not always completely neutral; bias toward one side or the other is at times evident (Jacobs 2002). Disputants' autonomy can be infringed upon when mediators go beyond representing a disputant's stated positions or arguments and instead produce their own arguments in favor of one side or the other (Garcia 1995). When mediators replace a disputant in an exchange, they are not letting the disputant speak for themselves. While in some mediation programs this type of representation is considered legitimate mediator practice if applied to both sides in a dispute, this position is controversial (Cobb and Rifkin 1991a).

In this chapter I investigate how mediators in all three data sets work to represent disputants' positions. While disputants have ample opportunities to represent themselves in these data, their options for self-expression are often limited in terms of when, to whom, and about what they may speak at any given point in the session. I will describe the range of ways mediators work to represent disputant's positions, and show how these representations affect disputant autonomy. The mediator's ability to display a neutral stance in these small claims and divorce mediation sessions is also affected by how they represent disputants' positions.

The types of mediator representation found will be discussed in the order of the least intrusive to the most intrusive. The least intrusive form of representation is paraphrasing. A mediator's summaries, rephrasings, or "upshots" of disputants' expressed statements and positions accomplish representation with minimal risk to the mediator's neutral stance or the autonomy of the disputant.

---

[1] See Bush (2013); Hanley (2010); Institute for the Study of Conflict Resolution (2011); Woolford and Ratner (2008).

[2] See Boulle et al. (2008); Cahn (1992); Donohue, Allen, and Burrell (1988); Ewert et al. (2010); Frenkel and Stark (2012); Goldberg et al. (2017); Picard (2016); Roberts (1988).

If a mediator moves beyond paraphrasing to "revoicing" a disputant's position, they reframe or reformulate it in an exchange with the opposing disputant. Revoicing involves extending or embellishing a disputant's argument, and may involve adding material that was not present in the disputant's original statement.

The most intrusive form of representation is "replacement." Replacement of a disputant by a mediator involves a mediator directly negotiating with one disputant on behalf of the other. The mediator goes beyond representing a disputant's expressed positions, and instead replaces the disputant in an exchange with the opposing disputant. When replacing a disputant the mediator still represents the disputant's interests, but goes beyond representing what they have articulated. Thus, disputant self-representation provides the most autonomy, and mediator replacement of a disputant provides the least.

Paraphrases, Summaries, and Upshots

As is typical in facilitative mediation, the mediators in these data make at least small changes in their restatements of disputant's positions and proposals rather than repeating them exactly. Mediators' paraphrases of disputants' statements can be functional for the process of mediation by enabling them to verify or correct their comprehension, and may help the disputant to feel understood or at least heard. In addition, a disputant may be more willing to listen to an opposing disputant's position if it is articulated by the mediator rather than by that disputant.

In this section I discuss how mediators paraphrase disputant's statements while creating a summary or upshot. An upshot is a formulation of talk that proposes a gloss or "gist" of what that person has said (Heritage and Watson 1979). Upshots are often prefaced with the transition marker "so."[3] In these data I found that upshots can be used to refocus or redirect the discussion, articulate the main point of a story or the main areas of disagreement, highlight common ground, or enable the mediator to serve as an intermediary between opposing disputants.

Refocusing or Redirecting the Discussion

Mediators can use summaries or upshots to refocus attention from the details of the dispute to underlying interests or problems. In Excerpt 5.1 the mediator uses an upshot to refocus attention on the disputant's emotions about the problem.[4]

---

[3] See Antaki, Barnes, and Leudar (2005); Barnes (2007); Bolden (2010); Hutchby (2005); Raymond (2004); van der Houwen (2009).

[4] See Bishop et al. (2015); Doneff and Ordover (2014); Poitras and Raines (2013); Whatling (2012).

Excerpt 5.1 Washer Dryer Midwest Small Claims Mediation, p. 18

```
382  Tish:  [Yes, well:      I] did call 'im [on thuh ] phone! (0.4) .h 'cause I
383         told him, I said we agreed that you would pay, you agreed
384         >that you would pay< half >uh thuh< bill!
385         (0.6)
386  Med:   Mm hm.
387         (0.1)
388  Tish:  >And you would< pay HALF (1.0) thuh next month, and half thuh
389         following month! In two month payments! (0.3) .h And he called me
390         (0.4) .h a: blankin' liar! (0.6) >And I hung up on 'im!< (0.8) There is
391         where my allegiance (0.8) went to (0.3) Robert (0.4) >uh hundred
392         percent!< (0.9) I don't deserve to be talked to that way? And I will
393         stand for [it!    ]
394  Med:            [>So] you were< offended.
395         (0.4)
396  Tish:  Yes Ma'am!
397         (2.5)
398  Med:   And (0.4) by now we're what, intuh August:? (0.9)
399         >September or something< [°like that?°       ]
400  Tish:                           [OH it's HHHH] °just-° eh July!
401         (0.5)
402  Med:   °July.° (1.0) .h (2.7) How close do you (0.5) live to: Anna and John?
403         (0.1)
404  Tish:  Thirty miles.
```

In Excerpt 5.1, Tish, a landlord, describes the events that led up to the dispute with her tenants (lines 382–384, 388–393). The mediator then draws an upshot which focuses attention on the emotional content of her story ("[>So] you were< offended."; line 394). By focusing on the disputant's emotions rather than on the details of what was done or said, the mediator's upshot can help the disputant convey what is important to her. Tish agrees with this upshot in line 396, but does not elaborate. After a long pause, the mediator then solicits a return to Tish's story, by asking her a question about the chronology of events (lines 398–399). This mediator's use of upshots worked to refocus or redirect the disputant's story to highlight the underlying issues for the disputants.

Articulating the Main Point of a Story

Upshots and summaries were also used to highlight the main points of a disputant's story or statement of the problem. In Excerpt 5.2 the mediator's upshot focuses on the substantive implications of the story rather than on the emotions behind the story. This dispute is between a homeowner (Jack) and the owner of the roofing company (Ed) who originally installed the roof on Jack's house.

Excerpt 5.2 Roof Repair Midwest Small Claims Mediation, p. 12

235 Jack: [°Okay?°] (0.5) So WHAT I started <u>doing</u> is I started doin' uh
236   little digging? (0.3) I called thuh (0.5) Metro County (0.7) °uh°
237   <u>zoning</u> commission. talked t' uh gentleman <u>there</u>? (0.5) He said
238   with that type (0.3) w' that's <u>under</u> two and twelve pitch, (0.6) you
239   don't, you just <u>don't</u> put <u>shingles</u> °on!° (0.5) tch .h So THEN I I
240   called up! °uh° (0.3) <u>Royal</u>! which °I° (0.3) I <u>think</u> is thuh- thuh
241   manufacturer of their <u>SHINGLES</u>! (0.5) .h And <u>they</u> Sent me
242   information saying (0.6) that on <u>every</u> bundle of <u>shingles</u>! they
243   send out, there's inforMAtion on them that says (0.5) .h when you
244   <u>have</u> under uh two and twelve pitch? (0.4) you <u>do</u> not put <u>shingles</u>
245   °on it!°
246   (0.5)
247 Med: tch .h So <u>your</u> feeling at this point? (0.4) was 'at thuh wro:ng? kind
248   of?
249   (0.1)
250 Jack: Ro[of! was put on! eXact-   ]
251 Med: [roof had been put on that] section of thuh house?
252   (0.1)
253 Jack: Exactly! (0.4) .hh And SO (0.2) um (0.5) <u>THEN</u> I CALLED th-
254   prior >owner uh thuh house! ...

The mediator draws an upshot from Jack's story ("thuh wro:ng? kind of? ... [roof had been put on that] section of thuh house?"; lines 247–248, 251). Jack projects the end of her utterance and provides a candidate sentence completion in line 250. The mediator completes her utterance in overlap with Jack (line 251). Jack's emphatic agreement is first issued in overlap in line 250 ("eXact-"), and then again in the clear in line 253 ("Exactly!"). As Li (2008) notes, a precisely positioned "exactly" can be used to show the correctness of a speaker's response. Jack uses "exactly" to agree with the mediator's upshot summarizing the chronology of events in terms of what they imply for Jack's position. Note that the mediator's upshot does not just convey Jack's point more succinctly, she articulates Jack's main complaint and his basis for claiming that Ed is responsible for the problems with the roof.

Articulating the Main Areas of Disagreement

Another common use of upshots by mediators in these data is to clarify the main areas of disagreement between the disputants. Excerpts 5.3–5.5 show how a mediator can use paraphrases and summaries to help disputants focus on the issues under dispute rather than staying stuck on complaints about the other party. Before Excerpt 5.3 began, Bob and Kate had discussed several problematic issues in their relationship. Excerpt 5.3 shows Kate detailing why she feels alienated from her partner Bob.

Excerpt 5.3 Bob and Kate Midwest Family Mediation, Session 1, p. 90

```
1948  Kate:  Even though HIS way of dea:ling with thuh stress is .h (1.2) just
1949         be light about it! (0.6) u:m: (0.6) You know, eh- (0.5) instead of:
1950         bein' down. I mean he even told me (in) frustration was, well I'm
1951         just not gonna be that way! (0.7) .h You kno:w?, If if if thuh
1952         situation comes up and YEAH, you know you hate it, and it is:
1953         thuh situation you're gonna be: down and bah bah bah! .h Oh I'm
1954         just not gonna BE that way. (0.9) .h But that's FINE? but not
1955         everybody can relate! and and HA:Ndle! (0.3) IT! (0.8) that way.
1956         And I admit, I just didn't feel like bein' close to him. (0.3) I didn't
1957         feel like makin' LO:VE!, I didn't feel like bein' TOUCHED!, I
1958         didn't feel like bein' HUGGED?, (0.4) .h or because, you know, it's
1959         just like WHAT FO:R?, (0.9) you know?, you know?, what's thuh
1960         point? (0.4) You know, I I .h (0.3) I don't feel uh real sense of
1961         security, a:nd so for me to keep GIVING of myself, (0.7) .h I just
1962         don't feel (1.0) °I don't feel good in doing it.°
1963         (0.5)
```

Kate has explained why she is keeping Bob at a distance and why she feels estranged from him. When Mediator A responds after Kate's turn, she works to draw an upshot (Excerpt 5.4, lines 1964–1968), summarizing Kate's immediately prior utterance as well as the issues raised by both disputants earlier in the session.

Excerpt 5.4 Bob and Kate Midwest Family Mediation, Session 1, p. 90

```
1964  MA:    SO: (0.9) it sounds like where we a:re?, is that (0.5) Bob is NOT
1965         ready, (0.6) to- (0.5) be married right now. (0.7) He LOVES you,
1966         he loves your children?, (0.7) he's committed to you?, (0.3) but he's
1967         not ready to be married right now. (0.9) Religiously, you cannot
1968         stay in this house?
1969         (0.4)
1970  Kate:   °Mm hm.°
```

The mediator begins her upshot with "so," signaling a transition (Bolden 2009). Mediator A frames the summary collectively, using the pronoun "we": ("SO: (0.9) it sounds like where we a:re?, . . ."; line 1964). She thus includes herself and Mediator B as participants in the collectivity. She first summarizes Bob's position (lines 1964–1967), and then summarizes Kate's position (lines 1967–1968). She uses questioning intonation with her summary of Kate's position, and Kate responds with an agreement-implicative minimal response (line 1970).

After a pause, Mediator A elaborates her upshot of Kate and Bob's situation (Excerpt 5.5, lines 1972–1975):

Excerpt 5.5 Bob and Kate Midwest Family Mediation, Session 1, p. 90

```
1971          (1.5)
1972   MA:    SO: there's uh NEED (0.4) to separate. (0.5) There's uh need for
1973          you: to- move somewhere else?, (0.6) for uh period of time, until
1974          (0.7) these issues get addressed. (1.7) to see if you're ready to come
1975          back together as uh married couple.
1976          (1.6)
1977   Kate:  °°Mm hm.°°
1978          (1.5)
1979   MA:    Is 'at right?
1980          (1.0)
1981   Kate:         °(That was pretty good)?°
1982          (2.6)
1983   Bob:   °Yeah?° (0.4) °That's° (0.6) that's what makes sense.  (0.5) phh!
1984          .hh (0.2) [(I know that)] (0.1) °I know that.°
1985   MA:               [SO:         ]
1986          (0.8)
1987   MA:    As HARD as that IS! for you folks, (0.7) um and as much as YOU
1988          feel, Kate, that (1.1) you wish: this had been articulated?, (1.6) two
1989          months ago, however long ago, would have made it better for you.
1990          (1.0) It's happening right now. (0.5) And it's clea:rly, on thuh
1991          table, that this is where you both are. (2.1) Are YOU: prepared to
1992          (1.8) move out when.
1993          (1.0)
1994   Kate:  .h I've been (0.4) desperately (0.8) °tryin' to find housing?°
1995          (0.7)
1996   MA:    So as soon as you would find hou[sing?,   ]
```

Having given both parties an opportunity to disagree with her upshot of the predicament the couple is in, and receiving none, Mediator A continues by drawing an "upshot from the upshot." In lines 1972–1975 she confirms the conclusion that the couple needs a temporary separation. The disputants agree with this upshot as well (lines 1977, 1981, and 1983–1984). Mediator A's upshots are functional for this mediation session because she clearly articulates the disputants' positions and what they need to do next, while at the same time effectively cutting off the repetitive complaining and discussion of the issues that had been occurring. Now the participants can move forward.

Highlighting Common Ground

Mediator training guides often recommend that mediators identify and highlight common ground or areas of agreement between disputants to help them see that they are not as far apart as they thought.[5] The belief is that this can facilitate the creation of further areas of agreement. In these data mediators use summaries or upshots as a technique for highlighting common ground between disputants. For example, in Excerpt 5.6 the mediator identifies the concern both disputants have for an injured dog:

Excerpt 5.6 Injured Dog Midwest Small Claims Mediation, p. 7

```
153  Mart:  Last year. (0.8) .h and (0.5) I GAve him PLENTY UH TI:ME? to:
154         (0.6) even recontact me, I know that (0.8) Mister Brown knew
155         where I lived! 'cause he came into my ho:use! (0.4) .h when I (0.3)
156         brought thuh dog in? (0.5) t' make sure >thuh dog was< (0.3) still
157         alive? and oKAY! (0.4) .h HE 'AD OFFERED t' take me to thuh
158         vet! But thuh vet< wasn't open at that time!
159         (0.7)
160  Med:   Sounds like! (0.6) 'm BO:TH! parties were very upset about °what
161         happened.°
162         (0.3)
163  Mart:  Yes! It's it's NOT SO MUCH! (0.8) .h WHAT HAPPENED.
164         WHAT HAPPENED had HAPPENED. >There's no way< (0.5)
165         >that can be< [changed!      ]
```

The mediator responds to Martin's description of what happened when the respondent's car hit his dog. Her statement is designed to highlight an area of agreement between the disputants, that they both care about the dog who was injured (lines 160–161). Martin agrees with this statement (line 163).

Mediators' attempts to highlight common ground between disputants are not always successful. If disputants resist or avoid these efforts, mediator pursuit may be necessary to get disputants to acknowledge areas of agreement or common ground between them. For example, in the second session of Bob and Kate's family mediation, Mediator A works to move the couple away from complaints and continued talk about their problems toward discussion of potential solutions. As Excerpt 5.7 begins, Bob is talking about the couple's problems making payments on the car Kate's parents gave her.

Excerpt 5.7 Bob and Kate Midwest Family Mediation, Session 2, p. 67

```
1440  Bob:   So that's- that's an issue. (1.4) also. >Or do we just-<
1441         (0.4) .h to keep them happy? or: y'know so that they're? (0.3)
1442         >out uh th-< picture? (0.9) >buy it off uh them?< And then take it
1443         ourselves and trade it in? or (0.5) tch °whatever.°
1444         (1.3) °But it's°
1445         (0.1)
1446  Kate:  >See uh lot of it< hinges on what >Bob and I are gonna< do.
```

---

[5] See Bishop et al. (2015); Doneff and Ordover (2014).

```
1447          (0.4)
1448  MA:    >See THAT'S WHY< [(                          ).]
1449  Kate:                    [>SEE AND IF I CAN] GET< BOB
1450          TUH FINALLY TELL ME WHAT we're gonna do:? then 'ere's so
1451          many things that can [fall    ] intuh place and 'en you can START
1452  MA:                         [WELL-]
1453  Kate:  making some direction and setting some goals and (0.4) .h and
1454          some (0.4) distant decisions. (0.3) .h >As LONG as< you're in
1455          limbo, (0.7) you can't do anything! everything comes? (0.3) ih- it's
1456          in limbo! (0.7) eh it's in limbo! You can't? (0.3) make uh u:h (0.3)
1457          any kind of (0.5) turn.
1458          (1.9)
1459  MA:    So thuh BOTTOM LINE it SOUNDS like! is that you really can't
1460          >make uh decision< about thuh car payment? (0.9) until? (0.5)
1461          you're >OUT uh this:< (0.7) transition period. (1.3) So:
1462          (1.3)
1463  Kate:  And since I kind uh feel like he's thuh reason why I'm havin'
1464          t' make this transitional? (0.9) >Then it's kin' uh< like I can't be
1465          without [uh car because I gotta-                      ]
```

Kate resists the mediator's efforts to make a transition from complaint talk to resolution talk. For example, in lines 1449–1457 Kate is complaining that she is stuck in limbo because her partner Bob can not decide whether they should get married or not. The mediator first tries to intervene in line 1452 ("WELL-"), but drops out when Kate continues speaking. When Kate is done, Mediator A responds with an upshot summarizing not just Kate's immediately prior turn, but the discussion as a whole and its implications for what the couple should do about the car payments (lines 1459–1461). Note that Mediator A begins with a "so" at the beginning of line 1459, setting up her statement as an upshot. After her summary there is a 1.3 second pause at the end of line 1461. When neither disputant responds, Mediator A produces another "So:". This second "so" may be setting up for or inviting an "upshot of the upshot." However, Kate's response (lines 1463–1465) does not produce a clear agreement or disagreement with this upshot, nor does it produce an upshot of the upshot – a statement of what Kate and Bob should do. Instead, Kate uses an "and-preface" (Heritage and Sorjonen 1994) to tie her utterance to Mediator A's turn. She then continues blaming Bob ("I kind uh feel like he's thuh reason why ..."; line 1463). She continues discussing the problem involving the car (lines 1464–1465). The mediator's attempt to shut down complaints and frame the issue in terms of the couple's shared involvement in the transition period was resisted by Kate.

As the exchange continues, Mediator A makes another attempt to highlight common goals:

Excerpt 5.8 Bob and Kate Midwest Family Mediation, Session 2, p. 67

```
1466  MA:    [WE:LL? I THINK I'VE I HEARD YOU] BOTH say
1467         you're thuh reasons. (0.8) .h Bob >Bob is thuh< reason beCAUSE
1468         >he's not ready to-< (0.4) to (0.5) ACTually take thuh marriage
1469         VOWS!
1470         (0.4)
1471  Kate:  Right.
1472         (0.9)
1473  MA:    On your part? (0.9) You're unwilling to live in his HOUSE for
1474         religious reasons [so        ]
1475  Kate:                   [°Right.°] which are supposed tuh be his same
1476         religious values too.
1477         (0.4)
1478  MA:    Yeah. [but BY- (thing-)]
1479  Bob:         [Well they are! I ] understand it. I'm not [(      ).]
```

Mediator A again tries to redirect the talk away from complaints, this time by articulating the reasons both partners have given for their trial separation (Excerpt 5.8, lines 1466–1469 and 1473–1474). This second attempt to create common ground is also unsuccessful in redirecting the talk. Note that Kate's response in lines 1475–1476, while responsive to Mediator A's turn, refocuses attention away from the proposed upshot and back to yet another criticism of Bob.

Excerpt 5.9 shows Mediator A making a third attempt to highlight common ground between Bob and Kate. Mediator A interrupts Bob to refocus attention on the common ground between them (lines 1480–1483):

Excerpt 5.9 Bob and Kate Midwest Family Mediation, Session 2, p. 67

```
1480  MA:                                  [>I THINK IT'S<]
1481         CLEARLY BOTH OF YOU! who are saying? (0.7) that (1.1)
1482         that >that this is HAPpening because of-< (0.3) reasons on both
1483         sides.
1484         (0.7)
1485  Kate:  Mm hm.
1486         (2.6)
1487  MA:    Bob would be >HAPPY t' have you< stay there?
1488         i[f thuh religious is]sue
1489  Kate:  [Indefinitely.      ]
1490         (0.3)
1491  Kate:  °Mm [hm?°]
1492  MA:        [was ]n't uh problem.
1493         (0.2)
1494  Kate:  °Mm hm? [I think] he would.
```

Mediator A interrupts Bob in line 1480, speaking loudly to talk over his turn. Bob drops out, leaving Mediator A to complete her utterance in the clear.

In addition to speaking loudly, Mediator A emphasizes the word "BOTH," thus drawing attention to the common ground between Bob and Kate. At this point, after several attempts, Mediator A is beginning to get the disputants to see each other's perspectives on this issue. In line 1494 Kate acknowledges that Bob has expressed willingness to let her live in the house during their separation, but that the religious issue makes that problematic for both of them. The process of achieving agreement on an issue is not necessarily straightforward or easy, but mediators' interventions can be helpful in getting disputants to see common ground.

Using Summaries to Serve as an Intermediary

As shown in Chapter 2, the disputants' interactions with each other are mediated, because they typically address their utterances to the mediators rather than to each other. In these data mediators may also serve as intermediaries by repeating summaries for the opposing disputant. The mediator may first summarize a disputant's statement in order to show that they were heard and provide an opportunity for the disputant to correct or clarify the accuracy of the summary. They may then resummarize the disputant's story, in an utterance addressed to the opposing disputant. Excerpts 5.10 and 5.11 show this use of repeated summaries. First, the mediator produces a summary of Pete's opening statement (Excerpt 5.10):

Excerpt 5.10 Camera Repair Midwest Small Claims Mediation, p. 18

```
379  Med:   'Nkay. (0.7) Alright Pete >what I'm gonna do 's:< (0.1) briefly
380          summarize what you've told me, (0.4) You're tellin' me that uhm
381          (2.1) that yuhp- thu:h (0.3) thuh camcorder's brought tuh you and as
382          uh matter of course which your business d's is fix thuh camera t'
383          determine what thee estimate will be for thuh pri:ce. (0.6) .hh A:nd if
384          thuh customer's not satisfied with tha:t then you'll just reverse thuh
385          work you'll put in thee (0.4) .hh thuh
386          (0.6)
387  Pete:  Take our parts out [and replace it.]
388  Med:                     [°Thuh° fau:lty] pa:rts, (0.4) a:nd (0.4) take your
389          parts back and (0.3) not charge them anything for it.=
390  Pete:                                          ='t's right.
```

The mediator's initial summary serves to determine whether his understanding of the disputant's position is accurate (lines 379–385, 388–389). Pete interjects in line 387 to clarify the mediator's summary. After asking Pete a few questions to clarify his position, the mediator then addresses the opposing disputant, Cindy, and produces a second summary of Pete's position for her benefit (Excerpt 5.11, lines 411–416).

Excerpt 5.11 Camera Repair Midwest Small Claims Mediation, p. 18

```
411  Med:    CINDY (0.3) u:h Pete's saying that (0.3) u:hm (2.4) what thuh
412          business would've done had you: (1.6) because you didn't like (0.4)
413          thuh price (0.3) didn't like >°thuh° fact that they went< ahead and did
414          thuh work was that they would've (0.3) returned thuh camera to:
415          (0.3) thuh state it was before they took it. (3.0) And they wouldn't
416          have charged you anything. (0.8) Why didn't you wanna do that?
417          (1.8)
418  Cindy:  Well they were rude and threatening in thuh conversation we had
419          about (0.4) doin' thuh work. And I never heard of anyone doing
420          (1.2) thuh work on something (0.6) for an estimate. (0.7) And (0.4)
421          besides that fact, (2.6) HH HOW DO I know they're gonna put it
422          back in thuh same condition. (0.4) How do I know it's not gonna be
423          in worse condition?
424          (2.4)
425  Med:    °Mhm° (0.2) What was wrong with thuh price? (1.0) What- did you
426          intend on having thuh camrecorder fixed?
427          (0.7)
428  Cindy:  It was my decision (0.3) our decision tuh have that camcorder fixed.
429          Not theirs tuh fix it.
430          (0.4)
431  Med:    Okay=
432  Cindy:       =Maybe I would have and maybe I wouldn't (0.3) maybe I
433          wouldn't 'ave wanted tuh
```

After this second summary of Pete's position, the mediator asks Cindy why she did not want to accept the camera back (line 416). The two summaries of Pete's position do different work for each disputant. While the first summary served to help the mediator ascertain that he understood Pete's position and to close down Pete's story, the second summary was addressed to Cindy and does different work. At this point, Cindy has heard both Pete's original statement and the mediator's first summary of Pete's statement. The mediator's second summary makes his role as an intermediary between the two disputants visible. The work this second summary does is to frame and set up the question the mediator asks Cindy.

In sum, there are several types of work mediators can do with summaries and upshots of disputants' statements. First, they can be used to reframe a disputant's story in terms of the underlying emotions which may help move the process of dispute resolution forward. Second, summaries and upshots can be used to articulate the main point of a story or areas of disagreement between disputants and help move them from further discussion of the problem to steps that can be taken to resolve the problem. Third, summaries and upshots can be used to highlight common ground or areas of agreement between disputants. Finally, summaries and upshots can be used to verify the accuracy of the mediator's understanding of disputant's positions and to accomplish his or her role as an intermediary between opposing disputants. In the next section I discuss mediator representations of disputants which go beyond summaries and paraphrases of their own words.

"Revoicing": Mediator Representation in Direct Exchanges with Opposing Disputants

Mediators may go beyond drawing summaries and upshots of disputants' stated positions, and instead represent one disputant's interests in direct exchanges with the opposing disputant. Excerpts 5.12, 5.13, and 5.14 illustrate how a mediator may represent one disputant to another by such "revoicing" of that disputant's expressed position. Excerpt 5.12 shows the divorced father Stan making a concession, by stating he's willing to cut in half the number of Thursdays he has each month to visit with his children.

Excerpt 5.12 Joint Custody West Coast Family Mediation, p. 92
              (Garcia 1995: 32)

```
2145  Stan:  Theh- twi:ns said well- (.) what happened duh Thursdays they-
2146         >you know they< speciFically brought that up tuh me and I said
2147         well?, .hh (0.3) 'looks like Mom wants to spend more time >with
2148         you (tw[o)< s ]o .hh if:: y[ou kno]w you wanna do Thu:rsday,
2149  Med:         [(Yeah)]           [(Right)]
2150  Stan:  Friday one week, and then: just uh Friday thuh next week?, (0.2) .h
2151         That's: (0.1) is compromising u[h little b] it?,
```

Stan characterizes his suggestion as a compromise (line 2151). A few minutes later the mediator paraphrases Stan's offer in an utterance directed to Karen (Excerpt 5.13, lines 2275–2278, 2282–2283).

Excerpt 5.13 Joint Custody West Coast Family Mediation, p. 97
              (Garcia 1995: 32)

```
2275  Med:    And then (0.1) what I hear, is thuh la:st month or so:, (0.2) it's
2276          been every other .hh (0.2) uh Thursday?, (0.3) And the::n (0.4)
2277          (but) that next wee:k is u::h (0.2) for thuh Friday?, (0.3)
2278          a[nd you're not ] wi:lling
2279  Stan:   [(Its been like)]
2280          (0.2)
2281  Karen:  Uh-=
2282  Med:       =to: (0.2) he's willing to relinquish!, (0.2) he used thuh word.
2283          .hh °u:hm (0.4) >one of those< (Fridays).
2284          (0.4)
2285  Stan:   No=
2286  Med:       =Instead of making it cons[iste]nt I MEAN THURSDAYS!
2287  Stan:                              [No ]
2288          (.)
```

```
2289  Stan:   Thursdays ri:ght.
2290          (0.2)
2291  Med:    Instead uh [mak]ing it °(I jus')
2292  Stan:              [I- ]
2293          (0.1)
2294  Stan:   I'm I'm willing tuh go along with thuh schedule that she said
2295          just tuh keep, (0.2) thuh [status] quo: and (0.3) you know?, (0.2)
2296  Med:                              [°(  )]
2297  Stan:   keep (.) keep her HAppy that she's: you know?,=
2298  Med:                                            =°Um=hmh
2299          (0.5)
2300  Med:    He's offering thuh two: (0.3) Thurs°day (0.3) °night.
```

By reformulating Stan's offer, the mediator simultaneously represents his position in a direct exchange with the opposing disputant (his ex-wife Karen), while also making changes that might bridge the gap between the two disputants and help them move toward agreement. Specifically, the mediator reformulates what Stan had referred to as a "compromise" in Excerpt 5.12 above (line 1251) to a statement in Excerpt 5.13 that Stan is "willing to relinquish" two Thursdays a month of visitation (line 2282). The implications of these two formulations are quite different. Stan's formulation of the offer as a "compromise" implies that he is meeting Karen half way, while the mediator's formulation of relinquishment implies that Stan is giving something up for Karen. This reformulation implies a greater level of self-sacrifice than was implied by his original statement.

This exchange is followed by a side sequence (Jefferson 1972) in which Stan and the mediator correct her mistaken reference to Fridays (Excerpt 5.13, lines 2285–2289).

Stan then restates his offer and adds an explanation of why he is making the offer (lines 2294–2295, 2297). Stan thus avoids directly challenging the mediator's reformulation of his offer, while at the same time revising it. In this reformulation Stan foregoes his original use of the term compromise and instead states that he is "willing to go along with the schedule that she said" (line 2294). The mediator again reformulates Stan's proposal in a way that indicates Stan is giving something up for Karen ("He's offering thuh two: (0.3) Thurs°day"; line 2300).

After some discussion of other issues, the participants return to a discussion of the Thursday visitations. The mediator again represents Stan by speaking in his place and reformulating his proposal.

Excerpt 5.14 Joint Custody West Coast Family Mediation, p. 103
(Garcia 1995: 33)

```
2398  Med:    [And HE IS]WILLing?, (0.2) tuh give up? (0.6)
2399          T[WO: of        ] those Thursdays!
2400  Karen:  [Two Thursdays]
```

```
2401          (0.3)
2402 Karen:   I know.
2403          (0.7)
2404 Med:     Number one I heard it (0.2) to make it consistent for thuh
2405          children!, (0.3) and (0.3) that that would please you!
2406          (8.1)
2407 Karen:   I'll jus': (0.2 ) I'll do it, just tuh meet him half way!,
```

In this reformulation of Stan's proposal the mediator again emphasizes that Stan is giving up visitation time (Excerpt 5.14, lines 2398–2399). Karen's acknowledgment of this reformulation is unenthusiastic and does not constitute either an acceptance or a rejection of the proposal (line 2402). The mediator then extends her representation of Stan's offer, by paraphrasing the reasons Stan has given to justify his proposal (lines 2404–2405). Karen's acceptance of the offer (in line 2407) is markedly unenthusiastic; note also the extended pause in line 2406. In spite of the mediator's work to revise and reformulate Stan's proposal to reframe it as him making a concession to Karen, Karen apparently does not experience it as a "gift," and instead feels that she is the one giving up something for him ("I'll do it, just tuh meet him half way!,"; line 2407).

Taken together, these examples illustrate the mediator's construction, conveyance, and reformulation of Stan's proposal in an attempt to resolve one of the issues under dispute. This mediator does not simply repeat his proposal, she works to present and represent it in ways that may be acceptable to the opposing disputant. While no guarantee that these reformulations will lead to resolution of an issue, revoicing a disputant's position to the opposing disputant may help transform the debate. While revoicing can be a constructive part of the dispute resolution process, it also has implications for the degree of autonomy disputants experience during mediation.

Mediator representation of a disputant's position is also a feature of the divorce and family mediation sessions. At times a mediator goes beyond representing a disputant's interests or stated positions and engages in "coaching" a disputant to get them to adjust their perspective. Coaching is also used to advise disputants by example as to how they could handle a problem. In Excerpts 5.15 and 5.16, the mediator works to represent Bob's position to his partner Kate. Bob has previously conveyed that he is uncomfortable when Kate goes out to dance clubs without him.

Excerpt 5.15 Bob and Kate Midwest Family Mediation, Session 2, p. 90

```
1953 Bob:  [>I mean< ih- and  ] 'ere's even uh r- uh reason? for my feeling
1954       °there.° like I've told you that- h. (0.5) if you wanted tuh go w:atch
1955       men str strip at uh bar where there's al- mostly (0.3) women!
1956       (0.5) watching these men? °That's not personal tuh me.° .h (0.5)
1957       But. (0.5) tuh go to uh place where people are mingling and
```

1958   dancing! (0.5) And I <u>know</u> for uh <u>fact</u> you're gonna be <u>hit</u> on?
1959   (0.4) umpteen <u>times</u> through thuh <u>night</u>! (0.6) And and and (0.3)
1960   thuh things that you wear when you go out? (0.4) That <u>bothers</u> me.

In Excerpt 5.15, Bob tries to explain why he does not object to Kate going out without him (lines 1953–1956), but that he is concerned with her going out to dance clubs without him (lines 1957–1960). Excerpt 5.16 shows Kate's response and Mediator A's intervention. The mediator revoices Bob's expressed position to Kate (in lines 1963–1964). She challenges Kate about the clothes she wears when going out dancing: "that's uh whole different story °though Kate.°". Kate then complains about Bob's criticisms of how she dresses (lines 1966, 1968). Mediator A then asks a question which works to clarify the problematic nature of her behavior (lines 1969–1970).

Excerpt 5.16 Bob and Kate Midwest Family Mediation, Session 2, p. 90

1961   (0.4)
1962 Kate: °Oh he hates [it if I wea-°   ]
1963 MA: [Okay >well see now< THAT'S?] (0.3) that's uh
1964   whole different story °though Kate.°
1965   (0.2)
1966 Kate: He hates if I wea:r? short skir:t? or (0.6) °any[thing!°]
1967 Bob: [Sure!]
1968 Kate: He just has uh fit.=
1969 MA: =D' you wear those >kind things when yuh
1970   go out< with Bob?
1971   (0.2)
1972 Kate: Oh <u>yeah</u>! (0.3) I mean ih- it has nothing tuh do with °oh! because
1973   I'm goin' out tuh shake my booty!° .h (0.4) <u>I</u> have always
1974   dressed? (0.4) I mean I have <u>always</u> dressed that wa:y? I dress
1975   that way with <u>him</u>? (0.4) with my ex-husband? I <u>dressed</u>. (0.4) that
1976   way? I never? (0.9) differentiated between any occasion o:r?
1977   situa[tion.]
1978 MA: [But] can you hear what Bob is saying about (0.7) <u>why</u> he
1979   feels differently? (0.3) if you're goin' to uh <u>bar</u>? than if you're
1980   (0.3) °goin' somewhere else?°
1981   (0.2)
1982 Kate: °Yea[h? ° I und   er]stand? But I just >feel like if you< °then
1983 MA: [or goin' danc-]
1984 Kate: you're just gon' have tuh get [over it.°]
1985 MA: [But he's] also sayin' (0.6) if there's
1986   alcohol? your inhibitions are <u>lowered</u>? And people do things that
1987   they'd <u>never do</u>! without (0.2) °couple drinks.°
1988   (0.5)
1989 Kate: °°Yeah! I think that's true.°°
1990   (0.2)
1991 Bob: And it happens? °And it and it it° hurts uh lot uh °relationships!°=

When Kate denies dressing differently when she goes out with Bob (lines 1972–1977), the mediator again intervenes to represent Bob's position (lines 1978–1980, 1983, 1985–1987). Kate finally acknowledges the truth of at least part of Bob's position, after Mediator A's final representation of it in this exchange ("°°Yeah! I think that's true.°°", line 1989). Mediator A's advocacy of Bob's position thus builds on his actual statements but goes beyond them in order to successfully challenge Kate to help her to see how Bob's position makes sense. This use of "revoicing" was successful in furthering the disputants' understanding of each person's positions.

In sum, the excerpts above have shown how a mediator can productively engage in an exchange with the opposing disputant on the original disputant's behalf. When "revoicing" disputants' positions, mediators restate and rephrase the disputant's previously expressed positions, and may also elaborate them. This type of mediation work involves representation of disputant's expressed positions, although often in a new or refocused way. However, mediators in these data at times go beyond revoicing disputant's expressed positions to replacing them in an exchange with the opposing disputant. Mediator replacement of the disputant is discussed in the next section.

Mediator "Replacement" of the Opposing Disputant

When a mediator's representation of a disputant's position is more extensive than revoicing (representing a disputant's expressed positions), the mediator replaces the disputant in an exchange with the opposing disputant. Replacement involves the mediator in creating their own arguments in support of the disputant's position, thereby acting more as a principal in the dispute rather than as a representative of a disputant. In the three mediation programs analyzed in this book, mediators at times went beyond paraphrasing or revoicing a disputant's stated position and instead replaced them in an oppositional exchange with the opposing disputant.

Replacement in Small Claims Mediation

The following excerpt illustrates how mediator replacement of a disputant in an exchange with the opposing disputant differs from revoicing. The complainant (Sheila) had agreed to buy a used car being sold by the respondent (Ted). After discovering that the title to the car was not in Ted's name, Sheila backed out of the deal. As Excerpt 5.17 begins, the mediator asks Ted why he refused to return Sheila's deposit.

Excerpt 5.17 Midwest Data, Car Deposit Small Claims Mediation, p. 13

270 Med: [Ju]st so what I'm (base,) ehm WHY didn't you redo- (0.4) 'turn
271   thuh deposit?
272   (0.5)
273 Ted: Becau:se! that's: that's (0.4) thuh NAture of uh uh uh down
274   payment or uh deposit. (0.6) you know? (0.3) >Which ever you
275   wanna< call it. (0.3) .h (0.2) It's money that you pa:y, so uh car
276   can be ho:ld, >so you have< thuh option tuh buy it. (1.4) They
277   had [their option (tuh)]
278 Med: [You say you o]:h ka:y?,=
279 Ted: =for uh good th[at whi:le   ]
280 Med: [(WELL) TH]AT
281   PART? (0.6) bu- (1.1) tch when something doesn't come- occu:r?,
282   thuhm- (0.4) th' 'POsit's usually returned? isn't it?
283 Ted: No. (1.0) >I mean just well they just opted not to buy thuh car!
284   (0.3) There was no problem with it. .h And I had every=
285 Med: =WHY?,
286   (0.3) WHY should she just give you two hundred dollars?=

The mediator's questions seek to clarify Ted's opening statement and his
position on the issues under dispute. However, many of the mediator's questions also challenge Ted's position that he should not have to return Sheila's
deposit. For example, while the mediator's question in lines 270–271 is informational (he asks Ted why he did not return Sheila's deposit), his question
in lines 280–282 suggests that Ted's position is wrong. After Ted disagrees
with that position (lines 283–284), the mediator asks a challenging question
("=WHY?, (0.3) WHY should she just give you two hundred dollars?="; lines
285–286). Note that the mediator spoke loudly and interrupted Ted before he
had reached a transition relevance place in his utterance.

The mediator has replaced Sheila in this exchange, and argued with Ted
on her behalf. While the mediator is still representing Sheila's interests, he
goes beyond paraphrasing, restating, or revoicing her expressed positions. The
mediator's questions seek clarification of Ted's positions and simultaneously
challenge Ted's position on Sheila's behalf. Rather than acting as an intermediary between the two disputants and facilitating their discussion of the
issues, the mediator is taking the place of a disputant and arguing in her place.

Excerpt 5.18 also shows how mediator replacement of a disputant differs
from revoicing. The two former roommates, Kris and Kurt, are in disagreement
over who should pay an electric bill. Kris has been billed for $122 because the
electricity account was in her name. After much discussion of the issues with
neither side willing to budge on their position that the other person should pay
the bill, the mediator asks Kris why the bill is worth fighting over (Excerpt 5.18):

Excerpt 5.18 Electric Bill Midwest Small Claims Mediation, p. 225

```
691  Med:  [May I      ] ask you uh question, Kris? (0.6) um (1.3) tch tch (0.9)
692         um (1.2) tch >lemme think about< how I'm gonna word this. (0.8)
693         °um° (1.0) uh HUNdred and twenty (0.2) two dollars: (0.3) seems
694         like uh drop in thuh bucket? (0.6) compa:red? (0.5) tuh thuh
695         money that you each exchanged (0.5) tuh one another. (0.5) .h I
696         mean uh (0.5) John says he paid rent? (0.4) for thuh- place while
697         Kurt was living there for uh while?, (0.6) .h You say that you: (0.3)
698         basically supported? (0.5) John for: (0.4) uh year?, (0.4) .h uh
699         hhundred! and twenty two dollars, seems real minor? (0.9) in thuh
700         whole scheme uh things. (1.8) um-
701         (0.6)
702  Kris:  >I WAS ON< (0.4) I was on welfare.
703         (0.3)
704  Med:   [°Okay]
705  Kris:  [UNti:l] .h (0.4) I became employed thuh same time John did in
706         September? of: (0.3) ninety three. (0.4) .h We both got our jobs on
707         thee exact same day.
708         (0.7)
709  Med:   So are you saying you are unABLE? tuh pay thuh hundred
710         [and twenty two?]
711  Kris:  [I WAS          ] paying my apartment? (0.9) and (0.3) I had gas
712         and electric?, I had thuh phone bill, (0.4) .h y'know? I had things
713         tuh pay at my own apartment? and I was TRYING TUH HELP
714         Kurt out as much as I could.
```

The mediator's replacement of John works to challenge Kris's position. Her use of a presequence ("May I ask you uh question, Kris?"; line 691) frames her question-to-come as a predelicate and gets the floor to present background information leading up to her implied question (Schegloff 1980). She does not actually ask the question, because Kris begins defending her position on line 702 before the mediator has explicitly asked her why she doesn't just pay the bill herself. The mediator has thus presented an argument in favor of John's position, that Kris should pay the bill. However, it is replacement rather than revoicing because although John has presented several arguments for why Kris should pay the bill, he has not used this argument. The mediator is creating an argument on his behalf in this exchange with Kris.

Replacement in Divorce Mediation

While mediator replacement of a disputant also occurs in the divorce mediation sessions, it is typically done differently than it is in small claims mediation. Excerpts 5.19–5.21 from Bob and Kate's family mediation illustrate mediator representation and replacement of disputants. Bob and Kate are in mediation to work on problems in their relationship, and between the second and third mediation sessions, they decided to get married. One of the challenges they face in their relationship is that Bob's parents are highly prejudiced against Kate (Bob is white and Kate is African American). In Excerpt 5.19 the mediator represents and replaces Bob in an exchange with his partner Kate about these issues.

Excerpt 5.19 Bob and Kate Midwest Family Mediation, Session 3, p. 105

```
2267  Kate:  [and white mixin'] by thuh ti[me I was do]ne! I bit my tongue out
2268  Bob:                          [Initially?    ]
2269  Kate:  uh respect for you. And see when I think about tho:se? (0.6) When
2270         I think about (0.4) thuh times that I will: (0.6) >that I had< (0.5)
2271         BIT! my tongue and kept my mouth shut or I've gone! and been
2272         supportive, .h an:d I don't feel like I: am being supported, (0.5)
2273         then I've reached and then I say, then, piss on >all of it.< I'm
2274         [not   ]
2275  MA:    [Well?] (0.6) NOW Bob is goin' to his parents sayin' (2.4) this is
2276         what's gonna happen. (0.3) Kate's comin' into our family, she's
2277         gonna be my wife, (0.6) I'm asking you to accept that. (1.4) So if
2278         they come into your [home,  ]
2279  Kate:                      [CHUH!] CHUH! chuh!
2280         (0.3)
2281  MA:    they're- >they can only< come in there! (0.8) Bob is telling them,
2282         these are thuh rules! (0.3) You can only come in there (0.5) if you
2283         accept my wife! (0.3) And if you treat her with deference and
2284         respect! and hopefully with love some day!
2285         (2.3)
2286  Kate:  Well I'd like° (0.4) °(for that.)°
```

Mediator A interrupts Kate's angry self-representation of her feelings about the problem with Bob's parents in order to represent Bob's side (e.g., lines 2275–2278, 2281–2284). Mediator A not only summarizes the upshot of what Bob has said earlier in the session, she puts words in his mouth, in effect replacing him in this exchange with Kate. Mediator A at the same time coaches Bob on what he could say to his parents when he has the conversation about these issues with them.

As the exchange continues, Mediator A asks Bob if she is "misinterpreting" him (Excerpt 5.20, line 2288); Bob's reply confirms that she has accurately summarized his position (line 2290).

Excerpt 5.20 Bob and Kate Midwest Family Mediation, Session 3, p. 105

```
2287         (1.3)
2288  MA:    eh- Am I misinterpreting you?
2289         (0.3)
2290  Bob:   No? (1.1) °No.°
2291         (3.6)
2292  MA:    It's not going to be easy? for you, Kate, to accept them: into your
```

```
2293        house?, but
2294        (0.4)
2295  Kate: No? a[nd I ] won't right away. (0.3) I mean I'm jus:t bein'
2296  MA:        [that's]
2297  Kate: hones:t. (0.7) I mean, (0.7) y'know? (0.4) He has empathy and
2298        sympathy for them, feels sorry for them, understands their position,
2299        well hey baby you've got tuh understand my position too right
2300        [now!]
2301  Bob:  [And I] do.
2302        (0.3)
2303  Kate: And that is I will not be open. (0.4) to. (0.5) [(          )]
```

Mediator A not only represents Bob's position and replaces him in this exchange with Kate, she also openly aligns with Bob (Excerpt 5.21, lines 2304–2314). By referring to Bob and the mediators as "we" when she says "maybe we're pushin' you too far too soon, Kate." (lines 2304–2305), Mediator A aligns with Bob and supports his side of the conflict when taking his place:

Excerpt 5.21 Bob and Kate Midwest Family Mediation, Session 3, p. 105

```
2304  MA:                              [Okay well] maybe
2305        we're pushin' you too far too soon, Kate. And (0.4) I guess (0.3)
2306        right now (0.4) we have Bob sayin' .h (0.6) he's gonna go talk to
2307        his parents. (0.2) [Maybe    ] tomorrow night, as soon as possible.
2308  Kate:                   [°Mm hm.°]
2309  MA:   (0.6) Tell them (1.2) this is thuh plan. (1.1) u:m (0.5) ASKing? for
2310        their (0.4) support. (0.4) Asking them to: (0.6) treat you (0.4) with
2311        respect and deference. (1.1) Hopefully love will (0.4) come in
2312        time. (2.7) I guess: (0.9) it is pretty unfair to ask you. tuh be
2313        willing to take (0.4) another step right away. (0.6) Maybe we need
2314        to see (0.4) how they respond!
```

Mediator A again speaks on behalf of Bob, representing him in her direct exchange with Kate. Mediator A's intervention also begins with a "we" statement which creates an alignment with Bob (lines 2304–2307).

In sum, mediator representation of a disputant through replacement goes beyond paraphrasing, summarizing, or revoicing a disputant's stated position. When replacing a disputant, a mediator represents the interests of a disputant in a direct exchange with an opposing disputant and effectively argues in his or her place. In the small claims mediation sessions replacement involved a bilateral exchange between the mediator and the opposing disputant, while in the divorce mediation sessions replacement was more complex. At times both disputants participated in the discussion, and at times the mediator formed an alliance with one disputant in an effort to convince the opposing disputant of his or her side of the debate. Mediators also combined advocacy with coaching, at times modeling or directly instructing disputants on how to handle problems they were facing.

Implications of Replacement for Dispute Resolution

When replacing a disputant in an exchange with the opposing disputant, the mediator risks violating the neutrality of the mediation process. Some mediators managed this concern by balancing their treatment of both disputants, first replacing one disputant and then the other, thus alternately supporting both sides of the dispute. There are varied opinions as to whether this is an effective method of supporting disputants while attempting to remain neutral. In this section I first discuss some instances in which replacement of the disputant has clear implications for disputant autonomy, and then discuss how replacement is tied to fairness in mediation more generally.

Replacement and Disputant Autonomy

One of the problems with mediator replacement of a disputant in an exchange with the opposing disputant is that the disputant must defend their position against two individuals – the mediator and the disputant he or she is representing. This may diminish the autonomy of both disputants; the replaced disputant because he or she is no longer self-representing, and the opposing disputant because there is now more pressure to defend his or her position.

For example, Excerpts 5.22–5.24 are from the dispute between an auto repair shop and a customer who believed that his vehicle was repaired incorrectly. As Excerpt 5.22 begins, Dan reissues a previous complaint, that the "water pump" in his vehicle was leaking (lines 1097–1099). He reminds the participants that this problem was not discovered until he had left the vehicle at the shop, and implies that a shop employee could have caused the problem ("Somebody could uh WHACKed it with uh HAMmer for all I: know!"; lines 1098–1099).

Excerpt 5.22 Vehicle Repair West Coast Small Claims Mediation, p. 48 (Garcia 1995: 38)

```
1097 Dan:  .hh We're A:lso forgetting thuh WAter pump was not leaking
1098        when I brought it in there! (0.5) Somebody could uh
1099        WHACKed it with uh HAMmer for all I: know!
1100        (0.1)
1101 MA:   °(Who [cares? and and you coulduh broken two] minutes
1102 Dan:        [(I don't                            )]
1103 MA:   after you drove outtah thuh gar[age   ]
1104 ?:                          [°(       )]
1105 RA?:                         [(       )]=
1106 MA:                              =Nobody's ever going to be
1107        able to decide when it cracked.
1108        (.)
1109 MA:   I'm not saying this is what you should accept I'm just saying
```

```
1110        [(          )]
1111  Dan:  [(          )] I've met mechanics tellin' me that uh water pump
1112        hou:sing, (0.1) on thuh {Car Brand} (0.5) NE::ver (0.2)
1113        cr[ack. ]
1114  MA:     [°(Um]hmh) (0.5) °Um [hmh.]
```

In this excerpt, Mediator A replaces the repair shop's representatives (Respondents A and B) and challenges Dan's position on their behalf (lines 1101, 1103, 1106–1107). Notice that Mediator A's first response is placed very quickly after Dan's statement, and begins with a strong challenge of it: "°(Who [cares? . . ." (line 1101). Mediator A uses repetition ("and and" to hold the floor during Dan's interruption of this utterance. He also challenges Dan's position that the dealership broke his vehicle's water pump housing ("and and you coulduh broken two] minutes after you drove outtah thuh gar[age]"; lines 1101 and 1103). Rather than repeating or paraphrasing an argument previously made by one of the respondents, Mediator A creates his own argument, thus replacing the respondents in this exchange with Dan. This approach challenges the assumption that mediators will display neutrality and support the autonomy of the disputants.

In this mediation hearing, Dan expressed his dissatisfaction with the proposed solution to the dispute. This suggests that mediator replacement of a disputant's self-representation can lead to forced agreements. In this case, at least one of the disputants is not satisfied with the agreement that was reached.

Excerpt 5.23 Vehicle Repair West Coast Small Claims Mediation, p. 72 (Garcia 1995: 38)

```
1643  Dan:  .hh hhh I'M not HA:PPY with >it at a:ll!,< (1.2) Well I mean
1644        there's GOT tuh be some, (0.2) Some RE:course for people who
1645        don't know any better, (.) that- take vehicles tuh people, and (0.4)
1646        this- (.) they let 'em go out like that.
1647        (2.5)
1648  Dan:  They had it uh week and uh ha:lf, they had thuh vehicle.
```

A few minutes later, Dan discovers he will have to pay about $400 more for the repairs than he had hoped. Dan continues arguing in favor of a lower bill (not shown), but both Mediators A and B continue replacing the respondents and arguing in their place. Dan then agrees to pay the amount they are recommending. Excerpt 5.24 shows that although he agrees with the proposed resolution, he does so only reluctantly:

Excerpt 5.24 Vehicle Repair West Coast Small Claims Mediation, p. 74 (Garcia 1995: 38)

```
1695  Dan:  Well I guess I have no other recourse!, (0.1) basically, (2.8) so-
1696        >pay it up< and uh=
```

In sum, although the mediators were able to get Dan to agree to the solution they supported, he did so only reluctantly, and with explicitly stated reservations. When replacing a disputant in a negotiation with the opposing disputant, the mediator represents their interests more directly than when simply paraphrasing or revoicing their stated positions. The mediator is negotiating instead of the disputant, rather than merely representing what that disputant has expressed. When mediators represent a disputant by replacing him or her in an exchange, they also intervene in the opposing disputant's self-representation, by challenging that disputant's positions. The opposing disputant may be led to change their position, or their justification for their position, as a result of this mediator intervention.

Replacement and Implications for Fairness

While the greatest degree of disputant autonomy in these mediation hearings occurs when disputants represent themselves, there are no instances of pure self-representation in these mediation hearings because disputants' actions are constructed within the speech exchange system of mediation. By such actions as addressing their remarks to the mediator rather than the opposing disputant, waiting to speak until offered the floor by a mediator, and referring to the opposing disputant in the third person, the disputant exercises their autonomy in a structured and somewhat constrained setting.

The types of mediator representation of disputants' positions analyzed in this chapter involve varying degrees of engagement. When mediators represent disputant's positions though paraphrasing, summarizing, or drawing upshots, they reproduce most closely what the disputant actually said. However, even restating or rephrasing a disputant's position may change the message produced by the disputant. For example, the mediator may choose to convey only parts of a disputant's position in their restatement, or they may reformulate it. Mediators' restatements of disputant's positions and offers thus may have implications for the autonomy of the disputants.

When representing a disputant's position in a direct exchange with an opposing disputant, mediators may revoice what the disputant actually said or go beyond revoicing to replace a disputant in the negotiation process. These actions may also impact the autonomy of disputants and may potentially affect their perceptions of the fairness of the mediation process.

While mediator actions such as replacing a disputant in a discussion of the issues can lessen disputant autonomy, there are also potential negative consequences when mediators choose not to intervene. Fairness in mediation has to do not just with how the process of mediation is conducted, but with the fairness of the resolution that is created (Frenkel and Stark 2012). For example, if a divorcing couple were to decide to split expenses equally, that decision may be fair or unfair depending on the equality of their incomes and other circumstances. Excerpt 5.25 serves to illustrate this situation. Just before this excerpt begins, the divorcing couple had been engaged in a discussion of the details of the parenting plan they are creating for their daughter Bethany. Jon had offered to pay the health insurance premiums for their daughter through his workplace insurance policy. As the excerpt begins, Jon states that any health care costs not covered by insurance would be split between him and his wife (lines 672–675).

Excerpt 5.25 Jon and Liz Midwest Divorce Mediation, Session 2, p. 31

```
672  Jon:   [>But what I'm sayin'< whatever! WHATEVER TH-] POLICY
673          does cover? (0.6) .h (0.5) >Thee uninsur-< are guess °ee uh-°
674          (0.7) °de- °>I guess-<° >whatever thee insurance< doesn't cover
675          >that we wou[ld< spl     ]it!
676  MA:                [°°Mm hm?°°]
677  MA?:   (0.7) Okay. (1.1) .h NOW?
678          (0.1)
679  MB:    °uh Nonreimbursed medical [expen]se is° °°is
680  MA:                              [Right.]
681  MB:    how you'd°° (0.4) °°call i[t ye    ]ah.°°
682  MA:                             [°Right.°]
683          (1.3)
684  MA:    .h SO: UM >IF YOU HAD UH PLAN< WHERE (1.4) .h uh
685          >she went tuh thuh< DOCTOR'S >AND IT WAS UH< SIXTY
686          DOLLAR BILL? (1.1) And you turned that in? and they covered
687          eighty percent.
688          (0.4)
689  Jon:   Mm hm?
690          (1.4)
691  MA:    tch .h um (0.8) Thee remainder? (1.4) you'd split (0.5) evenly
692          there.
693          (0.7)
694  Jon:   °°Right.°°
695          (0.4)
696  MA:    M[ight th]ere be uh deductible also?
697  Jon:    [Becah-]
698          (1.2)
699  Jon:   W[ell we- >I would th-<] >I would think that thuh< deductible
700  MA:     [uh yearly deduh-     ]
701  Jon:   would also be °uh° (0.5) split.
```

After John's statement that he and his wife will share the health expenses (lines 672–675) the mediators join the discussion and ask questions to clarify which medical expenses will be shared. Mediator A introduces the topic of the co-pays and deductibles for their insurance plan (lines 684–687,

691–692, 696). Jon reports that the couple has agreed to split those costs as well (lines 694, 699, and 701). Note that while splitting the medical costs between the spouses sounds fair, whether it is in fact fair depends on how much each spouse earns. The mediators do not raise the issue of fairness or have the spouses discuss their respective incomes and expenses. Jon currently holds two jobs, while Liz babysits children in her home. This is an instance in which a mediator's intervention might have been helpful to at least consider whether one spouse would be disadvantaged by an equal splitting of expenses. In short, mediator replacement of Liz in this exchange might have elicited information necessary to ascertain whether the proposed equal splitting of these costs was indeed fair, even though Liz did not raise this issue herself.

Some argue that even if a specific disputant's proposal or position is being handled in a way that may not seem fair, the mediation process can still be fair overall and can still lead to a good result (Frenkel and Stark 2012). For example, in the third session of the Mike and Kelly divorce mediation the mediators may have missed an opportunity for constructive replacement of a disputant when Mike gave Kelly an ultimatum. He declared that unless a parenting agreement that he was comfortable with was worked out in the next fifteen to twenty minutes of the mediation session, he would "let thuh court decide° °°thuh custody.°°" (Excerpt 5.26, lines 352–356).

Excerpt 5.26 Mike and Kelly Midwest Divorce Mediation, Session 3, p. 16

```
328  MA:    D' you have uh (0.4) uh parenting plan worked out? (0.4) or
329         d'[you  ] need tuh-
330  Mike:  [°No.°]
331         (0.3)
332  MB:    °(That's thuh best [thing we do uh)°]
333  MA:                       [tuh walk through] uh pa[rentin-]
334  Mike:                                            [Thi  ]s: (2.0)
335         thee only thing? (2.0) and I'm sorry I'm still not comfortable?
336         (0.3) with that situation. °And this is not° tuh be hurtful °because
337         I have° (0.1) weighed this situation over? .h (0.4) This is not tuh
338         be: .h (0.5) hh! (0.7) resentful? This is not: (0.5) uh way of getting
339         even or getting back? (0.3) or any of those things? (0.7) °u:m°
340         (1.0) Kelly is thuh mother of my children? (0.4) A:nd (1.5) I do
341         not want tuh take those- children? (0.5) away? (0.2) from her.
342         (0.9) >But thuh situation< that I've come to and and (1.5) I don't
343         want this (0.6) I als- >and I know< (0.6) >whatever it comes out-<
344         of- (0.5) where we're goin' now .h (0.5) I don't want this tuh
345         change thuh situation tuh where that- I can (0.9) >come tuh thuh<
346         house. >°And 'at we can< still be civil and 'ose things.° .h (0.3)
347         °And it's not meant° °for her tuh be angry with me, and I'm not
348         doin' this out of anger towards her?° (0.9) °uh° at all?
349         (0.1)
```

```
350  MB:    W' what is it, specifically °that you're° (0.2) (working
351         [with)   ]
352  Mike:  [Bottom] li:ne °is that-° (1.1) °I-° (1.7) unless >we can come tuh
353         some< other agreement? (1.0) >within thuh next< (0.6) °fifteen
354         tuh twenty minutes?° (1.0) °u:m° (1.3) °An':° (0.8) °on:
355         parenting?° (0.2) °Then then I'm gonna let thuh court decide°
356         °°thuh custody.°°
```

While Mike claims that he is not acting out of anger toward his wife, Kelly
(see lines 347–348), he clearly takes a strong stand and demands more rights
and control over the children than he currently has. He presents an ultimatum
(lines 352–356) in which he gives a time limit of fifteen to twenty minutes for
Kelly to agree to what he wants (custody of the children). If an agreement that
he is comfortable with is not reached in that time frame, he will "let thuh court
decide° °°thuh custody.°°"; lines 355–356). In other words, he will no longer
be willing to negotiate custody in mediation.

Instead of responding directly to Mike's ultimatum or criticizing it as
coercive, Mediator A continues to facilitate the discussion of parenting issues
(Excerpt 5.27, lines 358, 360, and 363). Note that while on the surface Mediator A ignores Mike's ultimatum and his demand to have custody of the
children, Mediator A's very first move subtly reasserts Kelly's agency in these
decisions by asking what "you both (0.6) want."; (line 358).

Excerpt 5.27 Mike and Kelly Midwest Divorce Mediation, Session 3, p. 16

```
358  MA:    >W' what is it< that you both (0.6) want. (0.3) What d' you [want]
359  Mike:                                                            [hh! ]
360  MA:    Mike.
361         (1.3)
362  Mike:  I nee:[d?  ]
363  MA:          [Wh]at >kind of uh plan.=
364  Mike:                            =What (0.5) thee only thing >that I
365         can< come up with .h (0.9) that I'm comfortable °with.° (0.3) And
366         that is .h (1.3) that as far as aye custody? h (0.5) or uh parental
367         right. (0.6) of thuh children. (0.9) that (0.8) I retain that. (0.5) And
368         that? (1.0) visitation can be extremely liberal. (0.8) And >that I
369         would still?< (0.4) be willin' tuh pay (1.1) an amount of support.
370         (1.1) °u:m° (0.8) >that we could< figure out. (0.8) going? (1.1)
371         towards her. (1.0) °'til° (1.1) things or whatever! (0.6) that's
372         straightened out? (0.3) But I'm not comfortable with? .h (0.7) not
373         having (1.1) thee: (0.4) strict parental (acts) right now.
374         (0.7)
375  MB:    [Y- ] (0.4) you're [uncomfortable with         ] sharing parent
376  MA:    [So-]              [REGARDLESS what thuh plan]
377  MB:    thing.
378         (0.6)
```

379 Mike: >°Not at this< moment, I'm >sorry? and at's:°< (0.4) I? (0.4)
380   y'know I- (1.0) °I thought° boy thee easy way out is >tuh do thuh<
381   shared °parenting?° .h (0.7) And (0.9) in my head?
382   [and in my mind though]
383 MB: [What is, what is   ] so har:d °about doing °thee other part.°

While Mediator A addresses her question in line 358 to both parents, Kelly does not immediately respond. Mediator A then solicits Mike's perspective (lines 358, 360, and 363). Mike explains his position, which is that he should have legal and physical custody of the children (lines 364–373).

The mediators have effectively ignored Mike's ultimatum. Instead, they continued the work of the session by discussing the issues related to the parenting plan. By the end of the fourth mediation session, the spouses have worked out a parenting plan that both are comfortable with and that gives them equal time with the children. The mediators' joint decision to ignore Mike's ultimatum in the third mediation session was a judgment call, and seems to have been the right one in this case.

In short, even though it may appear in a particular instance that the mediators have not dealt with a situation adequately or have failed to represent the interests of both disputants, the mediation process as a whole is not necessarily unfair. However, it could also be argued that this is an instance in which the mediators should have replaced Kelly in the interaction and represented her interests for her in a direct exchange with Mike.

Discussion and Conclusions

Mediators in these data used a variety of techniques to represent disputants' positions in small claims and divorce mediation sessions. Mediators summarized or paraphrased disputants' statements in order to refocus the discussion, articulate the main point of the story or main areas of disagreement, highlight common ground between the disputants, or serve as a liaison between opposing disputants. At times mediators went beyond direct representation of a disputant's statements to revoicing their expressed positions for them in an exchange with the opposing disputant. A more extreme form of representation involved actually replacing a disputant in a direct exchange with the opposing disputant, and creating arguments on their behalf rather than revoicing previously stated positions.

In the divorce mediation sessions, these different forms of representation also occurred, and in addition the mediators sometimes worked to instruct or coach disputants in how they might handle the problems under discussion. Another difference between the small claims and the divorce mediation sessions is that divorce mediators often worked to reframe the dispute between the spouses as a problem they all (the spouses and the mediators) needed to work together to solve.

This investigation of mediator representation of disputant's positions in small claims and divorce mediation has highlighted the problematics of mediator representation of disputants in terms of the goals of achieving disputant autonomy and mediator neutrality. Recall that in facilitative mediation, mediators are supposed to refrain from engaging in the substance of the dispute and instead focus on their roles as facilitators of the interaction. However, the more intrusive forms of mediator representation found in these data, especially replacement but to some extent also revoicing, may put the mediator in the position of extending or creating arguments in support of the disputant's position that they have not previously articulated. Mediator replacement of a disputant literally puts words in their mouth rather than assisting disputants to speak for themselves.

Mediators believe that compliance with mediated agreements is generally greater when disputants create their own agreement rather than having a third party make a decision for them.[6] The use of the replacement type of representation may therefore be problematic for mediation if it reduces satisfaction with and therefore compliance with mediated agreements.[7] The use of more intrusive types of representation may also decrease satisfaction with mediation if doubts about the mediator's neutrality are introduced through these actions.[8]

Paraphrasing can contribute to the dispute resolution process by allowing the mediator to reframe or reformulate a disputant's position to be more acceptable to the opposing disputant or to increase understanding of the other's perspective. In addition, mediator representation of disputants can be effective in cases where there is a high degree of conflict between the disputants, because disputants may be more willing to listen to the perspective of the opposing disputant when filtered through the voice of the mediator. Representation can also be one way that mediators may help balance the power of the disputants, by helping them formulate and convey their positions to the other disputant.[9]

However, problems often arose in these data when mediators replaced disputants in exchanges rather than limiting themselves to representation.

[6] See Blades (1985); Burrell, Donohue, and Allen (1990); Cahn (1992); Pearson and Thoennes (1984; 1988).

[7] Irving and Benjamin (1987); Regehr (1994).

[8] See also Cobb and Rifkin (1991a; 1991b); Cooks and Hale (1994); Fuller, Kimsey, and McKinney (1992); Karim and Dilts (1990); Kimsey et al. (1994). Some research connects disempowerment of disputants with a failure to reach an agreement (Kelly and Gigy 1989; see also Ewert et al. 2010). Merry's (1989) study suggests that settlement may be related to mediators avoiding appearing to coerce or pressure disputants.

[9] See Cooks and Hale (1994); Irving and Benjamin (1987); Regehr (1994).

When mediators not only represent disputants but replace them in an exchange with the opposing disputant, disputant autonomy may be affected. The autonomy of both disputants is reduced because while the mediator replaces one disputant in the exchange (thereby preventing that disputant from expressing themselves directly), he or she adds to the pressure on the opposing disputant (by adding the force of his or her own arguments to those put forth by the disputants). This makes it more difficult for the disputant to defend their position. The risks involved in refraining from intervening in disputants' exchanges were also discussed.

6   Soliciting Proposals for Resolution
of the Dispute

The goal of creating agreement is the primary purpose of any mediation session. In order for the disputants to come to an agreement, ideas for resolution of the dispute must be created and discussed. In this chapter I address the methods that mediators and disputants use to solicit or produce ideas for resolution.

After both disputants have made their opening statements with the help of the mediators, mediators work to move disputants from further discussion of problems to the generation of ideas for resolution of the dispute. Because disputants often have trouble leaving the phase of the hearing where they discuss complaints and problems (Poitras and Raines 2013), resistance to mediator solicits is fairly common. Mediators may therefore have to make several attempts to get disputants to move to the generation of ideas for resolution. I begin by illustrating two ways mediators can formulate proposal solicits: general and specific solicits. I then analyze how disputants may resist proposal solicits and how mediators may pursue solicits in the face of various types of disputant resistance.

General Solicits of Disputant Proposals

In a previous study of the Midwest small claims mediation sessions, I identified two types of mediator solicits, general and specific solicits (Garcia 2000). These types of solicits have different implications for the engagement of the mediator in the proposal-generation process and for the autonomy of the disputants in resolving their dispute.

A general solicit works to elicit an idea to resolve an issue without limiting the parameters of the suggestion. General solicits share some characteristics with topic initial elicitors (Button and Casey 1984). Topic initial elicitors "provide an open, though bounded, domain from which events may be selected and offered" (Button and Casey 1984: 170). In the context of mediation, questions such as "What would make you happy here?" or "Who would like to start with some ideas?" are what I refer to as general solicits. Mediators use general solicits to elicit proposals without limiting the type of proposal that can be suggested.

Excerpt 6.1 shows a mediator using a general solicit to elicit a disputant's perspective on how to resolve the dispute. This excerpt begins about forty minutes into the session, after the issues have been extensively discussed. As the excerpt begins, Herbert is explaining his hopes for the mediation session:

Excerpt 6.1 Two Brothers West Coast Mediation, Session 1, p. 46

```
987    Herb:  I hope that (0.5) there wi:ll be uh court order that thuh
988           house be so:ld!? (0.6) and that thee:: (0.2) property be split
989           fifty fifty? as: tenants in common? (1.5) Because if just
990           thee (0.2) phone bill or just thuh TAxes is taken care of.
991           (0.4) we'll be doing thuh same thing again in uh few
992           mo:nths. (3.0) At thuh same ti:me I'd like to:: (5.0) jus::t get
993           everything ah hhh! straightened OUT! (0.2) And (0.2)
994           where Bob can go on and lead his life as he ma:y, and I can
995           go on and lead mine as I °may!, (0.2) And with thuh
996           HOUS::E, (0.2) being commonly ours:!, there is absolutely
997           no way >that that's gonna happen.<
998           (1.2)
999    MA:    What is it that tu::h, (0.2) you'd like to see here Bob?
1000          (0.8)
1001   Bob:   Ah:::- as uh (0.3) good FAI:TH measure, (1.0) if- if (.) if
1002          we're E:ver gonna come to an agreement on thuh house.
1003          I'd- I'd (.) hopefully I would think, that we could firs:t
1004          come to an agreement, (0.2) on (.) th' BA:sic, (.)
1005          imm::ediate things that- inVO:LVE thuh care of thuh
1006          house. Such as utility, (0.2) .h and (0.2) RE:Ntal!, or occu-
1007          (.) PAtion, there o:f?, (0.5) A:h I would LI:KE, (0.6) to::
1008          (0.2) use A:LL my (.) resources, fiNANcial, (0.2) and, (.)
1009          skills available to me:, to see that Herbert!, (0.1) can get
1010          himself into uh house, (0.1) .h that he: will be HAppy with.
1011          (0.2) that (.) and that (0.4) I:: would be able to bu:y out his
1012          share. of Maple °Street.
```

Herbert says that he wants the house that he and his brother Bob inherited from their mother to be sold and the proceeds split between them (lines 987–997). Mediator A then produces a general solicit to get Bob's ideas for resolution on the table (line 999). Bob responds by listing several things that he would like to see happen (lines 1001–1012). While the mediator's general solicit succeeds in eliciting a proposal from Bob, Bob's proposal is the same as he had expressed earlier in the mediation session. The two brothers are still very far apart on what they want.

Mediators use general solicits to get proposals for resolution on the table or to get disputants to clarify their starting positions for negotiation. General solicits may result in disputants merely recycling the initial position they had communicated in the opening phase of the hearing rather than producing a new suggestion. Disputants often resist producing a proposal in response to general solicits (to be discussed below). For these reasons, mediators often use specific solicits.

Specific Solicits of Disputant Proposals

Specific solicits differ from general solicits in that they work to elicit ideas for resolution from disputants while limiting the parameters of the suggestions that can be made. First, a mediator may specify that only new ideas are being solicited (e.g., by asking for any *other* suggestions). Second, a mediator may specify that a specific issue or topic from among the issues under contention be addressed by the proposal. Third, a mediator may specifically solicit elaboration or refinement of an existing proposal. Finally, a mediator may include examples of appropriate ideas to guide the disputant's proposal construction. These techniques enable mediators to display an orientation to the autonomy of disputants while simultaneously guiding the solution-generation process and working to move disputants away from their initial positions.

Specific Solicits of New Suggestions

Mediators often specifically solicit new ideas for resolution of issues under dispute when disputants are engaged in repetitive discussion of complaints or otherwise display reluctance to move away from previously held positions. For example, in Excerpt 6.2, after considerable discussion of the issues, the mediator uses a specific solicit.

Excerpt 6.2 Bad Engine Midwest Small Claims Mediation, p. 43

```
1116  Med:  Dan? Do you have any (0.3) other suggestions about uh
1117        resolution?
1118        (0.7)
1119  Dan:  °°Hh::mm°°=
1120  Med:              =uh other than (0.9) °u:m°
1121        (1.3)
1122  Dan:  tch .h >I dunno what tuh [do< I tell   ] you what! (0.5)
1123  Med:                           [°any more?°]
1124  Dan:  This is so crazy? °And this has° cost me uh °fortune!° I
1125        would be willing °just tuh for-° (0.2) GET about this? (0.5)
1126        .h LET HER do whatever she's gotta do? >If she wants uh
1127        go on< her own way >and just forget about what she's<
1128        doin'. I'm (1.5) Eileen °I'm sorry-!° (0.6) °you-° Eileen?
1129        (0.6)
1130  Med:  s[-   ]
1131  Dan:   [>Yo]u know me °better than this man.°<
```

The mediator specifically solicits new ideas that have not already been discussed ("any (0.3) other suggestions ..."; lines 1116 and 1117). Dan responds by proposing that he and the complainant Eileen drop the cases they have brought against each other (lines 1124–1128). This new proposal is a major concession, because Dan is effectively offering to walk away from several hundred dollars he believes Ms. Eileen Jones owes him for work he has done on her car. The mediator's specific solicit successfully elicited a new proposal which is a significant departure from Dan's prior position.

Narrowing the Range of a Proposal Solicit

When disputants are having a difficult time reaching an agreement, mediators are advised to try to find a point of common ground in order to jump start the process of reaching agreement (e.g., Bishop et al. 2015; Moore 2014). Mediators' proposal solicits can narrow the discussion by specifying a suggestion about one issue or group of issues from those under dispute. For example, after previous failed attempts to solicit proposals for resolution, Mediator A produces a specific solicit (Excerpt 6.3, lines 1946–1947). This solicit limits the parameters of the proposal to just one of the many issues under dispute between the parties, a father ("Stan") and his children's stepfather ("Nick").

Excerpt 6.3 Blended Family West Coast Mediation, p. 85

```
1938 MA:    [So  ] O:NE A:rea of co:nflict: hh (0.5) °whether it's one
1939        sided or two sided, it has tuh do:: with
1940        (0.2)
1941 MB:    equal transp[ortation]
1942 MA:              [visiTA:]tion related de::tails:.
1943        (0.2)
1944 MB:    °Right°. .h
1945        (2.1)
1946 MA:    What (1.0) is:::: (1.1) your suggestion about (0.9)
1947        reSO:Lving (0.5) visitation related °details?°
1948        (2.3)
1949 Nick:  U:::HM (1.3) Well first there's thuh TRANSporTA:tion,
1950        (0.6) A:::ND DU::H
1951        (0.5)
1952 MA?:   °(W[ell-)]
1953 Nick:     [I    ]: GUESS: (1.9) SE:cond is U::H (1.0) is thuh
1954        TI::ME schedule!,
1955        (1.3)
1956 MA:    °Well, let's just take thuh transportation, (0.2) fi::rst, (0.2)
1957        °When you say you feel uh little bit put upo:n- (1.3) some
1958        times (0.5) because you seem to be doing MO::RE of thuh
1959        transportation than is you::r (0.8) fair share?
```

```
1960          (0.4)
1961  Nick:  Right.
1962          (5.4)
1963  MA:    Ho:w would you go about reso:lving that? hh
1964          (1.2)
1965  Nick:  I think BE:ST case for u:s would BE U::HM (0.6) if he
1966          wants tuh see them he (0.4) picks them UP, (0.4) and brings
1967          them ba:ck!
```

Nick responds to Mediator A's specific solicit by listing two areas of concern which are relevant to the visitation arrangements for his stepchildren: transportation and scheduling (lines 1949–1950 and 1953–1954). Mediator A then reissues the proposal solicit, narrowing it even further by asking Nick to focus only on the transportation issue (line 1956). He then reviews the issues around transportation that Nick has already raised earlier in the session (lines 1956–1959). After Nick's confirmation that these are his concerns (line 1961), Mediator A produces a second specific solicit (line 1963). This solicit is successful; Nick produces a suggestion starting in line 1965. While the transportation issue is just one of the problems these disputants face, getting disputants to focus on one problem at a time is often an effective way to start building an agreement.

Soliciting Elaboration of an Existing Proposal

Mediators can narrow the parameters of a proposal solicit by requesting an elaboration or refinement of a proposal that is already on the table. In Excerpt 6.4 the mediator solicits a specific proposal from the complainant Verona based on a proposal she had made earlier in the session.

Excerpt 6.4 Vacation Pay Midwest Small Claims Mediation, p. 30

```
644  Med:  >Would you accept< anything less then what choo've asked for
645          °so° far?
646          (1.4)
647  Ver:  Thuh very >lowest I would go:< 'uhd be four seventy five, 'cause
648          that's what I would've brought home after taxes.
```

In this excerpt the mediator works to try to save the original proposal (that the company give Verona $500) by specifically soliciting an extension or alteration of it (lines 644–645). This proposal solicit is successful – Verona revises her proposal to indicate she is willing to accept a (slightly) lower amount of vacation pay (lines 647–648). The mediator's specific solicit helped keep a potential idea for resolution alive by eliciting an adjustment to the proposal to make the proposal more attractive to the opposing disputant. Some movement from Verona's original position has therefore occurred.

Specific Solicits with Candidate Suggestions

Some mediators narrowed the parameters of potential solutions by including examples of the types of things that might be suggested in their proposal solicits. These specific solicits are analogous to the "candidate answers" to questions described by Pomerantz (1988). Pomerantz noted that providing a candidate answer in the question changes the response possibilities for the person answering the question. In Excerpt 6.5 the mediator produces a specific proposal solicit which provides a candidate suggestion as a model. The mediator raised the issue of the communication problems between the disputants which both sides had complained about during the session.

Excerpt 6.5 Washer Dryer Midwest Small Claims Mediation, p. 78

```
1698  Med:   °Mm kay.° (10.5) °Mm kay.° (2.2) .h (1.5) You said there
1699          were other issues Anna? particularly that you would like to:
1700          (0.3) address? S:om:e (0.5) kind of: (0.5) possible guides
1701          lines:? (1.0) tch °u:m° (0.4) Ho:w (0.4) everybody's gonna
1702          interact?, (1.0) .h with each other! (1.4) °to:° try to avoid any
1703          more (1.1) .h °°uh°° (0.6) stress? or confrontation! (1.0)
1704          Keep- (0.3) lines of communication open better. >D' you 've
1705          any< suggestions, Anna? how you'd like (0.6) .h=
1706  Anna:                                                    =Mm:?
1707          hh (0.6) >I would like tuh be< talked to wi' respect! Especially
1708          if I'm givin' it! (1.5) Definitely! liked tuh be talked as respec-
1709          with respect! ...
```

While the mediator's solicit (lines 1704–1705) is formulated as a general solicit, it works as a specific solicit because the mediator has prefaced it with candidate suggestions (lines 1698–1704). Anna responds with a suggestion related to the communication issues (line 1706–1709).

Summary

There are several ways in which mediators can formulate proposal solicits to narrow the parameters of the solicit. Mediators can use an "anything else" formulation to specifically exclude proposals previously made (hence requesting a new proposal). They can also narrow the range of possible suggestions by limiting the solicit to one of the issues under dispute, seeking an elaboration or refinement of a previously discussed proposal, or providing a candidate suggestion to demonstrate a type or category of solution that might be appropriate.

One of the weaknesses of general solicits is that disputants often simply repeat or rephrase their opening position or a proposal they have made earlier in the session. Specific solicits therefore may be more productive than general solicits, because disputants can be guided to focus on points not already made.

For example, in Excerpt 6.1, the mediator used a general solicit, and the disputant merely recycled the initial position they had communicated earlier in the hearing. Specific solicits are designed to move disputants away from a previously held position. In Excerpt 6.4 above the mediator asked the complainant whether she would be willing to accept less than her original request. She responded by proposing a new, lower amount of money that she would be willing to accept.

However, while there may be practical benefits to getting ideas for resolution of the dispute on the table through specific solicits, mediator's solicits may also limit disputant autonomy. In addition, there are potentially problematic implications for the mediator's display of neutrality. To some extent, these concerns apply to both general and specific solicits, but they are particularly relevant for specific solicits. While all solicits work to empower disputants, because they give them the floor to suggest their own ideas for resolution of the conflict, if a mediator works to limit or direct the scope of the solicited proposal, they could be seen as intervening in the production of ideas for resolution. Disputant resistance of mediator solicits may be one way of challenging this threat to disputant autonomy.

Resisting Mediator Solicits

At times disputants resist leaving the discussion of issues to move to the resolution stage (Poitras and Raines 2013). Disputants may delay producing a proposal when solicited in order to repeat or elaborate complaints or to further justify their position. When this happens, mediators may choose to allow further talk on these topics, or may choose to pursue production of a proposal and move the disputants from the storytelling to the resolution generation stage of the mediation session.

In addition, disputants may delay producing a proposal for strategic reasons, if producing a suggestion for resolution is not advantageous to them at that point in the mediation session (Goldberg et al. 2017). Hutchby's (1996a; 1996b; see also Sacks 1992) study of arguments in radio talk shows found that the second-position arguer has some advantages over the first speaker in an argument sequence. When the first position arguer states a position and justifies it, the second-position arguer then has the floor to challenge their position. This response does not have to include new positions or arguments which the first position arguer might then attack. The first position arguer can thus be put in a defensive position.

Similarly, by delaying producing a proposal, a disputant in a mediation session avoids having to commit himself or herself to a position. Waiting for the opposing disputant to make an offer first gives a strategic advantage, because the other disputant may offer more than expected. Finally, a delay in producing a proposal may benefit a disputant by enabling him or her to choose or create a more favorable interactional environment for the proposal. Resisting the mediator's attempt to solicit a proposal at a particular point in the session is one way a disputant can exercise their autonomy.

In these data there are several ways that disputants resist mediators' proposal solicits. First, a disputant may resist producing a proposal by claiming not to have a suggestion to make. Second, a disputant may resist a proposal solicit by passing on the opportunity and letting the opposing disputant make a proposal first. Third, a disputant may resist making a proposal by remaining silent in the face of a solicit. Finally, a disputant may resist a proposal solicit by producing talk on other issues instead of producing the requested suggestion for resolution.

Resisting Solicits by Claiming Not to Have a Proposal

A disputant can resist producing a suggestion for resolution when solicited by claiming not to have any ideas for resolution. In Excerpt 6.6 the mediator uses a general solicit (lines 1189–1190).

Excerpt 6.6 Bad Engine Midwest Small Claims Mediation, p. 46

```
1183   Jones:  So I was (0.2) kind uh please at that! (0.6) >'Cause I didn't
1184           think I get five hundred< out of them >I mean it was uh< nice
1185           body! and everything? (0.4) .h just thuh engine wasn't
1186           runnin'! (0.8) it was KNOCKIN'! it was runnin' >but it was
1187           just< °knockin' real loud.°
1188           (0.8)
1189   Med:    What's your suggestion Miss Jones about °how this: could
1190           be resolved.°
1191           (0.5)
1192   Jones:  I don' have none! I really don't! I mean like I said (0.4) °I
1193           have none!° (1.2) tch I really don't!
1194           (1.7)
1195   Med:    Well we've- (0.4) we've talked about it for a while?
1196           (4.3)
1197   Jones:  I don't see any way thoo it! I really don't! like I said I don't
1198           have thuh money t' get it fixed! (0.6) >That's th' reason why
1199           I was< wit' him 'uh make payments on it! (0.6) .h Because
1200           like- I'm an only providers? >Just me an' babies?<
```

Ms. Jones resists the mediator's solicit by claiming not to have a proposal to make (lines 1192–1193). The mediator pursues production of a proposal (line 1195), implying that the time for discussing the issues is over and it is now time to come up with ideas for resolution. In response, Ms. Jones repeats some of the arguments she had made earlier in the hearing. She explains why she can not make a proposal – because she does not have the money to get her car fixed (lines 1197–1199), and because she is a single provider for her family (line 1200). She thus avoids producing a proposal for a second time. Declining to produce a proposal when solicited is one way to avoid moving off of an initial position.

Resisting Mediator Solicits by Passing on the Opportunity

Disputants can resist proposal solicits by passing on the opportunity to make a proposal and instead letting the opposing disputant make a proposal (Excerpt 6.7):

Excerpt 6.7 Liz and Jon Midwest Divorce Mediation, Session 1, p. 14

```
559  Jon:  THE:N (0.4) and thos:e (0.6) and those issues ma:y (1.7)
560        may change! (0.4) uh (0.2) uh lot:. (1.0) °It's to- tuh whe:re
561        if we both° (0.5) agree with both of us (0.6) that we >would
562        be able tuh afford< it (0.8) and that we: (0.6) would have
563        both extra time with uh (0.3) °Bethany.°
564        (0.9)
565  MA:   .h So ffih- (0.8) n- (0.4) °eh-° d:- ah Are you interested in
566        makin' uh proposal? about? (1.0) how you could get uh
567        little bit more time right no:w? (0.8) Even while you have
568        an extra job?
569        (2.0)
570  Jon:  tch I: don't kno:w. (0.3) uh mean I don't know if I wanna
571        make it uh- uh propo:sal,
572        (0.9)
573  MA:   Or uh suggestion?=
574  Jon:              =ar (0.5) >You know I ji-< (0.3) I'd like
575        tuh know what she thinks. (0.6) wuh I mean how much
576        she's willing to: u:h (0.7) tuh compromise 'n thuh situation.
```

In lines 565–568 Mediator A produces a specific proposal solicit. However, Jon passes on the opportunity to produce a proposal (lines 570–571). When Mediator A reissues her solicit (line 573), Jon again passes on the opportunity, and instead requests that his wife Liz make a proposal (lines 574–576).

When a disputant passes on the opportunity to make a suggestion for resolution, they avoid having to make a commitment to a position. Waiting for the opposing disputant to make the first offer may be a strategic advantage. It is possible that the opposing disputant may offer more than they originally would have.

Resisting Mediator Solicits with Silence

In some instances mediator proposal solicits were met with silence. Mediator proposal solicits are first pair parts of adjacency pairs, and a disputant's second pair part – a proposal – is conditionally relevant in the next turn space. If the solicited disputant instead remains silent, the proposal is accountably absent. Repair of the absent response is thus relevant (Sacks et al. 1974; Schegloff and Sacks 1973). Mediators worked to repair the absent response if a disputant resisted a proposal solicit with silence. This silence, nevertheless, makes the disputant's declination of a proposal solicit visible.

Excerpt 6.8 shows a mediator's proposal solicit which was initially unsuccessful in eliciting a suggestion from the disputant.

Excerpt 6.8 Blended Family West Coast Mediation, p. 62

```
1419  MB:     Do YOU have any: suggestions about ho::w, eh eh- (0.2) we
1420          might help- (0.2) FI::ND some sort of work[ing re  ]la:tionship.
1421  Stan?:                                           [((sniff))]
1422  MB:     u:::h tch to: that would- (0.2) reso::lve thuh problems that've come
1423          up today. Duh you HA:VE anything you can throw out on thuh
1424          table? (0.1) Do you have ANy suggestions?, at all. ((MB gazes at
1425          Nick during this utterance.))
1426          (~6.0)
1427  MB:     And this is just thro::wing >it out on thuh table,< that's all it- this
1428          is not (0.2) casting ANything in concrete, this is just an exchA:nge
1429          of ideas tuh see if: .hh if SOME where within this ex- this- (0.2)
1430          discussion we can find something that'll- some WA:Y, some
1431          method tuh make thuh who:le (0.2) situation work for everyone
1432          smoo::ther?, (0.2) and I don't know that we're E:ver gonna fi:nd
1433          (0.7) thee:: °eh- this:° (0.2) final solution ah'm not sure that there
1434          is=
1435  Nick?:  =°chum=
1436  MB:            =aye final solution in this kind of situation. (0.2) but
1437          chou find thuh BE:st (0.4) a:venues:
1438          (0.4)
1439  Nick:   U::H (0.4) thee only thing I:: have tuh say it's not concrete at a:ll,
1440          but tuh .hh I THINK >Stan and I:< (0.2) (nert thee)
1441          (0.4)
1442  RB:     ((sniffs))
1443          (0.2)
1444  Nick:   NEE:D tuh LEA::rn, (0.2) to (0.2) speak from our hearts:. (0.4)
1445          rather than to be: in this competition, you know?, we NEE:D to
1446          (0.4) to REA::LLY come from thuh heart!, you know?, tuh (0.2) .h
1447          thuhhh- (0.2) thuh HEART that we both have for these children
1448          needs to come out between him an' I!, you know?, we need tuh
1449          REALize that WE:: are both here on EARTH!, (0.2) to deal with
1450          these children!, (0.5) a:n't that's: (0.2) and we have that in
1451          common an' an' it's really uh (0.2) quite uh gift!
```

There are several points in Mediator B's initial proposal solicit where her turn is possibly complete (for example, at the end of line 1420 and after "today." in line 1423). She then produces another solicit, this time using questioning intonation and pausing briefly after it ("Duh you HA:VE anything you can throw out on thuh table?"; lines 1423–1424). When the addressed recipient (Nick) does not respond, she produces an additional solicit (line 1424). Mediator B has been gazing at Nick throughout this turn. These proposal solicits are met with silence. After the lengthy silence in line 1426, Mediator B continues pressing for proposals, this time explaining the provisional nature of any ideas that might be presented. She works hard to create an environment where brainstorming is freely allowed. Nick finally responds beginning in line 1439, formulating his response not as a proposal for resolution but as something he has to "say" (line 1439). He then uses a preface to set his response up as not anything "concrete" (line 1439). When Nick eventually produces a suggestion (lines 1440, 1444–1451), it is very general and does not provide a concrete suggestion for how he and Stan could improve the care and transportation of the children.

At times mediators initially address a proposal solicit to both disputants. When such a collectively addressed solicit does not receive a response, the lack of response is due to the actions of two or more individuals, rather than just one. Disputants in these data often decline to respond to collective proposal solicits. It may be that because opposing disputants are not an association, they may resist attempts to treat them as aligned with each other in any way.[1] In these data mediators often responded by repairing collective solicits to individual solicits before succeeding in eliciting a disputant response.

In addition, the mediator's goal in producing the collective solicit may be to open the resolution stage of the session. In this circumstance, addressing both disputants at the same time lets them choose who will go first. This avoids a situation in which the mediator is perceived as treating the disputants unequally, which could have occurred if the mediator used an individual as opposed to a collective solicit to open this phase of the mediation process. Such an action could lead to perceptions of bias and could challenge the mediator's display of neutrality (e.g., Garcia et al. 2002; Jacobs 2002). In short, the fact that collective solicits are often unsuccessful does not mean that they do not fulfill useful functions in the context of the mediation session. The collective solicit may also serve as an attempt to reduce conflict between the disputants, by treating them as an association.

Resisting Mediator Solicits with Talk on Other Issues

Disputants may also resist a mediator's proposal solicit by responding with something other than a suggestion for resolution. They may produce a complaint

---

[1] See Lerner (1993); see also Goffman (1959) on teamwork.

about the opposing disputant, additional evidence supporting their position, or
more information about the history of the dispute. Excerpts 6.9 and 6.10 show
a disputant resisting a mediator solicit by revisiting the history of the dispute
from her perspective.

**Excerpt 6.9 Electric Bill Midwest Small Claims Mediation, p. 36
            (Garcia 2000: 329)**

```
918  Med:   I Kri- (0.2) Kris I s:ti:ll?, (1.0) would like you to offer uh
919         suggestion for resolving.
920         (0.7)
921  Kris:  tch (1.0) I: honestly! (0.5) You kno:w I (0.3) .h I realize
922         thuh bill is in MY NAME? But it was left in my NAme?
923         because .h (0.3) thee: place was: in Kurt's name? (0.7) And
924         (0.4) thuh day that we found out?, (0.4) that (0.7) um (0.4)
925         thuh- place was turned over tuh John?
926         (0.4)
927  John?: ((sniffs))=
928  Kris:          =I called?, (0.9) thuh gas and electric company tuh
929         have (0.3) thuh gas and electric taken out of: (0.3) our
930         name! (0.5) .h We were given till September first tuh move
931         out? (0.5) We wuh moved out, in July.
932         (1.0)
933  Med:   Okay.=
934  Kris:          =So we were OU:T of the:re (0.3) immediately. .h
935         Thuh DAY I CALLed tuh have thuh gas and electric bill
936         taken out of my NAME? [.hh I was to:              ]ld
937  John:                       [°This was already changed.°]
938  Kris:  (0.5) John had already called? (0.7) A:nd (0.5) changed it?
939         (0.5) >And I didn't know< anything about it. (0.7) HE
940         CHANGED it some time during thuh day, I called in thuh
941         afternoon! when I got home from work and found out that
```

In Excerpt 6.9 the mediator solicits a suggestion from Kris to resolve the
conflict over the utility bill (lines 918–919). However, Kris's response to the
solicit is not a proposal, it is a repetition of information she had provided
earlier about the history of the electric bill they are disputing over (lines
921–931, 934–936, and 938–941). This resistance leaves the mediator with
the option of reopening discussion of these issues or making another attempt to
refocus talk to potential solutions. The mediator makes another attempt to elicit
a proposal from Kris (Excerpt 6.10):

**Excerpt 6.10 Electric Bill Midwest Small Claims Mediation, p. 36
             (Garcia 2000: 330)**

```
942         (0.2)
943  Med:   °'kay.° (0.4) So, (0.4) Kris. (1.6) Wha:t (0.7) if you're
944         saying, tha:t (1.3) y'know? (0.5) ah- I understand you're
```

```
945            saying that he was living there. (0.7) What I! need from
946            you is uh suggestion to resolve this.
947            (0.7)
948   Kris:   tch LIKE I said like (0.6) I mean thuh LANDlord even says
949            so right there. He feels John should pay thuh bill. (0.6) .h
950            HE was there, ON thuh premises during thuh time. HE
951            knows who [was  ] there,
952   Med:             [Okay]
953            (0.4)
954   Med:    So you're- you'r:e asking for John tuh pay [thuh] hundred
955   Kris:                                              [Yes.]
956   Med:    and twenty two: (0.3) do[llars? and        ] some odd cents.
957   Kris:                            [Yes I AM that's]
958            (0.3)
959   Med:    Tha:t's what y[our       ] >idea for uh solution< is.
960   Kris:                 [Mm hm!]
961            (0.6)
962   Kris:   tch And that's why I brought it tuh [court.]
963   John?:                                      [((snif]fs))
964            (0.4)
965   Kris:   'Cause John told us he would pay (it/'em).
```

The mediator recycles her proposal solicit: "I understand you're saying that he was living there. (0.7) What I! need from you is uh suggestion to resolve this." (lines 944–946). The mediator thereby highlights Kris's failure to provide a suggestion for resolution of the problem. Kris responds with a proposal ("tch LIKE I said like (0.6) I mean thuh LANDlord even says so right there. He feels John should pay thuh bill ..."; lines 948–951). With the statement "He feels John should pay thuh bill ..." Kris conveys the landlord's position. By this formulation she is able to both convey her position (that John should pay the bill) while simultaneously providing evidence in support of this position (the landlord's position). In the mediator's response, she reformulates Kris's statement as a position report reflecting Kris's position (lines 954, 956, and 959). Kris then confirms the mediator's representation of her position (line 960).

Thus while the mediator's previous solicit in Excerpt 6.9 gave Kris the floor to produce a proposal, Kris continued complaining about the issues under dispute rather than producing a proposal. Excerpt 6.10 shows the mediator pursuing the production of a proposal by reissuing the solicit. Kris then produced a suggested resolution for how the disputed bill should be handled. However, Kris's proposal is not a new suggestion, it was a reiteration of her initial position from the start of the mediation session.

A disputant's resistance of proposal solicits and reissued proposal solicits can have strategic advantages for that disputant. By conveying information about the chain of events regarding the unpaid bill instead of producing a proposal, Kris creates an interactional context for the proposal she eventually

makes which is framed by information which supports her side of the dispute.
She has thus created a more persuasive context for her proposal than would
have occurred if she had placed her proposal after the mediator's earlier
solicits.

In Excerpt 6.11 a disputant avoids producing a proposal in response to a
mediator solicit by requesting and obtaining the floor to produce more information about their complaints.

Excerpt 6.11 Washer Plumbing Midwest Small Claims Mediation, p. 47

```
1022  Med:  So maybe?, (0.5) given that situation (0.4) .h it's helpful tuh say
1023        okay, what- what's gonna work (0.4) .h >tuh get us< through (0.4) .h
1024        maybe uh tru:ce! (0.7) maybe tuh get >some uh these< things
1025        resolved,
1026        (0.5)
1027  Tish: Can [I rebut? ] (0.2) tuh what they've? (0.7) brought up?
1028  Med:      [uh truce.]
1029        (0.3)
1030  Med:  Well? (0.3) .h (0.5) it doesn't >have tuh be uh< rebuttal!
1031        >This isn't uh< cou:rt! (0.5) °I'm°
1032        (0.6)
1033  Tish: Well, [I- ]
1034  Med:        [but] certainly su:re! [talk about ]
1035  Tish:                             [can I com ]ment! th[en!]
1036  Med:                                                  [.h ] sh: certainly!
1037        °yeah!°
1038        (0.8)
1039  Tish: tch Thee: u:m (0.8) thuh furnace! (1.0) °tuh° they CALLED me
1040        and said uh (2.5) tch I don't remember °uhw° what they said (0.4)
1041        >what they had a:sked s: sp specifically< >but thee answer< was
1042        (0.5) you can change thuh filters! they hadn't turned on thuh furnace?
1043        It was October? November? (0.6) .h December? they hadn't turned
1044        on thuh furnace! HOW d' they know it's broken!? (0.7) .h they hadn't
1045        chay- >I told ['em<]
1046  John:             [.hh  ]hh
1047        (0.6)
1048  Tish: tch They could buy=
1049  John:                    =hhhhh=
1050  Tish:                          =furnace filters! (0.5) .h they could
1051        change those themSELVES! (0.6) I mean? (0.2) don't call me up and
1052        tell me (0.5) .h that (1.2) that they THINK tha:t thuh paint's gonna
1053        chip! (1.3) >well is it< chipping? No! (0.4) it just >looks like it's<
1054        going to! (1.8) Until it HAPPENS until you do something (0.4) .h to
1055        help yourself? (1.3) I'm not your mom! (1.2) So they hadn't turned
1056        on thuh furnace!? (1.2) >°I I I you know if it 'ad<° blown BLACK
1057        SMOKE OUT OF IT (0.3) then there 'as probably uh problem! (0.6)
1058        but they hadn't turned it on! They were living there! (0.5) .h with no
1059        heat! (0.6) Now! (0.4) How much sympathy can I have for that! (0.7)
```

The complainant Tish interrupts the mediator's proposal solicit to request the floor for a rebuttal. Once given the floor, she ends up using this time to respond to complaints the respondents, her tenants, had made during their opening statement. She also introduces new complaints about the tenants.

Summary

Disputants in these data use four main techniques to avoid or delay producing an idea for resolution of issues in response to a mediator solicit. The disputant can claim not to have a proposal to make, pass on the opportunity to produce a proposal, remain silent in the face of a proposal solicit, or produce talk that is something other than a proposal. By these means, a disputant can resist producing a suggestion while conforming to the speech exchange system of mediation talk.

Mediator solicits of disputant proposals may or may not be successful in eliciting proposals from disputants. However, a solicit does not have to result in the immediate production of a disputant's proposal in order for it to be useful for the mediation process. The solicit is a technique mediators use to try to move disputants out of the storytelling stage of the hearing in which complaints, accusations, and claims are focused on, to the stage of the hearing in which ideas for resolution are proposed and discussed. While a mediator's solicit may work on the first try, disputants often need time to work toward talk about ideas for resolution. Failure to produce a proposal immediately when solicited by a mediator is therefore not a sign of mediator failure, but a sign that disputants either are not ready yet for resolution talk, or that at least one disputant is strategically holding back. Nevertheless, asking for a proposal may be helpful in getting the disputants to (eventually) refocus from complaints onto solutions.

Pursuing Proposals and Recycling Proposal Solicits

Conversation-analytic studies have found pursuit of absent responses occurring in a variety of institutional settings. For example, in televised news interviews, interviewers may pursue answers to questions when the answer is absent, inadequate, or evasive (e.g., Clayman 2001; Romaniuk 2013). Sidnell's (2004) study of legal testimony shows lawyers pursuing not just answers to questions, but specific explanations.

Regardless of the method disputants in mediation use to resist providing proposals when solicited, mediators have the option of pursuing responses in the face of such resistance. Mediators can follow the disputant's lead and facilitate continued talk on the disputant's complaints or evidence, or may instead pursue a response to the proposal solicit until the disputant has produced a suggestion for resolution. The decision as to whether to pursue a response to a proposal solicit is an area of mediator discretion which may expose them to perceptions of bias. For example, if only one disputant's avoidance of proposal production is pursued by the mediator, such differential treatment of the disputants may challenge the mediator's display of neutrality.

In Excerpts 6.12 and 6.13 the mediator makes repeated attempts to solicit proposals from the disputants. Excerpt 6.12 begins with the mediator producing a second general solicit:

Excerpt 6.12 Roof Repair Midwest Small Claims Mediation, p. 46

1018	Med:	.h [Well] lem- lemme ask you though-? (0.8) is is °h° (0.3)
1019	Jack:	[u:m]
1020	Med:	THE:RE? (0.4) <u>some</u> way that (0.5) that you and <u>Jack</u> can
1021		get this (0.5) .h worked out between thuh two of you!
1022		(0.5)
1023	Ed:	Well!
1024		(0.9)
1025	Med:	>D' you [have any< sugges]tions?
1026	Ed:	[>Y'know I dunNO! I mean<]
1027		(0.1)
1028	Ed:	I <u>DON'T</u> feel like I say! >that's what I said in th' beGIH!<
1029		(0.4) <u>I</u> DON'T <u>REALLY</u>? (0.6) .h I DON'T THINK! >I
1030		mean I in muh <u>OWN</u>?< (0.8) MIND? >and m' own< <u>heart</u>? <u>I</u>
1031		didn't <u>do any</u> thing (0.8) you know? (0.5) bro- I didn't
1032		<u>CHARGE</u> anybody for somethin' they never <u>got</u>? (0.7) I
1033		didn't (0.4) you know? I didn't try to (0.5) .h pull thuh <u>wool</u>
1034		over on somebody's eyes or anything like this! I mean ih
1035		we've been <u>doing</u> this °so° I have nothing tuh l- <u>gain</u>! by
1036		doing that! (0.4) .h >Y'know< I I <u>REALLY</u> didn' think
1037		y'know! (0.5) .h <u>WE</u> <u>HAD</u> any? (0.7) any wrongdoing! on
1038		this thing! (0.6) .h um This is what (0.4) they <u>wanted</u>? >'n'
1039		'is is what we've< <u>did</u>! (0.4) .h um (0.6) [thuh] <u>roof</u>
1040	Med:	[.h wuh-]
1041	Ed:	basically an' an' an' what you classify as (0.4) y'know? an'
1042		an' (0.4) weather conditions? °>with thuh ih wuh wih<° it's
1043		been <u>shedding water</u>! (0.5) .h u:m (0.6) .H °u:h° y'know it's
1044		been!

The mediator's general solicit (lines 1018 and 1020–1021) is addressed to the respondent Ed. The complainant Jack is referred to in the third person (line 1020). Ed's response to this general proposal solicit is rejection-implicative (note the between-turn silence in line 1022 and Ed's "Well!" in line 1023). The mediator produces another general solicit in line 1025, to which Ed responds quickly. Ed begins his turn in overlap with the mediator (line 1026). He first denies having any suggestions for resolving the dispute, and follows this with an explanation of why he is not responsible for the problems with the roof (lines 1028–1044). His explanation amounts to a reiteration of his starting position – that he should not have to pay for the problems with the roof.

In the continuation of this exchange the mediator produces two additional solicits (Excerpt 6.13):

Excerpt 6.13 Roof Repair Midwest Small Claims Mediation, p. 46

```
1044  Med:  .h [Well with-   ]
1045  Ed:       [been WORKI]NG!
1046        (0.4)
1047  Med:  withOUT? (0.7) going ba:ck an' a:n' (0.5) revisiting thuh
1048        problem >because I think< you've both been very articulate
1049        in in (0.4) .h talking about your own perspective, WHAT
1050        thuh problem is?
1051        (0.1)
1052  Jack: °Mm hm.°
1053        (0.3)
1054  Med:  u:m (0.7) .h Let's see if we can just (1.3) °see-° y'know
1055        (0.3) WITHOUT? (0.8) PUTTING RESPONSIBILITY on
1056        anybody? (0.3) .h >See if there's:<
1057        (0.1)
1058  Jack: °Ok[ay.°  ]
1059  Med:     [ANY] ANY WAY that thisk (0.3) can be resolved
1060        here!
1061        (0.3)
1062  Ed:   Okay.
1063        (0.4)
1064  Med:  .h Jack what-? (0.3) >d' you have<
1065        [any suggestions about how this might be worked] out?
1066  Jack: [.hhhhhhhhhhh                    hhhhhhhhhh ]
1067        (0.5)
1068  Jack: .hh (6.1) tch .h >Wellp-< hhh >I' be honest with you< I
1069        DON'T! I: I CAME IN HERE today thinking y' know I
1070        want I want them tuh replace my roof? Or (0.3) >maybe
1071        not replace it< but pay tuh have uh new roof °put on 'ere!°
1072        (0.9) tch .h I CAME in here with that intent! (1.4) because I
1073        r' I really feel like I'm right! (0.8) .h (0.7) reGARDless!
1074        >Bu' then I hear ED talking< °a:nd um° (1.2) .h °y'know°
1075        (1.0) h >I STILL think-< (0.5) °y'know° ED'S thuh
1076        professional he's thuh roofer! (0.7) .h And I usually go
1077        with what uh professional suggests °tuh me!° (0.4) °If he
1078        suggests that t'°shingle? (0.4) on my roof. I go wi' it! (0.3)
1079        He he knows °more than I do!° (0.4) .hhh hh! (1.0) t'
1080        SAME time? °I think kher- y'know? ° (0.4) I don't think!
1081        (0.6) I get uh feeling!? that Ed iS (0.4) >seems like< (0.6)
1082        pretty decent PERson and he's not tryin' tuh, he WASN'T
1083        intentionally! (1.7) trying 'uh rip anybody OFF! (1.0) .h
1084        °y'know >it was just an'°< (1.1) shingles were on 'ere? He
```

1085   went with shingles? °An'° (1.2) °°An' uh°° (1.3) .hh suh- hh
1086   I'm prePARED tuh BACK >OFF uh that!< But I >really
1087   don't have any figure< in my mind! (0.5) but I do! (0.4)
1088   um (1.0) °y'know!° after >listening tuh ED I realize< >it's
1089   not uh-< (0.4) >'s not uh!< >it WASN' uh!< (0.4) .h >i'
1090   wasn' uh< PURPOSEFUL! (0.6) inTENT!

The mediator produces another solicit (lines 1044, 1047–1050, 1054–1056, and 1059–1060). This solicit, which was addressed to both disputants, does not result in the production of a proposal. An additional solicit is then produced by the mediator in lines 1064–1065. In this solicit she addresses Jack directly. The beginning of Jack's lengthy response in lines 1068–1090 reveals that he is not making a specific proposal. However, he suggests that he is backing down from his original position that Ed replace the roof or pay for the replacement of the roof. The mediator's pursuit of the production of a disputant proposal in the face of repeated resistance by the disputants therefore did eventually get some movement on Jack's position. This is the beginning of a basis for a proposal to be worked out between the disputants.

In sum, while solicitation of proposals can provide for disputant autonomy by letting the disputants create the ideas for resolution of the dispute, pursuing proposal production by repeat solicits may in fact disempower disputants. It may also challenge a mediator's display of neutrality if proposal pursuits are directed to only one of the disputants. If a mediator pursues just one disputant and tries to elicit a proposal from them, the potential for perceptions of bias due to unequal treatment of disputants may arise. However, pursuit of proposal solicits can be an effective method to get movement on positions when disputants are stuck.

Proposal Solicitation in Divorce Mediation

The production of proposal solicits in divorce mediation is often done in the same way as it is done in small claims mediation. For example, in Excerpt 6.14 below Mediator A produces a general solicit ("°What would you like to have happen?°"; line 471):

Excerpt 6.14 Darryl and Belinda Midwest Divorce Mediation, Session 1, p. 21

457 Darr: I kind uh take thuh position I'm not gonna (0.2) .hh negotiate away
458   my childre=heh=n!=
459 MA: =Mm=muh=hmh (0.2) hm mm.
460   (0.3)
461 Darr: Y' kno:w ih I've .hh (0.2) provided uh- really! nice home for 'em.
462   (1.1) °And eh° (0.3) they got (0.9) everything they need! just about!
463   (0.2)

```
464  MA:   Mm [hmm    ]
465  Darr:      [in terms] of, material stuff. (1.1) .h And that's what I've
466             worked for all my life! And I (1.3) don't have intention of uh (0.7)
467             throwin' it all away!
468             (0.2)
469  MA:   Mm hm
470             (3.0)
471  MA:   °What would you like to have happen?°
472             (1.6)
473  Darr:  Mm eh mnh? (5.0) (Well!) (1.1) To get back tuh thuh good old
474             da=heh=ys I heh gue=hehss! .hh=
```

As Excerpt 6.14 begins, Darryl is complaining about the negative effects
a divorce would have on his children, particularly in terms of the economic
consequences (lines 457–467). Mediator A responds to Darryl's utterances
with minimal responses (lines 459, 464, and 469), thus positioning himself
as an addressed recipient of Darryl's utterances. This segment of the divorce
mediation session thus follows the speech exchange system of mediation.
When Darryl appears to be done with his statement (note the 3 second pause
in line 470), Mediator A produces a general solicit which Darryl responds to
with a statement of what he wants. Darryl would rather have a return to the
"good old da=heh=ys . . ." than a divorce (lines 473–474).

This general solicit and Darryl's response to it occur in a segment of
the mediation session in which the participants are following the speech
exchange system of mediation. However, in divorce mediation there are often
segments of system talk in which participants use a hybrid style that combines
elements of mediation format with the speech exchange system of ordinary
conversation. Proposal solicits are therefore often placed or produced differently in divorce mediation sessions than they are in small claims mediations.
For example, in Excerpt 6.15 below, Darryl and Belinda are engaged in a
disagreement over preparing food for the family. While Darryl persists in
addressing his remarks to the mediators and referring to his wife Belinda in
the third person (1318–1319, 1325–1330), she selects herself to speak and
addresses him directly (e.g., 1320–1321, 1324). The exchange thus has some
of the elements of a hybrid exchange. While Belinda's role in the exchange
becomes argumentative (note her adjacent placement of oppositional utterances), the exchange does not escalate to arguing. The mediators do not
sanction the disputants or interrupt the disagreement in progress, but they do
take steps to engage in the discussion. In line 1332 Mediator A produces a
general solicit. When Belinda produces an utterance in overlap with this
solicit, Mediator A reissues it in the clear, appending a direct address of Darryl
to it (lines 1332 and 1334).

Excerpt 6.15 Darryl and Belinda Midwest Divorce Mediation, Session 2, p. 60

```
1318  Darr:  [And  ] eh- if then she doesn't want tuh go through all that .hh she
1319         wants tuh buy something and shove it in thuh micro[wave!]
1320  Bel:                                                    [We're] not
1321         talking about every [night!]
1322  Darr:                     [And  ] and=
1323  MB:                              =Okay=
1324  Bel:   =[I don't want tuh do that every night!]
1325  Darr:   [>And and and< what would hap-  ] what would happen is (0.4)
1326         she eh I would go buy all thuh fresh fru food .hh and (0.3) and and
1327         she'd prepare what was left over ih ih wah of thuh hi- of thuh heat
1328         >heat and eat< food, .hh and then when on her week tuh go .h she
1329         would buy all thuh >heat and eat< foods and then that's all we'd
1330         have. .h and >then th' other< stuff would go bad!
1331         (0.7)
1332  MA:    Wh[at would you like tuh do?] (0.4) What would you like tuh
1333  Bel:     [You're talkin' about      ]
1334  MA:    do Dad?
1335         (0.5)
1336  Darr:  I don' know. Somebody probably ought tuh just take over thuh
1337         whole thing!
1338         (0.7)
1339  MA:    Hire somebody?=
1340  Darr:                 =hmph! no:=heh henh!
1341         (0.9)
1342  Bel:   °°Hm.°° You're talking about when I was working and uh
1343         try[ing tuh do everything ]
1344  Darr:     [Well it hasn't changed] none since you've ain't been
1345         workin'.=
1346  MA:          =°Yeah° (0.6) How- would you (1.7) maybe I'm not
1347         hearing this right um >would you-< prefer tuh do thuh shopping?
1348         (1.2)
1349  Darr:  Yeah. (1.9) Yeah I would.
1350         (1.1)
1351  MA:    Mom how'd that be with you!
1352         (0.1)
1353  Bel:   That's fine with me! .hh See you always wanted these made from
1354         scratch meals but you never wanted tuh help!
```

Mediator A's general solicit (lines 1332 and 1334) succeeds in getting Darryl to produce a suggestion (lines 1336–1337). After another question-and-answer pair to clarify Darryl's position (lines 1339–1340), Belinda resumes the disagreement with Darryl she had begun before the mediator's proposal solicit (lines 1342–1343). Again, she uses the speech exchange system of ordinary conversation to select herself to speak, and directly addresses an argumentative utterance to Darryl. His response is also argumentative, an interruptively placed oppositional utterance (lines 1344–1345). Mediator A pursues clarification and acceptance of Darryl's proposal regarding shopping rather than directly addressing this argumentative exchange (lines 1346–1347). Mediator A eventually succeeds in getting both disputants to agree to the suggestion about how shopping for food will be handled (lines 1346–1354).

Another difference between proposal solicitation in the divorce and small claims mediation sessions was how participants responded to collective solicits. In small claims mediation, collectively addressed proposal solicits were typically met with silence or some other resistance technique. However, in the divorce mediation sessions, collective solicits were more likely to successfully elicit suggestions of ideas for resolution. For example, in Excerpt 6.16 Mediator A asks both spouses whether they want their family to eat meals together or separately (lines 1178–1180).

Excerpt 6.16 Darryl and Belinda Midwest Divorce Mediation, Session 2, p. 64

```
1178  MA:   Now we come back tuh th- (0.5) same question that we had
1179        >before and that is< (1.3) would you all (meet this need) (0.5) eat
1180        thuh meal together? or (°would you°) (2.6) °eat separately.°
1181        (0.9)
1182  Darr: °Well we could-° u:h we could eat together y'know
1183        (0.6)
1184  MA:   °Mm hm.°
1185        (2.7)
1186  Bel:  I guess we'll continue, but I: I do have concerns (about) u:m (0.9)
1187        it's it's confusing, for thuh children.
```

In line 1182 Darryl produces the first response to Mediator A's collective solicit. Note that he uses "we" to refer to himself and his wife, Belinda. After a brief mediator response (line 1184), and a pause (line 1185), Belinda responds to the solicit as well. While her use of "we" mirrors Darryl's use of the plural pronoun, it is ambiguous as to whether she is constructing her position as a response to Darryl's or as a delayed response to Mediator A's solicit. While coming to the same conclusion as Darryl, she does not work to construct her utterance as a response to his. However, in this excerpt both spouses have produced a response to Mediator A's solicit, which is in stark contrast to the responses to collective proposal solicits typically seen in small claims mediations, in which several repetitions and reformulations are generally required before a response is obtained.

In sum, there are several ways in which proposal solicitation differs in small claims and divorce mediation. While some solicits in divorce mediation sessions are constructed and placed similarly to those in small claims mediation, these solicits often occur in the context of a hybrid interaction rather than in the speech exchange system of mediation. Mediators thus can simultaneously guide disputants toward resolution talk and idea generation while also managing segments of direct address between disputants which may become argumentative. In addition, because divorce mediation sessions are constructed from their initiation to foster a collaborative approach to problem solving rather than an adversarial approach, collectively addressed proposal solicits are more often successful in divorce mediation than in small claims mediation.

Discussion and Conclusions

As previous research has shown, the goal of mediation to achieve both the neutrality of the mediator and the autonomy of the disputants is potentially problematic.[2] Neutrality in mediation can be challenged not just with biased behavior such as siding with one disputant against another, but through how mediators and disputants construct their actions and coordinate their actions with each other.[3] Issues such as where a proposal solicit is placed or how it is formulated, whether a disputant responds by producing a proposal or not, and how a mediator responds to any disputant resistance to proposal production, are potentially relevant for the accomplishment of mediator neutrality and disputant autonomy in mediation.

For example, a mediator's choice to use a general or a specific proposal solicit has implications for the disputant's options. General solicits give disputants wide latitude for the type of proposal they may suggest, including recycling a previously articulated position. Specific solicits, on the other hand, put constraints on the types of proposals the disputant can produce.

Disputants can exercise control over whether or when to produce a proposal by resisting a mediator's solicits. Resisting production of a proposal when solicited may enable the disputant to withhold information on what they are willing to do until after the opposing disputant has revealed their position. If a disputant chooses to resist a solicit by avoiding or delaying producing a proposal, the mediator has the option of either pursuing a proposal by reissuing the solicit or abandoning the attempt to elicit a proposal. Pursuing a proposal solicit in spite of disputant resistance may reduce the disputant's autonomy by exerting pressure on him or her to respond. However, failing to pursue a proposal solicit may lead to perceptions of unfairness, since the absence of pursuit will be visible to all participants. Mediator decisions as to whether or not to pursue proposal production may be perceived as a failure of mediator neutrality, if disputants on opposing sides of the dispute are treated differently in this regard.

---

[2] See Cobb and Rifkin (1991b); Poitras and Raines (2013).
[3] See Garcia et al. (2002); Jacobs (2002).

Disputant resistance of a mediator's pursuit of a proposal solicit may benefit the disputant's position by providing an opportunity to create a more favorable interactional context for his or her proposal. The risk to this path of action is that disputant resistance may be seen as failure to cooperate with the mediator. The mediator's pursuit of proposal solicits in the face of the disputant's resistance makes their failure to cooperate with the mediator visible to all parties in the mediation session. Thus, there may be strategic costs for disputants who resist the mediator's pursuit of proposals.

The production of disputant proposals for resolution of issues under dispute is therefore a process that involves the participation of the mediator and the disputant. Mediators can attempt to choose a location in the mediation session for a disputant to produce a proposal, by producing a solicit. However, the disputant may delay or avoid the production of a proposal at that point. Disputants may differ in terms of their strategic judgments as to when to produce proposals, and some may more effectively place their proposals in locations advantageous to themselves, for example by first presenting background information or evidence that works to frame their subsequent proposal more favorably than it would have been if it occurred immediately after the mediator's first proposal solicit.

As this analysis of proposal solicitation has shown, participants in mediation use a variety of techniques to display an orientation to the norms of disputant autonomy and mediator neutrality. While the mediator's proposal solicits facilitate disputant autonomy by letting the disputant produce ideas for resolution, these actions may also work to disempower them. The exchanges between mediators and disputants over when and how ideas for resolution will be produced may be an aspect of mediation that paradoxically both facilitates and challenges disputant autonomy. For example, if a mediator selects which disputant makes a proposal first, or selects the point in the session in which a proposal is solicited, they are to some extent limiting the autonomy of the disputants.

7   Producing Ideas for Resolution of the Dispute

The goal of creating agreement is the primary purpose of any mediation session. In order for the disputants to come to an agreement, ideas for resolution of the dispute must be created and discussed. In Chapter 6 I investigated how mediators solicit proposals for resolution of the dispute in the small claims and divorce mediation sessions. In the current chapter I address how both mediators and disputants produce and respond to ideas for resolution of issues under dispute.

In an earlier study I found that when small claims mediators make proposals for resolution of issues under dispute they typically construct them as suggestions and do not imply that they are committed to that idea (Garcia 1997). Disputant's ideas for resolution were formulated and treated differently, as "position reports." Position reports are ideas for resolution of issues under dispute to which the proposer is committed (Carnevale and Pruitt 1992). Maynard (1984) notes that position reports are formulated to convey what the speaker wants, their personal preferences.

This difference in how ideas for resolution of issues under dispute are formulated by mediators and disputants reflects their institutional roles in the context of the mediation session. In most facilitative mediation programs, mediators are discouraged from contributing substantively to the resolution of the dispute (Goldberg et al. 2017). Formulating their ideas as suggestions rather than as position reports may enable them to contribute to the process of proposal production while displaying an orientation to disputant autonomy.

When disputants' ideas for resolution are constructed as positional commitments rather than as suggestions, previous research suggests they will not be as likely to contribute to mutually beneficial approaches to resolving the issues under dispute than are ideas presented as suggestions (Carnevale and Pruitt 1992; see also Pruitt et al. 1983). Research on mediation and negotiation more generally supports this finding, because providing opportunities to freely brainstorm ideas for solutions has been shown to be an effective mediation technique.[1]

---

[1] For example, see Boulle et al. (2008); Fisher and Ury (1991); Frenkel and Stark (2012).

These brainstorming techniques are referred to as "problem-solving approaches" and have been shown to increase the chance of reaching agreement, because they are most effective in generating new ideas.[2] Whether a proposal is formulated as a suggestion or a position report may therefore have implications for the success of the negotiation process.

In the next sections of this chapter I investigate how disputants and mediators formulate their ideas for resolution of issues in all three data sets. I will first show how disputants formulate and place their ideas for resolution as position reports, and then analyze how mediators formulate their ideas as suggestions or proposals. When mediators produce proposals they use a variety of techniques to display an orientation to a norm of disputant autonomy and mediator neutrality. In the final sections of this chapter I discuss variations of proposal production in divorce mediation.

Disputants' Ideas for Resolution as "Position Reports"

In these data disputants' ideas for resolution of issues under dispute are formulated to express a position in favor of the idea they are suggesting. Mediators help create an interactional context for the disputant's proposals by constructing position report solicits rather than proposal solicits; they thus frame the disputant's subsequent suggestion as a positional commitment. Excerpt 7.1 shows the mediator asking the respondent Jay to produce a position report:

Excerpt 7.1 Vacation Pay Midwest Small Claims Mediation, p. 24

```
510  Med:  uhm. (3.6) tch Are you willing tuh give Verona any money- (0.2)
511        towards what she's asking.
512        (0.4)
513  Jay:  Absolutely. (1.0) that's wh- that's you know: (1.1) we definitely
514        wanna work (0.4) just work this thing ou:t. (1.0) You know take
515        >care °of it°< we- we: (0.8) would (0.4) >be happy giving her
516        something.<
```

Mediator A's proposal solicit goes beyond asking Jay for a suggestion, he asks Jay what he's willing to do ("Are you willing tuh give Verona any money- (0.2) towards what she's asking.", lines 510–511). Mediator A is thus soliciting a position report (an idea for resolution and a positional commitment to that idea). Jay responds by specifying what he wants and what he is willing

---

[2] See Bishop et al. (2015); Boulle et al. (2008); Carnevale and Pruitt (1992); Ewert et al. (2010); Filley (1975); Fisher and Ury (1991); Frenkel and Stark (2012); Tyler (1987); Zubek et al. (1989).

to do (lines 513–516). In sum, both mediators and disputants display an orientation to disputants' ideas for resolution as position reports by how these suggestions are solicited and formulated.

Participants also display their orientation to disputants' ideas for resolution as position reports by their responses to these ideas. For example, in Excerpts 7.2 and 7.3, both the disputants and the mediators display an orientation to one disputant's suggestion as a positional commitment. In Excerpt 7.2 Mr. Porterville produces an utterance which is an unsolicited suggestion for resolution of the conflict.

Excerpt 7.2 Patched Carpet West Coast Small Claims Mediation, p. 23 (Garcia 1997: 233)

```
512  Port:  .hh Mi[ss Cen]terville, is there another- (0.1) is there
513  MA:           [(   )]
514  Port:  another- (0.3) u::h (2.0) closet (0.5) that's covered?,
515         (0.8)
516  Cent:  Thuh closets are covered!?
517         (2.2)
518  Port:  WHAT if we took u::h (.) what's your largest closet
519         °there, it's been °so long I °don' remember if it's: °uh (
520                      )°=
521  Cent:              =Pro:bably six by six I could not (.) be
522         positive [(                                )]
523  Port:            [>What if we< what if we took] it out of your
524         clo:set, (0.9) a:nd took this piece and put it in your closet
525         how would that °affect you.°
526         (1.4)
527  Cent:  .hh I don't know that we're going to, be any better o::ff:!=
```

Mr. Porterville suggests replacing the flawed piece of carpet in Mrs. Centerville's living room with a larger piece of carpet from her closet (see lines 512–525). Note that Mr. Porterville's idea for resolution is treated as a positional commitment (an offer) by the mediators, even though it was formulated as a question. After some more discussion of the idea (not shown), Mediator B asks Mrs. Centerville to respond to Mr. Porterville's "offer" (Excerpt 7.3). Mediator B thereby treats Mr. Porterville's suggestion as a positional commitment – a statement of what he is willing to do rather than merely a suggestion to be considered (lines 646–647).

Excerpt 7.3 Patched Carpet West Coast Small Claims Mediation, p. 29 (Garcia 1997: 233)

```
646  MB:   So how's it sound tuh you what tuh (0.4) Mister
647        Porterville's of:fered?
648        (0.3)
649  Cent:  Well, if thuh closets are la:rge enough for him to do this:,
```

Excerpt 7.3 shows how all four participants in the mediation session display an orientation to Mr. Porterville's suggestion as an offer to which he is committed. First, Mediator B explicitly characterizes the suggestion as an offer (lines 646–647). Second, Mr. Porterville and Mediator A implicitly agree with this characterization by refraining from disagreeing with it. Third, Mrs. Centerville implicitly agrees with the characterization of the suggestion as an offer by producing a disagreement-implicative response to it ("Well," followed by a reason why it might not work – the size of the closets; line 649).

As the discussion continues after Excerpt 7.3 (not shown), the mediators maintain their stance that Mr. Porterville's question was in fact an offer to take the carpet out of her closet and use it to replace the flawed carpet in the living room. It is treated throughout this discussion as a positional commitment. After several minutes of discussion in which the mediators engage with Mrs. Centerville in a discussion of the proposal, she agrees to accept the offer. At the same time, the mediators do not work to convince Mr. Porterville – he is treated as already committed to the idea.

Further evidence of participants' orientation to disputants' suggestions as positional commitments can be seen in how they are responded to by the opposing disputant. Since disputants' suggestions are positions they are committed to, revising those proposals once produced may be difficult. In a small claims mediation, Mr. Carter's offer in a dispute with his neighbor (Mr. Bryson) over the use of the land between their properties became a contentious topic of debate. The mediators had assisted Mr. Carter in creating the idea for this offer during a private caucus. When the joint mediation session was resumed, the idea was presented to Mr. Bryson. Mr. Carter (who was a contractor) proposed that he build a wooden box that they would fill with shrubs, in order to block off part of the yard between their houses. The presence of the box would prevent the land from being used to park cars, which was one source of conflict between the two families. Mr. Carter stated that he and Mr. Bryson should share the cost of buying the lumber needed to build the box. During the subsequent discussion of this idea, Mr. Bryson decided that he wanted the planter box to be much larger than initially conceived. Mr. Carter then countered that Mr. Bryson should pay for all of the lumber needed to build the box instead of just half. Mr. Bryson rejected this idea, arguing that Mr. Carter could not go back on his offer. Mediator B worked to persuade him that an offer could be revised, but Mr. Bryson refused to accept the legitimacy of this argument, insisting on holding Mr. Carter to his initial offer.

Mediator A then joined the discussion and explained that an offer can be revised, and that negotiations should be reciprocal. Although Mr. Bryson listened to Mediator A's explanation, his response was noncommittal as to whether he was convinced by the mediator's argument. In the end, the mediators did not succeed in convincing Mr. Bryson that Mr. Carter's offer could be altered. Several minutes later, Mr. Bryson repeated his position that Mr. Carter could not alter his original offer to pay for half of lumber, saying "That was what was propo:sed to start with, and that's was what I agreed to."

In short, Mr. Bryson treated Mr. Carter's initial offer as a positional commitment. Disputants in these data typically display an orientation to the opposing disputant's suggestions as position reports to which they are committed. A disputant who changes their position toward their own proposal risks being seen by the opposing disputant as backing down from a commitment.

In sum, in these data both mediators and disputants display an orientation to disputants' ideas for resolution of issues under dispute as positional commitments. Mediators formulate their proposal solicits as position report solicits, and disputants typically formulate the ideas they suggest as position reports. Disputants are thus limited to potentially contentious strategies (positional commitments) rather than problem-solving strategies such as brainstorming (Carnevale and Pruitt 1992).

In order to reach agreement, at least one disputant typically must shift at least somewhat from their initial position that they held when the mediation session began. Mediators work to help disputants negotiate proposals and change positions during the session. However, once having displayed commitment to a proposal by making a position report, disputants may be motivated to resist mediator attempts to get them to produce new proposals. This aspect of mediation may inhibit disputants' willingness to freely brainstorm ideas to help solve the conflict. Therefore proposals produced by mediators, even though officially discouraged in many mediation programs, can be helpful for the generation of ideas for resolution of the dispute. In the next section I analyze how mediators make proposals for resolution of issues under dispute.

Mediator's Ideas for Resolution as "Suggestions"

While mediation has a norm of disputant autonomy and mediator neutrality,[3] previous research has shown that the reality often challenges these assumptions.[4] Mediators' proposals in these data were typically constructed to display an orientation to the values of mediator neutrality and disputant empowerment. One way in which this was done was to avoid formulating their suggestions as position reports. Instead, mediators formulated their proposals as information-seeking questions. They also mitigated proposals (with uncertainty markers, hesitation, presequences, and prefaces), and performed footing shifts (Goffman

---

[3] See Bishop et al. (2015); Doneff and Ordover (2014); Poitras and Raines (2013).
[4] See Cobb and Rifkin (1991b); Garcia (1995); Garcia et al. (2002); Greatbatch and Dingwall (1989).

1981) to credit others for the ideas rather than presenting them as their own. The use of these techniques lessened the likelihood that mediators' ideas for resolution of the dispute would challenge disputant autonomy.

Information-Seeking Questions as Mediator Proposals

Mediator's ideas for resolution in these data were routinely formulated as questions. One advantage of using a question format for a proposal is that as a first pair part of an adjacency pair, the question specifically displays an orientation to the expectation that the disputant will be responding to it. The question formulation thereby enables mediators to display an orientation to disputant autonomy while at the same time contributing to the dispute resolution process by making a suggestion.

Another advantage of using an information-seeking question to make a suggestion is that its status as a proposal is ambiguous. These questions can be heard either as suggestions for resolution of an issue, or simply as questions seeking information. The ambiguous status of the informational question can make the proposal work being done by it quite subtle. Question-asking is a routine part of the work of being a mediator.[5] The informational question-as-proposal presents the suggestion in the same way as all the other questions the mediator asks during the session, rather than foregrounding its status as a proposal. Because the proposal-as-question is not explicitly a proposal and does not stand out as one, the disputant has discretion as to how to respond to it. The disputant can respond to it as a proposal, by accepting or rejecting it. On the other hand, they can respond to it as a request for information by providing the information requested.

Excerpts 7.4 and 7.5 show how mediators' information-seeking questions can do double duty as proposals. Excerpt 7.4 is from the second session of Kate and Bob's family mediation. Kate wants to move out of Bob's house and rent an apartment for a few months while they work out their differences.

Excerpt 7.4 Bob and Kate Midwest Family Mediation, Session 2, p. 35

```
745  MA:    °Okay.° >ONCE you make uh decision
746         [about this if you can do it? it beh-    ]
747  Kate:  [I'VE EVEN considered? moving intuh] uh hotel! (1.9) Or uh
748         situation where you pay. You know? (0.7) Have him help pay.
749         (0.4) along that line if he's still open? (0.6) .h Just- tuh start °gettin'
750         some relief.° (1.2) I've considered that. I mean it's like last LAST
751         weekend? (1.3) I was going tuh go spend uh couple nights away!
752         (1.4)
```

---

[5] See Madonik (2001); Picard (2016); Ranger (2010); Whatling (2012).

Kate elaborates her desire to move out of Bob's house temporarily (lines 747–751). As the exchange continues in Excerpt 7.5, Mediator A makes a suggestion for resolution of this issue. She formulates this suggestion as a question ("Is there any place you could go Bob? (0.4) temporarily?"; line 753).

Excerpt 7.5 Bob and Kate Midwest Family Mediation, Session 2, p. 35

```
753  MA:   Is there any place you could go Bob? (0.4) temporarily?
754        (0.1)
755  Bob:  °Mm hm.° I thought t[his     ]
756  Kate:                      [>B' I ] DON'T WANNA LIVE< in his
757        house.
758        (0.8)
759  MA:   But we're just TALKIN' 'BOUT uh couple weeks.
760        (0.3)
761  Kate: >I don't wanna stay in his house!<
762        (0.6)
763  Bob:  I've offered tuh do? It wou' [be much simpler!]
764  Kate:                              [He >and his-<  ] he and his ex
765        wife's house.
```

Note that Mediator A does not frame her utterance in line 753 as a suggestion (e.g., "Bob could move out so Kate could stay in the house."). Mediator A's question has a preference for a "yes" answer, and Bob's initial response appears to be agreement-implicative ("°Mm hm.° I thought t[his]"; line 755). Kate then interrupts Bob's utterance-in-progress to explain why this implied suggestion would not work (">[B' I] DON'T WANNA LIVE< in his house."; lines 756–757). Kate's response displays an orientation to the mediator's information-seeking question as an implied proposal. In line 759 the mediator also displays an orientation to her informational question as an implied proposal, by working to pursue its acceptance. By formulating her suggestion as an information-seeking question, the mediator clearly presents it as a suggestion rather than a position to which she is committed. She is asking for a response from a disputant rather than taking a position relative to her implied suggestion.

In sum, maintaining a neutral stance and protecting the autonomy of the disputants could potentially be challenged by mediator participation in the proposal-production process. By formulating suggestions for resolution as information-seeking questions, the mediator can engage in the production of ideas for resolution while at the same time displaying an orientation to the norms of mediator neutrality and disputant autonomy. A proposal formulated as a suggestion would have a preference for an acceptance of the suggestion in the next turn space, while rejection of the proposal would be the dispreferred response. By formulating the mediator proposal as a question rather than as a suggestion, the disputant does not have to either accept or reject the mediator's proposal. This formulation provides disputants more latitude in how they will respond.

Mitigated Proposals

Greatbatch and Dingwall (1999) found that British divorce mediators may characterize a proposal as "only a suggestion" in order to avoid appearing to pressure disputants into accepting the proposal. I found that the mediators in the small claims and divorce data used a variety of techniques to mitigate their proposals and to display an orientation to disputant autonomy. Hesitation or delay and the use of prefaces and presequences worked to foreground the disputant's prerogative to accept or reject the mediator's suggestion.

For example, in Excerpts 7.6 and 7.7 from the first session of Jon and Liz's divorce mediation, several of these techniques for mitigating the impact of a mediator-produced proposal are used. In Excerpt 7.6, Mediator B produces a proposal for how Jon can get more visitation time with his daughter Bethany, who lives with his wife Liz.

Excerpt 7.6 Jon and Liz Midwest Divorce Mediation, Session 1, p. 30 (Garcia 2012: 408–409)

```
1286  MA:  Who kno-h-ws (0.3) what you get in thuh court huhh! (0.4) It's far
1287       better if you can (0.2) figure out (0.2) what you wa:nt and
1288       hopefully negotiate with each other. (1.1) than (0.4) putting it in
1289       thuh court's hands.
1290       (3.3)
1291  MB:  If we look at thuh s::chedule again, Maureen? Can [we go ] back
1292  MA:                                                   [Mmm?]
1293  MB:  tuh this:? [for uh    ] moment?
1294  MA:            [Mm hmm]
1295       (0.6)
1296  MB:  uhm: (1.1) It's: appears tuh me that (0.2) one of thuh bes:t (0.5)
1297       blank periods is thee- (0.6) Friday e:vening perhaps if that's: (0.6)
1298       (okay) with Liz who values her weekend time as we:ll! (0.9) That
1299       week end that you're not having her full time if there would
1300       maybe be some (0.8) Fri:day evening time that Liz wouldn't feel
1301       (0.4) she was giving up her very precious time (0.8) because that's
1302       uh period where you don't really see: her sometimes for (0.5)
1303       perhaps seven days (0.6) at uh time! And Liz is (0.4) going to have
1304       forty eight good hours, with her Saturday and Sunday, (0.6) so
1305       that may be an area that: (0.9) one could (1.0) consider (0.4)
1306       suitable for both of you? (2.0) D'you have something special
1307       sometimes is Friday evening, (1.5) very important (0.6) for you:?
```

Mediator B uses a variety of techniques to mitigate her suggestion-in-progress and display her orientation to the autonomy of the disputants. First, she uses a presequence (lines 1291 and 1293; Schegloff 1980) in a question directed to her co-mediator ("Maureen"). This presequence serves to get the floor to discuss the visitation schedule. After getting the floor (note Mediator A's responses in lines 1292 and 1294), Mediator B produces an extended turn which culminates in an information-seeking question (lines 1296–1307).

While Mediator B's suggestion is simply that the spouses add Friday evenings to Jon's weekly visitation schedule, her extended production of this suggestion displays her orientation to her role as a neutral mediator working to maintain the spouses' autonomy. For example, Mediator B briefly hesitates after getting the floor (line 1295). In addition, she pauses several times during the production of her utterance, beginning with an error avoidance ("uhm: (1.1)"; line 1296; Jefferson 1974; see also Schegloff et al. 1977). Mediator B qualifies her claim that Friday evening is one of the best times in the schedule ("It's: appears to me"; line 1296), thus framing it as a personal opinion and displaying uncertainty. As soon as she produces the suggestion itself ("Friday e:vening"; line 1297) she immediately follows it with an uncertainty marker ("perhaps"), and then explicitly defers to Liz's concerns ("Friday e:vening perhaps if that's: (0.6) (okay) with Liz who values her weekend time as we:ll!"; lines 1297–1298). Note also that the mediator does not mark the turn constructional unit which is possibly complete at "Friday e:vening" (line 1297) as a transition relevance place (Sacks et al. 1974). She does not use completion intonation and does not pause at this point. There are additional uncertainty markers in Mediator B's explanation of her suggestion, such as "maybe be some" (line 1300), and "one could (1.0) consider" (line 1305). She ends with an information-seeking question (lines 1306–1307).

Liz's response (Excerpt 7.7, line 1309), treats Mediator B's turn as a proposal by accepting the proposal.

Excerpt 7.7 Jon and Liz Midwest Divorce Mediation, Session 1, p. 30 (Garcia 2012: 409)

```
1308        (1.3)
1309  Liz:  (°Um hm°) (0.2) I can do: Friday evening.
1310        (2.4)
1311  MB:   tch Looks like one tuh me that:
1312        (0.6)
1313  MA:   It would be uh poss[ibility  ]
1314  MB:                      [(would)] very nicely
```

Note that Liz does not answer the informational question posed by Mediator B, but instead treats her question as a proposal (by accepting it). In sum, by mitigating proposals, mediators can participate in the brainstorming process without violating the norms of mediator neutrality and disputant autonomy.

Footing Shifts

Threats to mediator neutrality from producing proposals can also be mitigated through the use of footing shifts (Clayman 1988; 1992; Goffman 1981).

A mediator can use a footing shift to produce a suggestion on behalf of another person, or to credit them with the idea. Footing shifts can work to display an orientation to disputant autonomy by distancing the mediator from the proposal.

For example, in Excerpt 7.8 from David and Kim's divorce mediation, Mediator B makes a footing shift during the production of a proposal. David has complained that his daughter Jenny (who lives with his wife), does not visit him often enough.

Excerpt 7.8 David and Kim Midwest Divorce Mediation, Session 1, p. 70

```
1510  MB:    °Okay.° (1.0) tch °Okay.° (0.3) .h Now I DON'T KNOW how
1511         this'll work in with your? °s- um° (0.4) work schedule. (0.4) .h
1512         But: (1.4) h- having spoken with uh number of child psychologists
1513         about children of (0.4) °uh° Jenny's age (0.6) .h >one uh thuh
1514         thing< that's important! for them ih- is their peers! (1.0) tch >In
1515         general!< (0.6) °children >wanna be with<° (0.4) °>uh they wanna
1516         spend< less time with their parents, and more time their friends!°
1517         (0.4) .h Are YOU? pretty? close by: yet? (0.6) D[avid?]
1518  Dave:                                                  [Two ] miles.
1519         (0.3)
1520  MB:    Two miles. Okay. (0.4) .h So do- would you have?, thuh
1521         where withall? to:, if Jenny wanted tuh have (0.3) °uh° (0.3) °an
1522         overni- uh- over°night with you? but ha:ve uh girlfriend come
1523         along? >Y'know like uh little< slumber party kind uh thing?
1524         (0.2)
1525  Dave:  °Sure.°
1526         (0.3)
1527  MB:    Would work?
1528         (0.5)
1529  Dave:  °°Sure.°°
```

Mediator B suggests that David find a way to let his daughter Jenny maintain her relationships with her peers and her routine activities (such as babysitting) when she visits him. The mediator uses a footing shift to attribute the advice she is giving to "uh number of child psychologists" (line 1512). She also makes reference to peers (">In general!< (0.6) °children >wanna be with<° (0.4) °>uh they wanna spend< less time with their parents, and more time their friends!°"; lines 1514–1516); thus using the perspective of others to buttress her suggestion.

In sum, footing shifts are a commonly used technique by which mediators can distance themselves from the suggestion they are making. Footing shifts enable mediators to participate in the brainstorming process of generating ideas for resolution of the dispute while managing potential concerns about mediator neutrality and disputant autonomy.

Mediator Proposals and the Display of Neutrality

While mediators typically display an orientation to neutrality and disputant autonomy when making suggestions, mediators did occasionally produce positional commitments to proposals. While this rarely happened in these data, participants worked to repair it when it occurred. Excerpts 7.9 and 7.10 show what can happen if a mediator formulates an idea for resolution as a position report. During this family mediation between Stan and his children's stepfather Nick, Mediator A produces a position report:

Excerpt 7.9 Blended Family West Coast Mediation p. 108 (Garcia 1997: 230)

```
4265  Nick:  >You know?, that< thuh PRO::blem seems tuh be:: mostly
4266         between me and STA:N?, .h I:: U::H
4267         (.)
4268  MA:    (If she)=
4269  Nick:         =I didn't know [heLE::N]
4270  MA:                         [You    ] and Sta::n shouldn't have a:ny
4271         conta::ct at A::ll!
4272         (0.3)
4273  Nick:  WE::LL, I- but we HA:[:VE had that contact.]
4274  MA:                        [(To question       )] uh child support
4275         check, through an attorney, yeah, you're gonna have two attorney,
4276         contact's indiRE:CT!, .hh But I can't think of A::Ny rea:son,
4277         for you tuh ca::ll up?, (0.9) STA::N! (0.9) about A::Nything! (3.1)
4278         and vice uh versa!,
```

Mediator A interrupts Nick's explanation of why he and Stan are the ones who need to communicate about problems and restates a proposal he had made earlier in the session: "[You] and Sta::n shouldn't have a:ny conta::ct at A::ll!" (lines 4270–4271). This proposal is directly addressed, and is produced without delay or mitigation. This utterance functions as a position report because Mediator A makes a definitive statement of what he thinks should happen, and does not use a questioning format which would display an orientation to the disputant's autonomy. Note that Mediator A does not say that Nick and Stan could choose not to have contact, he says that that they "shouldn't." Directives such as "should" are first pair parts and make a response the next relevant action (Goodwin 1988). Nick's response "WE::LL, I- but we HA:[:VE had that contact.]" (line 4273) is rejection-implicative (Davidson 1984; Pomerantz 1984). Mediator A interrupts Nick before he completes this disagreement. Mediator A restates his position and provides justifications for it (lines 4274–4278).

As the exchange continues, both mediators treat Mediator A's position report as problematic. They work together to repair his position report and reframe it as a suggestion. Excerpt 7.10 begins with Mediator B's response to Mediator A's position report ("Seems fai[:r?,]"; line 2479):

Excerpt 7.10 Blended Family West Coast Mediation, p. 109 (Garcia 1997: 231)

```
2479  MB:    Seems fai[:r?, ]
2480  MA:            [PE: ]Rsonal opinion!, I'm not tryna sa:y that that's
2481         what you're gonna aGREE:: °to that's just uh
2482         (thought.)°=
2483  Stan:          =I::::=
2484  Nick:               =Ri::[ght!,]
2485  Stan:                [I    ]: HO:PED it would come tuh thi:s!,
2486         (0.6) Yeah. That sounds grea::t!, you kno[w?, wh]ere do I
2487  ?:                                             [(    )]
2488  Stan:  si::gn?=
2489  MA:           =We're not here tuh tell you what thuh hell tuh
2490         do::!,=
2491  Stan:        =Right.
2492         (0.5)
2493  MA:    'Cause if you don't wanna do it you ain't gonna do it any now.
2494         (0.7)
2495  MB:    °Yeah. (1.1) And you'll end up in court.
```

By asking if Mediator A's proposal "Seems fai[:r?," (line 2479), Mediator B works to repair the lack of a questioning component in Mediator A's original proposal. She thereby displays an orientation to the disputants' right to accept or reject the proposal. However, Mediator B's "Seems fai[:r?," does not itself challenge Mediator A's proposal. Mediator B therefore only partially moves away from Mediator A's position report. She avoids a direct challenge of his position. This repair work helps her to display a united front with her co-mediator rather than opening disagreeing with him.

Mediator A takes the place of a disputant response at this point by over-lapping Mediator B's question at the earliest possible recognition point: "[PE:]Rsonal opinion!," (line 2480). By announcing that his proposal was his personal opinion, Mediator A works to distance his position from his proposal, which was equivalent to a position report. By separating his personal opinion from his earlier suggestion, he implies that the disputants may have a different opinion. As Mediator A continues his utterance, he highlights the disputants' right to agree or disagree with his suggestion (lines 2480–2482). Mediator A's repair work supports Mediator B's move by immediately retreating from his original position report.

Stan and Nick then respond to the mediators' reframed proposal. By virtue of its positioning, Nick's "Ri::[ght!,]" (line 2484) seems to be responding to Mediator A's prior turn rather than Stan's turn beginning in line 2483. Nick's utterance is an agreement with Mediator A's prior turn, in which he separated his personal opinion from the disputants' right to create an agreement. Nick therefore supports Mediator A's repair of his initial position report, that the disputants will decide whether they will have contact or not.

On the other hand, Stan's completed response conveys his enthusiasm with Mediator A's original proposal, that he and Nick should not have contact ("[I]: HO:PED it would <u>come</u> tuh thi:s!, (0.6) Yeah. That sounds <u>grea::t</u>!, you kno[w?, wh]ere do I <u>si::gn</u>?="; lines 2483, 2485–2486, 2488). Stan thus aligns with Mediator A's position report by expressing strong appreciation for and approval of Mediator A's suggestion. The two disputants therefore have opposing positions relative to the idea Mediator A has introduced. Stan is in favor of the proposal, while Nick's statement supports his right to either accept or reject the proposal.

After the disputants respond, Mediator A again works to emphasize the autonomy of the disputants and their right to decide how to respond (lines 2489–2490, 2493), emphasizing that he is not trying to force the disputants to agree. Mediator B agrees with Mediator A in line 2495.

In sum, these excerpts have illustrated that when a mediator formulates his or her ideas for resolution as position reports and displays a positional commitment to them, his or her neutral stance and the autonomy of the disputants may be challenged. In the context of facilitative mediation, taking a position relative to a potential solution is an action typically reserved for disputants.

Proposal Production in Divorce Mediation

While participants in small claims mediation sessions typically use the speech exchange system of mediation (in which talk is directed to mediators and disputants wait until selected to speak when the opposing disputant has the floor), in divorce mediation sessions segments of talk in a hybrid interactional format are more likely to occur. This quasi-conversational structure opens the possibility for a wider range of ways that proposals can be produced.

The latter sessions of the multisession divorce mediation cases were particularly likely to have segments of talk conducted in a hybrid format, involving a quasi-conversational speech exchange system rather than the typical mediation format. This shift in interactional style is often associated with an increased degree of comfort between the parties and a decrease in conflict between them, as they reach the stage of the mediation process where they have agreed on many of the issues and learned to trust the process and the mediators.

In these data I found that divorce mediators are more likely to engage with the spouses in a collaborative proposal solicitation and development process. Divorcing spouses may work together and collectively produce proposals, and at times one spouse may directly address the other in order to make a suggestion. These exchanges may also involve mediators coaching disputants on how to develop and implement proposals.

Mediators in the divorce mediation cases more often treat disputants as two people with shared interests rather than as individuals on opposing sides of a dispute. Disputants in the divorce mediation sessions occasionally referred to themselves and their spouses as "we" when making proposals. This type of collective self-reference is rarely seen in the small claims cases, where participants typically do not know each other well and are on opposing sides of an issue. In the divorce mediation cases, the spouses all have children so even after the divorce they will share responsibilities for their care. This "we-ness" is therefore intrinsic to their situation and may be reflected in their formulation of proposals. Proposals disputants produced in divorce mediation sessions were therefore more likely to be produced by a disputant directly addressing the opposing disputant than in the small claims sessions.

In addition, there is one type of proposal which occurred only in the divorce mediation sessions: the joking or semi-serious proposal. While a joking proposal can help to express emotions about an issue, there are also concrete ways joking proposals can be useful for the proposal-generation process. For example, stating an outrageous position that no one expects to be accepted can be useful because it enables participants to articulate challenging issues. Seemingly outrageous suggestions may be an effective part of the brainstorming process (Bishop et al. 2015). This difference between divorce and small claims mediation sessions suggests that the divorce mediation sessions may be more effective in facilitating brainstorming than the small claims cases. In this section I show how mediators engage in the process of proposal generation in the divorce mediation sessions.

Proposal Generation in Hybrid Exchanges

Proposal production often unfolds differently in divorce and small claims mediation sessions. In hybrid exchanges in divorce mediation there may be direct address between disputants as proposals are produced. In addition, mediators at times actively participate in the proposal-production process. While the disputants in the small claims mediation sessions tend to take an adversarial posture vis-à-vis each other, the dynamic between disputants in divorce mediation sessions is more complex. While there can be a high level of conflict and animosity between the spouses (Gulbrandsen et al. 2018), there is also a shared history and shared interest in their children. This may be one reason that collectively constructed disputant proposals occasionally occurred in the divorce mediation sessions, but not in the small claims cases.

Excerpt 7.11 from the third session of Darryl and Belinda's divorce mediation shows a disputant producing a proposal in an utterance addressed directly to the opposing disputant. The excerpt begins after a question-and-answer exchange between Mediator B and Belinda about the couple's son Marcus.

Excerpt 7.11 Darryl and Belinda Midwest Divorce Mediation, Session 3, p. 28

```
595  Bel:   And we've been working with Marcus' psychologist tryn' tuh get
596          him tuh pick (0.5) uh couple of activities and he still has not (1.0)
597          found anything that's acceptable tuh just get out, and get him
598          moving .hh (0.7) uh Get him burning off energy, and also get him
599          away from thuh other two kids.
600          (0.4)
601  MA:    °Mm hm.°
602          (0.5)
603  Bel:   tch (0.7) So maybe Darryl, (0.9) you know, we could sit dow:n and
604          you could back me up on this and sa:y okay when you get outta
605          control. (0.6) .h And when Mom or Dad says, (0.5) out you go or
606          in thuh basement, do your laps, (0.6) you go.
607          (1.7)
608  Dar:   °Sure.°
609          (0.1)
610  Bel:   'M'kay?
611          (1.4)
612  Dar:   °Sure.°=
613  Bel:          =I mean I think that would if they just had like uh °relea:se°
614          (0.8) y'know
615          (0.1)
616  MB:    I think they're probably feelin' uh split between you two, an' an' I
617          don't know if u:m (0.3) I mean does that feel right?
618          (0.3)
619  Bel:   Yeah.
```

Belinda's first turn in Excerpt 7.11 is part of an ongoing exchange with Mediator B about the couple's eldest son Marcus (lines 595–599). Belinda then directly addresses her husband Darryl and makes a proposal for how he could support her efforts to improve Marcus's behavior (lines 603–606). She asks him to "back me up" (line 604) by supporting her efforts to get Marcus more exercise. Darryl agrees with this suggestion (line 608). After a few more exchanges of turns Mediator B again joins the discussion (lines 616–617).

When compared to the adversarial relationship often seen between disputants in the small claims cases, there is a blurring of the lines of opposition in this divorce mediation session. However, note that although Darryl agrees with Belinda's proposal, there is some reluctance displayed. There are relatively long pauses prior to his responses (lines 607 and 611). Also, note that Darryl speaks very quietly when giving his assent in lines 608 and 612 ("°Sure.°"), which may indicate that his agreement is tentative or unenthusiastic.

Another way that proposal generation in divorce cases differs from that in small claims mediation is the role of the mediators in the proposal-production process. The divorce mediators in these data at times participate in the production and development of proposals and coach disputants in their implementation.

For example, in Excerpts 7.12 and 7.13 from the third session of Darryl and
Belinda's divorce mediation, the spouses at times address each other directly,
and the mediators participate in the proposal development process in several
ways. Excerpt 7.12 begins with Mediator B making a suggestion that Darryl
and Belinda talk to their children about their attempt to work together in
mediation:

Excerpt 7.12 Darryl and Belinda Midwest Divorce Mediation, Session 3, p. 119

```
2590  MB:  u:m (0.7) And whether it's both of yo:u (0.1) together, saying, (0.4)
2591       y'know we're in mediation and we don't know what's happening
2592       and, (0.2) y'know >but uh mean, can you do that. Can you? (0.4)
2593       I mean even kids like tuh hear it when you say, I don't know what
2594       I'm doin' but I'm doin' somethin'.
2595       (0.2)
2596  Bel: [Right.   ]
2597  MB:  [Y'know] I'm >tryin' tuh do< somethin'=
2598  Bel:                                      =I think we should have uh
2599       meeting >with 'em Darryl.< (0.2) >°Whatta you think.°< (0.3) °and
2600       just uh°
2601       (0.4)
2602  Dar: °(>Why don' we figure< this out >°What we're gonna< say tuh
2603       them first.)
```

As Excerpt 7.12 begins, Mediator B introduces the idea that Darryl and
Belinda should talk to their children about the ongoing divorce mediation
process (lines 2590–2594, and 2597). Belinda first produces an agreement-
implicative minimal response ("Right"; line 2596), and then addresses her
husband Darryl directly. Belinda produces a position report and solicits
Darryl's response to it (lines 2598–2600). Darryl's response to this suggestion
is not an outright rejection, but it refocuses the discussion onto the content
of their communication with their children rather than the mode or timing
of it (lines 2602–2603). As the exchange continues, Mediator A responds
(Excerpt 7.13):

Excerpt 7.13 Darryl and Belinda Midwest Divorce Mediation, Session 3, p. 119

```
2604       (0.4)
2605  MA:  .h Yea:h I think you have to
2606       (0.2)
2607  Bel: Yeah?
2608       (0.2)
2609  MA:  Believe °what you're gonna say too. (0.2) I [mean   ] you if you-
2610  Bel:                                             [Mm hm.]
2611  MA:  if you have uh feeling. (0.4) tha:t (0.3) you're not gonna be there
2612       for them. (0.8) then: you can't say that.
```

```
2613          (0.1)
2614   MB:    Yeah.
2615          (0.2)
2616   Bel:   Right.
2617          (0.1)
2618   MA:    I think (0.2) that if yo:u (0.3) and it may take uh (0.2)
2619          >while you know,< (0.2) tu:h tuh work this through is .hh (0.2) and
2620          when you talk tuh them and you SA:Y, (0.2) I wuh (0.1) Mom and
2621          Dad are having (0.1) for example! (0.2) Mom and I are obviously
2622          having some °difficulties° [we're try ]ing (0.2) we're (0.1) we're
2623   Bel:                             [Mm hm. ]
2624   MA:    working things out. (0.2) mm But no MATTER what happens!
2625          (0.8) >I'm gonna uh< be your Dad,
2626          (0.3)
2627   Bel:   Mm hm.
2628          (0.2)
2629   MA:    °Mom you're gonna be their Mom, and (we're gonna) be there for
2630          you.°
```

Mediator A responds to Darryl's contribution (lines 2605, 2609, 2611–2612). While Mediator A's line 2605 looks like a simple agreement with Darryl's position that he and his wife should begin by figuring out what they will say to the children, the continuation of his utterance reflects a different point. Mediator A references Darryl's statements from earlier in the mediation that if the divorce goes through he might essentially abandon the family (not shown). In lines 2609, 2611, and 2612 Mediator A takes the position that what the spouses tell the children has to be real. Therefore, what first looked like Mediator A agreeing with and siding with Darryl's proposal revision, is instead Mediator A bringing another point into the discussion. The mediator is thereby contributing to the proposal development process and helping to shape what the spouses decide to do. After Mediator B and Belinda respond to his contributions with agreement tokens (lines 2614 and 2616), Mediator A provides further input to the developing proposal by suggesting specific wording they might use as they talk to the children (lines 2618–2622, 2624–2625, 2629–2630).

In this and other of these divorce mediation sessions, the solicitation and discussion of proposals is integrated with mediator coaching of disputants. As Excerpt 7.14 begins, the participants are discussing how Bob should inform his parents that he has decided to marry Kate. Earlier in the mediation process the couple had revealed that Bob's parents have a strong prejudice against Kate. The excerpt begins with Mediator A soliciting a proposal from Bob as to how he should approach the discussion with his parents (lines 1936–1937).

Excerpt 7.14 Bob and Kate Midwest Family Mediation, Session 3, p. 89

1936	MA:	So: (0.7) what d' y' think (0.7) your approach could be, and
1937		when could you talk to them?
1938		(0.7)
1939	Bob:	tch Well I'd- I've I <u>wanna</u> get up there, and I- maybe even
1940		tomorrow <u>night</u>? (0.5) dependin' on what's goin' on. °hhh °h
1941		°h y'know try to get up there and talk to them? (0.7) AND I I
1942		MEAN I it's: (0.4) I don't know <u>what</u> my approach will be,
1943		it's one of those um (0.8) just play it by EAR? (0.6) u:h
1944		(1.9) °tch, y'know.°
1945		(0.1)
1946	MA:	So: you're gonna go over there and sa:y (0.8) Mom and Dad
1947		you probably already <u>know</u>, (0.7) Kate and I have set uh
1948		date to be married.
1949		(0.6)
1950	Bob:	°°°Mm hm!°°°
1951		(0.5)
1952	MA:	And prePARE yourself for (1.0) whatever they might say.

While Bob makes a suggestion in response to one of Mediator A's concerns (when he will talk to his parents), he denies having a suggestion about how he could approach the discussion, suggesting he will just play it by ear (lines 1939–1944). Mediator A responds by paraphrasing his suggestion (lines 1946–1948 and 1952). Note that Mediator A's paraphrase goes beyond a summary of what Bob actually said. She uses this summary to instruct or coach Bob in how he could conduct the interaction with his parents.

This process of proposal development differs markedly from proposal generation in small claims mediation sessions in that the mediator is an integral part of the proposal generation process. Even though the spouses are at times using a more conversational approach and speaking directly to each other, the mediator is still playing a major role in the discussion.

In sum, proposal generation in divorce mediation often works differently than in small claims mediation, because especially in sessions with relatively low levels of conflict between the spouses, they are able to engage in brief directly addressed hybrid exchanges. Disputant proposals which are produced in quasi-conversational hybrid exchanges may differ in placement and structure from the disputant proposals typically seen in small claims mediation. This can mean that a proposal (or position report) can be responded to directly by the other disputant. Their acceptance or rejection can thereby occur adjacently in these sessions. Institutional role is not as rigidly tied to proposal generation as it is in small claims mediations. Mediators may engage in and contribute to the development of proposals, and disputants may work together and direct proposals to each other rather than through mediated interaction.

Joking Proposals

Laughter can perform many functions depending on where it is placed.[6] Keyton
and Beck (2010) suggest that laughter in jury deliberations may create ambi-
guity which creates openness for solving problems. A nonserious or joking
proposal in a mediation session may provide opportunities for stress reduction
or expression of emotions. It may also serve as an opportunity for creating
alignment between opposing disputants. Joking proposals may also play a role
in the brainstorming process. For example, in the next two excerpts, Darryl and
Belinda use joking or nonserious proposals to express their thoughts about the
serious challenges they have with their eldest son Marcus. Excerpt 7.15, from
the couple's fifth mediation session, begins with Mediator A soliciting the
spouses' preferences for where their three children will live after the divorce.
He uses an informational question to introduce the idea that the children do not
necessarily have to live together (lines 1201–1204).

Excerpt 7.15 Darryl and Belinda Midwest Divorce Mediation, Session 5, p. 56

```
1201  MA:  But these are thuh kind uh things that y' (0.3) if you can, (1.0) (
1202             ) gimme some thoughts as to where thuh children
1203       will live. (1.6) (              ) no, whatta your thoughts
1204       about them all staying together?
1205       (2.3)
1206  Bel:  I don't know=
1207  MA:           =Where they're (living        )=
1208  Bel:                                         =Yet through today I
1209       was thinking, Go:d it'd be great if u:h just (1.6) if somebody adopt
1210       Marcus or jus:t (0.4) take him, [you-h-know?    ]
1211  Dar:                                 [Military school?]
1212       (0.9)
1213  MA:  Mm!
1214       (0.6)
1215  Dar:  whech=huh=henh=henh
1216       (0.2)
1217  Bel:  Because (0.4) Darryl has uh sister who occasionally, (1.2) fairly
1218       often actually takes Marcus for uh weekend. (0.9) uhh!
1219       (0.8)
1220  MA:  Mm hm.=
1221  Bel:          =Thuh difference in our house, is just amazing, it's quiet.
```

Belinda expresses the thought that "Yet through today I was thinking, Go:d
it'd be great if u:h just (1.6) if somebody adopt Marcus or jus:t (0.4) take him,
[you-h-know?]" (lines 1208–1210). Her laugh-implicative aspiration in line

---

[6] See Arminen and Halonen (2007); Glenn (2003; 2010); Holt (2010); Jefferson (1979; 1984b).

1210 is what Jefferson (2004b) refers to as an "in-speech" laugh. This suggests that she is treating her utterance as a candidate laughable (Jefferson 2004b). This nonserious proposal enables her to express her feelings about their situation. Her husband Darryl overlaps her turn with a second joking proposal ("[Military school?]"; line 1211). Mediator A responds to this with a laugh-implicative minimal response (line 1213). After a brief pause Darryl then laughs (line 1215). Belinda continues in a more serious vein (lines 1217–1218 and 1221), and the discussion of their son Marcus continues.

A few minutes later in the same mediation session another joking proposal occurs. Belinda asks her husband "You want Marcus, Darryl?" (Excerpt 7.16, line 1475). Darryl responds with an exclamation and a laughter particle ("phew=henh"; line 1477), thus treating this question as a joking proposal.

Excerpt 7.16 Darryl and Belinda Midwest Divorce Mediation, Session 5, p. 67

```
1462  MA:                                      =.hh Some uh thuh
1463        thoughts are you know you may wannas (              ) is that
1464        best °if they all stay together? or=
1465  Bel:                         =Mm hm.
1466        (0.4)
1467  MB:   or that thuh one goes with thuh Da:d=
1468  MA:                               =Ye:ah
1469        (0.4)
1470  MB:   two stay with thuh Mo:m or (0.3)
1471        [two (          ) go with Da:d and]=
1472  MA:   [Whatever combination works      ]=
1473  MB:                            =(        ) with thuh
1474        [Mom and Dad]
1475  Bel:  [Mm hm.     ] (0.2) You want Marcus, Darryl?
1476        (0.5)
1477  Dar:  phew=henh=
1478  MA:                 =I'm just I'm just (0.2) posing a:ll these when [( )]
1479        one possibility
```

Mediator A's statement in lines 1478–1479 does not respond to Darryl's laughter or otherwise treat Belinda's suggestion as a nonserious proposal. Here he seems to be doing work to avoid being seen to take a positional commitment. In sum, while joking proposals are rare in these data, disputants can use them to discuss ideas that might be seen as unrealistic or controversial. Difficult ideas can get on the table through these semi-serious suggestions, thus facilitating the brainstorming process and the disputants' understanding of the issues they face.

In Excerpt 7.17 a couple is using mediation to help work out issues they need to resolve before deciding whether to get married. Excerpt 7.17 shows them discussing the problem of Bob's jealousy when his partner Kate interacts with other men in dance clubs. The mediator produces a proposal solicit (lines 1152 and 1156). This is a specific solicit, because it focuses only on this issue rather than the many other issues they have been working on in the session.

Excerpt 7.17 Bob and Kate Midwest Family Mediation, Session 3, p. 53

```
1148  Kate:  [(Nor-)] eh yeah! that (0.7) I shouldn't feel (1.0) bad about
1149         having that innocent conversation? I shouldn't fe:el °I'm
1150         gonna get in trouble if I ever° (0.4) if I talk! to this gu:y!
1151         (0.2)
1152  MA:    Well LET'S BRAINstorm
1153         (0.4)
1154  Bob:   chuh! chuh! chuh
1155         (0.2)
1156  MA:    What would help in these situations. (0.3) There-
1157         (0.1)
1158  Kate:  For me t' put uh bag on my head? T' wear uh skirt down to
1159         here? and talk [to   ] nobody? unless it's uh female? or in
1160  MA:                   [.heh!]
1161  Kate:  it's- or it's him.
1162         (0.4)
1163  MA:    But then you wouldn't know when=
1164  Bob:                           =>Kate [was like-<]
1165  MA:                                   [Bob is eye]in'
1166         somebody else.
1167         (0.6)
1168  Bob:   hh=henh heh .h
```

First, note that Mediator A uses a collective approach in her general solicit, beginning line 1152: "Well LET'S BRAINstorm." With this formulation she creates an alignment between Bob and Kate and the two mediators. This formulation projects a collaborative approach to problem solving and brainstorming ideas for solutions. The collective proposal solicit is unsuccessful, and Mediator A pursues production of a proposal via a specific proposal solicit in line 1156. Kate responds to the mediator's specific solicit with a tongue-in-cheek suggestion that she wear a paper bag over her head in order to avoid attention from other men (lines 1158–1159, 1161). Mediator A participates in the joking frame Kate has introduced, by producing a short laughter particle (line 1160; Glenn 2003; Jefferson 1979), followed by a joking response (lines 1163 and 1165–1166). Bob displays his participation in the joking frame with his (slightly delayed) laugh (line 1168). This exchange has several characteristics of hybrid interaction, including collaborative talk, the use of a joking frame to contribute to the production of suggestions for resolution, and disputant's self-selection to speak.

In sum, proposal production in divorce mediation differs in several ways from that in small claims mediation. Due to the more flexible interactional organization of divorce mediation, in which participants at times use a hybrid speech exchange system involving disputant self-selection and direct address of the opposing disputant, disputants in divorce mediation sessions may address proposals directly to each other. In addition, a collaborative approach to proposal generation may be employed, in which mediators participate in brainstorming ideas for resolution and help shape and develop ideas in conjunction with disputants. Mediators may also engage in coaching of disputants as to how to implement proposals. Finally, joking or nonserious proposals were occasionally produced by disputants in the divorce and family mediations. This approach both displayed and reinforced the less adversarial approach which is often achieved in these divorce mediation sessions.

Discussion and Conclusions

As this analysis of proposal solicitation and production has shown, participants in mediation use a variety of techniques to display an orientation to the norms of disputant autonomy and mediator neutrality. While the mediator's proposal solicits facilitate disputant autonomy by letting the disputant produce ideas for resolution, they may also disempower them. The negotiation between mediators and disputants over when and how ideas for resolution will be produced is an interactional context in which the goal of disputant empowerment and autonomy promised by mediation may not be completely achieved. For example, when mediators produce position report solicits rather than suggestion solicits, select which disputant makes a proposal first, or select the point in the session in which a proposal is solicited, they are to some extent limiting the autonomy of the disputants.

Mediators and disputants play different roles in the proposal-production process. Since mediators' ideas for resolution are almost always suggestions rather than position reports, they can produce ideas without committing themselves (or the disputants) to that idea. The rare instances when mediators displayed a position in favor of a proposal they made were quickly repaired. By avoiding such positional commitments to suggestions they make during the session, mediators can maintain neutrality relative to the issues and increase the chances they will be perceived as fair and unbiased. They can thus effectively contribute to the brainstorming process and, ultimately, the resolution of the dispute.

In these data disputants' suggestions for resolution of issues under dispute were formulated as position reports. The opposing disputants routinely treated these position reports as offers to which the disputant was committed. Since position-taking can be contentious,[7] disputants have less freedom to brainstorm ideas for the solution-generation process than do mediators. Disputants can change their positions once they have made an offer, but repair work is required to accomplish this shift.

The organization of proposal production in divorce mediation can differ substantially from that in small claims mediation, especially when participants engage in hybrid exchanges which combine aspects of the speech exchange systems of mediation and ordinary conversation. First, mediators may treat the divorcing couple as a collectivity and ask them to come up with suggestions for resolution together. Disputants may at times direct proposals directly to the opposing disputant rather than to the mediators, and may engage in a collaborative proposal construction process involving the participation of the mediators. Second, discussion of proposals in divorce mediation may lead to instances of coaching of disputants, as the mediators not only respond to disputants' ideas for resolution, but also work to instruct participants as to how to better handle the problems they are facing. Third, the occasional use of joking or nonserious proposals may occur in the divorce mediation sessions.

Given previous research which shows that problem-solving strategies such as brainstorming are more effective negotiation tactics than positional commitments, how mediators facilitate the proposal-production process is critical for its effectiveness in creating agreement between disputing parties. Mediators may therefore need to take additional measures to maximize the contributions of disputants in proposal generation. It may be that private caucuses with individual disputants are a better environment for brainstorming sessions than the joint mediation session. If allowed to make suggestions for resolution in private, treating disputant's ideas for resolution as positional commitments can more easily be avoided. If mediators conduct brainstorming in the joint session, they should make a point of emphasizing that merely suggesting an idea does not mean that the disputant is committed to it. By producing proposal solicits (as in "suggest an idea for resolution"), rather than position report solicits (as in "what do you want?"), mediators may create a frame for disputant's ideas for resolution that supports such flexibility. Disputants' suggestions should not be taken as positional commitments until the ideas are on the table and have been discussed by the participants and agreed upon. However, in these data even mediators who emphasized the provisional nature of proposals and worked hard to explain the brainstorming process were often confronted by disputant reluctance to produce suggestions for resolution. A more formal process for brainstorming ideas for resolution may need to be created.

[7] See Carnevale and Pruitt (1992); Fisher and Ury (1991); Pruitt et al. (1983).

Another aspect of mediation that may need to be reconsidered is the common convention that mediators refrain from making suggestions for resolution. Such actions are often considered to be stepping beyond the facilitative role. Intervening in the substance of the dispute is something that mediators are trained to avoid. However, as this analysis of the process of producing ideas for resolution has shown, the fact that mediator's suggestions are not taken to be position reports may be a strength that outweighs any potential risk of intervening in the substance of the dispute. Mediation programs may want to consider including mediator assistance in creating ideas for resolution as part of the official process of facilitative mediation. Measures such as these may open the door for the production of more creative solutions to problems.

8   Mediator Teamwork

Mediation programs may choose to use teams of mediators rather than single mediators for a variety of reasons. Co-mediators can assist each other in facilitating the interaction and can balance each other's skills and knowledge (Bishop et al. 2015; Rosengard 2016). Teams of mediators can also model cooperative behavior for the disputants as they conduct the session (Boulle et al. 2008). While in the Midwest small claims program the mediators work alone, in the West Coast mediation program and the Midwest divorce and family mediations, the mediators routinely work in two-person teams. This chapter will explore a range of ways mediators can accomplish teamwork and present a united front vis-à-vis the disputants to best accomplish the goals of mediation.

Interactants can work together to put on a performance as a team by maintaining a definition of the situation (Goffman 1959). This performance is accomplished through coordinating activities with team members, avoiding disagreeing with or repairing actions of team members, and presenting teamwork as spontaneously achieved (Goffman 1959). While Goffman gives several examples of situations in which teams give successful or unsuccessful performances, he does not describe how these performances are maintained during extended verbal exchanges.

Francis (1986) identified routine interactional procedures as a resource that can be used to construct a team performance. In his study of industrial mediation, teams of disputants aligned and coordinated their actions to accomplish teamwork during negotiations. Management and labor formed separate teams, who constructed their team identities through interactional techniques such as supporting each other's actions, passing the floor to a team member who could more effectively respond, or intervening when they felt they could more effectively manage the exchange.

Previous research on mediation and other negotiation contexts explores how mediators accomplish team work in those settings. Pogatschnigg (2012) conducted interviews with mediators about co-mediation, and Greatbatch and Dingwall (1994) used conversation analysis to discover several ways that co-mediators can support each other's interventions in situations where disputants' actions are problematic. For example, they found that mediators may use agreement tokens and other types of supportive utterances to express agreement with their co-mediator.

Numerous techniques and procedures by which participants in interactions can create and display alignment have been described in previous research. Clayman (1985) found that disjunctures can be avoided or repaired by displaying realignment, retrospectively deconstructing disjunctures, or changing the topic. The use of perspective-display sequences facilitates the production of opinions while avoiding overt disagreement or disaffiliation with the party addressed (Maynard 1989). By first asking for the other's opinion, the initial speaker can then adjust their response to that opinion, thereby avoiding potential disjunctures between them. Unacquainted persons can avoid potentially problematic disjunctures by using pretopical sequences to screen inappropriate topics and identify topics with which they can both align (Maynard and Zimmerman 1984). Children may create alignments or display misalignment during argumentative exchanges (Maynard 1985a).

There are several ways in which preference organization (e.g., Pomerantz 1984; Sacks 1987a; Schegloff et al. 1977) can be used by interactants to avoid or mitigate misalignment. For example, the preference for agreement with assessments identified by Pomerantz (1984) provides for the immediate and direct production of agreements with assessments, while disagreements are typically delayed, formulated indirectly, and mitigated. The preference for self-correction minimizes the occurrence of other-correction, in which the misalignment of co-interactants is made visible.[1]

The display of alignment, so prevalent in ordinary conversation, is rendered problematic in situations of conflict. Under such conditions, participants may deliberately violate a norm of agreement in order to accomplish arguing.[2] Although not designed to be an adversarial process, mediation is an interaction between participants who are in disagreement over issues which are important to them. Mediators must therefore facilitate the session while managing or preventing overt conflict between the disputants. Ideally, a mediator will coordinate their actions with their co-mediator in a way that models respectful interaction and does not contribute to an escalation of conflict in the hearing.

In this chapter I analyze how co-mediators construct their performance as a team to display a united front to the disputants. I begin with a discussion of instances in which there were failures of teamwork to illustrate why successful teamwork matters for the mediation process. I then describe a range of techniques mediators use to create and display the coordination and alignment of

---

[1]   See Francis (1986); Jefferson (1979); Schegloff et al. (1977).
[2]   For example, see Garcia (1991); Goodwin (1983); Maynard (1985b).

their actions with their co-mediator's actions, enabling the display of a united front vis-à-vis the disputants. These techniques include displaying teamwork through silence, explicit negotiation, expressions of agreement, paraphrases, sentence completions, "and-prefaces," and complementary actions.

Failure of Alignment between Co-mediators

As Garfinkel (1967) notes, the work participants do in interaction becomes visible on occasions when that work failed. In these data I identified three categories of failures of alignment between co-mediators: activity misalignment, substantive misalignment, and interactional misalignment. While in practice these phenomena may overlap, failure on any one of these fronts may create a visible disjuncture between the mediators. Activity misalignment has to do with whether the mediators are working to achieve the goals of the same stage of the mediation session (for example, the opening stage, the facilitation of a disputant's story, the transition to the generation of ideas for resolution, or the negotiation over potential proposals for resolution). Substantive misalignment involves the mediators' display of disagreement over issues or the specifics of the dispute. Interactional misalignment involves the mediators' failure to coordinate the exchange of turns at talk as they work together to facilitate the session.

Activity Misalignment

Part of the work of facilitating a mediation session is managing transitions through the stages of the hearing. The small claims mediation sessions follow a fairly standard format. The introductory stage of the session is followed by the mediators' solicitation of opening statements from each disputant in turn. The disputants' opening statements are typically followed by discussion of the issues raised. In addition, there may be caucuses with individual disputants. At some point in this process, the mediators initiate a transition to the idea generation stage in which disputants are encouraged to produce suggestions for resolving the dispute. The discussion of these suggestions is followed by the creation of an agreement or a decision to terminate the mediation without an agreement.

While the Midwest divorce mediation cases differ in several ways from the small claims cases, in both types of mediation there are routine procedures for moving through the initial stages of mediation to the agreement creation stage. When two mediators are working together as co-mediators, the process of moving from one stage or activity to another must be coordinated between them. Failure to successfully coordinate transitions between such activities are rare in these data, but some instances did occur.

Transition from the Discussion Stage to the Solution-Generation Stage.
Failures of mediator alignment can occur during attempts to transition from
one stage of the hearing to another. Excerpts 8.1 and 8.2 show the mediators
misaligned as to whether they should move from the discussion stage of
the hearing to the solution-generation stage. Excerpt 8.1 begins with the
respondent Nancy answering a question about a letter she and her neighbors
wrote complaining about their neighbor, the complainant Ms. Kemper (lines
1743–1744).

Excerpt 8.1 Neighbors West Coast Small Claims Mediation, p. 76

```
1743  Nan:  =No!, (0.2) Maple Street:, management, to: .hh thee: o:wner of
1744        thuh complex.
1745        (0.2)
1746  MA:   .hh I[:: have uh question.]
1747  MB:      [>Okay. A        ]lright.< (0.2) Yeah.
1748        (0.1)
1749  MA:   >>Are you through (then)?<<
1750        (0.2)
1751  MB:   U::H?, (0.2) >I have uh couple< mo:re, but I can wait!
1752        (0.2)
1753  MA:   >(   go    )<
1754        (0.2)
1755  MB:   Don't- (0.2) don't loose your thought!?
1756        (0.2)
1757  MA:   tch I've had it for (0.2) twenty minutes. (0.2) (now)=
1758  MB:                                              =Oh! h
1759        huh hunh hunh heh heh heh hunh! .hhhh O:kay, (0.2) ALL right.
```

Mediator A initiates a presequence (Schegloff 1980) to get the floor to
ask a question (line 1746). Mediator B's listener responses in line 1747 refer
to Nancy's prior turn (lines 1743–1744). Mediator B's response overlaps
Mediator A's turn. The "Yeah." Mediator B produces in line 1747 is ambiguous as to whether it invites Mediator A to produce the question she has
projected, or whether it is part of Mediator B's response to Nancy's prior turn.
Mediator A works to repair this uncertainty with her question in line 1749.
Her question is formulated with a preference for agreement (Pomerantz 1984;
Sacks 1987a). However, Mediator B's response begins with a rejection-
implicative placeholder (line 1751), followed by a statement which confirms
that she has more questions to ask but also that she is willing to let Mediator
A go first. Mediator A's response to this is unfortunately inaudible (line 1753),
but Mediator B's next turn in line 1755 seems to be encouraging Mediator A
to ask her question. However, Mediator A defers in line 1757, indicating that
there is no rush to ask her question. Mediator B acknowledges this with a
surprise marker ("Oh!", line 1758; see Heritage 1984b) followed by laughter
(line 1759).

As the exchange continues, Mediator B initiates a transition to the solution-generation phase of the hearing instead of asking the question she had projected in line 1751. She does this by asking the disputants for a resolution (Excerpt 8.2, lines 1760 and 1763).

Excerpt 8.2 Neighbors West Coast Small Claims Mediation, p. 76

```
1760  MB:      (0.2) thuh poi:nt i::s:, (0.6) thuh resolu::tion,
1761           (0.2)
1762  Nan?:    >Umh.<=
1763  MB:                =of thuh ma:tter. (0.2) Not- (0.2) any: (0.9) uh- great:
1764           more de:tail will be needed to exPLAI::N to A:nybody!,
1765           .hh=
1766  Nan:      =>>Um hm<<,
1767           (0.1)
1768  MB:      u::h, that there is uh problem. (0.2) There is >de:finitely uh
1769           problem.< (0.2) There is de:finitely uh problem. .hhh u::hm, I
1770           (jus') said in in thuh begi:nning, I took thuh ti::me, tuh go do:wn
1771           and look at that complex, and it's tight!
1772           (0.1)
1773  Nan?:    Um=hm mm.
1774           (.)
1775  MB:      It's an A::Wful lottuh living space, put o:n to, .hh uh lo::t of >of
1776           of uhm<, (0.2) u::h uh uh small amount of ground.
```

Mediator B's transition to the solution-generation stage occupies the space for Mediator A's projected question and makes the activity misalignment between the two mediators visible. The misalignment between the mediators was resolved by Mediator A, who held back her projected question and let Mediator B proceed with the transition to the solution-generation phase. In sum, one type of misalignment that can occur in these mediation sessions is misalignment in transitioning between one stage of the hearing to another.

Transition from the Discussion Phase to Individual Caucuses. A caucus is a private individual conference between one disputant and the mediators. Mediators use caucuses for many reasons, including to defuse potential arguing between the disputants.[3] Caucuses can also be used to build disputants' trust in the mediators and help the mediators balance the goals of conveying empathy while remaining impartial (Poitras 2013). In Excerpts 8.3 and 8.4, a brief instance of activity misalignment between co-mediators as to whether a caucus should be held is quickly resolved. The participants in Excerpt 8.3

---

[3] See Bishop et al. (2015); Doneff and Ordover (2014); Ewert et al. (2010); Picard (2016); Welton, Pruitt, and McGillicuddy (1988); Whatling (2012).

have been engaged in a discussion of Mike's allegations that his wife Kelly
has abused drugs and alcohol.

Excerpt 8.3 Mike and Kelly Midwest Divorce Mediation, Session 1, p. 74

```
1677  MA:    [Can y]ou say, (0.3) °whom-° (0.3) thuh source of these
1678         allegations is?
1679         (4.1)
1680  Mike:  °Not-° (0.8) °not now.° °°No.°°
1681         (0.1)
1682  MA:    °Okay.°
1683         (1.0)
1684  MB:    And you're (flat) denying, all thee °allegations.°
1685         (0.5)
1686  Kelly: Never ever have been drunk around my kids at all? Ever? (0.4) .h
1687         And I don't use any kind of (1.0) drugs that >I don' know< (0.6)
1688         where >you come up with< this bull, (1.4) but I >think you need
1689         tuh< straighten out? whoever you think it is that's telling you these
1690         things? (2.3) Because they're lyin'!
```

During Kelly's response to Mike's allegations (lines 1686–1690) she speaks
directly to Mike in a challenging way. She addresses him as "you" rather than
directing her remarks to the mediator (lines 1688–1690), refers to his accusations as "bull" (line 1688), and claims that the people he got his information
from were lying (line 1690).

A long pause follows Kelly's utterance (Excerpt 8.4, line 1691). Mediator
B then responds, refocusing from the contentious topic under discussion to the
possibility of making at least a provisional agreement on the issues (lines 1692,
1694–1697).

Excerpt 8.4 Mike and Kelly Midwest Divorce Mediation, Session 1, p. 74

```
1691         (9.1)
1692  MB:    Okay.  Can you? (0.9) °two?° (0.4) agree? (0.7) [tuh this?] t' to
1693  Mike:                                                 [°I um?° ]
1694  MB:    (0.9) say this >woul' be an acceptable< °(home).° .hh (0.1)
1695         Y'know, once you make an agreement °like this.° it's never cast in
1696         concrete! (0.4) .h You can always come back? (0.3) to mediation
1697         and renegotiate. (2.0) >And we have< had that happen.
1698         (0.3)
1699  MA:    °°Lots uh times.°° (1.0) °tch° >I think I'd< like tuh- (0.4) caucus
1700         for uh couple minutes [°tuh°   ]
1701  MB:                          [>I think] that'd be uh very good idea.<
```

Mediator B avoids commenting on the argumentative aspects of Kelly's
utterance and instead addresses how the spouses could reach an agreement
that would be acceptable to both of them, at least provisionally. Mediator A
responds very quietly with "°°Lots uh times.°°" (line 1699), thus displaying

agreement with Mediator B's previous utterance. After a pause and a few hesitations and false starts, Mediator A goes on to suggest that the mediators caucus with each disputant individually (lines 1699 and 1700). Mediator B overlaps the end of this utterance to agree with Mediator A's suggestion: "[>I think] that'd be uh very good idea.<" (line 1701). Thus the two mediators were temporarily at odds as to what activity should be engaged in: discussing potential ways to resolve the dispute or caucusing with each disputant individually. Mediator A uses delay and tentativeness to downgrade her apparent disagreement with Mediator B as she proposes that they caucus. Mediator B's immediate abandonment of her plan and display of agreement with Mediator A's suggestion quickly repairs this misalignment and restores the display of a united front between the mediators.

In sum, misalignments between co-mediators as to what activity should be currently engaged in can challenge their coordination of teamwork. Most problematic (and rare) in these data are overt misalignments between the mediators. Mediators can also produce misalignments subtly and work to quickly repair them, thus avoiding or mitigating any potential damage to their presentation of themselves as a team for the disputants.

Substantive Misalignment

Substantive misalignment between mediators can occur when co-mediators express different positions relative to an issue. Although this type of misalignment occurs very infrequently, there are some instances of it in these data. For example, a substantive misalignment occurred in a family mediation in which Stan and his ex-wife's husband Nick are in conflict over transportation and visitation arrangements for Stan's three children. In Excerpt 8.5, Mediator A proposes that Stan's daughter Shelly visit Stan's household separately, in order to prevent arguing between her and her twin sisters (lines 2022–2024).

Excerpt 8.5 Blended Family West Coast Mediation, p. 89 (Garcia 1997: 228)

```
2022  MA:     It isn't uh question of where you take thuh twins, over tuh
2023          Sta:n's:, and pick up Shelly, and take her back to your hou::se, and
2024          then [(                          )]
2025  Nick:        [NO::, I kind uh LIKE that i]dea though?,
2026          (2.2)
2027  MA:     That would separate Shelly from thuh twi:::ns:!, may be uh little
2028          bit of this=
2029  Nick:             =I think that could be really constructive.
2030                 ( 0.4)
2031  Stan:   Actually I think that would be (.) de::structive.
2032                 (.)
2033  MB:     .hh Yeah.
2034                 (.)
```

```
2035  Stan:   u:h[m I:'M: I']m I ro- Helen and I are very ali::gned in
2036  MB:        [I'm ye:ah ]
2037  Stan:   trying to promote some semblance of uh normal,
2038          (0.3)
2039  Helen:  °Um hm=
2040  Stan:              =uh relationship and (0.2) the on[ly time she's]
2041  MA:                                   [Well, no:t on]ly THA:T,
2042          but lots uh times when (0.5) you want, (0.5) thuh twins tuh be
2043          awa::y, (0.4) you don't want, to be saddled with Shelly!, You're
2044          goin' off tuh TO:WN or someplace.
```

Nick immediately expresses approval of Mediator A's proposal (line 2025). After hearing Nick's response, Mediator A explains why the proposal would be a good idea (lines 2027–2028), and Nick again interrupts to express approval ("I think that could be really constructive."; line 2029). Stan then disagrees with the plan to separate the children ("Actually I think that would be (.) de::structive."; line 2031). Mediator B quickly joins in and expresses agreement with Stan's position (".hh Yeah."; line 2033; see Kangashargu 2002 on oppositional alignments). Stan then explains why he and his current wife Helen disagree with Mediator A's proposal (lines 2035, 2037, and 2040). Mediator A interrupts Stan's explanation to back down from his proposal and join Mediator B in aligning with Stan's position (lines 2041–2044). In short, the mediators in this excerpt initially displayed disagreement over the proposal, but Mediator A took advantage of the first available turn space after Mediator B expressed her disagreement to repair that misalignment.

While some examples of mediator misalignment are visible to all participants, others are subtle and quickly repaired. Excerpt 8.6 from the second session of Mike and Kelly's divorce mediation begins with Mediator B suggesting that the couple's three children should participate in the mediation process (lines 759–760).

Excerpt 8.6 Mike and Kelly Midwest Divorce Mediation, Session 2, p. 36

```
759  MB:  I have uh feeling Kris that somewhere °along thuh-° (0.4) line
760       >tha' we ought to< see thuh children.
761       (0.9)
762  MA:  tch .h We're WILLING >tuh see thuh< children if thuh two of you
763       (0.3) °agree?° that [that's?] (0.8) somethin' that would (0.4) be of
764  MB:                   [Right.]
765  MA:  benefit.
```

Mediator B suggests to her co-mediator Kris that they should talk to the couple's three children (lines 759–760). Although not disagreeing with this suggestion, Mediator A's response displays little enthusiasm for this idea. First, Mediator A delays her response by almost a second (line 761). She then says "tch .h We're WILLING >tuh see thuh< children ..." (line 762).

Mediator A emphasizes the word "willing" and raises her voice to further emphasize this word. Mediator A thus reformulates Mediator B's "we ought to" see the children to a downgraded "we're willing" to see the children; a strategy similar to the modified repeats described by Stivers (2005). However, note that even though there seems to be a disagreement between the two mediators about this issue, Mediator A does her best to downplay it.

In sum, there are a range of ways a mediator's misalignment on substantive issues can be repaired when they occur. When mediators are able to produce a misalignment in a subtle way and/or quickly move to repair it, it is not likely to provoke a lack of confidence in the competence of the mediators.

Interactional Misalignment

Mediators may be aligned in terms of what activity to engage in or their positions on issues, but still fail to present a united front. In this section I will discuss several types of interactional misalignment which can be found in these data. If the co-mediators are not able to coordinate the exchange of turns between themselves without interruptions or other problems, it may appear as if they are not listening to each other. Excerpt 8.7 illustrates an interactional misalignment between two mediators that was quickly resolved.

Excerpt 8.7 Jon and Liz Midwest Divorce Mediation, Session 1, p. 13

```
519  Jon:  (0.8) u:h As far as ti:me?, (0.4) You know I work (0.1) Monday
520        through Friday and that's my job. (0.9) uh I do! you know?, (0.4)
521        that could (leverage?) ways of time. (0.5) But u:hm (0.9)
522        y'know as far as thuh second jo:b?, (0.4) I can change that
523        °whenever I want to.°
524        (0.4)
525  MA:   [(This)]
526  MB:   [So s  ] 'm sorry [Maureen        ] is your second job over
527  MA:                     [(Doesn't matter)]
528  MB:   weekends at: all? Saturday and Sundays or: (0.5) >maybe in thee<
529        evenings?
530        (0.6)
531  Jon:  tch uhm (1.1) It's uh- (0.4) normally what I would work is u:hm
532        (1.6) >maybe like uh< Tue:sday?, (1.4) or: (0.8) °maybe° Friday
```

As Excerpt 8.7 begins Jon is explaining his work schedule, which limits his availability for visitation with his daughter. Mediators A and B simultaneously begin to respond to Jon's utterance (lines 525 and 526). Mediator A resolves the overlap by dropping out.[4] Mediator B immediately cuts off her utterance-in-progress and apologizes to Mediator A ("Maureen") for the interruption

---

[4] See Hutchby (1996b); Jefferson (1986); Lerner (1989); Oloff (2013).

(line 526). Mediator A's partially audible utterance in line 527 appears to be "Doesn't matter," which may refer to Mediator B's interruption. The mediators thus display an orientation to their interactional misalignment as problematic. The interruption is as brief as possible, and an apology was given and most likely acknowledged.

Excerpt 8.8 illustrates an interactional misalignment in which it appears that one mediator was not listening to the other. In this divorce mediation session, Mediator A has been asking the spouses questions and writing their answers on an easel. As Excerpt 8.8 begins, Mediator B then asks a question about whether the divorcing couple's three children attend the Morrison School (line 984).

Excerpt 8.8 Darryl and Belinda Midwest Divorce Mediation, Session 1, p. 46

```
984   MB:  They're all at Morrison?
985        (0.2)
986   Bel: °Mm hm°
987        (3.1)
988   MB:  So Melody: who is eleven, ih- would then be in, (0.5) sixth,=
989   Bel:                                                     =Sixth!
990        (3.1)
991   MA:  And Me:lody: i::s u:hm (0.4) eleven?
992        (0.3)
993   Bel: Mm [hm! ]
994   Dar:    [Yeah]
995        (0.6)
996   Dar: S:ixth grade
997        (3.8)
998   MA:  A:lso Morrison?=
999   Bel:               =Mm hm=
1000  Dar:               =Mm hm
```

After receiving Belinda's answer about which school her children attend, Mediator B then asks questions about the age and grade in school of their youngest daughter Melody (line 988). Mediator A subsequently asks for the same information (lines 991 and 998). Mediator A's question repeats demonstrate that he has not heard the information elicited by Mediator B's prior questions, presumably because he was engaged in writing on the easel during these exchanges. Mediator A's failure to hear Mediator B's questions and the spouses' responses makes an interactional misalignment between the mediators visible.

Arguments between co-mediators did not occur in these data. However, public disagreements or discoordination are other types of interactional misalignment that did occasionally occur. Excerpts 8.9 and 8.10 from a small claims mediation between neighbors in an apartment complex serve to illustrate how mediators can fail to seamlessly coordinate their joint actions and therefore fail to function smoothly together as a team. Prior to these excerpts, an argument had emerged between the disputants. Excerpt 8.9 begins with Mediator A intervening in this dispute and sanctioning the disputants for arguing (lines 1900, 1902, 1906, and 1908). However, in line 1909 a disagreement between the mediators as to whether they should break for a caucus emerges.

Excerpt 8.9 Neighbors West Coast Small Claims Mediation, p. 83

```
1900  MA:    [I DON'T WANT ANY CROSS TALK, thank you.]
1901  Kemp:  (        )=
1902  MA:              =If you wannuh talk [(about it), write it ] do::wn,
1903  Kemp:                               [(              )]
1904  MA:    .hh=
1905  Kemp:  =((sniff))=
1906  MA:              =and if it's importa[nt tuh you::, then you should]
1907  MB:                                  [(                           )]
1908  MA:    br[ing it up, A::::ND!, befo::re we caucus:,]
1909  MB:      [Oka:y, but I think    maybe it's time ] (that we) take
1910         uh break.=
1911  ?:                =>Um kay.<
1912         (0.1)
1913  MA:    We [will cau]cus, I mean- uh- I don't know that we will
1914  Nan?:     [(     )]
1915  MA:    caucus, is it uh brea:k or uh caucus?=
1916  MB:                                         =uhm! ih- Well- bo::th:.
```

In addition to disagreement (or at least uncertainty) as to whether they should break for a caucus, there are interruptions between the mediators (lines 1907 and 1909). After the mediators have discussed whether a break will be taken and whether it will be a break or a caucus (lines 1908–1916), one of the disputants asks a question about caucuses which leads to further display of misalignment between the mediators (Excerpt 8.10):

Excerpt 8.10 Neighbors West Coast Small Claims Mediation, p. 83

```
1917         (0.2)
1918  Kemp:  What duh you mean uh caucus?=
1919  MA:                              =Let me explai::n that to you.
1920         That means that [we will] talk to one person.
1921  MB:                    [(here.) ]
1922         (0.2)
1923  MB:    >Um hm<
1924         (0.2)
1925  MA:    And see where they're coming from and w[hat]
1926  MB:                                           [Ye]ah=
1927  MA:                                                 =and we will
1928         not divulge.
```

```
1929          (0.1)
1930  MB:     Yeah.
1931          ( .)
1932  MA:     What is said dur[ing that conversation.     ]
1933  MB:                    [When CROSS talk begins] to ha:ppen, it is
1934          uh U::H thuh it is uh U::H (0.2) uh- uh- an AME:Rican uh
1935          Association, of- Arbitration Association's, guideline
1936          that=
1937  Nan:     =>Um hm<=
1938  MB:                    =.hhh when thuh cross talk begins tuh get tangled,
1939          (0.5) it- it is GOO::D tuh caucus: (0.2) tuh get, thuh thoughts,
1940          (0.2) straightened out again. (0.3) .hhh It is no:t, (0.4)
1941          A:Nythi:ng, (0.2) that needs to be said in private that will not (.)
1942          make (0.1) mo:::re cross talk [.hh       ] will not be divu:lged, by
1943  Nan:                              [(Um hm)]
1944  MB:     either one of us::=
1945  Nan:                    =((chuh chum))=
1946  MB:                              =It's just uh chance (.) fo::r, you
1947          to: (0.5) to du:mp.
1948          (0.1)
1949  ?:      ((chuh))=
1950  MB:            =HEH=HEH! .hh (ed ad uh) withOU::T!, withOU:::T::!,
1951          (0.2) (eh) HA::ving thee other party ri::ght at your- (0.1) side.=
```

At first, Mediator B restricts herself to short supportive actions or continuers while Mediator A explains what a caucus is. Note Mediator B's minimal response ">Um hm<" (line 1923). Her transition to "Yeah." as a listener response in lines 1926 and 1930 may foreshadow her eventual transition to speakership (Jefferson 1984c). When she makes this transition in line 1933, her utterance is positioned interruptively with Mediator A's continuing explanation of caucuses. This interruption is resolved by Mediator A who drops out.[5] In short, these excerpts display several instances of failure of alignment between Mediators A and B. When one mediator interrupts another mediator there is a failure to model appropriate behavior for the disputants.

Summary

Teamwork between co-mediators can fail in a variety of ways. In this section I described instances of activity, substantive, and interactional misalignment. Typically mediators take steps to repair these misalignments when they occur. Through these corrective actions they display their orientation to the goal of presenting a united front in their work as co-mediators. When mediators do not

---

[5] See Jefferson (2004c); Schegloff (1987b; 2000); West and Zimmerman (1977; 1983).

successfully work together to restore a united front, their presentation as a team is challenged. This failure may have implications for their ability to manage the mediation session and for disputants' confidence in the competence of the mediators. In the next section I discuss how mediators work to successfully create and display alignment with each other as they do the work of facilitating the session.

Creating and Displaying Mediator Alignment

Instances of successful mediator teamwork are far more common in these data than failures of mediator alignment. In this section I describe how mediators can display alignment with each other through the coordinated use of silence, explicit negotiation, explicit expressions of agreement, repetition or paraphrasing of each other's utterances, constructive sentence completions, and-prefaces, and complementary actions.

Displaying Alignment through Silence

Mediators often display alignment with their co-mediator by remaining silent while the co-mediator works to facilitate the session. In some interactional contexts, such as after an adjacency-pair first pair part (Sacks et al. 1974) or an assessment (Pomerantz 1984), the absence of a response is noticeably absent and often repaired. However, there are also contexts in which silence on the part of a co-interactant will be typically seen as agreement. For example, in Excerpt 8.11, one mediator performs the tasks of facilitating the session (in this case, questioning a disputant about his story and soliciting the next disputant's story), while the other mediator remains silent. As the excerpt begins, Nick has just played a tape recording of an argument which occurred in his home. On the tape, Stan and his ex-wife Karen (Nick's current wife) were arguing over a child support check.

Excerpt 8.11 Blended Family West Coast Mediation, p. 30

```
682  Nick:  s:: SO U:::HM, (1.2) I'll also say, that's not thuh first time I've
683         been threatened with death by Sta::n. (0.7) NO::R: ha::ve- is that
684         thuh first ti:me, he's used that la::nguage around me!, (0.2) .h NOR
685         is that thuh first TI:ME (0.6) he's:: threatened tuh beat me U::p,
686         nor is it thuh first time he's been nose tuh nose with me!, (0.8)
687         A::nd u::h (0.7) tch (0.2) he SEE:MS tuh call that being uh ma::n,
688         but I- think it's: really about thee opposite uh tha:t and I °hope!,
689         (0.7) thah some day he re:alizes that.
690         (3.3)
691  MB:    °(Okay) (0.3) Is thee i:ssue just is thee issue that you don'- duh
692         thah- (0.5) you have these- these ki::ds: and that you can't get
```

```
693          along?, Or is it thee issue that thuh money's not the:re? >is it it:<
694          (0.5)
695  Nick:   tch U:::HM (2.5) I think theh i:ssue is: (3.3) U:::HM (2.1) I-
696          I mus' SA:Y that- O::Ften (0.7) U:::H (2.1) we are able tuh get
697          alo::ng we are a:ble to: (0.4) at least, comple:te thuh business at
698          ha:nd:, whi[ch is      ]:
699  ?:                [Um hmh]
700          (.)
701  MB:     °Um hmh°=
702  Nick:                =bu:t (0.4) thuh pro:blem seems tuh be these incidents
703          that crop up (0.5) once in uh whi::le, [wher    ]e (0.4) HE IS (.)
704  Stan:                                          [((sniff))]
705  Nick:   verbal- (.) verbally:: and perhaps physically abusive!
706          (.2)
707  MB:     Um hmh.
708          (0.2)
709  Nick:   A::nd du::h (0.5) you kno:w?, it's s'no:t ONly with ME::, you can
710          s:ee how he talks with his ex [wi:     ]fe!,
711  Stan:                                 [((sniff))]
712          (.)
713  MB:     °Um hmh=
714  Nick:                =AND THAT has HAppened in front uh thuh kids, (0.6)
715          uh NUMber of ti:mes a::nd, I- you know I- (0.8) I- just
716          think it's really SA:d for them.
717          (.)
718  MB:     °Um hmh, (.) °um hmh!=
719  Stan:                          =((blows nose))
720          (0.2)
721  MB:     °tch (0.3) °Duh you wanna respond?°
722          (0.4)
723  Stan:   YEA:H, I sure wou:ld, I have uh whole bunch uh things tuh
724          talk about.
```

Mediator B takes an active role in facilitating the discussion about the taped argument. She asks Nick a question in lines 691–693 and provides listener responses during his answer (see lines 701, 707, 713, and 718). Mediator B then solicits Stan's response to Nick's story (line 721). By not intervening in this exchange, Mediator A displays his acceptance of Mediator B's handling of it. This example illustrates how silence on the part of a mediator can be a technique through which mediator alignment is displayed.

Mediator Teamwork through Explicit Negotiation

In these data it was unusual for mediators to explicitly negotiate the coordination of their activities or to decide how to proceed. Perhaps, as Goffman

(1959) argued in his analysis of team work, such public negotiation would display that the agreement was not achieved spontaneously and naturally. Teamwork achieved by public negotiation may not be as convincing as that achieved by a co-mediator's agreement-implicative silence. In Excerpt 8.12 mediator teamwork is achieved through a public decision-making process. The participants are engaged in a discussion of how much advance notice one divorcing spouse should give the other when making vacation plans that will involve their children.

Excerpt 8.12 Mike and Kelly Midwest Divorce Mediation, Session 4, p. 27

```
558  Mike:   Just w- y'know two weeks uh
559          [year (y'know >u   ]h lot uh< times)?
560  MB:     [(to advise thee um)]
561          (0.1)
562  MB:     >Does 'at- you think 'at's enough< time Kris?
563          (0.4)
564  MA:     Well USually people give (0.4) THIRTY DAYS or as soon as you
565          know! you tell thee other parent.=
566  Kelly:                               =Well yeah that would- °(that
567          [would be)°    ]
568  MB:     [Why don't you] make it thirty days? °tuh- >just so it's< more°
569          (0.3) >°acceptable at court?°<
570          (0.1)
571  Mike:   °°Okay.°°
```

After Mike has suggested that he and his wife Kelly give each other two weeks notice (lines 558–559), Mediator B asks her co-mediator ">Does 'at- you think 'at's enough< time Kris?" (line 562). Mediator A (Kris) recommends that they give thirty days' notice (lines 564–565). After one of the spouses expresses approval of that idea (lines 566–567), Mediator B endorses Mediator A's suggestion, and provides an additional reason in support of Mediator A's suggestion – that it would be acceptable to the court when the divorce agreement is finalized (lines 568–569). In sum, explicitly asking a co-mediator for input can be an effective way to engage him or her in the process of facilitating the session while displaying an orientation to their status as a team.

Mediator Teamwork through Expressing Agreement

Mediators in these data can also create and display alignment by explicitly expressing agreement with each other's utterances. In Excerpt 8.13 one mediator's positive assessment of the disputants' success in resolving an issue is followed by the co-mediator's second assessment in which she produces an equally enthusiastic approval.

Excerpt 8.13 Jon and Liz Midwest Divorce Mediation, Session 1, p. 27

```
1160  Jon:  And had Halloween. (0.5) She then dropped her off (1.3) Yeah you
1161        did drop her off right I didn't pick her up. (0.3) Yeah she dropped
1162        her off, (0.8) and from se:ven until ei:ght: (0.5) she went around
1163        my neighborhoo:d, (0.8) uh (0.6) you know I got tuh see her, well I
1164        got tuh see her co:stu:me (0.3) And then I think (0.8) around: (0.8)
1165        eight: (0.6) Liz came by and picked her up and I think (0.7) tch
1166        (0.6) had thuh rest of thee hour with her ih.
1167        (0.3)
1168  MA:   Well that's splendid.
1169        (0.5)
1170  MB:   And you two are doing great! [You  ] worked that one out
1171  MA:                                [Yeah.]
1172  MB:   beautifully on your [own! And] it's uh wonderful start.
1173  MA:                       [Yea:h   ]
```

Both mediators compliment the divorcing couple on how well they have handled sharing time with their daughter during the divorce process. Mediator A responds in line 1168 ("Well that's splendid."), and Mediator B produces second assessments in lines 1170 and 1172. Mediator A then expresses agreement with Mediator B's assessments in lines 1171 and 1173. While in general, silence may be taken as agreement, a mediator's failure to respond when a co-mediator compliments the disputants may be heard as a disagreement with the compliment (Pomerantz 1984). There is also a preference for agreement with assessments which may come into play (Pomerantz 1978a; 1984).

Mediators sometimes use agreement tokens or minimal responses to convey their support of each other's utterances.[6] In Excerpt 8.14, Mediator A produces most of the substantive contributions and Mediator B supports those contributions with agreement tokens and minimal responses.

Excerpt 8.14 Kim and Dave Midwest Divorce Mediation, Session 1, p. 95

```
2072  MA:   °I think there's health care decisions also.°=
2073  MB:                                              =°Yes.°=
2074  MA:                                                    =°That
2075        need tuh be discussed.
2076        (0.1)
2077  MB:   °That's [right.°  ]
2078  MA:          [°(As uh] lawyer)°? (0.5) °(an' 'at bane) of thee insurance.°
2079        (0.4)
2080  MB:   °That's right.°
2081        (0.5)
2082  MA:   °°Yeah.°°
2083        (0.4)
```

---

[6] See Bolden (2010); Fishman (1978); Schegloff (1982).

2084 MB: °On reimbursed medical expenses?°
2085   (0.7)
2086 MA: And and just thuh decision! (0.8) tuh ha:ve aye pro<u>ce</u>dure! >done
2087   on thuh< child. °also.°
2088   (0.6)
2089 MB: °Right.°=
2090 MA: =°°u:m°° (0.6) °°Y'know >who who's gonna< need uh°°
2091   °and I° <u>here</u>? (0.9) °at least I° thought- >THOUGHT I heard you<
2092   say that <u>you</u> were going tuh be thuh °person who would make
2093   those decisions° °°Kim.°° (0.5) °°Is 'at right?°° (0.6) °°Okay.°°
2094   (1.7) But [it   ] needs tuh be spelled ou:t?
2095 Kim: [°°Well°°]
2096   (0.9)
2097 MB: °R:ight.°

With her "°Yes.°" in line 2073, Mediator B expresses agreement with Mediator A's previous utterance (line 2072). After Mediator A finishes the continuation of her utterance in line 2075, Mediator B again expresses agreement in a short utterance ("°That's [right.°]"; line 2077). She does so again in lines 2080, 2089, and 2097. In sum, the use of explicit agreements and agreement tokens by mediators in response to their co-mediator's utterance accomplishes the display of agreement.

Mediation Teamwork through Paraphrasing

Mediators can also display their agreement and cooperation with each other through repetition or paraphrasing of their co-mediator's contributions. As Excerpt 8.15 begins, Mediator A makes a statement about children's ability to "survive" divorces.

Excerpt 8.15 Belinda and Darryl Midwest Divorce Mediation, Session 1, p. 70

1527 MA: .hh Because (1.1) <u>ki:ds</u> (1.9) kids can survi::ve (0.6) °from my
1528   experience they, kids survive divorces.°
1529   (0.2)
1530 Bel: Mm hm
1531   (0.1)
1532 MB: Their re<u>sil</u>ience (is [amazing   )]
1533 MA: [They're <u>very</u> resilient. Thuh thing that] <u>does</u>
1534   follow them, (0.2) is, (0.1) thuh con<u>tin</u>uing conflict between Mom
1535   and Dad. (0.5) They [pick it] up.<

Mediator B adds a comment which supports Mediator A's statement (line 1532). Mediator A then picks up on Mediator B's contribution in his next turn, and repeats her position. Note that his response is an upgraded second assessment (line 1533, "They're <u>very</u> resilient."; Pomerantz 1984). This non-argumentative use of format tying (Goodwin and Goodwin 1987) makes the

mediators' agreement with each other visible and displays that the mediators
are listening to each other.

In Excerpt 8.16 from Mike and Kelly's divorce mediation, an argument
between the spouses over Kelly's drinking reemerges.

Excerpt 8.16 Mike and Kelly Midwest Divorce Mediation, Session 3, p. 18

```
382 MB:    Wha- [let- let- ] let's hear >°what she has tuh say.< okay.°
383 MA:         [°Okay.°]
384        (0.1)
385 Kelly: He got angry about somethin'. (1.2) u:h (1.6) I won't say what-
386        (0.4) thuh kids say but .h (0.9) he >all of uh sudden< was yellin'
387        he >wants 'uh take< my CAR away? >he wants 'uh take<
388        >thuh kids away he's gonna do this!< (0.5) He has custodian? .h
389        (0.5) He gets angry like that. (0.6) He's gonna do it for- (0.2)
390        >all thuh time!< (0.6) He did it (0.4) throughout this- (0.3) from-
391        beginning, >thuh whole of this!< (1.2) >All th' time!<
392        (0.1)
393 Mike:  Thuh situation where that came from? (0.8) was uh halloween
394        party where adults were
395        (0.6)
396 MA:    >Well [I think< we already]
397 Mike:       [inebriated?        ] >And [we had gone over it?<        ]
398 MB:                                    [Yeah, we've >gone over that.<]
```

Mediator A begins a turn in line 396 which appears to be a deflection of
Mike's reintroduction of this contentious topic. When Mike continues his
utterance and speaks over Mediator A's response, Mediator B joins in (line
398) to repeat and support Mediator A's challenge of Mike's persistence
in reopening the topic of what happened at the Halloween party. Based on
what was said earlier in the mediation session, Mike's reintroduction of this
topic appears to be leading up to a repetition of his accusation that his wife
Kelly has abused alcohol. This topic has already been discussed extensively,
and Mediator B displays her support of her co-mediator by reinforcing her
response to it. By these means the mediators display a united front vis-à-vis
this topic.

In sum, paraphrasing a co-mediator's action can be done through direct
repeats, format tying, or reformulations which make the same point as the
co-mediator. These paraphrases are yet another way that co-mediators can
work to display a united front to the disputants.

Mediator Teamwork through Sentence Completion

Interactants can display that they are listening to a fellow speaker and support
the production of his or her utterance-in-progress by offering a candidate

sentence completion when a current speaker pauses before completing a turn constructional unit (Jefferson 1974; see also Lerner 1991). The current speaker may be pausing to avoid an error or to search for a word or phrase needed to complete their utterance (Jefferson 1974). In these data mediators rarely intervened to help their co-mediator finish a sentence, but when they did so successfully it served to further their display of a united front. Excerpt 8.17 shows a mediator completing a co-mediator's utterance (line 870). Mediator A accepts the suggested sentence completion in the continuation of his turn (line 872), thus displaying a shared perspective with his co-mediator.

Excerpt 8.17 Darryl and Belinda Midwest Divorce Mediation, Session 1, p. 40

```
859  MA:   Thee other? concept, (0.5) is whe:re, there is not shared parenting.
860          (0.7) A:nd (0.4) where sh theh where one parent, (0.4) u:h ha:s thee
861          primary responsibility for raising thuh children, (0.4) and thuh other
862          parent, (0.4) ha:s thuh right (0.4) >to visit with thuh children.< (0.5)
863          °But really does not participate in decision making.° (2.4) Our
864          courts? are been mo:re and more to:wards, shared parenting.
865          (0.4)
866  Bel:   Hmm?
867          (0.3)
868  MA:   tch .h In fact it used tuh be thee aye: presumption:
869          (0.9)
870  MB:   That thuh mother?
871          (0.2)
872  MA:   Thuh mother was thuh considered called thuh na:tural custodian.
```

However, mediators' attempts to provide sentence completions for co-mediators' utterances-in-progress are not always successful. In Excerpt 8.18 a mediator provides two possible completions for her co-mediator's utterance-in-progress, neither of which is accepted.

Excerpt 8.18 Mike and Kelly Midwest Divorce Mediation, Session 2, p. 38

```
803  MA:    Let's try NOT tuh use thuh word custody. (0.3) >So that thuh<
804          kids don't ever hear that word.
805          (0.1)
806  Kelly: Well that's what they said- [°°t' me.°°   ]
807  MA:                                [CUSTODY] is: (0.7) uh word that
808          means somebody owns thuh kids? It's kind uh like they're
809          (0.6)
810  MB:    Possessions?
811          (0.1)
812  MA:    they [have uh]
813  MB:          [Proper ]ty.
814          (0.1)
815  Mike:  >W'it's kind [uh< >it's kind uh< necess-? right.        ]
816  MA:                 [Uh fence aROUND THEM FROM THEE ] OTHER
```

```
817          PARENT?=
818 Mike:        =°Exactly.°=
819 MA:                =.h So! (0.4) Let's TRY to- (0.4) avoid using
820          that word. because? (0.3) no matter WHAT HAPPENS here? thuh
821          children are >going tuh go< back and forth between Mom and
822          Dad. (0.7) An- (0.4) TRY t' communicate that tuh them. (0.4) that
823          no matter WH:AT happens in thuh court? (0.6) you children are
824          gonna have uh mother >and uh father?< (0.5) You're gonna go
825          >back and forth< between Mom's house and Dad's °house.°
```

Starting in line 803, Mediator A is engaged in explaining why she does not want the parents to use the term "custody" to refer to arrangements made for the children's care postdivorce. In line 808 she reaches a point in her turn where it is not possibly complete and then pauses (line 809). Mediator B provides a candidate sentence completion in line 810: "Possessions?" However, the continuation of Mediator A's utterance in line 812 suggests that her pause was part of an error correction process rather than an error avoidance or word search (Jefferson 1974). Note that when she continues her utterance in line 812 she has changed "they're" to "they have uh". Before this utterance is completed, Mediator B overlaps Mediator A and provides a second possible sentence completion ("Proper]ty."; line 813). However, when Mediator A continues her utterance after Mike's interjection, she uses neither of the terms Mediator B has suggested. Instead, Mediator A's completion of her utterance (in lines 812 and 816–817) criticizes the term "custody," not because it treats the children like possessions or property, but because it puts "[Uh fence aROUND THEM FROM THEE] OTHER PARENT?=". Mediator B's failure to correctly project Mediator A's sentence completion challenged the display of a united front between them.

In sum, sentence completions at points in a co-mediator's utterance where they appear to be working to avoid an error or searching for a word to complete an utterance can be a way for a mediator to support a co-mediator. If the sentence completion is successful, it may enhance the display of teamwork between the mediators. If unsuccessful, it may challenge the display of teamwork.

Mediator Teamwork through "And-Prefaces"

An "and-preface" is used to precede an utterance in order to indicate its relationship to prior utterances and actions. And-prefacing has been found to be useful not only in ordinary conversation, but also in talk in a range of institutional settings (Heritage and Sorjonen 1994; Nevile 2006). In these mediation data I found several ways mediators used and-prefaces to display that their current utterance is connected to their own or their co-mediator's prior utterance.

In Excerpt 8.19 both mediators use and-prefaces as they extend and elaborate on each other's contributions, as the participants are discussing the disadvantages of resolving a divorce through the courts as opposed to through mediation.

Excerpt 8.19 Belinda and Darryl Midwest Divorce Mediation, Session 1, p. 81

```
1754  MA:   u:h (0.3) Usually what happens is just what happened to you.
1755        (1.2) You [go    ] and sit on thuh bench.
1756  Bel:          [Hmh!]
1757        (0.3)
1758  Bel:  Mm hm
1759        (0.2)
1760  MA:   °And nothing happens.°
1761        (0.1)
1762  Bel:  Right
1763        (0.2)
1764  MB:   And all thuh two professionals went with you that time.=
1765  MA:                                                    =Yeah
1766        (0.1)
1767  MA:   And t[wo professionals]
```

As the excerpt begins, Mediator A points out that Belinda and Darryl would likely spend a lot of time waiting in court for their divorce case to be heard (lines 1754–1755). After Belinda's responses in lines 1756 and 1758, Mediator A uses an and-preface (line 1760) to extend and emphasize this point. After Belinda agrees (line 1762), Mediator B selects herself to speak and mirrors Mediator A's turn construction by also beginning with an and-preface (line 1764). This formulation presents her contribution as a continuation of Mediator A's previous utterance. Mediator A briefly agrees, using "Yeah" in line 1765 – a transition-to-speakership implicative continuer (Jefferson 1984c). He then uses an and-preface to construct his turn in line 1767 as a confirmation of Mediator B's prior utterance. The use of and-prefaces therefore can contribute to mediators' display of the cooperative nature of their work and their agreement on issues being discussed.

Another use of and-prefaces in mediation is as a subtle repair of a co-mediator's utterance. For example, in Excerpt 8.20 from the fourth session of Mike and Kelly's divorce mediation, Mediator A uses an and-preface (line 959) to present her utterance as a continuation of Mediator B's prior turn (line 957).

Excerpt 8.20 Mike and Kelly Midwest Divorce Mediation, Session 4, p. 44

```
946  Mike:  So: (0.4) I've gotta call my attorney today? Couldn't
947         >get uh hold of her:?< (0.3) Thursday or Friday? .h (0.4) Call my
948         attorney today? (0.3) °tell her what we:'ve agreed upon?° .h (0.9)
949         A:nd h! (0.3) ask her (0.5) >what step I need 'uh take–<
950         >Do I need tuh call< CHILD- (0.4) support? (0.6) exec- eksetra
```

```
951          eksetra? (0.3) A:nd .h (0.4) send thuh check down tuh there? (0.4)
952          or .h (0.3) >And then I'm-< (0.2) >gonna get it< set up where it'll
953          be taken >out uh my< check.
954          (0.4)
955  MA:     Yeah [that's-]
956  Mike:        [But   ] >I can [do that.<   ]
957  MB:                          [THAT'S th'] easiest way.
958          (0.3)
959  MA:     >AND THEY'LL INsist< on doin' that. (1.5) °°Okay.°°
960          (0.4)
961  MB:     >°(Because they want you) liable< to°=
962  Mike:                                       =°S[ure.°   ]
963  MA:                                          [°Right.°] (0.8) You can
964          modify that as your- circumstances change?
```

Mike describes his plan to have his child support payments automatically withdrawn from his paycheck (lines 946–953). Mediator B endorses this plan in line 957 ("THAT'S th']easiest way."). Mediator A then joins in (line 959) and uses an and-preface to present her turn as a continuation of Mediator B's turn. Through the use of the and-preface as opposed to, for example, using "but" as a preface (as found by Romaniuk 2013 in interviewers' challenges to interviewees' answers in televised news interviews), Mediator A presents her utterance as an agreement with or continuation of Mediator B's turn. However, it is actually a repair. Note that Mediator B has said that having the child support payments deducted from Mike's paycheck will be "th'] easiest way." (line 957). However, Mediator A – the more experienced mediator – knows that this procedure is required rather than optional. Mediator A's turn in line 959 thus subtly corrects Mediator B's representation. She provides Mike with more accurate information on what he can expect from the child support payment process, while at the same time constructing her turn as an agreement with her co-mediator. The use of the and-preface to construct her turn as a continuation of Mediator B's prior turn, rather than a correction of it, contributes to the successful display of a united front between the mediators.

In Excerpt 8.21 from a small claims mediation hearing, a mediator also uses an and-preface to respond to his co-mediator's prior turn, such that his repair of that utterance is implicit rather than explicit. A landlord (Robert) has brought the small claims case to try to recover late rent and loan payments from his tenant (Loren). At this point in the mediation hearing, Robert has been expressing his dissatisfaction with Loren's position that she can not pay the monies due.

Excerpt 8.21 Childcare Center West Coast Small Claims Mediation, p. 170

```
3882  Rob:    Uh hundred and sixty is: (0.2) tch (0.4) that ma- maybe this
3883          isn't within thuh scope [of (what )]
3884  Loren:                          [We:ll    ]=
3885  MB:                                       =But
```

```
3886          (0.2)
3887  Rob:    Yeah, and then I ha[ve here      ]
3888  MB:                        [No, I'm (sorr]y) it isn't.
3889          (0.1)
3890  Rob:    >I mean it was brought up-< (0.2) as one of my
3891          (0.2)
3892  MB:     I=s: I'm sympathetic, to your problem!
3893          (0.4)
3894  MA:     And I'm symp- pasetic to yours AND yours!
3895          (0.6)
3896  MA:     Both of you folks are in uh (0.2) °in uh° dreadful set of straights!
```

In line 3892 Mediator B expresses sympathy with Robert's concerns ("I=s: I'm sympathetic, to your problem!"). Mediator A then selects himself to speak and provides a subtle repair of Mediator B's utterance, conveying that the mediators are sympathetic to both disputants, not just to Robert ("And I'm symp- pasetic to yours AND yours!"; line 3894). By using an and-preface, Mediator A presents his turn as a continuation of (and in agreement with), Mediator B's prior turn. Mediator A's utterance thus works to maintain the neutrality of the mediators as they express their concern for the problems facing the disputants, by correcting Mediator B's implication that they were sympathetic to only Robert's problems rather than to both disputants.

In sum, the use of and-prefaces is one way mediators can work to convey a united front with respect to their co-mediators' actions during the mediation session. This technique can be used both to convey agreement and to subtly repair the co-mediator's actions, while successfully accomplishing teamwork and modeling cooperation for the disputants.

Mediator Teamwork through Complementary Actions

While the methods of accomplishing teamwork discussed above primarily involve ways that one mediator can coordinate with or support the other's actions, mediators can also successfully accomplish teamwork by complementing the other's actions. By using a "tag team" approach, instead of duplicating or reinforcing each other's actions, mediators can seamlessly alternate actions or roles in the session. For example, they may switch back and forth between speaker and listener roles, or alternate responding to a disputant's turn or initiating new topics. In Excerpt 8.22, the two mediators almost seamlessly alternate actions as they assist the divorcing couple in a discussion of visitation arrangements for their three children.

Excerpt 8.22 Mike and Kelly Midwest Divorce Mediation, Session 1, p. 10

```
212  MB:    What about weekends.
213         (0.9)
214  Mike:  tch u::h (0.9) She: has 'em throu:gh (1.0) Saturday night? (0.1) 'n I
```

215   pick 'e[m up] Sunday- °morning.° (0.5) t' have 'em through?
216 Kelly: [(Sun-)]
217   (0.1)
218 Kelly: CHUM!
219   (0.1)
220 Mike: Saturday night 'til Sunday morn- I pick 'em Sunday mornin'.
221   .h (0.5) Have 'em Sunday? Monday. Tuesday, Wednesday!
222   °(Another week).°=
223 MA: =°Okay.° W' lemme get this: straight.
224   Okay? So thuh CHILDREN are with Dad? (5.0) four days uh week
225   (0.9)
226 MA: On[e week?]=
227 Mike: [U:m   ]=
228 Kelly: =We switch.
229   (0.6)
230 Mike: Fours days one week. Three day thuh °next week.°
231   (4.2)
232 MB: Are there- they consecutive days?
233   (0.6)
234 Mike: >°Yes they are.°<
235   (0.7)
236 MA: Okay.
237   (0.4)
238 MB: It's easier on thuh kids.

As the excerpt begins, Mediator B asks a question (line 212). After the spouses respond, Mediator A then works to clarify her understanding of the visitation arrangements (lines 223–224, 226). After the spouses provide the requested information (lines 228 and 230), Mediator B asks a follow-up question ("Are there- they consecutive days?," line 232). Note that it is Mediator A who provides a receipt token for Mike's answer to this question (line 236), and it is Mediator B who makes the next comment (line 238).

In Excerpt 8.23 from the first session of Bob and Kate's family mediation session, the mediators also make complementary contributions to the facilitation of the session. The mediators perform a wide range of complementary actions including complimenting disputants, making suggestions, and summarizing an agreement that has been reached on an issue. They also use minimal responses and alternate between speaker and listener roles as they perform successful mediation teamwork.

Excerpt 8.23 Bob and Kate Midwest Family Mediation, Session 1, p. 92

1998 Kate: .hh You know, just to: (0.9) tch .h BECAUSE I JUS' startin- I
1999   NEE:D, and it may be selfish:?, but (0.5) honestly, I just need
2000   some relief now.
2001   (0.4)
2002 MA: °Right.°

```
2003          (0.1)
2004   Kate:  You know I just nee:d? some? (1.5) some AIR.
2005          (0.4)
2006   MB:    Okay. I think that's very WI:SE?, that you recognize you own (0.7)
2007          needs. (0.6) .h And that you're gonna °act on them.°
2008          (0.5)
2009   MA:    tch (0.7) .h Okay. LET'S TRY TO WRITE DO:WN what (0.1)
2010          we've said, and and the:n?, (1.0) talk abou:t, (1.3) what you agree:
2011          you'll say to thuh children. (1.0) So that you're both sayin' thuh
2012          same thing. (0.3) Or may be you SAY it to them together.
2013          (0.8)
2014   Kate:  Mm [hm.]
2015   MB:       [Can] you say it together? I think [that might be better?]
2016   Kate:                                       [They already kn    ]ow?
2017          (1.3) °W' mine do.°
2018          (1.0)
2019   MB:    Do yours know?
2020          (0.7)
2021   Bob:   °Mm hm.° (0.6) They kno:w (0.5) that it's (0.7) °been talked
2022          about.°
2023          (2.7)
2024   MA:    Okay. [So we' ]re- (0.7) we HAVE an agreement that (1.2) there
2025   MB:          [Un hunh]
2026   MA:    will be uh TEMPOrary period of separation. (14.5) ((writes on
2027          easel)) in orde:r (0.5) to addre:ss (2.7) thee issues expressed. (12.2)
2028          And Kate you've agreed to be thuh one moving out.
```

In line 2002 Mediator A produces an agreement token in response to Kate's prior turn, thus positioning herself as a recipient of Kate's turn. After Kate's next turn in line 2004, Mediator B is the one to respond. She produces a different type of response. "Okay" can be used to mark transitions from one section of talk to another (Rendle-Short 1999; 2002). Barske (2009) notes that "okay" can be used to indicate an impending topic shift. Using "Okay." as both a listener response and a transition to speakership, Mediator B goes on to compliment Kate and acknowledge the emotional aspects of her situation (lines 2006–2007). She works to reframe Kate's statement from an expression of need to a statement about her strengths. Mediator A then begins to speak, also using "Okay." as a transitional action. She thus both responds to Mediator B's comment, and makes a transition from a listener to a speaker role. Mediator A suggests that they create a plan for what Bob and Kate will say to their children (lines 2009–2012). After Kate's minimal response (line 2014), Mediator B contributes to the topic Mediator A has introduced with an information-seeking question which is an implicit suggestion (line 2015). After some discussion of this issue, Mediator A uses another transition-implicative "Okay." and the transition marker "So" to draw an upshot from the prior talk (line 2024). Mediator A begins to summarize the agreements they have made so far (lines 2024, 2026–2028). In sum, the tag team approach is an effective way for mediators to share the work of facilitating the mediation session while smoothly coordinating their actions with each other and displaying and modeling teamwork for the disputants.

In sum, co-mediators have many interactional resources at their disposal to create and display their alignment with each other, and present a united front vis-à-vis the disputants. By these means they not only effectively share the work of facilitating the session, but also model constructive methods of resolving disagreements and cooperating in the performance of tasks.

Discussion and Conclusions

In this chapter I examined how teamwork is accomplished in mediation sessions facilitated by two mediators. I showed how co-mediators work to create a united front, and how breaches or lapses of such team impressions may occur. The infrequency of misalignment between mediators in these data is one type of evidence that co-mediators are typically successful as they work to facilitate the mediation session as a team. In addition, when misalignments do occur, they are generally treated as problematic and repaired by the mediators. I found that often teamwork is invisible – that is, a mediator can display a united front with their co-mediator by remaining silent while the other does the work of facilitating the session. One mediator will do most or almost all of the speaking, and the other will remain largely silent (or the mediators will alternate the roles of active and silent participant). When done well, the work of the two co-mediators is almost indistinguishable from the work one mediator would do alone, because the mediators act as if they are interchangeable actors both working seamlessly toward the same goal.

There were occasions in these data when mediators accomplished teamwork in the hearing through explicit negotiation, but this occurred relatively infrequently. This is consistent with Goffman's (1959) position to the effect that explicit public negotiation between team members can undermine the team performance by making it appear unspontaneous or unnatural. Another factor, more specific to the mediation context, is that disputants need to feel confidence in the mediators' ability to facilitate the hearing and create a safe environment for discussion of the issues. Disputants may feel vulnerable because mediation brings them in close contact with the person with whom they are in conflict. When mediators explicitly discuss what to do next, they are displaying that they do not know what to do next – this type of display has the potential to make the disputants feel as if they are on a rudderless ship.

Mediator misalignments may lessen disputants' confidence in the ability of the mediators to successfully facilitate the session. When mediators interrupt each other, have a noticeable difference of opinion about an issue, or express different ideas about how the session should proceed, the breakdown of their united front is visible to participants. Part of the work of mediation is therefore displaying their team membership as the co-mediators work together to facilitate the conflict resolution process for the disputants.

Mediators working in teams therefore face challenges and organizational issues that mediators working alone do not face. In spite of these challenges, co-mediation may benefit the mediation process by increasing the authority of mediators. Their united front, when successfully achieved, may have more persuasive strength than that of a single mediator. This is particularly likely to be the case for programs such as the West Coast mediation program, which is staffed by volunteer rather than professional mediators. Creating and displaying alignment therefore is a mediator skill that may affect both the success of the process and disputant confidence in the process.

9   Autonomy, Empowerment, and Neutrality in Divorce and Small Claims Mediation

As previous research and mediation textbooks have revealed, mediators use many techniques to facilitate the session and help the disputants achieve their goals, such as summarizing and paraphrasing disputants' positions, soliciting ideas for resolution, and asking questions.[1] However, whether these techniques are effective in a given mediation session depends not just on the specific technique used, but on the interactional skill of the mediators to effectively formulate and place their interventions in the ongoing flow of interaction. Mediation is an interactional process that involves the coordinated action of all participants. The interactional competence of both mediators and disputants is critical for its successful completion, regardless of whether an agreement is reached.

At its best, mediation can not only help disputants resolve conflicts, but can transform high-conflict relationships into cooperative ones. For example, in the first session of Mike and Kelly's divorce mediation, the spouses held widely disparate positions which led to the emergence of arguing. However, during the last of four mediation sessions, the divorcing spouses were able to joke and laugh together as they cooperatively discussed the details of the shared parenting agreement they had created. Their interaction during four mediation sessions with the skilled guidance of the mediators enabled them to resolve their conflicts and regain a degree of comfort and trust so that they could communicate directly, productively, and pleasantly with each other.

Small claims mediation cases also often achieve the goal of resolving conflicts between disputants by providing a safe interactional environment in which disputants tell their stories, listen to each other's positions, and attempt to reach agreement. For example, in a small claims mediation between a hotel and a bus company which had been hired to transport hotel guests to a ball game, the companies' representatives not only discussed the issues without arguing, but reached a mutually agreeable resolution. During the course of the session, the complainant was so convinced by the respondent's explanation

---

[1] For example, see Boulle et al. (2008); Ewert et al. (2010); Frenkel and Stark (2012); Madonik (2001); Ranger (2010).

of what had happened that she decided to drop the case against the hotel. At the end of the session, both employees agreed that their companies could work together in the future. As the mediation session ended, they engaged in pleasant, cooperative exchanges with shared laughter.

However, mediation sessions do not always result in mutually agreeable resolutions, and do not always improve the relationship or communication patterns between disputants. For example, in Darryl and Belinda's divorce mediation, the mediators declared an impasse at the end of the fourth mediation session because the spouses were still in disagreement as to whether they should get divorced or not. They did not yet have a sufficiently shared perspective on what they wanted in order to negotiate the details of their divorce. Similarly, several of the small claims mediation sessions did not result in agreement. When this happened in the Midwest small claims cases, the disputants would be taken back to small claims court and a judge would decide the case for them. While it may be tempting to view such cases as failed mediations, recall that autonomy of the disputants is a core value of mediation. Disputants agree to participate in mediation with the understanding that they have the right to decide how to resolve the conflict. Deciding not to settle or compromise with the opposing disputant is a valid alternative for genuinely autonomous disputants. The success or failure of the mediation session should therefore be evaluated not on its outcome (settlement reached or not reached), but on the quality of the process used to reach that outcome.

The in-depth analysis of the interactional process of mediation from a conversation-analytic perspective contributes to our understanding of mediation as a conflict resolution procedure. This analysis reveals how mediation's unique interactional organization creates opportunities for conflict resolution, and shows how mediators work to achieve the goals of disputant autonomy and empowerment, mediator neutrality, and equal treatment of the disputants. However, the analysis also reveals some ways mediation may fail to meet these goals. In this chapter I first summarize the results of the analysis in this book and then discuss ways in which mediation and the role of the mediator could be changed to improve divorce and small claims mediation. I conclude with a discussion of ideas for further research.

Summary of Findings

The Speech Exchange System of Mediation

Participants in both small claims and divorce mediation typically interact within the speech exchange system of mediation. In the small claims mediations, disputants were almost always instructed to direct their remarks to the mediator instead of to each other. The small claims mediation session is thus largely a series of alternating two-party exchanges between the mediator and each disputant individually, with the mediator acting as liaison between the opposing disputants. The mediator is typically the addressed recipient, and the opposing disputant is treated as an overhearing audience or unaddressed recipient, and does not have the right to reply immediately.

There are a number of ways disputants in small claims mediation sessions display an orientation to the speech exchange system of mediation. When one disputant has the floor to tell his or her story, the opposing disputant is expected to wait until that story is complete and his or her response is solicited by the mediator. However, mediators may intervene in a disputant's ongoing story to ask questions, refocus the topic, or perform other actions. While mediators can both select themselves to speak next and select a next speaker, disputants typically wait to be selected to speak by a mediator. Disputants typically do not use the current speaker selects self option, except to continue a story-in-progress if they have the floor. Mediators can display an orientation to the turn-taking system of mediation both implicitly (e.g., by soliciting a disputant to speak), and explicitly (e.g., by reminding a disputant of the turn-taking system and/or sanctioning them for violations of it).

Disputants typically display an orientation to the speech exchange system of mediation by waiting until solicited to speak or by requesting permission to speak if the opposing disputant has the floor. Mediators typically grant disputants' requests for permission to speak, but they do not always do so. Their use illustrates how the mediator's role as facilitator of the session enables them to place limits on the autonomy of disputants. The mediator's role of facilitating the session gives them discretion over which complaints or accusations may be addressed immediately and which must wait for responses.

There were times when disputants did self-select as next speaker when an opposing disputant had the floor to tell their story. I found that under certain conditions these brief intrusions were not treated as problematic or as violations of the speech exchange system. In these data six types of potentially nonproblematic intrusions were found: error repair, sentence completions, alignments with the mediator, brief oppositional utterances, informational questions, and relevant information.

While both divorce and small claims mediation sessions differ from ordinary conversation, they also differ in some ways from each other. As found in previous research on divorce mediation sessions (Greatbatch and Dingwall 1997), the divorce and family mediation sessions analyzed in this book are much more likely to have segments of talk in which the interactional organization is closer to a conversational speech exchange system than to the typical mediation format. I refer to this as a hybrid speech exchange system. There is increased flexibility and freedom to volunteer to speak in the divorce mediation sessions than in the small claims sessions.

While in the small claims sessions, the mediator typically begins by soliciting the complainant's opening statement, in the divorce mediation sessions the
substantive portion of the session typically begins with a discussion of joint
concerns. While disputants in small claims mediation are typically instructed
not to interrupt each other, and to direct their remarks to the mediators, divorce
mediators may specifically invite the spouses to ask questions at will. The
mediators thus frame the interaction in divorce mediation sessions as a collaborative process, while the interaction in small claims mediation sessions is
framed as an interaction between disputants on opposite sides of a dispute.

However, even though disputants in a divorce mediation session may at
times address each other directly, the presence and interventions of the mediators make the structure of the interaction different from an ordinary conversational exchange. The mediators may intervene in the interaction when
needed, either to interrupt, redirect or defuse conflict or escalation into arguing,
or to ask questions or redirect the topic.

These differences between small claims and divorce mediation are important
because divorced spouses with children typically will have continuing interaction with each other after the mediation process ends and their divorce has
been finalized.[2] Mediation helps these couples learn how to maintain productive communication and cooperation with each other after the divorce. In
particular, the multisession structure of the divorce mediation process provides
divorcing spouses with an opportunity to learn and practice cooperative interactional techniques as they work to resolve their dispute.

Managing and Minimizing Arguing in Mediation

Chapter 3 investigated how the speech exchange system of mediation works
to minimize arguing, and how mediators manage and facilitate disputants' exit
from arguments when they emerge. Arguing does not occur frequently in these
data. While the turn-taking system of ordinary conversation allows for the
adjacent exchange of oppositional utterances which may escalate into arguing,
the turn-taking system of mediation works to avoid directly addressed, adjacent exchanges between disputants.

In ordinary conversation, oppositional utterances such as accusations or
complaints, return accusations, counterassertions, or denials make further
oppositional responses relevant, and make exiting from the argument challenging.[3] However, accusations in mediation typically do not engender oppositional responses as next actions because denials are not immediately relevant.

---

[2] Workplaces are another setting where mediation can be helpful in helping people restore and
maintain relationships after the conflict is resolved (McKenzie 2015).
[3] See Coulter (1990); Dersley and Wootton (2001).

While in ordinary conversation, accusations and denials are adjacency pairs and an omitted denial would be noticeably absent, disputants in mediation hearings can fail to respond immediately to an accusation without implying guilt. When disputants wait for a mediator solicit before responding to an opposing disputant's complaints or accusations, the possibility of arguing is minimized because arguing requires adjacently placed oppositional utterances.

When denials are delayed in mediation, some of the accusations and complaints produced may never receive a response. Participants may choose to focus on key issues of the dispute rather than to address each and every complaint. Or, a disputant may strategically avoid responding to a particular complaint. In these mediation sessions, by-passed accusations are typically allowed to lapse rather than being pursued by a disputant. Thus, disputants can minimize the number of accusations on the table by choosing not to respond to every accusation.

In addition, the norms of mediation encourage the production of mitigated rather than aggravated accusations and denials. The techniques used to mitigate the production of accusations in these data included third person attributions of blame, elision or displacement of the agent, and other techniques for downgrading the accusation. By these means, the occurrence of adjacent and directly addressed oppositional utterances that may escalate into arguments are minimized in mediation.

When arguing does occur, mediators have the option of sanctioning disputants for arguing. However, mediators often choose to avoid sanctioning in favor of less obvious types of intervention, or to withhold intervention altogether as long as the disagreement is constructive and does not escalate. Mediator interventions include using questions to redirect the topic and restore mediator address, using strategic interruptions to forestall further argumentative talk, and using continuers or minimal responses to insert the mediators' contributions between disputants' oppositional utterances. Mediators may also rephrase or repeat a disputant's previously expressed position in order to help the disputants understand what each other is saying.

Mediators' use of such active listening techniques displays their status as a recipient of disputants' utterances, even in segments of talk where a disputant directly addresses the opposing disputant. The mediator thus retrospectively redefines the disputant's utterance as addressed to the mediator as well as the opposing disputant, subtly shifting the structure of the exchange from a purely argumentative exchange between the two disputants to a three-party, nonargumentative exchange which includes the mediator. These types of actions may keep the argument from escalating and refocus the discussion to the issues under dispute.

In sum, through these and other interactional techniques, mediators can break up argumentative exchanges by separating oppositional utterances which otherwise would be adjacent. By interrupting or talking over argumentative exchanges mediators can often refocus attention onto other issues while officially ignoring the argument. Extended arguments between disputants interacting directly with each other without mediator intervention are rare in these data. The mediators in these examples made judgment calls as to whether or when to actively intervene in direct argumentative exchanges between disputants.

Mediator Solicitation and Facilitation of Disputants' Opening Statements

The disputant's opening statements or extended "stories" telling their version of the dispute are a critical part of mediation sessions, particularly in the small claims mediations. The mediation programs studied in this book have different protocols for deciding which disputant will be the first to produce an opening statement. In the small claims data sets, the complainant is typically selected to go first. Occasionally a mediator asked the disputants to choose who goes first. Some mediators explicitly communicate why that disputant is selected to go first, while others do not. Mediator's choices about how to solicit the first opening statement may be consequential for disputants' perspectives on the fairness of the process. If a disputant does not know why the other disputant was selected to go first, they may feel they are being treated unfairly.

Mediator solicits of disputant's opening statements in the divorce mediation sessions differ from those in small claims mediations. The small claims sessions typically begin with a starker separation between the two disputants than in divorce mediation, because their position as opposing disputants is emphasized by the distinction made between complainant and respondent. The mediators in the divorce mediation sessions typically begin with a collective approach which attempts to engage both spouses rather than choosing one or the other to go first. The fact that the spouses are in disagreement on at least some issues surrounding their divorce is therefore de-emphasized initially. Instead, an issue on which they have common ground (such as their children) is addressed first. Since one of the stated goals of small claims mediation is to create a less adversarial process for resolving disputes than the typical options provided by the legal system, small claims mediators should consider adopting the approach used in divorce mediation.

Once they have the floor to produce an opening statement, disputants in mediation sessions use a variety of techniques to maximize their effectiveness. They can construct chronological accounts or narratives, present evidence to support their claims, claim the moral high ground, or impugn the standing of the opposing disputant. Disputants also used the quoted or reported speech of others as evidence to buttress claims, and told stories describing how facts were ascertained to support claims they were making in their opening statements.

In addition, disputants in these data often made preemptive moves in their opening statements, projecting potential accusations or claims that could be made by the opposing party, and presenting evidence to controvert them prior to their production. These preemptive moves depend on the interactional organization of the mediation session for their production since the opposing disputant must wait for the first disputant to complete their statement and for a mediator to solicit the opposing disputant's statement.

Since the interactional competence of disputants in a mediation session may differ greatly, mediators may need to assist disputants in producing their opening statements. Mediators should be aware of these techniques and intervene as necessary to balance the rights of the second storyteller. By these actions mediators can work to empower weaker disputants, but they also run the risk of interfering with disputant's autonomy and freedom to express themselves.

While previous research by Cobb and Rifkin (1991a) showed that the disputant who makes the first opening statement has certain advantages over the disputant who goes second, the analysis in this book shows that there are also advantages to going second.[4] For example, while the first disputant is free to construct their opening statement as they wish, he or she also must produce a coherent account of what happened. The second disputant, on the other hand, does not have to repeat or revisit the details of the chronological account of events unless they feel it is to their benefit to do so. The ground work has already been laid by the complainant's opening statement, so the respondent can build upon or refer back to that statement as they construct their response. The second disputant typically frames his or her opening statement as a response to selected elements of the first disputant's story. The respondent can also use inaccuracies in the complainant's story to challenge his or her credibility. Even when mediator solicits of second disputants' opening statements provide a great deal of latitude for how the respondent constructs their opening statement, respondents often begin their statements with a rebuttal of specific accusations made by the complainant. The relatively narrow focus of respondents' opening statements therefore seems to be a strategic choice on the part of second disputants rather than an inherent problem with the interactional organization of mediation.

Mediator Representation of Disputants' Positions

When compared to other options offered by the legal system, disputants in mediation have a greater opportunity to tell their own stories and to create their own agreements rather than giving lawyers, juries, or judges those powers.

---

[4] See Arminen (2005); Hutchby (1996a; 1996b); Sacks (1992).

However, how representation of disputants' positions is done in these small claims and divorce mediation sessions may limit disputants' autonomy and the mediator's ability to display a neutral stance.

As shown in Chapter 5, the greatest degree of disputant autonomy in mediation occurs when disputants represent themselves. However, as mediators facilitate the discussion of issues and proposals for resolution of issues under dispute, disputants' opportunities for self-representation may be reduced in terms of when, to whom, and about what they may speak. By such actions as addressing their remarks to the mediator rather than the opposing disputant, speaking only when offered the floor by a mediator, and referring to the opposing disputant in the third person, disputants experience constraints on their autonomy as they self-represent their positions. In addition, mediators in these data typically engage substantially in disputants' construction of their positions and claims (for example, through questions), even when disputants are representing themselves.

These concerns are amplified when mediator representation of disputants' positions is considered. Mediators' representations of disputants' positions differ in the extent and manner in which they alter the disputant's original statements, including paraphrasing, revoicing, and replacing. The least intrusive form of mediator representation is restating or paraphrasing a disputant's statement. This type of representation enables the mediator to verify that the disputant has been heard correctly and may also may help the disputant to feel that someone is listening to them. In addition, the opposing disputant may be more willing to listen to that disputant's position when it is rearticulated by the mediator rather than when produced by that disputant.

Mediator restatements of disputants' utterances can be used to articulate the main point of a story or areas of disagreement between disputants and to help them to transition to a discussion of potential solutions. Restating or paraphrasing a disputant's position can contribute to the dispute resolution process by allowing the mediator to reframe a disputant's position in a form more acceptable to the opposing disputant. However, even restating or rephrasing a disputant's position may change the message produced by the disputant. For example, the mediator may choose to convey only parts of the disputant's position in their restatement, or they may reformulate it. Mediators' restatements of disputants' positions thus may have implications for the autonomy of the disputants' resolution of the dispute.

The analysis in Chapter 5 showed that mediators in these data do not restrict themselves to restating or rephrasing disputants' positions. Mediators at times intervened more extensively by representing a disputant's position through revoicing or replacement. When revoicing, a mediator extends or elaborates a position articulated by a disputant, reframing or reformulating it in an exchange with the opposing disputant. When replacing a disputant, a mediator takes the place of a disputant in the negotiation and acts on their behalf. They go beyond expressing positions previously articulated by that disputant and create new arguments in support of those positions.

Mediator representation of disputants' positions can be constructive in facilitative mediation, for example if there is a need to empower a weaker disputant. By representing disputants who are not as effective in representing themselves, mediators may work to create equality between the disputants, thus balancing the power between them.[5]

While disputant self-representation provides the greatest degree of disputant autonomy, mediator replacement of a disputant may constitute a challenge to disputant autonomy. Disputant autonomy is decreased for both the disputant who is being replaced (whose interests are now represented by the mediator) and for the disputant who is being challenged by the mediator. The replaced disputant loses the opportunity to present their own justifications for their position, while the opposing disputant is further pressured to revise their position. The authority of the mediator as facilitator of the process may give them more persuasive power over the opposing disputant.

Another potential risk of mediator replacement of disputants is that disputants may feel pressured to accept solutions they are unenthusiastic about. In general, mediation practitioners agree that compliance will be greater when disputants create their own agreement than when a third party imposes a solution on them.[6] Reluctant agreement with solutions may reduce compliance rates, and hence mediation's effectiveness.[7] Thus, the extent of mediator intervention in the dispute resolution process which replacement entails may not be appropriate.

Mediator representation of disputants in divorce mediation differs from the approach typically taken in the small claims cases. For example, the divorce mediators may form an alliance with one disputant in an effort to convince the opposing disputant of their side of the debate. Mediators also went beyond representing a disputant's interests or stated positions and engaged in coaching the disputant to adjust their perspective or to advise them as to how they could handle a problem.

In sum, when replacing a disputant in an exchange with the opposing disputant, the mediator risks violating the neutrality of the mediation process. When a mediator directly supports one disputant's position, and disagrees with the opposing disputant's position, a posture of neutrality may be difficult to support.[8] Cooks and Hale (1994) argue that in order to be conducted ethically, mediation must provide for disputant autonomy, and the mediator must remain

---

[5] See Cooks and Hale (1994); Irving and Benjamin (1987); Regehr (1994).
[6] See Blades (1985); Burrell et al. (1990); Cahn (1992); Pearson and Thoennes (1984; 1988).
[7] See Irving and Benjamin (1987); Regehr (1994).
[8] See also Cobb and Rifkin (1991b); Cooks and Hale (1994).

impartial and neutral. Other studies have found a relationship between these factors and mediation outcomes.[9] Some mediators attempted to manage these concerns by balancing their treatment of both disputants, first replacing one disputant and then replacing the other, thus alternately supporting both sides of the dispute. There are varied opinions as to whether this is an effective method of supporting disputants while attempting to remain neutral.

Facilitating the Solution-Generation Process

A major goal of mediation is to empower disputants to create an agreement themselves rather than having the mediator create one for them. Mediators are therefore typically trained to avoid making suggestions, and instead to solicit ideas for resolution from disputants. However, while mediators are advised to solicit disputant's suggestions for resolution, they are not typically instructed in how to produce those solicits.

Chapter 6 revealed a variety of ways mediators can solicit disputant's proposals and disputants can comply with or resist the solicitation of a proposal. When mediators used general solicits, they worked to elicit an idea for resolution from a disputant without limiting that idea. Specific solicits, on the other hand, limited in some ways the parameters of the idea sought. The mediator can specify that only new ideas are being solicited (e.g., by asking for any *other* suggestions), that a specific issue or topic from among the issues under contention be addressed by the proposal, or that an elaboration or refinement of a previous proposal be produced. Finally, the mediator can include specific examples of the types of things that might be suggested to guide the disputant's proposal construction.

Mediators often choose to use specific solicits, because disputants often respond to general solicits by reissuing their original position rather than suggesting a new idea for resolution. Specific solicits are typically more effective in getting disputants to produce an idea for resolution, but may have a negative impact on the mediator's display of neutrality and the autonomy of the disputant. The specific solicit engages the mediator in the proposal's construction by defining or limiting the parameters of the proposal.

Resistance to mediator proposal solicits is fairly common in these data. A disputant may resist producing a proposal by claiming that they do not have a suggestion to make, by passing on the opportunity and letting the opposing disputant make a proposal first, by remaining silent in the face of a solicit, or by talking about other things instead of producing the requested proposal. By resisting proposal solicits, disputants avoid having to commit themselves to a

---

[9] See Fuller, Kimsey, and McKinney (1992); Karim and Dilts (1990); Kimsey et al. (1994).

position. Waiting for the opposing disputant to make an offer first may be a strategic advantage because the other disputant may offer more than expected. A delay in producing a proposal also enables a disputant to wait for a better time to produce their proposal, rather than letting the mediator choose the location of their proposal.

Regardless of the method disputants use to resist producing proposals when solicited by a mediator, mediators have the option of pursuing a response in the face of such resistance. The mediator can follow the disputant's lead and drop the attempt to solicit a proposal, or can pursue production of a proposal by reissuing the solicit. Mediator pursuit of proposal production by repeat solicits may counter the empowering effect of proposal production by working to elicit a proposal in spite of disputant resistance or avoidance of that action. Another potential problem associated with mediator pursuit of proposals is that unequal treatment of disputants can create a perception of a failure of mediator neutrality. If a mediator pursues a proposal solicit with one disputant but not the other, perceptions of bias due to unequal treatment of the disputants may arise. Disputants who persist in resisting a mediator's repeated proposal solicits may risk appearing uncooperative, which may put them in a disadvantageous position relative to the opposing disputant.

A solicit does not have to result in the immediate production of a disputant's proposal in order for it to be useful for the mediation process. For example, proposal solicits can be used by mediators to try to move disputants out of the storytelling stage, in which complaints, accusations, and claims are focused on, to the stage in which ideas for resolution are proposed and discussed. A mediator's proposal solicit may not work on the first try, because disputants often need time to become ready to talk about ideas for resolution. Failure to elicit a disputant proposal in response to the first mediator solicit is therefore not a sign of mediator failure. The disputants may not be ready to move to talk about resolution, or one disputant may be strategically holding back. Nevertheless, asking for a proposal may be helpful in getting the disputants to (eventually) refocus from discussing complaints to suggesting ideas for resolution of the dispute.

Mediators display a neutral stance and facilitate disputant autonomy when they solicit disputants' proposals to elicit ideas for resolution rather than making suggestions themselves.

Mediator proposal solicits facilitate disputant autonomy by letting them make the proposals for resolution, but disempower them by choosing (and selectively enforcing through pursuit of proposals) who makes a proposal and when in the session a proposal occurs. Mediator participation in proposal solicitation is therefore simultaneously helpful in facilitating and encouraging the production of ideas for resolution, and potentially problematic for disputant autonomy and disputant empowerment. Disputants' skill at proposal production or evasion of proposal solicits may vary, and mediators' actions may or may not assist them in furthering their position or their goals.

Mediators' proposal solicits in divorce mediation differ in several ways from those in the small claims mediation sessions. In these data, the latter sessions of the multisession divorce mediation cases were particularly likely to have segments of talk conducted in a hybrid format, involving a quasi-conversational speech exchange system rather than the typical mediation format. While in the small claims mediation sessions proposals were typically solicited by mediators, the divorce mediators were more likely to engage with the disputants in a collaborative process of proposal solicitation and development. Mediators may treat the divorcing couple as a collectivity and ask them to come up with suggestions for resolution together. On occasion a disputant may directly address the opposing disputant (their spouse) and make or solicit a suggestion. In addition, solicitation of proposals in divorce mediation may lead to instances of coaching of disputants, with the mediators not only responding to disputants' proposals as suggestions, but also working to instruct them on how to better handle the problems they are facing.

In sum, by producing proposal solicits mediators display an orientation to the goal of disputant autonomy, but their success in this display depends on the disputant's actions in terms of complying with or resisting proposal solicits. This analysis therefore supports previous research that revealed contradictions between disputant autonomy and mediator neutrality in facilitative mediation.[10] The tension is between mediator facilitation of disputant proposal production, on the one hand, and mediator pressure on disputants (through choice of when to produce proposal solicits, and whether to pursue proposal production when solicits are evaded or resisted) on the other hand. Mediator success in achieving and displaying neutrality is thus not achieved solely by avoiding taking a position on an issue, but also through the ways that mediators and disputants construct their actions and coordinate their actions with each other.

Proposal Production and Disputant Autonomy

In most mediation programs mediators are discouraged from making proposals, because the belief is that when ideas for resolving the conflict come from the disputants, they are more likely to be satisfied with the agreement and more likely to comply with it. The principle underlying this policy is that mediation should empower disputants to make their own solutions; when mediators make suggestions they may be infringing on the autonomy of the

---

[10] See Cobb and Rifkin (1991b); Poitras and Raines (2013).

disputants. It is also believed that disputants will be more likely to comply with agreements if they come up with the ideas for resolution of the dispute themselves.

The mediators in these data worked to construct their proposals to display an orientation to the values of mediator neutrality and disputant empowerment. While mediation programs value these norms,[11] previous research has shown that the reality often challenges these assumptions.[12]

However, in each of the three data sets analyzed in this book, there were at least some instances of mediators producing proposals for resolution of issues under dispute. While technically a violation of mediation procedure, when the proposals mediators make are examined in their interactional context, it becomes evident that these proposals often further the process of creating agreement in mediation.

As shown in Chapter 7, disputants' suggestions for resolution of issues under dispute are typically both formulated and framed as position reports (ideas to which the disputant is committed). This commitment to the ideas they suggest may limit disputants' ability to freely participate in brainstorming ideas for resolution. Because mediators' proposals are not position reports, they can characterize their ideas as suggestions (per Greatbatch and Dingwall 1999), or use a footing shift to produce a suggestion on behalf of another person. These techniques work to display an orientation to disputant autonomy by distancing the mediator from the proposal, thus lessening the impression that the mediator is personally invested in the proposal. A mediator who makes a suggestion can therefore more freely contribute to the brainstorming process, thus facilitating the resolution of the dispute while at the same time accomplishing a display of neutrality.

In addition, mediators typically formulate their proposals as information-seeking questions, thus allowing disputants to avoid their potential proposal-relevance altogether. The ambiguous status of the informational question can make the proposal work being done by it quite subtle. Question-asking is a common way for mediators to interact with disputants at all phases of the mediation, and is a routine part of the work of being a mediator.[13] The disputant can therefore formulate their response as either provision of information or acceptance or rejection of a proposal. By providing a slot for the disputant to respond to the proposal, the question formulation enables mediators to display an orientation to disputant autonomy while at the same time contributing to the dispute resolution process by making a suggestion.

---

[11] See Bishop et al. (2015); Doneff and Ordover (2014); Poitras and Raines (2013).
[12] See Cobb and Rifkin (1991b); Garcia (1995); Garcia et al. (2002); Greatbatch and Dingwall (1989).
[13] See Madonik (2001); Picard (2016); Ranger (2010); Whatling (2012).

Because mediator suggestions are not position reports, they can let their actions be guided by disputant responses to their suggestions. If disputants do not support a mediator's suggestion, the mediator can retreat from it or even argue against their own proposal. They do not defend their own suggestions or engage in contentious discussion about them. In these data mediator proposals are treated as suggestions by both the mediators and by the disputants. This lack of attachment to the suggestion enables the mediators to display neutrality and further the goal of disputant empowerment.

Mediator proposal-making, even though not officially approved of in most facilitative mediation programs, may well be helpful to the disputants as they work to resolve their dispute. As noted in Chapter 1, mediators in facilitative mediation are trained to avoid engaging with the content or substance of the dispute, and instead to focus on facilitating the process.[14] However, there are a variety of ways mediators assist disputants in the creation of agreement on issues under dispute. Although some mediation programs discourage mediators from making suggestions or giving advice, when they can use appropriate techniques for contributing to idea generation without compromising mediator neutrality or disputant autonomy, these contributions can be constructive (Garcia 2012). Even if a mediator's idea for resolution is rejected, it may serve to focus the disputants' attention on the production of ideas for resolution rather than continuing to detail complaints and argue over issues. Mediator proposals can help shift the disputants to the next stage of the mediation process or spark other ideas for resolution, thereby constructively contributing to the agreement creation process.

The potential weakness of disputant suggestions is that, precisely because they are formulated and/or framed as positional commitments or "offers," their contributions to brainstorming and other problem-solving strategies are limited. As prior research has shown, positional commitments in negotiation and bargaining contexts may be contentious.[15] While mediators may easily and unproblematically revise, retract, or retreat from their own proposals, these actions are much more difficult for disputants relative to their own proposals. These differences suggest that mediator participation in the production of proposals is likely a positive contribution to agreement creation, even in the context of facilitative agreement where such participation is likely to be officially proscribed.

Proposal Generation in Divorce Mediation. Proposal generation in divorce mediation is often done differently than in small claims mediation, especially in those segments of the session in which participants use a quasi-conversational hybrid speech exchange system rather than a typical mediation

---

[14] See Bishop et al. (2015); Doneff and Ordover (2014).
[15] See Carnevale and Pruitt (1992); Fisher and Ury (1991); Pruitt et al. (1983).

format. In divorce mediation sessions a disputant may at times produce proposals in utterances directly addressed to the opposing disputant; this type of proposal production rarely occurred in the small claims sessions. This can mean that proposals (or position reports) and their acceptance or rejection can occur adjacently in these sessions.

While the disputants in the small claims mediation sessions tend to take an adversarial posture vis-à-vis each other, the dynamic between disputants in divorce mediation sessions is more complex. While there can be a high level of conflict and animosity between the spouses, there is also a shared history and shared interest in their children. This may be one reason that collectively constructed disputant proposals occasionally occurred in the divorce mediation sessions.

Disputants in the divorce mediation sessions occasionally referred to themselves and their spouses as "we" when making proposals. This type of collective self-reference is rarely seen in the small claims cases, where participants typically do not know each other well and are on opposing sides of an issue. In the divorce mediation cases, the spouses all have children so even after the divorce they will share responsibilities for their care. This "we-ness" is therefore intrinsic to their situation and may be reflected in their formulation of proposals. Mediators in the divorce mediation cases more often treat disputants as a unit with shared interests rather than as individuals on opposing sides of a dispute. Divorce mediators may also engage in and contribute to both the production and development of proposals.

One type of proposal which occurred only in the divorce mediation sessions was the joking or semi-serious proposal. One interpretation of a joking proposal would be that its purpose is to blow off steam or express emotions about an issue. However, there are concrete ways joking proposals can be useful for the proposal-generation process. For example, stating an outrageous position that no one expects to be accepted can be useful for the dispute resolution process because it enables participants to articulate challenging issues. Seemingly outrageous suggestions may be an effective part of the brainstorming process (Bishop et al. 2015).

In sum, this analysis of position-taking while making proposals in small claims and divorce mediation suggests that the impact of position-taking will depend on the type of mediation, the interactional context and the formulation and framing of the proposals. In order to understand the best ways to make proposals in mediation, these actions must be examined in detail in naturally occurring interactions.

Mediator Teamwork

In Chapter 8 I analyzed how co-mediators in the Midwest divorce and West Coast small claims mediation sessions conduct their performance as a team to successfully display a united front to the disputants. Failures of alignment between co-mediators (activity misalignment, substantive misalignment, and interactional alignment) only occasionally occurred. Failure on any one of these fronts may create a visible disjuncture between the mediators which is potentially problematic for their successful facilitation of the session.

When misalignments between co-mediators occur, they are generally treated as problematic and are repaired. Through these corrective actions the mediators display their orientation to the goal of presenting a united front to the disputants and function as role models for how to peacefully resolve disagreements or differences of opinion. When mediators interrupt each other, have a noticeable difference of opinion about an issue, or express different ideas about how the session should proceed, the breakdown of their united front is visible to participants. This failure may have implications for their ability to successfully manage the mediation session or retain the confidence of the disputants in their ability to fairly and effectively manage the process.

Instances of successful mediator teamwork are far more common in these data than failures of mediator alignment. A mediator can display a united front with their co-mediator by remaining silent while their co-mediator does the work of facilitating the session. One mediator may do most or almost all of the speaking, or the co-mediators may alternate the roles of active and silent participant. Co-mediators can also display alignment with each other through explicit expressions of agreement, repetition or paraphrasing of each other's utterances, constructive sentence completions, and-prefaces, and complementary actions.

There were occasions in these data when mediators accomplished teamwork through explicit negotiation, but this occurred relatively infrequently. This is consistent with Goffman's (1959) observation that explicit public negotiation between team members can undermine the team performance by making it appear unspontaneous or unnatural. Another factor, more specific to the mediation context, is that disputants need to feel confidence in the mediators' ability to facilitate the session and to create a safe environment for discussion of the issues. Disputants may feel vulnerable because mediation brings them in close contact with the person with whom they are in conflict. When mediators explicitly discuss what to do next, they are displaying uncertainty – this type of display may reduce the disputants' confidence in the mediators.

Mediators working in teams face challenges that mediators working alone do not face. In spite of these challenges, co-mediation may benefit the mediation process in a number of ways. Their united front, when successfully achieved, may have more persuasive strength than that of a single mediator. This is particularly likely to be the case for programs such as the West Coast data set, which is staffed by volunteer rather than professional mediators. They can reinforce each other's actions, thus increasing their authority in the session. Two co-mediators can also more effectively contribute to the brainstorming process when disputants need help generating ideas for resolution of the dispute. Having two mediators in the room may also more effectively balance the oppositional relationship of opposing disputants, especially in high-conflict mediations. The ability to create and display alignment with their co-mediator therefore is an interactional skill that may affect both the success of the process and disputant confidence in the process.

Implications for Mediation Practice

In this section I will discuss several ways the results of this research could be used to improve the effectiveness of mediation. The findings of this book can be helpful to mediators, mediator trainers, and potential disputants who intend to participate in mediation.

Mediation practitioners believe that mediation benefits disputants even if they do not settle their dispute in mediation. This belief was reaffirmed for me as I studied the transcripts and tapes of these mediation sessions. Even in sessions where disputants did not reach a mediated agreement, they had ample opportunity to explain what happened and to convey their side of the story. They got to process emotions and convey things that mattered to them to a mediator who listened to them closely. They also had the experience of expressing problematic issues in the presence of the person with whom they were in conflict. In addition, they were able to decide whether to negotiate a settlement in mediation, drop the case, or pursue other avenues of dispute resolution such as small claims court. With a few exceptions, mediation was an effective approach for assisting people attempting to resolve their disputes. The analysis in this book also revealed specific ways that mediators and disputants could alter their behavior to make the process of mediation more effective and fair.

Recommendations for Mediators and Disputants

In his book on the problematics of achieving neutrality in mediation, Mayer (2004) notes that a participant's power in mediation is not unidimensional. An individual's influence or control over what happens in an interaction is related to such factors as institutional roles, the specific situation, and the personal characteristics of each individual (Mayer 2004). Part of mediator training is learning to notice and work to balance power between disputants. For example, mediators may be explicitly trained in identifying common sources of power such as differences in gender, age, social status, level of education, or hierarchical position.[16] However, these attempts to balance power may also

---

[16] For example, see Landau (1995); Neumann (1992); Roberts 2008; Ver Steegh (2008).

create challenges for mediators as they work to display neutrality.[17] The
analysis in this book has shown how the interactional techniques used by
participants can contribute to differences in effectiveness in the context of
mediation. In order to fairly facilitate the mediation process through the
storytelling, discussion, and solution-generation stages, mediators must understand not just the actions that need to be engaged in at different stages of
the mediation session (e.g., storytelling, complaint making, or solution generation), but how the interactional techniques they and the disputants use work
together in the speech exchange system of mediation.

For example, Chapter 4 revealed the extent to which skillful disputants
can strengthen their claims and make persuasive arguments through how
they construct their opening statements and support their claims with various
types of evidence. When mediators are trained to observe how participants are
constructing their arguments and to notice differences in skill or interactional
competence between the disputants, they can constructively manage their
facilitation of the session to empower disputants and provide for the maximum
possible level of autonomy.

Chapter 5 revealed several ways that mediators' representations of disputants' positions can either increase or decrease disputant autonomy and
mediator neutrality. Mediators should choose to maximize opportunities for
disputant self-representation of their positions, as this is the approach that leads
to greatest disputant autonomy. When it is necessary to represent disputants'
positions for them, mediators should limit their representations to summaries,
paraphrases, and upshots designed to reflect back a disputant's position to
them, verify their understanding of a position, or display to the opposing disputant what that person's perspective is. These types of representation should
be favored over the most intrusive type of representation in which a mediator
replaces a disputant and argues in their place.

Chapter 6 and 7 analyzed the proposal solicitation, production, and negotiation process in both divorce and small claims mediation. Chapter 6 shows
that in order to provide for the autonomy of the disputants, mediators must
be aware of the implications for disputants' autonomy of how and when in
the session they choose to solicit disputants' proposals for resolution of the
dispute, and whether and to what extent they pursue proposal production when
avoided by a disputant. Chapter 7 highlighted the dilemmas mediators face
when deciding whether to make suggestions for resolution of the conflict
themselves, or leave the production of ideas to the disputants. Even though
most mediators are trained to avoid substantive contributions to the process of
dispute resolution and to refrain from giving advice or making suggestions, in

---

[17] For example, see Garcia (1995); Garcia et al. (2002); Kolb and Kressel (1994); Rifkin, Millen,
and Cobb (1991).

both the small claims and divorce mediation sessions studied here, mediators contributed effectively to the process of creating ideas for resolution of the dispute. As long as these proposals were treated as suggestions rather than as positional commitments, mediators could contribute without diminishing the autonomy of the disputants. Mediators were not always as effective in providing for disputants to do the same; their contributions were typically both constructed and responded to as position reports. One implication of these findings is therefore that mediators should work to facilitate the free use of brainstorming processes in the session.

Both divorce and small claims mediators would do well to use caucuses more frequently, in particular to help support disputants in planning or articulating their positions so that the mediator does not have to represent them to the opposing disputant. In addition, caucuses can effectively be used to provide a safe environment for brainstorming ideas for resolution of the dispute. When a disputant's ideas for resolution are produced in the context of a private caucus with the mediators they can both formulate and have their ideas responded to as suggestions rather than as positional commitments.

Recommendations for Mediation Procedures and Processes

There are several ways in which mediation programs could be strengthened by adopting practices from other approaches to mediation. For example, there were several aspects of the divorce mediation sessions that could effectively be applied to small claims cases to further decrease the adversarial relationship between the participants in these types of mediation and improve the dispute resolution process.

Redesign the Solicitation of Opening Statements. The small claims mediators could adopt the approach used by the divorce mediators to open the substantive portion of the mediation. One of the techniques the divorce mediators used was to open the first mediation session with a question on a topic of mutual interest addressed to both parties. This differs markedly from the approach used in the small claims sessions, in which one disputant is asked to describe their side of the dispute. The mediator's approach to soliciting the opening statements in the small claims cases emphasized the division between the opposing disputants and may have increased the adversarial relationship between them. The disputants' opening statements often included accusations and complaints, as well as responses to them.

On the other hand, in the divorce mediation sessions the mediators began by addressing both disputants collectively and by discussing a mutual interest (such as their children). This approach enables the spouses in divorce mediation to begin by identifying some common ground which can then be built on during the session. Small claims mediators, on the other hand, structure the process to start out with areas of disagreement, and then try to introduce or discover areas of common ground later on.

The results of this analysis suggest that it might be more beneficial to begin the substantive part of small claims mediations by having the disputants articulate what they agree on, rather than their areas of disagreement. A history of the dispute could therefore be developed out of shared beliefs and perspectives, followed by identifying and discussing areas of disagreement. This change could affect the path of the entire session, since the job of mediation would no longer be to inch two widely disparate positions closer together, but to build on and discuss ways to add to a foundation of agreement. This approach could decrease oppositional thinking and the interactional patterns associated to it. Further research could test whether this method improves the process of mediation, and/or the experience and satisfaction of participants with the process.

Utilize the Co-mediation Model. The analysis in Chapter 8 revealed several ways in which teams of co-mediators can support each other in the work of facilitating the mediation session. The co-mediators can serve as a resource for information, ideas, or guidance for each other during the course of the session. The co-mediators can support and reinforce each other's actions when interventions need to be made, for example when a disputant must be sanctioned or redirected. In addition, co-mediators can model cooperative behavior for the disputants, thus serving as role models for how to engage in constructive disagreements. These benefits of the co-mediation model suggest it should be more widely adopted.

Design the Proposal-Generation Process to Maximize Brainstorming. There are ways in which mediator engagement in the proposal-generation process could be strengthened. Given the analysis in Chapter 6, it is clear that soliciting proposals may be more likely to be productive than soliciting position reports. In general, mediators should do work to increase the likelihood that genuine brainstorming will occur, rather than statements of positional commitments. This can be done through framing solicits as proposal solicits rather than a position report solicits, reminding disputants that making suggestions does not imply that they are committed to those suggestions, and using private caucuses for brainstorming to increase disputants' freedom to suggest ideas for resolution. In addition, mediators should take care to consider when and why they pursue proposal solicits when disputants display reluctance to produce a proposal at that point in time.

Mimic the Multiple-Sessions Model of Divorce Mediation. The multiple session model of the divorce mediation has many positive advantages for those participants. It enables them to make progress on their own between sessions, and to learn and practice constructive communication techniques over a span of time. While having multiple sessions will be impractical for most small claims settings, some programs are able to schedule individual meetings with each disputant prior to scheduling the small claims mediation itself. Or, the small claims mediation could be designed as a two-part process. An initial information gathering stage could be followed by an idea generation stage in which ideas for resolution and negotiation over proposals could be held.

Suggestions for Further Research

Comparing Different Types of Mediation

As new varieties of mediation gain in popularity and are used more often, studies of their interactional organization, strengths, and weaknesses should be done. Researchers should investigate the interactional organization of the narrative, transformative, evaluative, and other approaches to mediation and compare them to the more popular facilitative approach.

Transformative mediation sessions differ most markedly from the facilitative mediation sessions analyzed in this book. In the transformative mediation model disputants speak directly to each other for the entire session rather than speaking to the mediator (Institute for the Study of Conflict Resolution 2011). Transformative mediators may reflect back disputant's positions and statements to them using almost identical words and phrases,[18] while in facilitative mediation programs such as those analyzed in this book, mediators rarely reflect back exactly what was said. Facilitative mediators typically paraphrase, summarize, or restate what disputants have said, thus working to achieve a range of goals (e.g., helping bring a disputant's story to a close, working as an intermediary between disputants, or checking for accurate comprehension of a disputant's position) while representing their position. The transformative mediator also refrains from sanctioning arguing when it occurs, thus giving priority to respecting the autonomy of the participants and helping them learn to manage their own disagreements. The transformative mediator also leaves the solution-generation process in the hands of the disputant, by refraining from making proposals or suggestions for resolution of issues under dispute. The transformative approach to mediation thus achieves the goals of mediator neutrality and disputant autonomy more consistently than does facilitative mediation.

---

[18] See Bush (2013); Institute for the Study of Conflict Resolution (2011); Woolford and Ratner (2008).

While the mediator in transformative mediation may be more neutral, some of the advantages for the disputants of a more interventionist model are lost in that approach. For example, as mentioned above, in facilitative mediation mediator suggestions for resolution are often extremely helpful for the process of creating agreement, even when a mediator's suggestions are rejected by the disputants. Second, especially for the small claims cases where participants will not have a relationship after the mediation process is over, time spent engaging in arguing might simply increase stress and hostility rather than benefiting the disputants. Mediator intervention and refocusing onto other, more constructive forms of talk, may therefore be preferable to letting the disputants argue. The transformative model of mediation is therefore likely to be most useful for disputants with a higher degree of interactional skill, a lower degree of conflict, and an ongoing relationship that will continue after the mediation. Research into the interactional organization of other varieties of mediation, including transformative mediation, should be done to explore the effect of these differences on the resolution of disputes.

The Need for Cross-Cultural Comparisons

Mediation sessions involving cross-cultural exchanges are likely to be increasingly prevalent in coming years. Stringer and Lusardo (2016) give recommendations for mediators on bridging cultural differences between disputants. Several previous studies analyze cultural differences in mediation; more work on how cultural differences affect the interaction in mediation needs to be done from a conversation-analytic approach.[19] Previous research has documented cultural differences in conflict style, such as the practice and value given to silence (Shi 2010), how cultural differences in politeness and etiquette affect communication (Polly 2007), and cultural conventions about directness and indirectness (Loi and Evans 2010). There are also cultural differences in how listener responses are produced (Philips 1983; Sorjonen 1996), how turn taking is organized (e.g., Fox, Hayashi, and Jasperson 1996) and how preference organization works (Tanaka 2008), all of which may well impact how mediation work is done.

Conversation-Analytic Research on Caucuses in Mediation

Previous conversation-analytic studies have not yet examined the process of interaction in the caucuses held with individual disputants in divorce and small claims mediation sessions. While mediators are advised to use caucuses for

---

[19] See Campbell (2013); Garcia (2013); Tjosvold and Wang (2013); Yuan (2013); Wei (2018).

several purposes, including defusing anger between disputants or facilitating brainstorming about ideas, the nature of the interaction should be studied to determine how these private exchanges contribute to dispute resolution.

Improving Access to Data

While getting permission to collect the data used in this book (during the 1980s and mid 1990s) was relatively easy, my efforts in recent years to get permission to collect more data have been resisted by the directors of a number of mediation programs. The main reason they cite for their refusal to allow recording of mediation sessions is to protect the confidentiality of the mediation process. Another common justification is the belief that participants in mediation would not act the same way, say the same things, or come up with the same solutions, if they knew they were being recorded. I conclude this chapter with a plea for directors of mediation programs to reconsider their reluctance to participate in research on mediation. This reluctance is particularly ironic especially given the goal of mediation to increase disputant autonomy; if the right to decide whether to participate in research is not given to the disputants, they are deprived of autonomy. Mediation program director's decisions to not allow research may deprive disputants of the right to decide for themselves whether they want to participate or not.

My experience with studying mediation over the years is that data collection does not change the process in a significant way. First, several participants told me they had forgotten they were being recorded. Second, some research suggests that videotaping interactions is unlikely to change interactions significantly (e.g., Semeniuk and Riesch 2011). Third, the findings of this book reveal that even when participants know they are being recorded, they still engage in a range of positive and negative behaviors; clearly they are not significantly censoring their actions for the benefit of the camera. The occurrence of occasional bad behavior on the part of disputants, or less than ideal mediation work on the part of mediators, shows that putting a recording device in the room does not mean that you will obtain an artificial, highly censored mediation session.

As this book has shown, there is important information about how mediation works that can only be obtained from recordings of the sessions. There are a variety of measures that can be taken to protect the privacy of the participants and the confidentiality of the data, including making agreements regarding access to the videotapes, using electronic means to blur faces or delete spoken identifiers from taped data, agreeing to turn off the recording devices if participants become uncomfortable for any reason, and agreeing to erase the recording if a participant changes their mind after the mediation session.

One of the earliest conversation-analytic studies was Harvey Sacks's study of calls to a suicide hotline (Sacks 1987b; 1992). Conversation analysis has thus from its very beginnings been an analytical approach that is simultaneously basic and applied science. The findings of conversation analysis can be used to learn how interaction works and to enable participants in a wide variety of settings to make better decisions about how to act in given situations. The hope is that the findings reported in this book will be useful for mediators seeking to extend their training beyond understanding recommended techniques, and useful to disputants as they seek to understand what will happen in a mediation session and how they can best present their case and most constructively work to reach a fair resolution.

Appendix: Transcription Symbols

The following symbols are adapted from Gail Jefferson's system; see Atkinson and Heritage (1984: ix–xvi).

Symbol	Definition
.hh hh	Inhalations and exhalations, respectively
ta::lk	Colons indicate a syllable is drawn out
that-	Dash indicates a word was cut off abruptly
lot	Underlining indicates stress or emphasis
YOU	Capital letters indicate increased volume
°cost°	Degree signs indicate decreased volume
(1.4)	Numbers in parentheses indicate length of pauses (in seconds)
(talk)	Words in parentheses are tentative transcriptions
( )	Empty parentheses indicate nontranscribable talk
.,?!	Punctuation indicates intonation, not grammatical structure
heh, hunh	Laughter particles are transcribed as pronounced
A: [a copy of it]	Brackets indicate simultaneous speech
B: [I have]	
A: yeah=	Equal signs indicate one utterance or word is attached to another
B: =in order	
A: are yuh gonna?	Words spelled as pronounced
>words spoken<	Caret symbols pointing in indicate increased rate of speech
<words spoken>	Caret symbols pointing out indicate decreased rate of speech
((Turns gaze to B))	Information in double parentheses describes nonverbal behavior or details about how the words were spoken

References

Abramson, Harold. 2005. "Problem-solving advocacy in mediations: A model of client representation." *Harvard Negotiation Law Review*, 10: 103–134.

Alberts, Jess K., Brian L. Heisterkamp, and Robert M. McPhee. 2005. "Disputant perceptions of and satisfaction with a community mediation program." *The International Journal of Conflict Management*, 16(3): 218–244.

American Arbitration Association (ed.). 2016. *Handbook on Mediation*, 3rd ed. Huntington, NY: Juris.

American Arbitration Association, American Bar Association, and the Association for Conflict Resolution. 2005. *The Model Standard for Conduct of Mediators*. Washington, DC: American Bar Association. www.americanbar.org/content/dam/aba/migrated/dispute/documents/model_standards_conduct_april2007.authcheckdam.pdf

Antaki, Charles, Rebecca Barnes, and Ivan Leudar. 2005. "Diagnostic formulations in psychotherapy." *Discourse Studies*, 7(6): 627–647.

Arminen, Ilkka. 2005. *Institutional Interaction: Studies of Talk at Work*. Aldershot, UK: Ashgate.

Arminen, Ilkka, and Mia Halonen. 2007. "Laughing with and at patients: The roles of laughter in confrontations in addiction group therapy." *The Qualitative Report*, 12(3): 484–513.

Atkinson, J. Maxwell, and Paul Drew. 1979. *Order in Court: The Organisation of Verbal Interaction in Judicial Settings*. London: Macmillan.

Atkinson, J. Maxwell, and John Heritage (eds.). 1984. *Structures of Social Action: Studies in Conversation Analysis*. Cambridge: Cambridge University Press.

Bahr, S. J. 1981. "Mediation is the answer: Why couples are so positive about this route to divorce." *Family Advocate*, 3(4): 32–35.

Barnes, Rebecca. 2007. "Formulations and the facilitation of common agreement in meetings talk." *Text and Talk*, 27(3): 273–296.

Barske, Tobias. 2009. "Same token, different actions: A conversation analytic study of social roles, embodied actions, and *ok* in German business meetings." *Journal of Business Communication*, 46(1): 120–149.

Barsky, Allan E. 1996. "Mediation and empowerment in child protection cases." *Mediation Quarterly*, 14(2): 111–134.

2013. "'Med-Arb': Behind the closed doors of a hybrid process." *Family Court Review*, 51(4): 637–650.

Beach, Wayne. 1993. "Transitional regularities for 'casual' 'Okay' usages." *Journal of Pragmatics*, 19: 325–253.

Beck, C. J. A., and L. E. Frost. 2007. "Competence as an element of 'mediation readiness'." *Conflict Resolution Quarterly*, 25(2): 255–278.

Beck, C. J. A., and B. D. Sales. 2001. *Family Mediation: Facts, Myths and Future Prospects*. Washington, DC: APA Books.

Benjamin, Michael, and Howard H. Irving. 1995. "Research in family mediations: Review and implications." *Mediation Quarterly*, 13(1): 53–82.

Bingham, Lisa Blomgren, Cynthia J. Hallberlin, Denise A. Walker, and Won-Tae Chung. 2009. "Dispute system design and justice in employment dispute resolution: Mediation at the workplace." *Harvard Negotiation Review*, 14(1): 1–33.

Bishop, Peter, Cheryl Picard, Rena Ramkay, and Neil Sargent. 2015. *The Art and Practice of Mediation*. Toronto, ON: Emond Montgomery.

Blades, J. 1985. *Family Mediation: Cooperative Divorce Settlement*. Englewood Cliffs, NJ: Prentice Hall.

Boden, Deirdre, and Don H. Zimmerman. 1991. *Talk and Social Structure: Studies in Ethnomethodology and Conversation Analysis*. Berkeley: University of California Press.

Bolden, Galina B. 2009. "Implementing incipient actions: The discourse marker 'so' in English conversation." *Journal of Pragmatics*, 41: 974–998.

2010. "'Articulating the unsaid' via and-prefaced formulations of others' talk." *Discourse Studies*, 12(1): 5–32.

Borg, Marian J. 2000. "Expressing conflict, neutralizing blame, and making concessions in small-claims mediation." *Law and Policy*, 22(2): 115–141.

Bottomley, Ann. 1985. "What is happening to family law? A feminist critique of conciliation." Pp. 162–187 in J. Brophy and C. Smart (eds.), *Women in Law*. London: Routledge and Kegan Paul.

Boulle, Laurence J., Michael T. Colatrella Jr., and Anthony P. Picchioni. 2008. *Mediation: Skills and Techniques*. Newark, NJ: Lexis Nexis.

Brenneis, Donald, and Laura Lein. 1977. "'You fruithead': A sociolinguistic approach to children's dispute settlement." Pp. 49–65 in Susan Ervin-Tripp and C. Mitchell-Kernan (eds.), *Child Discourse*. New York: Academic Press.

Brett, Jeanne M., Zoe I. Barsness, and Stephen B. Goldberg. 1996. "The effectiveness of mediation: An independent analysis of cases handled by four major service providers." *Negotiation Journal*, 12(3): 259–269.

Brown, Daniel G. 1982. "Divorce and family mediation: History, review, future directions." *Family Court Review*, 20(2): 1–44.

Burns, Sarah E. 2007. "Thinking about fairness and achieving balance in mediation." *Fordham Urban Law Journal*, 35(1/2): 39–81.

Burns, Stacy. 2000. "Impeachment work in the Menendez brothers' murder trial: The interactional achievement of facticity, credibility and accountability." Pp. 233–256 in Jeffery T. Ulmer (ed.), *Sociology of Crime, Law and Deviance*, vol. 2. Amsterdam: JAI.

Burrell, Nancy A., William A. Donohue, and Mike Allen. 1990. "The impact of disputants' expectations on mediation: Testing an interventionist model." *Human Communication Research*, 17(1): 104–139.

Burton, L. 1986. *A Training Manual for Mediators*. Santa Monica, CA: Los Angeles County Bar Association.

Bush, Robert A. Baruch. 2013. "Mediation skills and client-centered lawyering: A new view of the partnership." *Clinical Law Review*, 19: 429–488.

Bush, Robert A. Baruch, and Joseph P. Folger. 2004. *The Promise of Mediation: The Transformative Model for Conflict Resolution*. San Francisco, CA: Jossey-Bass.

Bush, Robert A. Baruch, and Sally Ganong Pope. 2002. "Changing the quality of conflict interaction: The principles and practice of transformative mediation." *Pepperdine Dispute Resolution Law Journal*, 3(1): 67–96.

Button, Graham. 1992. "Answers as interactional products: Two sequential practices used in interviews." *Social Psychology Quarterly*, 50(2): 160–171.

Button, Graham, and Neil Casey. 1984. "Generating topic: The use of topic initial elicitors." Pp. 167–190 in J. Maxwell Atkinson and John Heritage (eds.), *Structures of Social Action: Studies in Conversation Analysis*. Cambridge: Cambridge University Press.

Cahn, Dudley D. 1992. *Conflict in Intimate Relationships*. New York: Guilford Press.

Campbell, Duncan. 2013. "A mediator's experiences in dealing with cultural differences in commercial mediations." *China Media Research*, 9(4): 53–57.

Carnevale, Peter J., and Dean G. Pruitt. 1992. "Negotiation and mediation." *Annual Review of Psychology*, 43: 531–582.

Carper, Donald L., and John B. LaRocco. 2016. "What parties might be giving up and gaining when deciding not to litigate: A comparison of litigation, arbitration and mediation." Pp. 3–25 in American Arbitration Association (ed.), *Handbook on Mediation*, 3rd ed. Huntington, NY: Juris.

Center for Dispute Settlement. 1988. *Parent/Adolescent Mediation: A Training Manual*. Washington, DC: Center for Dispute Settlement.

Cerino, A. M., and S. M. Rainone. 1984. "The new wave: Speedy arbitration hearings – but are they fair?" *Villanova Law Review*, 29(6): 1495–1503.

Chandler, D. B. 1990. "Violence, fear, and communication: The variable impact of domestic violence on mediation." *Mediation Quarterly*, 7(4): 331–346.

Charkoudian, Lorig, Deborah Thompson Eisenberg, and Jamie L. Walter. 2017. "What difference does ADR make? Comparison of ADR and trial outcomes in small claims court." *Conflict Resolution Quarterly*, 35(1): 7–45.

Charkoudian, Lorig, and E. K. Wayne. 2010. "Fairness, understanding, and satisfaction: Impact of mediator and participant race and gender on participants' perception of mediation." *Conflict Resolution Quarterly*, 28(1): 23–52.

Clayman, Steven E. 1985. "Managing disjunctures in conversation: Their avoidance and repair." MA thesis, Department of Sociology, University of California, Santa Barbara.

1988. "Displaying neutrality in television news interviews." *Social Problems*, 35(4): 474–492.

1992. "Footing in the achievement of neutrality: The case of news-interview discourse." Pp. 163–198 in Paul Drew and John Heritage (eds.), *Talk at Work: Interaction in Institutional Settings*. Cambridge: Cambridge University Press.

1993. "Reformulating the question: A device for answering/not answering questions in news interviews and press conferences." *Text*, 13(2): 159–188.

2001. "Answers and evasions." *Language in Society*, 30: 403–422.

Clayman, Steven E., and John Heritage. 2002. *The News Interview: Journalists and Public Figures on the Air*. Cambridge: Cambridge University Press.

Clayman, Steven E., and Douglas W. Maynard. 1990. "Turn-taking and address in the achievement of an institutional setting: The case of the news interview." Paper presented at Midwest Sociological Association, April, Chicago, IL.

Clayman, Steven E., and Jack Whalen. 1988/89. "When the medium becomes the message: The case of the Rather–Bush encounter." *Research on Language and Social Interaction*, 22: 241–272.

Cobb, Sara. 1993. "Empowerment and mediation: A narrative perspective." *Negotiation Journal*, 9(3): 245–259.

   1994. "Theories of responsibility: The social construction of intentions in mediation." *Discourse Processes*, 18(2): 165–186.

Cobb, Sara, and Janet Rifkin. 1991a. "Neutrality as a discursive practice: The construction and transformation of narratives in community mediation." *Law, Politics, and Society*, 11: 69–81.

   1991b. "Practice and paradox: Deconstructing neutrality in mediation." *Law and Social Inquiry*, 16(1): 35–62.

Cohen, R. 1995. *Students Resolving Conflict: Peer Mediation in Schools*. Glenview, IL: GoodYearBooks.

Conley, John M., and William M. O'Barr. 2005. *Just Words: Law, Language and Power*. Chicago: University of Chicago Press.

Cooks, Leda M., and Claudia L. Hale. 1994. "The construction of ethics in mediation." *Mediation Quarterly*, 12(2): 55–76.

Coulter, Jeff. 1990. "Elementary properties of argument sequences." Pp. 181–204 in George Psathas (ed.), *Interaction Competence*. Washington, DC: International Institute for Ethnomethodology and Conversation Analysis and University Press of America.

Davidson, Judy. 1984. "Subsequent versions of invitations, offers, requests, and proposals dealing with potential or actual rejection." Pp. 102–108 in J. Maxwell Atkinson and John Heritage (eds.), *Structures of Social Action: Studies in Conversation Analysis*. Cambridge: Cambridge University Press.

Depner, Charlene E., Karen Cannata, and Isolina Ricci. 1994. "Client evaluations of mediation services: The impact of case characteristics and mediation service models." *Family Court Review*, 32(3): 306–325.

Dersley, Ian, and Anthony J. Wootton. 2000. "Complaint sequences within antagonistic argument." *Research on Language and Social Interaction*, 33: 375–406.

   2001. "In the heat of the sequence: Interactional features preceding walkouts from argumentative talk." *Language in Society*, 30(4): 611–638.

de Vera, Carlos. 2004. "Arbitrating harmony: 'Med-Arb' and the confluence of culture and rule of law in the resolution of international commercial disputes in China." *Columbia Journal of Asian Law*, 18: 149–194.

Dingwall, Robert. 1986. "Some observations on divorce mediation in Britain and the United States." *Mediation Quarterly*, 5: 5–23.

Doneff, Andrea, and Abraham P. Ordover. 2014. *Alternatives to Litigation: Mediation, Arbitration, and the Art of Dispute Resolution*. Boulder, CO: National Institute for Trial Advocacy.

Donohue, William A. 2006. "Managing interpersonal conflict: The mediation promise." Pp. 211–233 in John G. Oetzel and Stella Ting-Toomey (eds.), *The Sage Handbook of Conflict Communication: Integrating Theory, Research, and Practice*. Thousand Oaks, CA: Sage.

Donohue, William A., M. Allen, and N. A. Burrell. 1988. "Mediator communicative competence." *Communication Monographs*, 55: 104–109.

Donohue, W. A., L. Drake, and A. J. Roberto. 1994. "Mediator issue intervention strategies: A replication and some conclusions." *Conflict Resolution Quarterly*, 11: 261–274.

Douglas, Susan. 2012. "Neutrality, self-determination, fairness and differing models of mediation." *James Cook University Law Review*, 19(2012): 19–40.

Drew, Paul, and John Heritage. 1992. *Talk at Work: Interaction in Institutional Settings*. Cambridge: Cambridge University Press.

Edwards, Derek, and Elizabeth H. Stokoe. 2007. "'Black this, black that': Racial insults and reported speech in neighbour complaints and police interrogations." *Discourse and Society*, 19(3): 337–372.

Ewert, Charles, Gordon Barnard, Jennifer Laffier, and Michael L. Maynard. 2010. *Choices in Approaching Conflict: Understanding the Practice of Alternative Dispute Resolution*. Toronto, ON: Emond Montgomery.

Fairhurst, Gail. 2007. *Discursive Leadership: In Conversation with Leadership Psychology*. Thousand Oaks, CA: Sage.

Felstiner, William L. F., and Lynne A. Williams. 1978. "Mediation as an alternative to criminal prosecution." *Law and Human Behavior*, 2(3): 223–244.

Fighting Fair. 2006. *Parent-Adolescent Mediation*. Mediation Training DVD. Bangalow, NSW: Fighting Fair.

2010. *Workplace Mediation*. Mediation Training DVD. Bangalow, NSW: Fighting Fair.

Filley, A. C. 1975. *Interpersonal Conflict Resolution*. Glenville, IL: Scott, Foresman.

Fisher, Roger, and William Ury. 1991. *Getting to Yes: Negotiating Agreement without Giving In*. New York: Penguin.

Fishman, Pamela M. 1978. "Interaction: The work women do." *Social Problems*, 25: 397–406.

Fitzgerald, Pamela, and Ivan Leudar. 2010. "On active listening in person-centred, solution-focused psychotherapy." *Journal of Pragmatics*, 42(2010): 3188–3198.

Folberg, Jay. 1983. "A mediation overview: History and dimensions of practice." *Mediation Quarterly*, 1(1): 3–13.

Folberg, Jay, and A. Taylor. 1984. *Mediation: A Comprehensive Guide to Resolving Conflicts without Litigation*. San Francisco, CA: Jossey-Bass.

Fox, B. A., M. Hayashi, and R. Jasperson. 1996. "Resources and repair: A cross-linguistic study of syntax and repair." Pp. 185–237 in Elinor Ochs, Emanuel A. Schegloff, and Sandra A. Thompson (eds.), *Interaction and Grammar*. Cambridge: Cambridge University Press.

Francis, David W. 1986. "Some structures of negotiation talk." *Language in Society*, 15(1): 53–79.

Frenkel, Douglas N., and James H. Stark. 2012. *The Practice of Mediation: A Video-Integrated Text*, 2nd ed. New York: Wolters Kluwer Law and Business.

Fuller, Rex M., William D. Kimsey, and Bruce C. McKinney. 1992. "Mediator neutrality and storytelling order." *Conflict Resolution Quarterly*, 10(2): 187–192.

Gale, Jerry, Robyn L. Mowery, Margaret S. Herrman, and Nancy L. Hollett. 2002. "Considering effective divorce mediation: Three potential factors." *Conflict Resolution Quarterly*, 19(4): 389–420.

Garcia, Angela Cora. 1989. "Mediation talk: The interactional organization of mediation hearings." PhD dissertation, Department of Sociology, University of California, Santa Cruz.

1991. "Dispute resolution without disputing: How the interactional organization of mediation hearings minimizes argument." *American Sociological Review* 56(6): 818–835.

1995. "The problematics of representation in community mediation hearings: Implications for mediation practice." *Journal of Sociology and Social Welfare*, 22(4): 23–46.

1996. "Moral reasoning in interactional context: Strategic uses of care and justice arguments in mediation hearings." *Sociological Inquiry*, 66(2): 197–214.

1997. "Interactional constraints on proposal generation in mediation hearings: A preliminary investigation." *Discourse and Society*, 8(2): 219–247.

2000. "Negotiating negotiation: The collaborative production of resolution in small claims mediation hearings." *Discourse and Society*, 11(3): 315–344.

2010. "The role of interactional competence in mediation." *Conflict Resolution Quarterly*, 28(2): 205–228.

2012. "Advice-giving and disputant empowerment in divorce mediation sessions." *Language and Dialogue*, 2(3): 398–426.

2013. "Mediation talk in cross cultural perspective: The contribution of conversation analysis." *China Media Research*, 9(4): 85–101.

2016. "Air Traffic Control interactions in routine and emergency contexts: A case study of Flight 1549 'Miracle on the Hudson'." *Journal of Pragmatics*, 106(2016): 57–71.

Garcia, Angela Cora, Kristi Vise, and Stephen Whitaker. 2002. "Disputing neutrality: When mediation empowerment is perceived as bias." *Conflict Resolution Quarterly*, 20(2): 205–230.

Garfinkel, Harold. 1967. *Studies in Ethnomethodology*. Cambridge: Polity Press.

Gaughan, R. A. 1982. "The family mediation service." In H. Davidson, L. Ray, and R. Horowitz (eds.), *Alternative Means of Family Dispute Resolution*. Washington, DC: American Bar Association.

Gaybrick, A., and D. Bryner. 1981. "Mediation in a public setting: Arlington, Virginia." *Family Law Reporter*, April 14.

Gerhart, Paul F., and John E. Drotning. 1980. [Untitled]. *Industrial Relations*, 19(3): 254–259.

Gewurz, Ilan G. 2001. "(Re)designing mediation to address the nuances of power imbalance." *Conflict Resolution Quarterly*, 19(2): 135–162.

Gibbs, W. 1963. "The Kpelle Moot: A therapeutic model for informal justice settlement." *Africa*, 33: 1–11.

Gill, Virginia Teas, Anita Pomerantz, and Paul Denvir. 2010. "Pre-emptive resistance: Patient's participation in diagnostic sense-making activities." *Sociology of Health and Illness*, 32(1): 1–20.

Gilligan, Carol. 1982. *In a Different Voice: Psychological Theory and Women's Development*. Cambridge, MA: Harvard University Press.

Gilman, James E. 2017. *How to Resolve Conflict: A Practical Mediation Manual*. Lanham, MD: Rowman and Littlefield.

Girdner, Linda K. 1985. "Adjudication and mediation: A comparison of custody decision-making processes involving third parties." *Journal of Divorce*, 8: 33–47.

Glenn, Phillip. 2003. *Laughter in Interaction*. Cambridge: Cambridge University Press.
  2010. "Interviewer laughs: Shared laughter and asymmetries in employment interviews." *Journal of Pragmatics*, 42(2010): 1485–1498.
Goffman, Erving. 1959. *The Presentation of Self in Everyday Life*. New York: Anchor Books.
  1963. *Behavior in Public Places*. New York: Free Press.
  1981. *Forms of Talk*. Philadelphia: University of Pennsylvania Press.
Goldberg, Stephen B., Jeanne M. Brett, and Beatrice Blohorn-Brenneur, with Nancy H. Rogers. 2017. *How Mediation Works: Theory, Research, and Practice*. Bingley, UK: Emerald.
Goodwin, Charles. 1984. "Notes on story structure and the organization of participation." Pp. 225–246 in J. Maxwell Atkinson and John Heritage (eds.), *Structures of Social Action: Studies in Conversation Analysis*. Cambridge: Cambridge University Press.
  1986. "Between and within: Alternative sequential treatments of continuers and assessments." *Human Studies*, 9(2): 205–217.
  1987. "Forgetfulness as an interactive resource." *Social Psychology Quarterly*, 50(2): 115–130.
  2006. "Retrospective and prospective orientation in the construction of argumentative moves." *Text and Talk*, 26(4/5): 443–461.
Goodwin, Charles, and Alessandro Duranti. 1992. "Rethinking context: An introduction." Pp. 1–42 in A. Duranti and C. Goodwin (eds.), *Rethinking Context: Language as an Interactive Phenomenon*. Cambridge: Cambridge University Press.
Goodwin, Marjorie Harness. 1980. "He-said-she-said: Formal cultural procedures for the construction of a gossip dispute activity." *American Ethnologist*, 7(4): 674–695.
  1983. "Aggravated correction and disagreement in children's conversations." *Journal of Pragmatics*, 7: 657–677.
  1988. "Cooperation and competition across girls' play activities." Pp. 55–96 in Alexandra Todd and Sue Fisher (eds.), *Gender and Discourse: The Power of Talk*. Norwood, NJ: Ablex.
Goodwin, Marjorie Harness, and Charles Goodwin. 1987. "Children's arguing." Pp. 200–248 in S. Philips, S. Steele, and C. Tanz (eds.), *Language, Gender and Sex in Comparative Perspective*. Cambridge: Cambridge University Press.
Granzner-Stuhr, Stefanie, and Ilse Pogatschnigg (eds.). 2012. *Ich kann doch nicht Androgyn werden: Geschlechtsspezifische Aspekte in der Mediation*. Vienna: Peter Lang.
Gray, Barbara. 2006. "Mediation as framing and framing within mediation." Pp. 193–216 in Margaret S. Herrman (ed.), *The Blackwell Handbook of Mediation: Bridging Theory, Research, and Practice*. Malden, MA: Blackwell.
Greatbatch, David. 1988. "A turn-taking system for British news interviews." *Language in Society*, 17: 401–430.
Greatbatch, David, and Robert Dingwall. 1989. "Selective facilitation: Some preliminary observations on a strategy used by divorce mediators." *Law and Society Review*, 23(4): 613–641.
  1994. "The interactive construction of interventions by divorce mediators." Pp. 84–109 in Joseph P. Folger and Tricia S. Jones (eds.), *New Directions in Mediation: Communication Research and Perspectives*. Thousand Oaks, CA: Sage.

1997. "Argumentative talk in divorce mediation sessions." *American Sociological Review*, 62(1): 151–170.

1999. "Professional neutralism in family mediation." Pp. 271–292 in Srikant Sarangi and Celia Roberts (eds.), *Talk, Work, and Institutional Order: Discourse in Medical, Mediation and Management Settings*. Berlin: Mouton de Gruyter.

Green, Alexander R., Dana R. Carney, Daniel J. Pallin, Long H. Ngo, Kristal L. Raymond, Lisa I. Iezzoni, and Mahzarin R. Banaji. 2007. "Implicit bias among physicians and its prediction of thrombolysis decisions for Black and White patients." *Journal of General Internal Medicine*, 22(9): 1231–1238.

Greenspan, Deborah, Fredric M. Brooks, and Jonathan Walton. 2018. "Recent developments in alternative dispute resolution." *Tort Trial and Insurance Practice Law Journal* 53(2): 199–225.

Greenwald, Anthony G., and Linda Hamilton Krieger. 2006. "Implicit bias: Scientific foundations." *California Law Review*, 94(4): 945–967.

Greenwald, R. F. 1978. "C. R. S.: Dispute resolution through mediation." *American Bar Association Journal*, 64: 1250–1254.

Gulbrandsen, Wenke, Hanne Haavind, and Odd A. Tjersland. 2018. "High-conflict parents in mediation: An analysis of dialogues and sources to conflict." *Conflict Resolution Quarterly*, 35(2018): 335–349.

Halkowski, Timothy. 1990. "'Role' as an interactional device." *Social Problems*, 37(4): 564–577.

Hanley, Jim. 2010. "Transformative mediation." *HR Magazine*, April, 64–65.

Heath, Christian. 1992. "The delivery and reception of diagnosis in the general-practice consultation." Pp. 235–267 in J. Maxwell Atkinson and John Heritage (eds.), *Talk at Work: Interaction in Institutional Settings*. Cambridge: Cambridge University Press.

Heisterkamp, Brian L. 2006a. "Conversational displays of mediator neutrality in a court-based program." *Journal of Pragmatics*, 38: 2051–2064.

2006b. "Taking the footing of a neutral mediator." *Conflict Resolution Quarterly*, 3(3): 301–315.

Heritage, John. 1984a. *Garfinkel and Ethnomethodology*. Cambridge: Polity Press.

1984b. "A change-of-state token and aspects of its sequential placement." Pp. 299–345 in J. Maxwell Atkinson and John Heritage (eds.), *Structures of Social Action: Studies in Conversation Analysis*. Cambridge: Cambridge University Press.

1987. "Conversation analysis." Pp. 256–261 in Anthony Giddens and Roy Turner (eds.), *Social Theory Today*. Cambridge: Polity Press.

Heritage, John, and J. Maxwell Atkinson. 1984. "Introduction." Pp. 1–17 in J. Maxwell Atkinson and John Heritage (eds.), *Structures of Social Action: Studies in Conversation Analysis*. Cambridge: Cambridge University Press.

Heritage, John, and Steven E. Clayman. 2010. *Talk in Action: Interactions, Identities, and Institutions*. Cambridge: Wiley-Blackwell.

Heritage, John, and David Greatbatch. 1991. "On the institutional character of institutional talk: The case of news interviews." Pp. 95–137 in Deirdre Boden and Don H. Zimmerman (eds.), *Talk and Social Structure*. Cambridge: Polity Press.

Heritage, John, and Douglas W. Maynard (eds.). 2006. *Communication in Medical Care: Interaction between Primary Care Physicians and Patients*. Cambridge: Cambridge University Press.

Heritage, John, and Marja-Leena Sorjonen. 1994. "Constituting and maintaining activities across sequences: *And*-prefacing as a feature of question design." *Language in Society*, 23(1): 1–29.

Heritage, John, and Rod Watson. 1979. "Formulations as conversational objects." Pp. 123–162 in George Psathas (ed.), *Everyday Language, Studies in Ethnomethodology*. New York: Irvington Press.

Herrman, Margaret S., Nancy Hollett, and Jerry Gale. 2006. "Mediation from beginning to end: A testable model." Pp. 19–78 in Margaret S. Herrman (ed.), *The Blackwell Handbook of Mediation: Bridging Theory, Research, and Practice*. Oxford: Blackwell.

Holt, Elizabeth. 1996. "Reporting on talk: The use of direct reported speech in conversation." *Research on Language and Social Interaction*, 29(3): 219–245.

2000. "Reporting and reacting: Concurrent responses to reported speech." *Research on Language and Social Interaction*, 33(4): 425–454.

2010. "The last laugh: Shared laughter and topic termination." *Journal of Pragmatics*, 42(2010): 1513–1525.

Huebler, Alex. 1983. *Understatements and Hedges in English*. Amsterdam: John Benjamins.

Hutchby, Ian. 1996a. "Power in discourse: The case of arguments in talk radio." *Discourse and Society*, 7(4): 481–497.

1996b. *Confrontation Talk: Arguments, Asymmetries, and Power on Talk Radio*. Mahwah, NJ: Lawrence Erlbaum.

2005. "'Active listening': Formulations and the elicitation of feelings-talk in child counseling." *Research on Language and Social Interaction*, 38(3): 303–329.

2006. *Media Talk: Conversation Analysis and the Study of Broadcasting*. New York: Open University Press.

Institute for the Study of Conflict Resolution. 2011. What the Parents Know: A Transformative Mediation. Mediation DVD. Affiliated with the Maurice A. Deane School of Law at Hofstra University. www.TransformativeMedia tion.org/.

Irving, Howard H., and Michael Benjamin. 1987. *Family Mediation: Theory and Practice of Dispute Resolution*. Toronto, ON: Carswell.

1992. "An evaluation of process and outcome in a private family mediation service." *Mediation Quarterly*, 10(1): 35–55.

2002. *Therapeutic Family Mediation*. London: Sage.

Jacobs, Scott. 2002. "Maintaining neutrality in dispute mediation: Managing disagreement while managing not to disagree." *Journal of Pragmatics*, 34: 1403–1426.

Jefferson, Gail. 1972. "Side sequences." Pp. 294–338 in David Sudnow (ed.), *Studies in Social Interaction*. New York: Free Press.

1974. "Error correction as an interactional resource." *Language in Society*, 13(2): 181–199.

1978. "Sequential aspects of storytelling in conversation." Pp. 219–248 in Jim Schenkein (ed.), *Studies in the Organization of Conversational Interaction*. New York: Academic Press.

1979. "A technique for inviting laughter and its subsequent acceptance declination." Pp. 79–96 in George Psathas (ed.), *Everyday Language: Studies in Ethnomethodology*. New York: Irvington Press.

1984a. "Transcript notation." Pp. ix–xvi in J. Maxwell Atkinson and John Heritage (eds.), *Structures of Social Action: Studies in Conversation Analysis.* Cambridge: Cambridge University Press.

1984b. "On the organization of laughter in talk about troubles." Pp. 346–369 in J. Maxwell Atkinson and John Heritage (eds.), *Structures of Social Action: Studies in Conversation Analysis.* Cambridge: Cambridge University Press.

1984c. "Notes on a systematic deployment of the acknowledgment tokens 'yeah' and 'mmhm'." *Papers in Linguistics,* 17(2): 197–216.

1986. "Notes on 'latency' in overlap onset." *Human Studies,* 9(2/3): 153–183.

1990. "List-construction as a task and resource." Pp. 63–92 in George Psathas (ed.), *Interactional Competence.* New York: Irvington Press.

2004a. "Glossary of transcript symbols with an introduction." Pp. 13–31 in Gene H. Lerner (ed.), *Conversation Analysis: Studies from the First Generation.* Amsterdam: John Benjamins.

2004b. "A note on laughter in 'male–female' interaction." *Discourse Studies,* 6(1): 117–133.

2004c. "A sketch of some orderly aspects of overlap in natural conversation." Pp. 43–59 in Gene H. Lerner (ed.), *Conversation Analysis: Studies from the First Generation.* Amsterdam: John Benjamins.

Jenks, Christopher, Alan Firth, and Liz Trinder. 2012. "When disputants dispute: Interactional aspects of arguments in family mediation sessions." *Text and Talk,* 32(3): 307–327.

Kangasharju, Helena. 2002. "Alignment in disagreement: Forming oppositional alliances in committee meetings." *Journal of Pragmatics,* 34(2002): 1447–1471.

Karim, A., and D. Dilts. 1990. "Determinants of mediation success in the Iowa public sector." *Journal of Collective Negotiations,* 19(2): 129–140.

Kelly, J. B. 1989. "Mediated and adversarial divorce: Respondents' perceptions of their processes and outcomes." In J. B. Kelly (ed.), *Empirical Research in Divorce and Family Mediation.* San Francisco, CA: Jossey-Bass.

Kelly, J. B., and M. A. Duryee. 1992. "Women's and men's views of mediation in voluntary and mandatory settings." *Family and Conciliation Courts Review,* 30(1): 34–49.

Kelly, J. B., and L. Gigy. 1989. "Divorce mediation: Characteristics of clients and outcomes." Pp. 263–283 in Kenneth Kressel and Dean G. Pruitt (eds.), *Mediation Research.* San Francisco, CA: Jossey-Bass.

Keyton, Joann, and Stephenson J. Beck. 2010. "Examining laughter functionality in jury deliberations." *Small Group Research,* 41(4): 386–407.

Kimsey, William D., Rex M. Fuller, Andrew J. Bell, and Bruce C. McKinney. 1994. "The impact of mediator strategic choices: An experimental study." *Mediation Quarterly,* 12(1): 89–97.

Kishore, Shyam. 2006. "The evolving concepts of neutrality and impartiality in mediation." *Commonwealth Law Bulletin,* 32(2): 221–225.

Kolb, Deborah M. 1981. "Roles mediators play: State and federal practice." *Industrial Relations,* 20(1): 1–17.

1983. *The Mediators.* Cambridge, MA: MIT Press.

Kolb, Deborah M., and Kenneth Kressel. 1994. "The realities of making talk work." Pp. 459–461 in Deborah M. Kolb (ed.), *When Talk Works: Profiles of Mediators.* San Francisco, CA: Jossey-Bass.

Kotthoff, H. 1993. "Disagreement and concession in disputes: On the context sensitivity of preference structures." *Language in Society*, 22(2): 193–216.

Kressel, Kenneth. 2000. "Mediation." Pp. 522–545 in M. Deutsch and P. T. Coleman (eds.), *The Handbook of Conflict Resolution: Theory and Practice*. San Francisco, CA: Jossey-Bass.

2007. "The strategic style in mediation." *Conflict Resolution Quarterly*, 24(3): 251–283.

Landau, B. 1995. "The Toronto Forum on Women Abuse: The process and the outcome." *Family and Conciliation Courts Review*, 33(1): 63–78.

LeBaron, Michelle. 2002. *Bridging Troubled Waters: Conflict Resolution from the Heart*. San Francisco, CA: Jossey-Bass.

Lerner, Gene H. 1989. "Notes on overlap management in conversation: The case of delayed completion." *Western Journal of Speech Communication*, 53(2): 167–177.

1991. "On the syntax of sentences in progress." *Language in Society*, 20(3): 441–458.

1993. "Collectivities in action: Establishing the relevance of conjoined participation in conversation." *Text*, 13(2): 213–245.

Li, Ingrid. 2008. "Exercising entitlement in next turn: The use of exactly as a success-marker." Paper presented at the Language, Interaction and Social Organization conference, University of California, Santa Barbara.

Lieberman, Amy L. 2016. "The 'A' list of emotions in mediation: From anxiety to agreement." Pp. 137–143 in American Arbitration Association (ed.), *Handbook on Mediation*, 3rd ed. Huntington, NY: Juris.

Liebmann, Marian. 2000. *Mediation in Context*. London: Jessica Kingsley.

Little, J. Anderson. 2007. *Making Money Talk: How to Mediate Insured Claims and Other Monetary Disputes*. Chicago: American Bar Association, Section of Dispute Resolution.

Livingood, John M. 2016. Pp. 467–479 in American Arbitration Association (ed.), *Handbook on Mediation*, 3rd ed. Huntington, NY: Juris.

Loi, C. K., and M. S. Evans. 2010. "Cultural differences in the organization of research article introductions from the field of educational psychology: English and Chinese." *Journal of Pragmatics*, 42: 2814–2825.

Lynch, Michael, and David Bogen. 1996. *The Spectacle of History: Speech, Text, and Memory at the Iran-Contra Hearings*. Durham, NC: Duke University Press.

Madonik, Barbara G. 2001. *I Hear What You Say, but What Are You Telling Me? The Strategic Use of Nonverbal Communication in Mediation*. San Francisco, CA: Jossey-Bass.

Maggiolo, Walter A. 1985. *Techniques of Mediation*. New York: Oceana.

Malizia, Deborah A., and Jessica Katz Hameson. 2018. "Hidden in plain view: The impact of mediation on the mediator and implications for conflict resolution education." *Conflict Resolution Quarterly*, 35(2018): 301–318.

Mantle, Marjorie. 2017. *Mediation: A Practical Guide for Lawyers*, 2nd ed. Edinburgh: Edinburgh University Press.

Matoesian, Gregory. 2005. "Nailing down an answer: Participations of power in trial talk." *Discourse Studies*, 7(6): 733–759.

Mayer, Bernard. S. 2004. *Beyond Neutrality: Confronting the Crisis in Conflict Resolution*. San Francisco, CA: Jossey-Bass.

Mayer, Bernard S., Joseph B. Stulberg, Lawrence Susskind, and John Lande. 2012. "Core values of dispute resolution: Is neutrality necessary?" *Marquette Law Review*, 95(3): 805–828.

Maynard, Douglas W. 1984. *Inside Plea Bargaining: The Language of Negotiation*. New York: Plenum Press.

1985a. "How children start arguments." *Language in Society*, 14: 1–29.

1985b. "On the functions of social conflict among children." *American Sociological Review*, 50(2): 207–223.

1989. "Perspective-display sequences in conversation." *Western Journal of Speech Communication*, 53(2): 91–113.

1992. "On clinicians co-implicating recipients' perspective in the delivery of diagnostic news." Pp. 331–358 in Paul Drew and John Heritage (eds.), *Talk at Work: Interaction in Institutional Settings*. Cambridge: Cambridge University Press.

2003. *Bad News, Good News: Conversational Order in Everyday Talk and Clinical Settings*. Chicago: University of Chicago Press.

Maynard, Douglas W., and Don H. Zimmerman. 1984. "Topical talk, ritual, and the social organization of relationships." *Social Psychology Quarterly*, 47(4): 301–316.

McCorkle, Suzanne, and Melanie J. Reese. 2015. *Mediation Theory and Practice*, 2nd ed. Los Angeles, CA: Sage.

McEwen, Craig A. 2006. "Examining mediation in context: Toward understanding variation in mediation programs." Pp. 81–98 in Margaret S. Herrman (ed.), *The Blackwell Handbook of Mediation: Bridging Theory, Research, and Practice*. Oxford: Blackwell.

McGowan, Deirdre. 2018. "Reframing the mediation debate in Irish all-issues divorce disputes: From mediation vs. litigation to mediation and litigation." *Journal of Social Welfare and Family Law*, 40(2): 181–194.

McKenzie, Donna Margaret. 2015. "The role of mediation in resolving workplace relationship conflict." *International Journal of Law and Psychiatry*, 39(2015): 52–59.

Meierding, N. R. 1993. "Does mediation work? A survey of long-term satisfaction of divorce mediating couples." *Mediation Quarterly*, 11(2): 157–170.

Menkel-Meadow, Carrie J., Lela Porter Love, Andrea Kupfer Schneider, and Jean R. Sternlight. 2011. *Dispute Resolution: Beyond the Adversarial Model*. New York: Wolters Kluwer.

Merchant Dispute Resolution Center. 2006. [Untitled]. DVD of Role Play of Mediation Session. TX, USA: Merchant Dispute Resolution Center.

Merry, Sally Engle. 1989. "Myth and practice in the mediation process." Pp. 239–250 in Martin Wright and Burt Galaway (eds.), *Mediation and Criminal Justice: Victims, Offenders, and Community*. London: Sage.

1990. *Getting Justice and Getting Even: Legal Consciousness among Working Class Americans*. Chicago: University of Chicago Press.

Merry, Sally Engle, and Susan S. Silbey. 1986. "Mediator settlement strategies." *Law and Policy*, 8(1): 7–32.

Mikkelsen, Jes Anker. 2014. "Mediation: What is still to be learned in Scandinavia?" *Defense Counsel Journal*, 81(3): 288–315.

Moore, Christopher W. 1986. *The Mediation Process: Practical Strategies for Resolving Conflict*. San Francisco, CA: Jossey-Bass.

　2014. *The Mediation Process: Practical Strategies for Resolving Conflict*, 4th ed. San Francisco, CA: Jossey-Bass.

Morrill, C., and P. C. Facciola. 1992. "The power of language in adjudication and mediation: Institutional contexts as predictors of social evaluation." *Law and Social Inquiry*, 17(2): 171–212.

Mulcahy, Linda. 2001. "The possibilities and desirability of mediator neutrality – towards an ethic of partiality?" *Social and Legal Studies*, 10(4): 505–527.

Muntigl, Peter. 2013. "Resistance in couples counselling: Sequences of talk that disrupt progressivity and promote disaffiliation." *Journal of Pragmatics*, 49(2013): 18–37.

Neumann, Dianne. 1992. "How mediation can effectively address the male–female power imbalance in divorce." *Mediation Quarterly*, 9(3): 227–239.

Neves, T. 2009. "Practice note: Community mediation as a social intervention." *Conflict Resolution Quarterly*, 26(4): 481–495.

Nevile, Maurice. 2006. "Making sequentiality salient: And-prefacing in the talk of airline pilots." *Discourse Studies*, 8(2): 279–302.

Notz, William W., and Frederick A. Starke. 1978. "Final-offer versus conventional arbitration as a means of conflict management." *Administrative Science Quarterly*, 23(2): 189–203.

Oloff, Florence. 2013. "Embodied withdrawal after overlap resolution." *Journal of Pragmatics*, 46(2013): 139–156.

Pearson, Jessica, and Nancy A. Thoennes. 1984. "Mediating and litigating custody disputes: A longitudinal evaluation." *Family Law Quarterly*, 17(4): 497–524.

　1985. "A preliminary portrait of client reactions to three court mediation programs." *Conciliation Courts Review*, 23(1): 1–14.

　1988. "Divorce mediation research results." Pp. 429–452 in Jay Folberg and Ann Milne (eds.), *Divorce Mediation: Theory and Practice*. New York: Guilford Press.

Peräkylä, Anssi. 1995. *AIDS Counselling: Institutional Interaction and Clinical Practice*. Cambridge: Cambridge University Press.

Peräkylä, Anssi, and David Silverman. 1991. "Reinterpreting speech-exchange systems: Communication formats in AIDS counselling." *Sociology*, 25(4): 627–651.

Philips, Susan U. 1983. *The Invisible Culture: Communication in Classroom and Community on the Warm Springs Indian Reservation*. Prospect Heights, IL: Waveland Press.

Picard, Cheryl A. 2016. *Practising Insight Mediation*. Toronto, ON: University of Toronto Press.

Pines, A. M., H. Gat, and Y. Tal. 2002. "Gender differences in content and style of argument between couples during divorce." *Conflict Resolution Quarterly*, 20(1): 23–50.

Pogatschnigg, Ilse M. 2012. "Einfluss des Geschlechts in der Co-mediation." Pp. 29–48 in Stefanie Granzner-Stuhr and Ilse M. Pogatschnigg (eds.), *"Ich Kann Ja Nicht Androgyn Werden." Geschlechtsspezifische Aspekte in der Mediation*. Frankfurt, Germany: Peter Lang.

Poitras, Jean. 2013. "The strategic use of caucus to facilitate parties' trust in mediators." *International Journal of Conflict Management*, 24(1): 23–39.

Poitras, Jean, and Susan Raines. 2013. *Expert Mediators: Overcoming Mediation Challenges in Workplace, Family, and Community Conflicts*. Lanham, MD: Jason Aronson.

Polkinghorn, Brian, and E. Patrick McDermott. 2006. "Applying the comprehensive model to workplace mediation research." Pp. 148–174 in Margaret S. Herrman (ed.), *The Blackwell Handbook of Mediation: Bridging Theory, Research, and Practice*. Oxford: Blackwell.

Polanyi, Livia. 1985. "Conversational storytelling." Pp. 183–201 in Teun A. Van Dijk (ed.), *Handbook of Discourse Analysis: Vol. 3. Discourse and Dialogue*. New York: Academic Press.

Polly, Matthew. 2007. *American Shaolin: Flying Kicks, Buddhist Monks, and the Legend of the Iron Crotch: An Odyssey in the New China*. New York: Gotham Books.

Pomerantz, Anita. 1975. "Second assessments: A study of some features of agreements/disagreements." PhD dissertation, Department of Sociology, University of California, Irvine.

   1978a. "Compliment responses: Notes on the co-operation of multiple constraints." Pp. 79–112 in Jim Schenkein (ed.), *Studies in the Organization of Conversational Interaction*. New York: Academic Press.

   1978b. "Attributions of responsibility: Blamings." *Sociology*, 12(1): 115–121.

   1984. "Agreeing and disagreeing with assessments: Some features of preferred/dispreferred turn shapes." Pp. 57–101 in J. Maxwell Atkinson and John Heritage (eds.), *Structures of Social Action: Studies in Conversation Analysis*. Cambridge: Cambridge University Press.

   1987. "Descriptions in legal settings." Pp. 226–243 in Graham Button and John R. E. Lee (eds.), *Talk and Social Organisation*. Clevedon, UK: Multilingual Matters.

   1988. "Offering a candidate answer: An information seeking strategy." *Communication Monographs*, 55(4): 360–73.

Potter, Jonathan, and Alexa Hepburn. 2010. "Putting aspiration into words: 'Laugh particles,' managing descriptive trouble and modulating action." *Journal of Pragmatics*, 42(2010): 1543–1555.

Presser, Lois, and Cynthia A. Hamilton. 2006. "The micropolitics of victim–offender mediation." *Sociological Inquiry*, 76(3): 316–342.

Program on Negotiation. 2009–2010. Landlord–Tenant Mediation. Mediation DVD. Cambridge, MA: Harvard University.

Pruitt, Dean G., P. J. Carnevale, L. Ben-Yoav, T. H. Nochajski, and M. Van Slyck. 1983. "Incentives for cooperation in integrative bargaining." Pp. 22–34 in R. Tietz (ed.), *Aspiration Levels in Bargaining and Economic Decision Making*. Berlin: Springer.

Psathas, George. 1995. "'Talk and social structure' and 'studies of work'." *Human Studies*, 18(2/3): 139–155.

Ranger, Frank. 2010. *Conflict Resolution and Mediation: Your Opportunity to Learn and Grow*. Denver, CO: Outskirts Press.

Raymond, Geoffrey. 2004. "Prompting action: The stand-alone 'so' in ordinary conversation." *Research on Language and Social Interaction*, 37(2): 185–218.

Regehr, C. 1994. "The use of empowerment in child custody mediation: A feminist critique." *Mediation Quarterly*, 11(4): 361–371.

Rendle-Short, Johanna. 1999. "When 'okay' is okay in computer science seminar talk." *Australian Review of Applied Linguistics*, 22(2): 19–33.

2002. "Talk and action in the computer science seminar." PhD thesis, Department of Linguistics, ANU.

Rifkin, J., J. Millen, and Sara Cobb. 1991. "Towards a new discourse for mediators: A critique of neutrality." *Mediation Quarterly*, 9(2): 151–164.

Roberts, Marian. 1988. *Mediation in Family Disputes*. Hants, UK: Wildwood House.

2008. *Mediation in Family Disputes: Principles of Practice*. Aldershot, UK: Ashgate.

Roebuck, Derek. 2017. *Arbitration and Mediation in Seventeenth-Century England*. Oxford: Holo Books/Arbitration Press.

Romaniuk, Tanya. 2013. "Pursuing answers to questions in broadcast journalism." *Research on Language and Social Interaction*, 46(2): 144–164.

Rosengard, Lee A. 2016. "Learning from law firms: Using co-mediation to train new mediators." Pp. 317–323 in American Arbitration Association (ed.), *Handbook on Mediation*, 3rd ed. Huntington, NY: Juris.

Rouncefield, Mark, and Peter Tolmie (eds.). 2011. *Ethnomethodology at Work*. Farnham, UK: Ashgate.

Sacks, Harvey. 1987a. "On the preferences for agreement and contiguity in sequences in conversation." Pp. 54–69 in Graham Button and John R. E. Lee (eds.), *Talk and Social Organisation*. Clevedon, UK: Multilingual Matters.

1987b. "You want to find out if anybody really does care." Pp. 219–225 in Graham Button and John R. E. Lee (eds.), *Talk and Social Organisation*. Clevedon, UK: Multilingual Matters.

1992. *Lectures on Conversation*, 2 vols. Gail Jefferson (ed.). Oxford: Blackwell.

Sacks, Harvey, Emanuel A. Schegloff, and Gail Jefferson. 1974. "A simplest systematics for the organization of turn-taking for conversation." *Language*, 50(4): 696–735.

Saposnek, Donald T. 1983. *Mediating Child Custody Disputes*. San Francisco, CA: Jossey-Bass.

Saposnek, Donald T., J. Hamburg, C. D. Delano, and H. Michaelson. 1984. "How has mandatory mediation fared? Research findings of the first year's follow-up." *Family and Conciliation Courts Review*, 22(2): 7–19.

Savoury, George R., Harold L. Beals, and Joan M. Parks. 1995. "Mediation in child protection: Facilitating the resolution of disputes." *Child Welfare*, 74(3): 743–762.

Schegloff, Emanuel A. 1968. "Sequencing in conversational openings." *American Anthropologist*, 70: 1075–1095.

1979. "Identification and recognition in telephone conversation openings." Pp. 23–78 in George Psathas (ed.), *Everyday Language: Studies in Ethnomethodology*. New York: Irvington Press.

1980. "Preliminaries to preliminaries: 'Can I ask you a question?'" *Sociological Inquiry*, 50(3/4): 104–152.

1982. "Discourse as an interactional achievement: Some uses of 'uh huh' and other things that come between sentences." Pp. 71–93 in Deborah Tannen (ed.), *Georgetown University Roundtable on Languages and Linguistics; Analyzing Discourse: Text and Talk*. Washington, DC: Georgetown University Press.

1987. "Recycled turn beginnings: A precise repair mechanism in conversation's turn-taking organisation." Pp. 70–85 in Graham Button and John R. E. Lee (eds.), *Talk and Social Organisation*. Clevedon, UK: Multilingual Matters.

1992. "Repair after next turn: The last structurally provided defense of intersubjectivity in conversation." *American Journal of Sociology*, 97(5): 1295–1345.

2000. "Overlapping talk and the organization of turn-taking for conversation." *Language in Society*, 29(1): 1–63.

2005. "On complainability." *Social Problems*, 52(4): 449–476.

2007. *Sequence Organization in Interaction: A Primer in Conversation Analysis*, vol. 1. Cambridge: Cambridge University Press.

Schegloff, Emanuel A., Gail Jefferson, and Harvey Sacks. 1977. "The preference for self-correction in the organization of repair for conversation." *Language*, 53(2): 361–82.

Schegloff, Emanuel A., and Harvey Sacks. 1973. "Opening up closings." *Semiotica*, 8(4): 289–327.

Seaman, Roger. 2016. *Explorative Mediation at Work: The Importance of Dialogue for Mediation Practice*. London: Palgrave Macmillan.

Sellman, Edward. 2008. *Mediation Matters: Creating a Peaceful School through Peer Mediation*. Cambridge: LDA.

Semeniuk, Yulia Y., and Susan K. Riesch. 2011. "Analysis of participant reactivity in dyads performing a videotaped conflict-management task." *International Scholarly Research Network* 2011: 596820.

Shailor, J. G. 1994. *Empowerment in Dispute Mediation: A Critical Analysis of Communication*. Westport, CT: Praeger.

Shapiro, Debra L., and Jeanne M. Brett. 1993. "Comparing three processes underlying judgments of procedural justice: A field study of mediation and arbitration." *Journal of Personality and Social Psychology*, 65(6): 1167–1177.

Shi, Xingsong. 2010. "Intercultural language socialization of a Chinese MBA student in an American negotiation class." *Journal of Pragmatics*, 42(9): 2475–2486.

Shun, Choong Jia. 2018. "And never the twain shall meet? An analysis of the benefits of caucus mediation and conference mediation." Pp. 87–95 in Joel Lee and Marcus Lim (eds.), *Contemporary Issues in Mediation*, vol. 2. Singapore: World Scientific.

Sidnell, Jack. 2004. "There's risks in everything: Extreme-case formulations and accountability in inquiry testimony." *Discourse and Society*, 15(6): 745–766.

2010. *Conversation Analysis: An Introduction*. Oxford: Wiley-Blackwell.

Silverman, David. 1993. *Interpreting Qualitative Data: Methods for Analysing Talk, Text and Interaction*. London: Sage.

Singer, J. 1992. "The privatization of family law." *Wisconsin Law Review*, 5: 1443–1567.

Smithson, Janet, Anne Barlow, Rosemary Hunter, and Jan Ewing. 2015. "The 'child's best interests' as an argumentative resource in family mediation sessions." *Discourse Studies*, 17(5): 609–623.

2017. "The moral order in family mediation: Negotiating competing values." *Conflict Resolution Quarterly*, 35(2): 173–195.

Sorjonen, Marja-Leena. 1996. "On repeats and responses in Finnish conversations." Pp. 277–327 in Elinor Ochs, Emanuel A. Schegloff, and Sandra A. Thompson (eds.), *Interaction and Grammar*. Cambridge: Cambridge University Press.

Stimec, Arnaud, and Jean Poitras. 2009. "Building trust with parties: Are mediators overdoing it?" *Conflict Resolution Quarterly*, 26(3): 317–331.

Stivers, Tanya. 2005. "Modified repeats: One method for asserting primary rights from second position." *Research on Language and Social Interaction*, 38(2): 131–158.

Stivers, Tanya, and John Heritage. 2001. "Breaking the sequential mold: Answering 'more than the question' during comprehensive history taking." *Text*, 21(1/2): 151–185.

Stokoe, Elizabeth. 2003. "Mothers, single women and sluts: Gender, morality and membership categorization in neighbor disputes." *Feminism and Psychology*, 13(3): 317–344.

Stokoe, Elizabeth, and Derek Edwards. 2007. "'Black this, black that': Racial insults and reported speech in neighbour complaints and police interrogations." *Discourse and Society*, 18(3): 337–372.

Stokoe, Elizabeth, and Alexa Hepburn. 2005. "'You can hear a lot through the walls': Noise formulations in neighbour complaints." *Discourse and Society*, 16(5): 647–673.

Stoner, Katherine E. 2018. *Divorce without Court: A Guide to Mediation and Collaborative Divorce*, 5th ed. Nolo: Law for All.

Stringer, Donna M., and Lonnie Lusardo. 2016. "Bridging cultural gaps in mediation." Pp. 447–465 in American Arbitration Association (ed.), *Handbook on Mediation*, 3rd ed. Huntington, NY: Juris.

Szmania, Susan J. 2006. "Mediators' communication in victim offender mediation/dialogue involving crimes of severe violence: An analysis of opening statements." *Conflict Resolution Quarterly*, 24(1): 111–127.

Szmania, Susan J., Addie M. Johnson, and Margaret Mulligan. 2008. "Alternative dispute resolution in medical malpractice: A survey of emerging trends and practices." *Conflict Resolution Quarterly*, 26(1): 71–96.

Tanaka, Hiroko. 2008. "Delaying dispreferred responses in English: From a Japanese perspective." *Language in Society*, 37: 487–513.

ten Have, Paul. 2007. *Doing Conversation Analysis: A Practical Guide*, 2nd ed. London: Sage.

Theobald, Maryanne. 2013. "Ideas as 'possessitives': Claims and counter claims in a playground dispute." *Journal of Pragmatics*, 45(2013): 1–12.

Thoennes, Nancy A., and Jessica Pearson. 1985. "Predicting outcomes in divorce mediation: The influence of people and process." *Journal of Social Issues*, 41(2): 115–126.

Tjosvold, D., and E. Van De Vliert. 1994. "Applying cooperation and competitive conflict theory to mediation." *Mediation Quarterly*, 11(4): 303–311.

Tjosvold, Dean, and Lin Wang. 2013. "Developing a shared understanding of conflict: Foundations for Sino-Western mediation." *China Media Research*, 9(4): 76–84.

Trachte-Huber, E. Wendy, and Stephen K. Huber. 2007. *Mediation and Negotiation: Reaching Agreement in Law and Business*. Newark, NJ: Lexis Nexis.

Tracy, Karen, and Anna Spradlin. 1994. "'Talking like a mediator': Conversational moves of experienced divorce mediators." Pp. 110–132 in Joseph P. Folger and Tricia S. Jones (eds.), *New Directions in Mediation: Communication Research and Perspectives.* Thousand Oaks, CA: Sage.

Tyler, Tom R. 1987. "The psychology of disputant concerns in mediation." *Negotiation Journal*, 3(4): 367–374.

Uwazie, Ernest E. 2011. "Alternative dispute resolution in Africa: Preventing conflict and enhancing stability." *Africa Security Brief*, 16: 1–6.

van der Houwen, Fleur. 2009. "Formulating disputes." *Journal of Pragmatics*, 41(2009): 2072–2085.

Vasilyeva, Alena L. 2010. "The treatment of fallacies in argumentative situations during mediation sessions." *Argumentation and Advocacy*, 46: 173–192.

Ver Steegh, N. 2008. "Yes, no, and maybe: Informed decision making about divorce mediation in the presence of domestic violence." Pp. 205–214 in J. B. Singer and J. C. Murphy (eds.), *Resolving Family Conflicts.* Aldershot, UK: Ashgate.

von Lehm, Dirk. 2014. *Harold Garfinkel: The Creation and Development of Ethnomethodology.* Walnut Creek, CA: Left Coast Press.

Wahrhaftig, Paul. 1983. "Nonprofessional conflict resolution." *Villanova Law Review*, 29: 1463–1476.

Waldron, J. A., C. P. Roth, E. H. Fair, E. M. Mann, and J. E. McDermott Jr. 1984. "A therapeutic model for child custody dispute resolution." *Conflict Resolution Quarterly*, 3(1): 5–20.

Wall, Victor D., Jr., and Marcia L. Dewhurst. 1991. "Mediator gender: Communication differences in resolved and unresolved mediations." *Conflict Resolution Quarterly*, 9(1): 63–85.

Wallensteen, Peter, and Isak Svensson. 2014. "Talking peace: International mediation in armed conflicts." *Journal of Peace Research*, 51(2): 315–327.

Webb, Eugene J., D. Campbell, R. Schwartz, L. Sechrest, and J. Grove. 1981. *Nonreactive Measures in the Social Sciences.* Boston: Houghton Mifflin.

Wei, Justin Low Ching. 2018. "Mandatory mediation in Singapore: Cultural compatibilities." Pp. 37–47 in Joel Lee and Marcus Lim (eds.), *Contemporary Issues in Mediation*, vol. 2. Singapore: World Scientific.

Welton, Gary L., Dean G. Pruitt, and Neil B. McGillicuddy. 1988. "The role of caucusing in community mediation." *Journal of Conflict Resolution*, 32(1): 181–202.

West, Candace, and Don H. Zimmerman. 1977. "Women's place in everyday talk: Reflections on parent–child interaction." *Social Problems*, 24: 521–29.

1982. "Conversation analysis." Pp. 506–541 in Klaus R. Scherer and Paul Ekman (eds.) *Handbook of Nonverbal Communication.* Cambridge: Cambridge University Press.

1983. "Small insults: A study of interruptions in cross-sex conversations between unacquainted persons." Pp. 103–118 in Barrie Thorne, Cheris Kramarae, and Nancy Henley (eds.), *Language, Gender and Society.* Rowley, MA: Newbury House.

Whalen, Jack, and Don H. Zimmerman. 1998. "Observations on the display and management of emotion in naturally occurring activities: The case of 'hysteria' in calls to 9-1-1." *Social Psychology Quarterly*, 61(2): 141–159.

Whatling, Tony. 2012. *Mediation Skills and Strategies: A Practical Guide*. London: Jessica Kingsley.

Williams, Ashley M. 2005. "Fighting words and challenging expectations: Language alternation and social roles in a family dispute." *Journal of Pragmatics*, 37(2005): 317–328.

Wing, Leah. 2009. "Mediation and inequality reconsidered: Bringing the discussion to the table." *Conflict Resolution Quarterly*, 26(4): 383–404.

Winslade, J., and G. Monk. 2008. *Practicing Narrative Mediation: Loosening the Grip of Conflict*. San Francisco, CA: Jossey-Bass.

Wissler, Roselle L. 1995. "Mediation and adjudication in the small claims court: The effects of process and case characteristics." *Law and Society Review*, 29: 323–358.

  1999. *Trapping the Data: An Assessment of Domestic Relations Mediation in Main and Ohio Courts*. Grant report prepared for the State Justice Institute, Washington, DC.

  2002. "Court-connected mediation in general civil cases: What we know from empirical research." *Ohio State Journal on Disputes Resolution*, 17(3): 641–704.

  2004. "Barriers to attorneys' discussion and use of ADR." *Ohio State Journal on Dispute Resolution*, 19: 459–508.

  2006. "The role of antecedent and procedural characteristics in mediation: A review of the research." Pp. 129–147 in Margaret S. Herrman (ed.), *The Blackwell Handbook of Mediation: Bridging Theory, Research, and Practice*. Oxford: Blackwell.

Woofitt, Robin. 1992. *Telling Tales of the Unexpected: The Organization of Factual Discourse*. London: Harvester Wheatsheaf.

Woolford, Andrew J., and Robert Ratner. 2008. *Informal Reckonings: Conflict Resolution in Mediation, Restorative Justice, and Reparations*. Abingdon, UK: Routledge-Cavendish.

Worley, Susan M., and Andrew L. Schwebel. 1985. "The effect of cooperation on egocentrism in divorce mediation: A simulation study." Pp. 151–165 in C. Everett (ed.), *Divorce Mediation: Perspectives on the Field*. New York: Haworth Press.

Xu, Seah Ern. 2018. "The paradox of power and neutrality in mediation. Pp. 97–106 in Joel Lee and Marcus Lim (eds.), *Contemporary Issues in Mediation*, vol. 2. Singapore: World Scientific.

Yuan, Kiaohui. 2013. "Face representation in interpreting politician–journalist interactions." *China Media Research*, 9(4): 102–113.

Zamir, Ronit. 2011. "Can mediation enable the empowerment of disadvantaged groups? A narrative analysis of consensus-building in Israel." *Harvard Negotiation Law Review*, 16: 193–257.

Zetzel, Geraldine W. K., and Sandra Wixted. 1984. *A Mediator's Manual for Parent–Child Mediation*. Cambridge, MA: Children's Hearings Project.

Zimmerman, Don H. 1984. "Talk and its occasion: The case of calling the police." Pp. 210–228 in Deborah Schiffrin (ed.), *Meaning, Form, and Use in Context: Linguistic Applications*. Washington, DC: Georgetown University Press.

Zimmerman, Don H., and Candace West. 1975. "Sex roles, interruptions and silences in conversation." Pp. 105–129 in Barrie Thorne and Nancy Henley (eds.), *Language and Sex: Difference and Dominance*. Rowley, MA: Newbury House.

Zondervan, Deborah Boersma. 2000. "Community mediation in the USA." Pp. 111–125 in Marian Liebmann (ed.), *Mediation in Context*. London: Jessica Kingsley.

Zubek, J. M., Dean G. Pruitt, R. S. Pierce, and A. Iocolano. 1989. "Mediator and disputant characteristics and behavior as they affect the outcome of community mediation." Paper presented at the 2nd annual meeting of the International Association of Conflict Management, Athens, GA.

Zumeta, Zena D. 2006. "A trainer responds to the model." Pp. 412–425 in Margaret S. Herrman (ed.), *The Blackwell Handbook of Mediation: Bridging Theory, Research, and Practice*. Malden, MA: Blackwell.

Index

accusations
  formulation of, 67–70
  mitigating, 70
  responses to, 66
  separation from denials, 63–66
activity misalignment, between co-mediators, 199–203
agreement, mediator teamwork through expression of, 211
American Arbitration Association, 3
and-prefaces, mediator teamwork through, 216–219
approaches to mediation, 3–4
argument, 60–88
  avoiding, 61, 63–71
  direct exchanges between disputants and, 71–77
  disputant self-exit from, 71–73
  focusing on facts to manage, 82
  formulation of accusations and denials and, 67–70
  interruptions, questions, and sanctions to manage, 80–82
  managing and minimizing, 227
  mediator-assisted disputant exit from, 73–77
  mediator responses to, 77–88
  minimal responses and topic shift to manage, 78–80
  mitigated, 62
  in ordinary conversation, 61–63
  responses to accusations and, 66
  separation of accusations and denials and, 63–66
  stepwise departures from mediation format to, 83–88
Arnold Institute, 21
Association of Family and Conciliation Courts, 3
attorney representation, 4
autonomy of disputants, 9
  proposal production and, 235–238
  replacement of disputant and, 141–143

bias. *See* neutrality of mediators
blame, third person attributions of, 68
brief oppositional utterances, in participation framework of mediation, 48

clarification of main areas of disagreement, by mediator, 124–126
community-based mediation, 12
complementary actions, mediator teamwork through, 219–222
consumer complaint cases. *See also* small claims mediation
conversation analysis, 15
  need for research on caucuses in mediation and, 245
cross-cultural comparisons, need for, 245

data collection, 18, 22
data preparation, 23
denials
  formulation of, 67–70
  separation from accusations, 63–66
disputants
  autonomy of. *See* autonomy of disputants
  direct exchanges between, 71–77
  ideas for resolution, as position reports, 174–177
  mediator representation of positions of. *See* mediator representation of positions
  nonproblematic intrusions by, in participation framework of mediation, 44–50
  opening statements of. *See* disputants' opening statements
  opposing, replacement by mediator, 136–147
  recommendations for, 242–244
  replacement by mediator. *See* replacement of disputant
  requests for permission to speak from, 41
  resistance to proposal solicits, 156–164
  self-representation by, 120

269

For EU product safety concerns, contact us at Calle de José Abascal, 56–1°, 28003 Madrid, Spain or eugpsr@cambridge.org.

www.ingramcontent.com/pod-product-compliance
Ingram Content Group UK Ltd.
Pitfield, Milton Keynes, MK11 3LW, UK
UKHW020336140625
459647UK00018B/2168